# Cultivating Army Leaders:
## Historical Perspectives

---

The Proceedings of the Combat Studies Institute
2010 Military History Symposium

**Kendall D. Gott**
General Editor

Cover Photo is a composite of the following images left to right: *"General John J. Pershing. General Headquarters, Chaumont, France,"* DA photo, 19 October 1918, NARA, ARC Id #530766, CGSC copyright registration #11-670 C. *"Lt. Gen George S. Patton, U.S. Third Army Commander, 10/13/1946,"* DA photo, October 13,1946, LOC (LC-USZ62-25122), CGSC copyright registration #11-667 C. 4) *"General Dwight D. Eisenhower, talks with Lt. General Lucus B. Clay at Gatow airport in Berlin, Germany during the Potsdam Conference. Gen. Omar Bradley is in the background,"* DA photo, July 20, 1945, NARA, ARC Id#198840, CGSC copyright registration #11-672 C. *"General William C. Westmoreland, Commanding General, MACV, watches the ceremonies on the arrival of the Royal Thai Volunteer Regiment in Vietnam,"* DA photo, ca. 1974, NARA, ARC Id #530616, CGSC copyright registration #11-669 C. *"General Winfield Scott,"* War Department photo, ca 1860-1865, NARA., ARC Id # 528333, CGSC copyright registration #11-671 C. *"Lt. General Ulysses S. Grant standing by a tree in front of a tent, Cold Harbor, Va,"* War Department photo, ca. June 1864, NARA, ARC Id #524455, CGSC copyright registration #11-668 C.

**Published by Books Express Publishing**
**Copyright © Books Express, 2011**
**ISBN 978-1-78039-567-8**

**Books Express publications are available from all good retail and online booksellers. For publishing proposals and direct ordering please contact us at: info@books-express.com**

## Foreword

These Proceedings are the eighth volume to be published in a series generated by the annual Military History Symposium hosted by the Combat Studies Institute. Each year, these conferences bring together both military and civilian historians, as well as formal and informal students of military history, literally from around the world. They gather for the purpose of presenting ideas and points of view on current military issues from a historical perspective. The 2010 symposium was sponsored by the US Army Combined Arms Center (CAC) and was held 21-23 September 2010 at Fort Leavenworth, Kansas.

This symposium will explore the development of leaders within the US Army in order to attain national goals and objectives in peace and war within a historical context. The symposium also included the discussion of current issues and trends, as well as sister services and international topics. This year we were extremely fortunate to have three distinguished featured speakers who all have exceptional experience in leader development and US Army officer education. Our panelists were also experts in their fields, and we were delighted that thay made the time and effort to present their work.

This eighth volume of proceedings contains the papers or the presentation transcripts of the participating speakers and panelists. It includes transcriptions of the question and answer periods following the presentations as well. These materials can also be found on-line at the CSI Web site at http://usacac.army.mil/cac2/csi/csipubs.asp.

These annual symposiums continue to be an important event for those within the Army who believe that insights from the past are relevant to current military challenges. The attendees have uniformly found them to be of great benefit. We hope that the readers of this and past volumes will find the experience equally useful. *CSI—The Past is Prologue.*


Roderick M. Cox
Colonel, US Army
Director, Combat Studies Institute
Fort Leavenworth, Kansas

# Contents

*page*

**Foreword** .................................................................................................................. iii

**Day 1: Keynote Presentation** ................................................................................... 1

    Cultivating Army Leadership: A Historical Overview by
        Brigadier General (R) John S. Brown ................................................................ 1

    Questions and Answers .......................................................................................... 19

**Day 1, Panel 1: Antebellum Officer Education, 1800-1865** ................................ 23

    Looking Beyond West Point: Life in the Old Army as Education for
        War by Wayne Wei-siang Hsieh, Ph.D. ......................................................... 23

    The Development of Successful Non-professional Officers in the
        Army of the Tennessee, 1861-1863 by Steven E. Woodworth, Ph.D. ........... 35

    Questions and Answers .......................................................................................... 43

**Day 1, Panel 2: Emergence of a Modern Officer Corps, 1866-1905** ................... 51

    The 1891 Infantry Tactics by Perry D. Jamieson, Ph.D. ...................................... 51

    The 1891 Infantry Tactics by Todd Brereton, Ph.D. ........................................... 57

    Questions and Answers .......................................................................................... 63

**Day 1, Panel 3: Changing Leadership for a Changing World Role, 1906-1939** ......... 75

    The Leavenworth Schools, Professional Military Education, and
        Reform in the Old Army, 1900-1917 by Tim Nenniger, Ph.D. ...................... 75

    So Rigorously Trained and Educated: Leader Development in the US
        Army, 1919 to 1939 by Peter J. Schifferle, Ph.D. .......................................... 89

    Questions & Answers ........................................................................................... 107

**Day 2: Featured Speaker:** ...................................................................................... 113

    History Strengthens by General (R) Gordon Sullivan ........................................ 113

    Questions and Answers ........................................................................................ 125

**Day 2, Panel 4: Conventional and Unconventional Challenges of the Cold War, 1945-1975** ............................................................................................................. 131

    Soldiering as an Affair of the Heart by Lewis Sorley, Ph.D. ............................. 131

    Soldiering as an Affair of the Heart Leadership: DePuy, Slim, and
        You by Henry Gole, Ph.D. ............................................................................. 143

    Questions and Answers ........................................................................................ 149

**Day 2, Panel 5: Rebirth of the US Army, 1976-2001** ........................................ 155

*page*

    Thoughts in Spring on Professional Identity by Richard Swain, Ph.D. ....................155

    Presentation by James Carafano, Ph.D. ...................................................................165

    Questions and Answers ............................................................................................173

**Day 2, Panel 6: Educating Leaders for a New Era, 2002 to Present** ......................**183**

    Mission Command: An Old Idea for the 21st Century by
      COL (R) Gregory Fontenot ..................................................................................183

    A New "Melody Report" Educating Officers for the 21st Century by
      Kevin Benson, Ph.D. ...........................................................................................191

    Questions and Answers ............................................................................................195

**Day 3, Panel 7: Sister Services Perspectives** ................................................................**197**

    Historical and Cultural Foundations of Navy Officer Development by
      Gene R. Andersen, Ph.D. ....................................................................................197

    "It was More Than Just Doctrine!" Reflections on the Preparation
    of the US Marine Corps and Its Officers for World War II by
      Donald F. Bittner, Ph.D. ......................................................................................205

    Questions and Answers ............................................................................................219

**Day 3: Featured Speaker** ...............................................................................................**223**

    US Army Leader Development: Past, Present, and Future by
      Brigadire General Sean B. MacFarland ..............................................................223

    Questions & Answers ..............................................................................................231

**Day 3, Panel 8: Foreign Perspectives** ...........................................................................**235**

    Making Australian Military Leaders: A Historical Reflection Based
    on the Changing Face of Wars and the Australians That are
    Selected to Fight Them by Lieutenant Colonel Craig Burn ....................................235

    Finding the Balance Between Timeless Fundamentals and Temporal
    Adjustments by Colonel Jean-Claude Brejot ..........................................................239

    A British Perspective by Colonel Graham Norton ..................................................243

    Questions and Answers ............................................................................................247

**Appendix A Conference Program** ................................................................................**255**

**Appendix B Biographies** ................................................................................................**261**

# Day 1: Keynote Presentation

## Cultivating Army Leadership: A Historical Overview by Brigadier General (R) John S. Brown

(Transcript of Presentation)

**Dr. Wright:**

It is my distinct pleasure and honor to welcome Brigadier General Retired John S. Brown, who gave more than 34 years of service to the United States Army, and now teaches as an adjunct professor and serves as a historical consultant. His most recent duty assignment was Chief of Military History for the United States Army.

Previously, General Brown served as Chief of Programs and Requirements for Supreme Headquarters Allied Powers Europe, Executive Officer to the Army Deputy Chief of Staff Operations, Commander of the 2d Brigade for his Cavalry Division in Texas and Kuwait, G3 Operations through our III Corps, G3 of the 24th Infantry Division, and Commander of 2-66th Armored Battalion in Germany. He has commanded Army units at every level from Platoon through Brigade, and has served on staffs at every level from Battalion through Theater.

General Brown has published, edited, and lectured at home and overseas. Notable publications include, *Draftee Division*, a case study of divisional mobilization in World War II, and the forthcoming *Kevlar Legions*, a history of Army transformation, 1989-2005. The author has a monthly column, *Historically Speaking*, in *Army Magazine*, and has written numerous articles and chapters. And that's an understatement on General Brown's part—he has written many, many things.

His education is outstanding—the United States Military Academy, Indiana University, United States Army Command General Staff College, United States Naval War College, and earned his PhD at Indiana University. Ladies and gentlemen, General John S. Brown.

**BG Brown:**

Thank you for that kind introduction. Hopefully, everybody can hear me. Well, it's good to see everybody here, and good to see so many old friends and faces, and meet and see some new folks. Can I have my first slide? Subject is Cultivating Army Leadership: Historical Perspectives. I was asked to give a speech that would kind of speak to the whole program, recognizing that we're going to parse it down into greater detail as we move long. And of course, as historians—or as folks interested in history—you know, we've got a certain responsibility towards the smaller details of who, what, when, where, why, when we're talking about cultivating Army leadership.

One theory holds that there's kind of timeless principles of leadership, and so that if you could just figure them out, distill them, grasp them, that you would be able to have a feel for what all leaders need—forever, whenever. I do believe that there are certain timeless principles, with respect to leadership.

But I think the story beyond that is a lot more complex, and a lot more given to an understanding of culture, of history, of timeframes, of circumstances. And that's where I think we, as historians, can be particularly useful. Because we can work the detail, and flesh out a contribution that goes to both the timeless and the time-sensitive.

Let me go with my next slide. Hopefully you're looking at the definition of leadership. It comes from Army Regulations 600-100, FM 6-22. They're in synch; they both have the same definition. Those are two surprisingly good pieces of work. If you were to read through them, you'll find that they don't take as long as you might think to get through. They're very interesting, a lot of detail. That's the defection they proposed for leadership, and I think that's the one that I want to go ahead and use today, just as a starting point.

I would say it's not a universally-agreed definition—there are other definitions. The standard college dictionary, Harcourt Brace, speaks to, "The office, position, or capacity of a leader," as leadership. Of course, then you have to go and define what a leader is. And you find the leader, basically, is someone who makes things happen. Another definition is, "Authoritarian control or guidance." But I think that this finer notion of a process of influencing people, and having responsibilities both to the mission and the organizing—I think that's something we want to carry forward in our definition.

Some time ago, General Reimer and a number of his four-star colleagues sat together in a room, and they tried to articulate the Army values that they believed were timeless, and they thought you would believe were. The things they thought were timeless, and they came up Army values—we ended up with a card, I don't know how many of you still have the card in your wallet, but you were reminded of the things that the Army considered to be its timeless, essential values that all soldiers should carry forward with them.

Now you'll notice, if you lay out the letters, you get an acronym. And the acronym, very curiously, matches up, "leadership." Now, was that an accident? You know, was it divine intervention? No. It was a conscious effort by General Reimer and his colleagues to make a connection between the timeless values that they believed represented leadership, and the timeless values of soldiers as a whole. And so, there was a linkage. You know, and to be a leader, who had to represent these timeless values. Now, these do appear in FM and AR 600-100, and they appear in FM 6-22. They're very thoughtfully contrived.

But there's a lot else that appears in the lines. These are also attributes of leadership that are taught and sought in our current doctrine that, in my view, are valid, but represent items that are time-sensitive and culture-sensitive. And should times and circumstances change, the validity of these values will change. For example, solve complex problems.

At great danger, I'll paraphrase Frederick the Great, who was the leading soldier of his day. And he led an army in a time in which the formula for success was to march forward resolutely, and the musketry to deliver a greater volume of musketry of his own. And with respect to leadership he said, you know, if you give me something, somebody, a young officer—he was talking about the young aristocracy, the Junkers, if you give me one of these young men who's energetic and stupid, it's OK. He'll make a fine infantry line officer. If you give me someone who's lazy but smart, that's great. He'll do a great job on the staff. If you give me somebody who's lazy and stupid, I can use him too. We'll figure something out. But the one who will be *very* difficult is the officer who is energetic and smart.

In the army of his day, when you marched forward into that musketry fire, and you had to be resolute, and you had keep all your men on line, and everybody had a single function, you didn't want a whole lot of creative thinking. You didn't want a whole lot of second-guessing. You didn't want a whole lot of folks who were trying to work their way through the intricacies of a complex problem. You wanted a very simple, methodical, trained solution. That was the warfare of his day. It's not the warfare of our day. So, I think that that's a little bit time-sensitive.

Take another anecdote. Communicate, coordinate, and negotiate with a variety of personnel. Certainly, that's exactly what we're asking our soldiers to do at almost every level. Certainly in Iraq and Afghanistan, but preceding that, in the Balkans and all of the Operations in which you have the notion of—and it's a valid one—the strategic private. The guy who's on a blocking position, or at a checkpoint, whose role is so important that, in moments, whatever he does can become an international issue.

But just a few years ago, during Desert Storm, I can remember, you know, our battalion was out in the desert, we were in Iraq—we were occupying Iraq. But our instructions were very clear to have nothing to do with the locals. To keep them at an arm's distance. There were a very select group of people who were supposed to deal with, talk to, have any interface with the locals. Our job there was to occupy the oil fields, and to make sure the oil fields were not put into use until such time as Saddam Hussein signed the treaty and everything was validated, so that we would leave and go home.

And so, the instructions to our soldiers, at that time, were not communicate, coordinate, and negotiate with a variety of personnel. And the expectation was not that it would be done at all levels. There was a very, very narrow group of selected soldiers who were responsible for doing that kind of coordination, or that kind of interface. And we're only talking about events 20 years ago, I'd say. It's not Frederick the Great, you know? It's some time ago.

Adapt to advances in communications technology. For at least 1500 years, between the time of the Romans and the time of the late Renaissance, there were no advances in communications technology. So, one presumes that the leaders of that time didn't have to adapt to changes in communications technology to be successful. Maintain positive expectations and attitude. Obviously, that's something that's very valuable to our Army and our culture. We like to have people happy.

But how many of you know Steve Colbert? Yeah, you know, right now, in the aftermath of Glenn Beck's march on Washington, you know, Jon Stewart's going to have a march on Washington that's kind of going to go the other way. And it's going to try to be broad-minded, and comprehensive, and inclusive. But Colbert says, well, he's going to have a march on Washington too, because he thinks that the imperative, now, is to bring back fear. And so he wants to restore the notion of intimidation, fear to the political process.

Well of course, I think he's joking. You know? But the point is, in cultures other than our own, and in times other than our own, there have been other incentives that were relied upon to develop the morale, and to exercise the leadership of soldiers in the ranks. And there are some armies in which fear is the traditional means of gaining compliance and exerting leadership. And there was a time in our own Army when fear a higher priority than it does now.

A testimony to time-sensitiveness. I would suggest to you that our contemporary adversaries have far different techniques of leadership and motivation than we do, to get their rank and file to execute the missions that they believe are important. And I don't think that Al-Qaeda sets a huge emphasis upon their soldiers having a positive mental attitude, in the way we think of a positive mental attitude.

Finally, another point is pent athlete. You know, in my mind, there are number of places in each of the volumes where folks speak of the requirement, the necessity, and the virtue of the leader being a pent athlete. To me, this implies he'd have five basic skills, but I've never found a list in which they actually numerated five. There's one place where they say you have to be a pent athlete, and they list about 30 different things you're supposed to be able to do. And so, the notion that he's multi-capable is there. But in earlier times, or in different times, the list would be different. Your pent athlete would respond to a different list. Let me have my next slide.

Leadership is obviously position-sensitive. It depends upon where you are in the hierarchy, what your techniques and attributes are. The direct leadership, organization leadership, and strategic leadership—that's the paradigm that appears in our AR and our FM. It's meant, I think, to match up with the levels of [who are?] tactical, operation, or strategic.

Although in my mind, it makes a kind of curious match at the break-off point. Because the break-off point between organizational leadership in the book is brigade, you know, brigade is the lowest level of organizational leadership. And in my view, that would mean a battalion commander would be involved in direct leadership. And my experience with privates is that they tend of battalion commander as a pretty lofty position, a pretty distant guy. The battalion commander is working through the prism of a trained staff of professional soldiers, each of whom have their specialty.

And so I think the battalion commander, from the point of view of leadership levels, is the break-off point between the direct leadership that occurs at the company grade and below, and the leadership by the virtue of staff and delegation. That's more common at the organizational level. But the point having been made that there are these levels, I think all of you—if you think back through your memories—can think of somebody who is a superb company commander. An excellent company commander, or an unmatched company commander, who simply did not have the attributes and character that it would have taken to command a brigade or a division.

And within our historical inventory, we can find all kinds of folks who made excellent division commanders, but failed when called upon to command at the corps or higher level, to be theater commanders. And it's not just that the leadership to be a captain is the lesser, in included attributes of the leadership to be a brigade, or the lesser-included attributes to be a theater. The character of the responsibility can be so different that you can bring somebody who would've been a poor company commander who, nevertheless theoretically, would make a great theater commander.

In our Army, we don't test that theory. Because of course, we bring people through the layers of command so that they achieve success without ever having someone advance who hasn't proven themselves at the lower level. But in many cultures and armies other than our own, folks literally did come in at the highest level. Julius Caesar, for example, had never commanded anything other than a boat before he commanded four legions in the Battle of Bibracte that began his career in Gaul. And he came in as a senior leader with great vision, but served by a highly professional army who absolutely knew what it was, the tactics of the time involved. And he was able to think at the highest level without having to worry about what happens to the lower level, because his centurions took care of that.

Now, on that subject, when I graduated from West Point, and for most of you who graduated from West Point too, you'd been through Military Art, you'd taken all the courses, you were perfectly capable of deciding what needed to happen in the Pacific or European Theater during World War II. You graduated from West Point as an excellent theater commander. What was hard was commanding a platoon. That whole learning experience, that whole coming up requires a set of skills that's different than the one that you can get through academics alone. And so what's the mix? What do you teach? And what do you *have* to learn on the job? What do you have no option for, except that first-hand experience?

Also from our FM, "Leadership is institutional, operational, self-development with respect to how it is you derive it." And we've already touched on this a little bit in an earlier comment. Institutional, obviously, is what you learn in the schoolhouse, and the things that you were taught, and it's a curriculum that is consciously instilled in the expectation that, somehow, you will take something away that will be relevant to your responsibilities. Operational is learning by doing. You know, just being a part of the program. You're on the job, and the words we use all gravitate around the notion of on-the-job experience. And then self-development are things that you do for yourself outside of the requirements of either your job or your education. The things you do to improve yourself.

Now I'd suggest to you that, within our own system, for much of our history, on-the-job training was the way it was done. That these other two options, institutional and self-development, were much thinner. I think when we get to panel one, we're going to have a great opportunity to kind of go over this. I think Dr. Wayne Hsieh is going to be able to speak to us from his background, having written about West Pointers in the Civil War, the old Army in war and peace. The notion of the role West Point played in cultivating this generational leadership.

But what we have to remember is that West Point was founded in 1802, and it didn't really start producing general officers until the Civil War. That was the first occasion where you saw general officers being produced by the virtue of an institution that was designed, in theory, to promote leadership. So for two generations, West Point, really, was a repository of engineering skills, of ballistics, of technical skills, and military technique.

And many of your leaders of the time felt that that was the only thing education could do for you. And that more to the point, that your cavalry officer and your infantry officer, and your line officer was going to be such a person by the virtue of talent, and temperament, and character. And that he was going to rise to the top without much need for education. That he was going to be the great militia leader, like Green. You know? Or Bedford Forrest. And that education was not particularly contributive. But that you did need it for people who were going to make maps, and people who were going to build buildings, and people who were going to construct fortifications, and people who were going to deal with artillery ballistics.

Now, in fact, where we got our general officers was by and large by the virtue of political connections. But the West Point leavening proved itself in the Mexican War as being a great way to produce very capable junior officers. And by the Civil War, as we're going to see in the panel, I believe, it bears fruit in this proliferation of general officers that have marked the course of the notion of institutional education, ever since.

In that same panel Dr. Steven Woodworth will be speaking to us, and amongst a proliferation of other publications, many publications, you've got his book, *Nothing but Victory: The Army of the Tennessee*. A great discussion and case study of the war in the West, and how that army achieved a very high state of competence and prestige, even though it's often overlooked for the Army of the Potomac. But it's interesting to note, as you take a look at the key players, the big stars, you know, you've got people like Grant, and Sherman, and Sheridan. These guys were not at the pinnacle of their class as West Pointers. They were not, incidentally, on the top of their game as army officers, either, in the pre-war Army. And the guys who *were* the superstars were guys like McClellan and Halleck.

And in the crucible of the Civil War, there was a disconnect that we probably need to discuss. And I'm sure panel one is going to address it a lot more than I'll be able to, here. What is the disconnect between the preparations and expectations of army officers before the war, and what played out and paid off in the Civil War? Had times changed? Or was there a flaw in the leadership that was being developed? And I'm going to come back to that point here, in a little bit, when we talk about it today.

Self development. You know, what exactly is the self development that's relevant to developing leaders? Well you know, for many generations, it was thought to be personal character. And the officers of the time had a classical education. And there were not a few of them who could read *Plutarch's Lives* in the original Latin or Greek. Now of course, *Plutarch's Lives*, consciously, was an effort to develop standard emulation which would allow you to develop worthy military leaders. I mean, now, the reason Plutarch wrote the book was, he wanted to provide examples that were worthy of emulating.

Now, when you get into self development that is going to create the officer who's going to command on the field of battle, character is important, but it can't be everything. And for a long time, there was a relative thinness of the literature that was going to be able to advance your capacity for self development. Before the Civil War, there wasn't all that much to read in order to develop yourself. A little bit, not all that much.

In our second panel, Dr. Perry Jamieson will be talking about, amongst other things, I saw him last night and he said he might mention *Crossing Deadly Grounds*, his book, *The United States Army Tactics, 1865-1899*. That reading, that fine piece of work, is important not just for the tactics that were being developed during the period, but more importantly, for the interplay and exchange of ideas back and forth in the professional literature that propelled this forward. And so self development, in part, is participation in this process of exchanging ideas and the deliberation.

In the same panel, Todd Brereton, who is the author of *Educating the US Army: Arthur L. Wagner and Reform*, hopefully will speak to this period as being a period in which, for the first time, education gained parity with experience. As the framework of reference of how it was officers were going to develop. But again, when we're talking about leadership, time-sensitive. Or time and culturally sensitive, in some respects.

Right now, what I want to do is belabor you with a little family history, family story. Bear with me, because as hard as it may be to believe, it'll lead somewhere eventually. 1912, my grandfather shows up at Battery DeRussy and he walks in to the battery. He's met at the door by a sharp-looking NCO speaking in a little bit of an Irish accent. And the NCO says, "Sir, we're very", I can't imitate an Irish brogue, I'd try, but I wouldn't do very well with it. You know, "Sir, we're very pleased to have you. All the men here are very proud to have an academy graduate as their new lieutenant. You're going to have a wonderful career, and we're going to have a great time, as long as you do your job and let me do mine. You go to all the meetings, you tell us what you want to do, you attend to the company commander, but when it comes to telling the soldiers what to do, you let me do that. Officers lead NCO's, NCO's lead men."

When my father showed up in 1942, it was to the 88th Infantry Division, which was the first of the all-draftee division in the combat in World War II, and everything was in turmoil. 15,000 soldiers had showed up, they all came across the Camp Gruber site. Out of this huge mass of draftees, there was a very tiny sliver of experienced officers. There were 200 experienced officers and 200 experienced NCO's out of the whole mass. And so, my father didn't have a platoon sergeant that showed up and told him what to do. He had a young E-6 who he went and found, who upon finding him, he said, "Well oh, I'm so happy you're here. You can help me out. Sir, what am I supposed to do?"

And it was this huge process of the Army trying to grow overnight, from being a small organization to being a massive one. And might as well tell you, probably at some point. My father had been my grandfather's aide until such time as he eloped with the boss's daughter and got kicked off of the division staff. And you know, that was what carried him down to be in a newly-formed battery with the E-6 as his NCO counterpart. But endearingly, my grandfather wrote my father a note shortly before he arrived, and said, you know, he called him Brownie, "Brownie, about time for you to show up. Look forward to seeing you. We got a big job on our hands, because everybody here knows even less about the Army than you do." So, you know, family pride.

But when I showed up, in 1972 as this 2-37 Armor Battalion in Erlangen, Germany, the Vietnam War was winding down, but we weren't set to Vietnam. My whole West Point class was sent to Germany, because at that time, Germany was in trouble with respect to force structure, with respect to assets, with respect to resourcing, with respect to the noncommissioned leadership. The commissioned officer leadership was as good as I've ever seen. But when you got to the noncommissioned officers, by and large for seven or eight years, they'd had a choice of a follow-on assignment coming out of Vietnam. And by and large, they would choose not to go to Germany as their follow-on assignment coming out of Vietnam.

And so, there was a window of time where you were very underrepresented by noncommissioned officers, and the arriving lieutenant, when I arrived, it was the first day of the use for alert. And that's where, you know, Lariat Advance, everybody's rolling out of the motor pool, all of the tanks are supposed to be on the road. Went to find my platoon sergeant, he was drunk. The next ranking man after this guy, who was a E-6, was a E-5, and he was drunk too. So it was E-4's and privates. This was a very narrow window of time, but a window of time when the noncommissioned officer presence just wasn't present in Europe. And if you want your idea of either hell or purgatory, try commanding a tank company without a noncommissioned officer. And so, you ended up with privates and lieutenants trying to do each other's job.

When my son reports into Vicenza, Italy, the 503d Airborne, he walks into the door, he's met by a sharp-looking NCO speaking with a slight Latin accent. Noncommissioned officer says, "Sir, welcome aboard. All of the men are very proud to have an Academy graduate as their new lieutenant. You're going to have a wonderful career, and we're going to have a great time, if you do your job and let me do mine. You go to the meetings, you attend to the battalion commander, you take notes, you tell us what you want done. But when it comes to telling the soldiers what to do, you let me do that. Officers lead NCO's, NCO's lead men." So, how far have we come in 85 years?

I would say though, you know, beyond the charm of having a personal connection with each of these folks, who are of course all dear to me, is the kind of larger picture that I believe that it gave me an intimate look at the fact that each of these soldiers was walking into a *different* Army.

Under the able supervision of Richard Stewart, right now, I'm working on a book, *Army Transformation*, it was mentioned. We call it *Kevlar Legions*, subtitled, *The Army Transformation 1989-2005*. You know, to get there, we need to talk about the previous transformations of the Army. And you know, when I'm talking about transformations, I mean your major changes, your sea changes. Your changes that take your Army from being one thing to being another. The expectation of some kind of exponential change in the results. Either you're ten times more lethal, or you're ten times more capable, or ten times less likely to take causalities. And it's adoption, not just of new technology, it's also socioeconomic change, strategic change, big picture.

These are the transformations I believe have occurred. I believe my grandfather walked into an Army for empire. And that that existed from the Spanish-American War through 1941, with a brief intermission for World War I, and that it was a very special army that had some characteristics that we'll talk about later, that transitioned to be the mobilization-based Army that we're familiar with from World War II. That there was a rehearsal for the mobilization-based Army in World War I, but the rehearsal didn't take, in the sense of radically altering the Army as it existed on the ground in 1920. But with World War II, that second bout of mobilization, followed by your strategic responsibilities in the aftermath of the war, did change the Army permanently into the mobilization-based Army.

The mobilization-based Army was coterminous, in some respects, with the early Cold War Army. Although the early Cold War Army was substantially different, by the virtue of its overseas responsibilities and nuclear munitions. The late Cold War Army was in the aftermath of Vietnam, but more importantly to the nature of the Army, it was all-volunteer. And then of course, the purpose of my book is to establish that, at some point in time, that late Cold War Army itself, transitioned to the digitized, expeditionary Army that we live in today.

And I believe that today's Army is appreciably different than the late Cold War Army, and certainly different than the early Cold War Army. And that's a little bit advanced advertisement on the book. But now, let's take a look at each of those cultures that these men walked into.

The lieutenant of 1912, he was, at the time up front, America, the United States was the most egalitarian country in the world. And was in fact in the midst of the Progressive Era, and it was in fact supportive of and trying to advance democratic processes. But nevertheless, the soldiers of that time were comfortable with and mindful of class and race in a way that would make us very uncomfortable today, but was generally accepted as kind of the way things were.

Officers, by and large, were drawn from the middle class. The middle class was relatively small compared with the middle class that we have today. There was a much larger working class. The working class was the locus from which soldiers were drawn. The working class included a very, very high proportion of immigrants, in the case of the Northeast. In the case of the South and West, a very large proportion of, essentially, agriculturally, you know, folks who had lived and been raised on farms. The officers had strikers, but this was nothing unusual, because the middle class had hired help.

There was a social division that translated itself comfortably into the ways that the Army did business. And in a lot of respects, the culture of the time was the reason that the Army worked. The most outstanding example, of course, is the high caliber and quality of the 9th and 10th Cavalry and the 24th and 25th Infantry, which were your black infantry and cavalry regiments. The NCO structure, there, was incredibly capable because, of course, for those individuals, a method of advance, and an opportunity for advance existed in the Army that existed nowhere else. There was a ceiling, but it was an opportunity for advance.

Similarly, the high proportion of Irish NCO's as a character, I mean, Irish NCO's is almost a stereotype of the time, but it had to do with the opportunities that existed. And so you had men who had a great deal of talent, that could not otherwise advance in society by the virtue of the social structure, who had an outlet for their success by the virtue of being the highly-capable Noncommissioned officers that we know from this period.

Now, the middle class, the ones who would go to West Point, would become officers, along with other aspirations, they put a great stock on personal knowledge, education, erudition. Getting to college, not many people went to college, a relatively few went, at the time. The education gave them an advantage, with respect to grasping the larger issues that they were supposed to apply to the problems that they faced. Up through 1920, advancement in the Army through major was by the virtue of competitive examination. You took a test to move forward. Because that was true, you had an institutional incentive to be well-read that matched up with the social imperative that was already there for people of your class.

The lieutenant of 1912, as he matured, would value school assignments. This wasn't just by the virtue of the kind of Progressive Era instinct towards book-learning, and the late 19th century professionalization, the major professions, to say, emerged at the time. But it also was the fact that the lieutenant of 1912 *knew* he was going to be a captain for a long time. Knew he was going to be a lieutenant for a long time. Knew that he was going to have as much troop duty as he wanted, or could absorb. That he was going to see an awful lot of soldiers. And the exceptional assignment, the one that would set him apart, the one that would give him an opportunity, would be to teach at Fort Leavenworth. Or to teach in one of the branch schools. And to have the time to learn, to be educated, to impart knowledge to others, to reflect on things.

And so, that generation set a great stock by assignments within the Army school system. You know, my grandfather taught here, my wife's grandfather taught here, Patton taught here, Eisenhower taught here. They all taught here at the same time. They all thought that this was a great opportunity to advance their professional skills and to deal with things that they could not encounter in the course of troop duty. Because of course troop duty, at the time, meant company level and below. There was not division maneuvers and battalion operations. It was a modest touch.

This Army, the lieutenant of 1912, was committed to imperial service. He knew that he would travel around the world within a relatively narrow paradigm of the Philippines, Puerto Rico, Panama. If he was assigned within the United States, he'd be in the sticks, you know, some Western outpost. And this, incidentally, this exposure gave him the opportunity to, I'll give you an illustrative example of the value that learning added to the equation that this guy brought to the Army.

This was the period of time of the great medical breakthroughs. The reason the Europeans were able to colonize Africa during this period, and the United States was able to develop the Panama Canal in this period, or the Philippines were effectively occupied, is because the American Army, for the first time, along with its other imperial counterparts, figured out and conquered disease. The lethal diseases that had taken tens of thousands of troops in early eras, you know, Yellow Fever, dysentery, they didn't exactly eliminate them, but they figured them out to the point that you could keep the casualties from them exceptionally low. With good reason, the builder of the Panama Canal estimated that, by the virtue of medical knowledge, they'd saved 70,000 they otherwise would've lost on the project. 70,000 lives represent the entire strength of the US Army at the time.

The people who brought this to bear were, of course, the people who were reading books, the people who had a little bit of knowledge, the people who were trying to bring in this new notion of germ theory to the active build of the Army. The Army officer was professionalizing at about the same time that the medical profession was professionalizing, and about the same time lawyers and everybody else were becoming professions.

So when you kind of take a look at it, the noncommissioned officer didn't have any of the time, hadn't given a whole lot of thought to germ theory. I mean, that wasn't high on his list of things to worry about or think about. But if the lieutenant said, "OK, you're going to put the latrine downstream from the mess hall. You're going to have the latrine at least 100 meters from everybody else. We're going to put oil on all of these water spots where mosquito larva had developed. And all the men are going to wash their hands before breakfast." The NCO didn't have any strong feelings one way or the other, but if the officer said it was going to happen, it was going to happen, and he made it happen.

And that kind of medical discipline was a unique attribute of this generation of officers in a way that that it never was before, and really hadn't been since. We've never reached the point of having the consciousness of hygiene that this generation had. Where, right now, we kind of are of the opinion that doctors are so good, medicine is so advanced, that whatever I get, they'll give me a pill and I'll be all right. So you know, we don't worry about medical implications in the way that these guys did, because there was no failsafe. There was no, you know, once you caught it, you were gone.

The junior officer, the lieutenant of 1942, couldn't afford the kind of frame of reference or attitude, the authoritarian class system that the lieutenant of 1912 lived with. It no longer existed. It really didn't exist in society as a whole, but in particular, it didn't exist in the Army of 1942. Because you didn't have that very solid, robust cadre of noncommissioned officers to run the show in the way that it had been run in the earlier Army. The class system, in a lot of respects, had broken down in the Great Depression. The movement, from that point on, would ever enlarge the middle class, to the point that the middle class would be the dominant demographic, rather than the minority demographic.

And of course, the lieutenant was thrown into circumstances where everybody was of relatively little experience, and all kind of things had to be done at once, in the course of this massive mobilization. The technique that was settled upon in the 88th Division, and in most other divisions, with respect to training, was not that the folks who knew what they were doing would teach everything to everybody who didn't know what they're doing. You know, which is kind of the obvious thing. You'd think that, "Well OK, you've got 200 NCO's, so they'll each take X number of soldiers, and they'll teach them what it is that they need to know."

That was not what was done. The alternative was that you took the lieutenant, who you were going to put in charge, and you trained him the night before. He trained his subordinates on whatever it is that they were supposed to know. And the same thing was true with the NCO. And you know, the formula you had, at Camp Ruby, you had night classes where the lieutenants went and learned what it was that they were supposed to know. And within a few days time, they were teaching that same material to the privates.

And the imperative was, whether you know it very well or not, you're in charge, you need to take charge. And the people who are going to be serving underneath you need to go to you, and see you as being the source of leadership, the source of knowledge, the source of guidance. And it reinforced the chain of command as it went along.

This was a generation that developed a huge thirst for troop duty. They wanted to be with the soldiers, and the wanted to be as often as they could. And the reason was, things were moving very quickly, and ranks moved very quickly, and the expansion of the Army was happening at a breakneck pace. And if you missed out on an operational assignment, you might miss the next step, because the steps were coming quickly. This was not an Army in which you were going to be a lieutenant for 20 years. You had to capture your moment, and you had to move quickly.

The generation was defined by World War II. Whenever my father would meet one of his colleagues, one of the first questions would be, "Well, where did you serve?" Well, what was meant by the question was, "Where did you serve in World War II? What unit were you with? What campaign were you in?" There were several generations in which, then, all the Chiefs of Staff came through, you know, had crossed Omaha Beach. The World War II experience defined them.

One thing I didn't comment on and should have. The branch experience was very distinctive and very unique in the pre-World War II army. And so, coast artillery men, and cavalry men, and infantry men lived in very different worlds, and they did different things. And it was not at all unusual for an infantryman to do infantry operation, and that was the only branch or specialty that was represented. It simply didn't happen in World War II. In World War II, the imperative of combined arms warfare manifested itself and never left. Every operation involved engineers, artillery, tanks, tight-knit and very capable combat arms performance.

With respect to the occupationist aftermath, this affected the World War II generation in a way analogous to the World War II combat experience affected them. But in kind of a reverse sort of way. When they were occupying Germany and occupying Japan, this generation was automatically catapulted into the unstated mission of helping the Germans and Japanese kind of figure out democracy, and civil rights, and Western culture. And you know, there was this whole effort in the mind of the United States to re-educate the Germans and Japanese in the direction of the virtues that we believed we had.

But of course, the first thing out of your mouth, if you're a lieutenant, or a captain, or a major, and you're trying to develop this kind of instruction is, "You know, the reason we had to bomb Germany to smithereens is because you all are racist and authoritarian." And then of course suddenly, you reflect as the German asks, "Well what about your black soldiers? What about your own race relations?" And this generation came to grips with the notions of racism and the notions of authoritarianism.

This is the period of time in which the integration of the Army began. This is the period of time in which the Uniform Code of Military Justice took its present form. Wherein which, for generations, the law was whatever the 1st sergeant decided it was. And instead, you had a Uniform Code of Military Justice which codified and which had fail-safes. That's the lieutenant of '42.

World War II was fought by two generations, not one. Maybe more. But in my own case, my grandfather and my father both fought, and fortuitously, in the same division. And so, you can kind of get a feel for the fact that you had both generations in play at once, and you had the character of both generations in play at once. And it was a narrow of time in which that could have happened.

One of the articles I've written dealt with general officer leadership in World War II, and if you take a look at the general officer level, you'll find virtually all of them had faculty experience. My grandfather taught the Dardanelles Campaign, here at Fort Leavenworth. And the Dardanelles Campaign, of course, is amphibious landing in the Mediterranean, and dealt with all the difficulties and miscarriages that occurred in that particularly amphibious landing. This was not a bad set of skills to have when you were fighting in the Mediterranean, again, in 1942-45.

Habits of reading and reflection. These guys, remember, they hadn't really served in units above the size of company. They'd never seen tanks or airplanes that actually worked. And yet, they had the capability and the imagination to put together the Army groups that fought World War II and effectively lead them. They had the capability to fight *Blitzkrieg* with capabilities that exceeded those of the Germans who had invented it. They governed all these strange lands and different places in the aftermath of World War II.

And so, somehow, they got, by the virtue of their learning and education, the things that they could not possibly have experienced, in fact. They all had operational or combat experience—not as much combat as you might have thought. A couple of months in World War I in about a third of the cases. But they were all very familiar with the artillery-infantry combination, and they all had served with that.

Interestingly enough, the litmus between the successful and unsuccessful general officers in World War II seems to have been the relative experience with field-grade command or high-level staff at that critical point between 1938 and about 1942. There were about 20 officers who were either division commanders or corps commanders who were relieved in the course of the war. And if you compare them with 20 commanders who were demonstrably successful, you'll find that the successful commanders went through their entire interwar experience, had done all of these schools and other things.

But when the mobilization began, and the Army began growing in earnest, they were fortunate enough to be assigned, in many cases, as battalion commanders, and in some cases, as regimental commanders. But as the Army expanded, one thing led to another, and they went to battalion, to regiment, to division, to corps. And so, as they progressed up the ladder, they had a good, strong feel for the commands that were immediately underneath them.

You had yet another cohort of officers who were popped onto the high-level staff because you need staff officers, and someone has to do it. And they started off on corps staff, and then they advanced to theater staff. And they moved, and they stayed in the high-level staff. And they become too valuable to move. And then, when they got their opportunity to be division commanders or corps commanders, they didn't have the depth of experience that would've allowed them to succeed. And too many of them failed.

But the combination between the two generations can be illustrated by the example of the 88th Infantry Division. Its first combat was Operation Diadem in World War II. This was in Italy. The senior officers had a big picture of what was supposed to happen. They had the Leavenworth solution, they knew how all of the different parts were supposed to be. They deployed their forces on the ground, they had given the guidance of how everything was supposed to happen.

In the opening moments of the campaign, the artillery went in right on time, the troops came out right behind the artillery, the troops went right up behind this curtain of artillery. They were within 30 seconds of the artillery lifting as they hit the next position. Mount Damiano fell, which was the critical piece of the Gustav Line, which is the Monte Cassino line. And so, this original battle plan had worked. They broke through, and they broke through with minimum casualties, and they were on the road.

But as they broke through, they were trying to get through to the Senger Line, called the Hitler Line, the next line of resistance. And they needed to get there before the Germans could redeploy to get there. And as this initial breakthrough had succeeded, as the initial pieces on the board had worked, as the plan had worked, you began to get this unraveling. Because, of course, no plan survives the initial contact with the enemy. And communications broke down. Things became difficult.

All the sudden, the battle migrated from being in the control of the senior leaders, like my grandfather, and it migrated down to being in the control of the junior officers who were trying to make things happen on the ground, and their noncommissioned counterparts. And the communications broke down. There was improvisation that was necessary. Somebody figured out that the artillery had the best radios. And that they generally could rely upon the artillery men to be in communications with each other if the ground permitted. But the ground didn't permit because the mountains were so steep, and there was such a difficulty with the defiles.

But the artillery also had observer planes, they had spotter planes. So, the spotter planes could fly. And so, you ended up with this improvised solution of flying the planes above the moving columns, and having the communications come through the artillery forward observers who had the radios that would work. Improvised on the ground.

As the advance progressed, it was quickly determined that you couldn't advance on the roads. The roads were too clogged; the Germans were too smart to let you use them. You had to go over the back of hills. Well, you couldn't get your supplies over. And traditionally, campaigns had broken down over supplies. But you had Italian mule tiers, you had mule trains. And the solution that had been improvised at the time was, you needed to lay as in, with the Italian mule tiers. You need to have something to make sure you could work with these guys, so you could get your mule through this absolutely forbidding landscape, and keep the pace of the advance going.

Well, there were some soldiers from Missouri who knew everything about mules. And there were some soldiers from New York who were of Italian descent, and knew everything about Italians. The Missourians knew nothing about Italians, the Italians knew nothing about mules. But between the two of them, they made the liaison that allowed the Italian mule team to be a party to the success of the advance.

And so, you had this improvisation that occurred at the grassroots level by the virtue of this kind of participate advantagement that was an instinctive characteristic of the 1942 generation. At the same time that you had a thoughtful, capable, and likely-to-succeed master plan that had been designed, with the Leavenworth solution, by men who had been in the class of 1912. And had, in fact, participated in the Leavenworth experience to the point of having taught on the faculty here. So, a good combination.

The lieutenant of 1972 comes in, you know, that ethnic diversity is the issue. Affirmative action is kind of a call sign. And although the Army had integrated earlier, this particular period was the time in which the integration, the successful integration of the Army, was the priority topic.

Now incidentally, I've missed the opportunity to make a point that I wanted to make. I apologize. But when talking about the general officer leadership in World War II, I did want to flag panel number three and Tim Nenninger, and his discussion of "The Leavenworth Schools and the Old Army." And Peter Schifferle, and his "America's School for War: Fort Leavenworth, Officer Education, and Victory in World War II." And the outstanding opportunity we're going to have with these two men to probe into the contribution of Leavenworth, through several generations, in creating the intellectual framework that allowed us to win World War II. And to provide that overarching capability for having the right plan that I spoke to, when speaking of the experience of the 88th Infantry Division.

The lieutenant of 1972 would be a cold warrior. His frame of reference would be the Soviet, and the army he would design himself against would be the Soviet Union. Now, I say this fully recognizing that the lieutenant of 1971 was coming in when the Vietnam War was still in progress.

I think when panel four gets together, we're going to have, from Dr. Lewis Sorley, Bob Sorley, amongst his other insights, he wrote *A Better War: Unexplained Victories and Final Tragedy of America's Last Years in Vietnam*. I think we owe Bob an enormous debt, in that, he's the first I know of to kind of turn around the paradigm that Vietnam was fought by a Cold War Army that just stumbled around in the woods, and got lost in the forest, and didn't know what it was doing. That in fact, the Army in Vietnam indicated a high success of adaptation to the circumstances, and a prospect of success overall, but that we walked away from the Vietnam experience. And in my own experience, the Vietnam experience was not part of the professional expectation of what the future was going to be like.

I think the Army left Vietnam behind, and is rediscovering it now. And I think that Dr. Henry Gole, who's the expert on *General William E. DePuy: Preparing the Army for Modern War*, will capture the frame of reference that we tend to become imbued with, as lieutenants of 1971, this notion that we were going to need to deal with a Soviet, or Soviet-like conventional adversarial. That was the mission at-hand. And to their credit, at the time, that was true. That was the greatest danger.

As a lieutenant, I would already be concerned with career management. And the notion of one generation was, "Well, get to the schoolhouse as often as you can." And the other generation was, "Get to troops as often as you can." By my time, the notion was, "You know, you have to get certain things done at certain times. You have to make certain gates. You have to be branch-qualified as a major. If you're a captain, you need to command a company just as quick as you can, and as often as you can. You're going to lose your window." You know, "When's your school time? You're going on two tracks. What is your other track going to be?"

And so, the whole idea of career management became an issue for the lieutenant of '71, in which, career management hadn't really been an issue in earlier generations. I mean, it wasn't thought of in those terms. And of course, you affectionately referred to the fellow in Washington, who you talked to once a year, as your "career mangler", you know? Because he was the one who was responsible for seeing to you got to the right jobs, and you got the right school, and did the right things along time.

Training management and expectation of the GDP. Those were, similarly, tightly organized, tightly constrained, tightly choreographed, highly structured. To the Army's credit, it did recognize that the noncommissioned officer level is the most difficult to replace. And it's the most vulnerable to the vagaries of war, deployment, all the rest of that.

And so, you ended up with a noncommissioned officer educational system, that developed over time, that was every bit as effective and capable as the officer's education system, that had long existed. And of course, all of us served as members of alliances. You know, wherever we were, that was the expectation. That we would be serving with soldiers, from countries other than our own, alongside them. Primarily in NATO.

For my son, the issue was no longer race. That was considered to be resolved. The issue was gender. And trying to accommodate circumstances in which you figured out whatever the implications were of the Exclusion Policy. And you had, you know, 12% women. And this was the social issue of the day. My son's digitized. Knows how to use a GPS, knows how to use Blue Force Tracking, intrinsically knows it, didn't have to be taught it. Could figure it out on the fly. They live in an expeditionary Army. Going back and forth overseas at a pace, and with a rotational, is a circumstance that's unparalleled in our previous experience.

Multitasking. It's not at all unusual for a unit, today, to send the officers off to participate in a CPX. The Bradley gunner's off to shoot at Bradley gunnery under the supervision of one set of NCO's. The infantrymen off to do whatever it is infantrymen are supposed to do, under the supervision of another set of NCO's. And you have the organization, it's not a company or battalion that's all in the same place at the same time, even during training.

And it's, of course, professionalized. Professionalized by the virtue of, you know, this huge emphasis upon all-volunteer Army. And then the amount of education, and the depth of investment that goes into that all-volunteer Army. With panel five, we're going to be able to have Rick Swain talking to us about *Lucky War*, hopefully, or the Desert Storm as the *before*.

You know, for me, Desert Storm was a culmination of a career. It was the point in time in which the Army arrived at demonstrating the capabilities that it truly had. So Desert Storm was the *after*. We've gone through all of this, and now we're at Desert Storm. For my son, Desert Storm was *before*. You know, in Desert Storm, you did all this wrong, and you were all screwed up, and these were all the things you couldn't do. And *now*, we're going to get so much better, because we're going to learn the lesson—we're going to learn from all the things you screwed up in Desert Storm.

Well, I think it's very interesting that we'll be able to have this expertise on Desert Storm, here. Because I really think that, from the point of view of Army transformation as I'm writing about it, Desert Storm is the tipping point. *It* is the litmus.

But along with this professionalization has gone a shrinkage of the Army, and a huge reliance on contractors. One of our experts, James Carafano, wrote, *Private Sector, Public Wars: Contractors in Combat*. That's going to be an opportunity to expose and experience the extent to which we have, in fact, contracted out things that the Army used to believe were intrinsic to leadership. This is not necessarily a problem. It's not necessarily wrong. But it is, you know, a new aspect to professionalism we haven't experienced in the past.

I have four grandsons. Every female, in their bloodline, is trying to convince them to do *anything* except go into the Army. And they've, of course, intimidated all the males into not pushing things too hard. But one of those guys is likely to screw up, and go in the Army. You know, the law of averages. If so, he'd be the lieutenant of 20-something. What will the Army be like for him? What will the leadership requirements be like for him?

In my view, age diversity is going to be an issue. With a shrinking population of traditional military aging, and expanding recognition of the value of health, and exercise, and all of that, and a diversification of the kinds of things soldiers are supposed to do. It's inevitable that we're going to have older and older soldiers, and we already do.

Robotics. Is that the next great wave? What are the implications of globalization? Physical criteria, what does it take to make a soldier? Is a soldier who is, you know, definition of combat is a soldier who's flying a drone from Lackland Air Force Base in combat. We already know that they're capable of getting PTSD. So, is that, those are the kind of paradigms or circumstances that we look forward to, with this next generation.

And I think that with panel six, Colonel Fontenot and Dr. [Kevin] Benson are going to be looking forward, into that aspect of it. You know, it's not enough to prepare today's leaders for today's circumstances. We also need prepare tomorrow's leaders—or anticipate tomorrow's leaders. Anticipate what we're going to do with the leaders we don't even have aboard yet. *And next slide*.

Think we're running to the point of an intermission. I'd just like to conclude by saying that leadership is, in some respects, timeless. But in some respects, it is relevant to the culture, positions, circumstances, and technology of the time. And the whole point that I hope I've brought across, with my extended story, is that each of those different armies I spoke to required a slightly different mix of leadership skills. There were some things that were timeless, but there were a lot of skills and capabilities that were time-sensitive.

And I think the historian's role, and the conference role, will be well-served if we're able to flag up and articulate the timeless. But we'll also be able to, with sufficient nuance, identify those things that are time sensitive, time constrained, or how things have changed over time. And if we do, then we are best able to provide the good service of matching today's circumstances with today's leadership development.

But perhaps more importantly, anticipating the needs of future leaders, in such a manner that we can design the programs that will train them for their roles. And the lieutenants of 202X are anticipated before they arrive, they're not getting their experience on the job. There's something the education system can offer them that prepares them for their responsibility. Thank you very much.

**Dr. Wright:**

Thank you very much, Sir. I'll just take a moment. I will be very brief, and then we'll go right into the discussion and question and answer session. Thank you again, Sir, for your overview of the symposium, and how the topic is going to be developed over the course of this event. That the leadership is time, culture-sensitive, and position-sensitive. You gave historical examples all the way back to Rome, all the way to present, and the role of West Point.

Each generation has a different Army. I thought that was very unique, and very unique to say. From 1912 to '42, '71 and '97, able to walk through the time period, and then personalize it, that was really neat too, with the family connection to each of those. Came full-cycle with the NCO Corps, showed how the NCO's developed. And also, to look to the future. You know, perhaps while the future's unknown yet, but it's coming. Our future is the history of tomorrow.

So, I will open this up. If you would please, if you have a point to make, or a question for General Brown, please raise your hand, I'll call on you. And again, push that button in front of you on the microphone, which will activate it.

## Day 1: Keynote Presentation

## Questions and Answers
(Transcript of Presentation)

## Moderated by Dr. Donald Wright

**Dr. Wright:**

Yes, Sir?

**Mr. King:**

Sir, Ben King, TRADOC. How you doing?

**BG Brown:**

Good! How are you today?

**Mr. King:**

Good, thanks. All these things you've touched on, from 1942 on, basically to the 21st Century—the Army leader has had to deal with an incredible amount of intellectual and social turmoil. From the leavening of the classes in World War II, integration, nuclear weapons, communications, the end of the women's Army Corps, that sort of thing. So all these leaders have had to deal with these things, until you get kind of all bunched up into the 80's and 80's, where you have the Nintendo generation that's kind of disturbing the old class of leaders. Do you see a leveling out now, in the 21st Century, where this social, intellectual turmoil that's been going on in the last half of the 20th Century will be less of a challenge in the 21st? I guess that's a loaded question, but yeah.

**BG Brown:**

I don't think so. I think that there are some things that will sort themselves out, and there are some things, aspects in which we'll kind of reduce our expectations, as our place in the world settles into a little less, a circumstance of primacy. But I think that our society is always going to be in turmoil. And I think, in the immediate future, we're going to have some very huge challenges. With respect, in particular, the demographic pressure of fewer and fewer young people to draw from, a broader and broader experiential base that they will be bringing into the Army. I think the culture wars, the social wars, the political turmoil, I don't think it will get worse, but I don't think it's going to get better. I think it's the kind of social analogy to whatever the law is, that computers get downsized by half, with every five years, or whatever.

**Mr. King:**

Moore's Law.

**BG Brown:**

I mean, there's going to continue to be this powerful pressure on us. And so, we're always going to have to draw upon our educational systems to deal with an uncertain and ever-changing future.

**Mr. King:**

Thank you.

**BG Brown:**

But that's only opinion, of course. 'Cause we're not there, yet.

**Mr. Gole:**

This is a follow-on to the excellent question—

**Dr. Wright:**

And excuse me, Sir. Just a moment, if you would. These proceedings are being transcribed—it's something I should have mentioned before—please state your name, your organization clearly, so that we can have that on the transcription. And then proceed to your comment, Sir.

**Mr. Gole:**

Henry Gole, disorganized. The question of the "we" of it, and the "I" of it, goes on. The question is very, very good, but I'm afraid it's [terrible?], and if anything, exacerbated by what I see around me right now. Projecting into the next year, two, three, four, five, this struggle between where one figures his role is as an individual human being, and his place in the society, the community at-large, the beat is going to go on. As a matter of fact, I think it's somewhat ominous.

**BG Brown:**

I agree with everything except your last comment. You know, the ominous part. Yeah, I believe the beat will go on, but I think it presents exciting and interesting prospects for our children and grandchildren, who know that they will be every bit as challenged and inspired as we were.

**Dr. Wright:**

Clay?

**MAJ Mountcastle:**

Good morning, Sir. Major Clay Mountcastle from here at CSI.

**BG Brown:**

Good to see you, Clay.

**MAJ Mountcastle:**

My question is geared, primarily, towards your experience or your opinion from the time you spent at CMH [Center of Military History], what was during a very pivotal point in our Army's transformation. You know recently, General (Retired) Bob Scales wrote, in our Army history, an article talking about the Army's too busy to learn habit it has developed recently, with the current OPTEMPO [Operational Tempo] during the Global War on Terror. And I was wondering your thoughts on, you know, you were presiding over CMH during 9/11, you got to see the Army's willingness to learn in the years leading up to 9/11, and then the transformation after 9/11. I have been assuming, recently, that the Army is using the Global War on Terror as an excuse to not do something that it really wasn't doing all that well, with leading up to 9/11. Basically, I'm directing that towards your digital generation of leadership. How well was the Army officer cohort doing, or taking the responsibility of learning its own history, in the lead-up to 9/11, in your estimation?

**BG Brown:**

It's an interesting question, Clay. I think that we often, and almost always, as historians, have found ourselves a bit put off by the insensitivity to history that the organization, as a whole, seems to have. And as you know, your father preceded me as Chief of Military History. And one of the insights he shared with me, as we were going through a transitional discussion, was the imperative of making sure that the services of historians were visible and available within the Army school system. And he had kind of energized a program that was called the Department of the Army Historical Advisory Committee, DAHAG. He had kind of refurbished it into an oversight committee that brought outsight, insight, and brought professors from a number of different locations to look in on the Army, see how well we were doing, see how well we were writing our history. And what I found was that, contrary to our opinion, these outside observers, who had been in venues other than the US Army, thought that, on a comparative basis, the Army was creditably attentive to history. That it was, in fact, trying to learn from its own experience. And that we were being critical of ourselves because we had a frame of reference that was different than theirs, in which they weren't counting, for example, the average student coming into Indiana University, or whatever. That is not at all to be dismissive of your point. I do think that we could make far more use of history, and far better use of history, and could learn more from our experience. And it's almost become an article of faith that an after-action review, once written, will be read once. And that'll be by the author, you know? Not by the guy who's got to do it again. And so, you know, there's an awful lot that we are avoiding. But I would say that our greatest danger is, if we not only fail to learn from those things that would contribute to the immediate event, but also, we fail to kind of step back and take a broad enough view to see deep. To allow the lessons we've learned from history to apply, not only to current circumstances, but to future circumstances. You know, to things that are out there at a greater distance. Did I do OK by your question?

**MAJ Mountcastle:**

Yes, sir, thank you.

**BG Brown:**

OK.

**Dr. Wright:**

We have approximately five minutes left. This will end up being one or two questions, perhaps. Sir?

**Dr. Wright:**

I'm Don Wright from CSI, and my question has to do with something that's current right now, out there being debated by both military officers and people outside the Department of Defense, even. And that's, what kind of leaders should we, as an institution, be preparing? Should we be preparing for the war that we have, or the war that, either, we want, or we think is on the horizon? And I think that the comments that you made about Vietnam, the Vietnam experience, and other things that we've read, that Vietnam really didn't have a major effect on the leader development system, according to system. Certainly below the field-grade level. So a general question about, what should the institution, looking back at its history, and maybe a little bit forward, how should it be thinking about what type of conflict to prepare for? Or should it be focusing on what we have at hand, right now?

**BG Brown:**

Hmm, great question. In just a few months, maybe a year, there's going to be a wonderful book, called *Kevlar Legions*, that is going to speak to the very point that you've made. And the recurrent balance that is struck between having to deal with contemporary circumstances, and trying to see deep. You know, for General Reimer, it was Army transformation, and the Army after next. You know, there was something that needed to happen right now, and there was something that was going to be downstream. For others, there are variations on that theme, or that model. The priority always goes to the immediate mission, with respect to the psychological energy your senior leaders can spend. Because they have lives on the line, people are actually dying, there's nothing that's hypothetical. You know, everything is happening right now, and needs immediate attention and circumstance. So, that's where your flow of energy and resources are going to go. But you have to set aside somebody, you have to parse somebody out who's sufficiently senior to have clout, authority, and access, and also, has a responsibility for seeing deep. And the traditional rule of thumb, that the Army staff is dealing with the immediate, and is churning in a squirrel cage of its own dealing with the deep future. And that TRADOC sets aside somebody to think of the deep future. And so, in answering your question, we really have to do both, but it's not likely to be that the Chief of Staff is going to be able to exclusively focus on either. You know, you have the Vice Chief of Staff, traditionally, is given responsibility of running the contemporary Army. So he takes all of that off of the Chief. The Chief is supposed to be thinking deep, and tries to think deep, but he will keep getting distracted by contemporary events. Somebody has to be set aside that is, in fact, your deep thinker, and is preparing for that more distant future. And by and large, there have been either exceptional organizations that have been set up to do that, like the Objective Task Force, or the Louisiana Maneuvers. But beyond that, also, there's the habit of faculties, and staffs, and schools everywhere to generate young faculty members who contribute, by also thinking deep. Was that a help?

**Dr. Wright:**

Absolutely. Ladies and gentlemen, this concludes our first section for this morning. Thank you very much.

# Day 1, Panel 1: Antebellum Officer Education, 1800-1865

## Looking Beyond West Point: Life in the Old Army as Education for War by Wayne Wei-siang Hsieh, Ph.D.

(submitted paper)

In much of both the popular and scholarly imaginations, the West Point background of Civil War commanders had a profound effect on their conduct of the war. In the past year we have seen Tom Carhart's *Sacred Ties: From West Point Brothers to Battlefield Rivals*, which aimed to be a group biography of sorts on young West Point graduates in the Civil War, and my own *West Pointers and the Civil War*, which obviously has implicit within its title the idea that that West Point background had a special significance.[1] While as an instructor at a service academy, I would like to think that some future historian can draw a straight line between what I teach in plebe Naval History and the I MEF commander's Joint Campaign Plan for Operation Iron Hammer in Zorgistan in 2030, but my own guess is that a deliberately overwhelmed and sleep-deprived plebe is going to do just enough to stay SAT in my course while fending off plebe Chemistry and his or her upperclassmen. For similar reasons, historians might wish to be cautious about drawing lines of influence between West Point classroom and Civil War battlefields, even if the same individuals occupied both spaces at different times in their lives. The antebellum careers of future Civil War generals in the "Old Army" had a profound effect on the way they waged war, but those effects came not from vaguely remembered lectures in "Old Cobben Sense" Mahan's capstone course on military science, or the close associations built between cadets at the academy, but on the more humble minor tactics and administrative knowledge regular army officers mostly acquired first at the academy, but later carried with them through their time in the "Old Army's" frontier and seacoast garrisons.

Military schools, like the schools attached to Fort Leavenworth and my own home institution at the Naval Academy, share the dilemma of trying to prepare their students for the next war. Unfortunately, the only wars we have sure knowledge are wars in the past, and the road between the past, present, and future is usually obscured by confusion, misdirection, and uncertainty. From the practical perspective of what cadets actually learned under the "Thayer system" (named for Sylvanus Thayer, who instituted crucial reforms at West Point after the end of the War of 1812), the answer must be that they learned little of great use for their roles as senior commanders during the Civil War. Indeed, outside of the small numbers of cadets who entered the Army's "scientific" branches such as the Engineers and the Ordnance Bureau, much of what they learned at West Point had little relationship to their day-to-day duties in line infantry, artillery, and cavalry regiments. A West Point graduate did receive a technical and scientific education second-to-none in antebellum America, but as a school for war, much of this scientific education remained, to put it bluntly, superfluous.

For most of the antebellum period, only a scant six days of Dennis Hart Mahan's first-class capstone course covered issues such as strategy, grand tactics, and other operational questions. As for the more rudimentary practical military training cadets received, which proved far more important, instruction in these subjects had their own problems. Furthermore, although substantial amounts of time at the academy were devoted to the drill field, a cadet's marks in tactics constituted in 1833 only 14 percent of a cadet's standing in his class. By 1854, that figure declined to 13 percent. In contrast, in the same year, the academy devoted 71 percent of classroom time to math, science, and engineering coursework, which was worth 54 percent of the order of merit.[2] In an army without established branch schools, practical military training probably should have occupied a higher proportion of a cadet's time at West Point.

Indeed, the academy's leadership recognized as much, and the first five-year course proposed in 1845 allotted more time to practical military training. The academic board for that year heartily endorsed reforms "to correct what is felt as an evil, particularly as upon no point is public censure found to bear more heavily and with a less disposition to excuse its errors, than upon that of professional ignorance." However, that academic board had still stuck by the position that nothing should be taken away from scientific training.[3] The five-year curriculum actually instituted in 1854 did use the extra year at the academy to add significant time to practical military training, while taking away nothing from the scientific curriculum instituted by Thayer shortly after the War of 1812. It is telling, however, that the increase in practical military training later provoked a backlash from the academy's engineering-orientated leadership.[4]

Indeed, the Corps of Engineers formal monopoly on the academy's administration would not be broken until after the Civil War, when the Army finally opened the position of West Point superintendent to officers outside the Corps of Engineers. The engineering-heavy curriculum instituted by Thayer and continued by his students, Mahan being the most important, had created a culture at the academy where, in John Tidball's words, "it becomes a kind of fixture in our minds that the engineers were a species of gods... The line was simply the line, whether of horse, foot, or dragoons...For the latter a good square seat in the saddle was deemed of more importance than brains. These ideas were ground into our heads with such Jesuitical persistency, I do not believe anyone of the old [1840s] regime ever entirely overcame the influence of it."[5] The striking irony of this scientific curriculum was that it almost completely ignored the predominant task of the nineteenth-century regular army (in terms of years of duty, at least), constabulary duty and Indian fighting on the western frontier.[6] The Old Army's most important, indeed, its only professional institution, thus became tied up with only one component of American military policy—harbor defense. Considering the fact that there would be no foreign attack on American soil between the end of the War of 1812 and Pearl Harbor, the engineering focus at West Point ended up wasting much of the Old Army's limited intellectual capital.

Indeed, as early as 1822 Alexander Macomb, future commanding general of the army, gently admonished Thayer that "you are aware that the character of the institution is Military and not philosophical, and while the several branches of the sciences, which are taught at the Academy are deemed highly important and essential in forming Scientific officers, the main object of the institution is to predominate over all others."[7] While William T. Sherman would be a staunch supporter of the academy in his later years, he would also declare in an address to the Class of 1869 that "the only schools where war and its kindred sciences can be properly learned are in the camp, in the field, on the plains, in the mountains, or the regular forts where the army is."[8] However, even after ending the Corps of Engineers' private monopoly on West Point's administration, the academy's curriculum during the rest of the nineteenth century remained focused on engineering and the physical sciences. Indeed, during the postwar period, the Thayer system became an inbred and stifling dogma at the academy in a way it had not been under the influence of the likes of Mahan.[9]

Nevertheless, as superfluous as this highly technical education was, superfluous really is the best way to describe it, because there is no compelling evidence that it actually had negative effects on the military performance of future Civil War generals. Some historians have attempted to trace the defensive mindset of generals such as George B. McClellan to the engineering heavy focus of the West Point curriculum. However, in the "Old Army," with its incredibly weak institutions for the formulation and promulgation of anything we would now call "doctrine," an individual Civil War commander's attitude toward issues such as the utility of entrenchments or the role of the rifle-musket depended more on individual preference and personality, as opposed to half-remembered courses at West Point. While the defensive mindsets of both McClellan and Henry W. Halleck might be connected in some way to the cult of the Corps of Engineers, with D. H. Mahan as its high priest, Robert E. Lee's and P. G. T. Beauregard's innate aggressiveness certainly was not inhibited by his membership in that exclusive fraternity. Furthermore, D. H. Mahan, the high priest of the Engineers at West Point, was hardly an apostle of defensive warfare in all circumstances, and even the defensively minded McClellan spent part of his antebellum career translating and compiling a bayonet fencing manual. Bayonet fencing represented an attempt to adapt cold steel, the characteristic weapon of shock tactics and offensive action, to both the rise of improved infantry arms such as the rifle musket and the increased use of aimed fire.[10]

Both Sherman's and Grant's somewhat checkered careers at West Point also serve as another lesson in the uncertain relationship between academic excellence and actual leadership ability, or even intellectual creativity. Sherman, perhaps the most intellectually gifted officer of the entire century, did well at West Point, but seems to have been somewhat bored by the curriculum and more interested in making mischief. His good nature and marks earned him some indulgences from the likes of Mahan, but his indifference toward cadet regulations led to a regular stream of demerits for minor offenses. Grant's record of general mediocrity at West Point is well known, and he was hardly enamored of the place.[11]

"Battles and Leaders" in some circles of Civil War studies is almost as disreputable a phrase as "drums and trumpets" was during the high tide of the "new military history" a generation ago, but that earlier approach to the Civil War struck at a fundamental truth in Civil War military history—that because of the weak institutional basis of both the Union and Confederate armies, individual commanders had a disproportionate effect on the outcome of military operations. While an American commander in Afghanistan and Iraq might need to reconcile his intent with a massive military bureaucracy and multiple layers of staff officers toiling away at PowerPoint slides in a martial version of Dilbert, while coordinating his efforts in a lateral direction with civilian agencies and various foreign partners, a George B. McClellan or Robert E. Lee could put his stamp on a field army to a degree unimaginable in this current age of bureaucracy and electronic communications.

For that reason, a more plausible line of influence between Trophy Point and Civil War battlefields can be found in the tight personal connections made between West Point cadets during their four difficult years at the academy. West Point's small classes, forty-to-fifty graduates a year during this period, and its demanding academic and disciplinary regime could not help but build strong personal connections (not always positive ones) among the institution's graduates. These were only intensified by the relatively small size of the antebellum army. Grant commented in his memoirs on the importance of these associations, writing in his memoirs that at West Point and in the Mexican War he "learned of the characters of those to whom I was afterwards opposed." Most importantly, in his view, "The natural disposition of most people is to clothe a commander of a large army whom they do not know, with almost superhuman abilities. A large part of the National army, for instance, and most of the press of the country, clothed General Lee with such qualities, but I had known him personally, and knew that he was mortal, and it was just as well that I felt this."[12]

For better or for worse, the high premium West Point graduates placed on antebellum associations in the regular army helped solidify the regular army's extraordinary hold on senior command positions in both armies, and this may indeed have had a negative effects on command selection during the war. West Point dominated the professional ethos of the old army, and the old army's veterans in turn dominated the high commands of both the Union and Confederate armies. Roughly two-thirds of major generals and higher in both armies had some sort of experience from the antebellum United States regular army,[13] and most of these men were West Point graduates. Considering the comparatively small size of the academy and the gargantuan size of the citizen-soldier armies they led, this is an astonishing proportion.

West Point and the regular army's officer corps did not exactly overlap, but in 1860, over 75 percent of old army officers had graduated from the academy. After 1838, when the army had overcome the mass resignations caused by the Second Seminole War, the proportion of West Point graduates increased almost every year above the 1838 figure of 64 percent.[14] Not only did the school on the Hudson educate future officers, it drew its instructors and superintendents from the army's self-styled intellectual elite (including Robert Anderson, George B. McClellan, George Thomas, William Hardee, Robert E. Lee, P. G. T. Beauregard, among others). Most importantly, its faculty included the Old Army's most noteworthy writer and thinker, Dennis Hart Mahan. Unlike the Navy's current attitude toward Annapolis, a teaching assignment at West Point was both a reward and a career enhancing post for officers. The periodic attempts to formulate and revise tactics utilized review boards that met at West Point, where they could use the Corps of Cadets as a test battalion and the West Point library as a convenient source of military books. Indeed, part of the academy's value was simply as a place where foreign military books could be centrally housed and utilized by interested officers—the actual rationale of Thayer's post War of 1812 mission to Europe. For example, and major tactical reforms such as the boards that formulated the army's first successful artillery manual and Hardee's Tactics all met at the academy.

Furthermore, in the absence of stable branch schools in the antebellum army, West Point had the noteworthy advantage of institutional stability. Unlike the branch schools, it was not potentially prey to the Army's need to police an ever-expanding frontier, or the occasional major conflict like the Mexican War or even the wars against the Seminoles. West Point cadets did not learn much in their academic classes of direct military relevance, but they at least received an introduction to the broader professional life of the regular army. For example, during the tactical reforms that led to the promulgation of Hardee's tactics in 1854, some of the cadets who served as guinea pigs showed some awareness of the larger professional issues involved.[15]

For better or for worse, their shared experiences at the academy caused West Pointers to have a greater confidence in fellow old army men than even the most qualified citizen-soldier generals. Lee in the Army of Northern Virginia made it an informal but important "rule that professional soldiers could be appointed to command without consideration of the Sate of their birth and without regard to seniority except among themselves," to use the words of the author of the most important command study of the Army of Northern Virginia. These sorts of policies led to grumbling among volunteer officers in the Army of Northern Virginia regarding what they saw as an unfair prejudice in favor of West Pointers. Perhaps most striking about Lee's policies favoring academy graduates was his willingness to give only regular army men the benefits of the old army's heavy respect for seniority.[16] In the antebellum U. S. Army, for the most part, seniority governed promotion up to the grade of colonel, with each officer waiting his turn. This respect for seniority probably did more harm than good in both sections' armies, even when limited to professionals, and it helped result in such mediocre figures as Ambrose Burnside and John Pemberton retaining positions of high responsibility through the sheer force of inertia established by their early general's commissions at the beginning of the war.

On the Federal side, while the close-knit relations of McClellan's West Point trained subordinates in the Army of the Potomac is well known, the academy had a strong monopoly on high positions even in the more flexible western armies. William T. Sherman appointed O. O. Howard to command of the Army of Tennessee over the more senior John Logan, perhaps the finest citizen-soldier general in the Union army, after the death of James McPherson. Talking of both Logan and Francis P. Blair, Sherman later wrote in his memoirs that "both were men of great courage and talent, but were politicians by nature and experience, and it may be that for this reason they were mistrusted by regular officers like Generals Schofield, Thomas, and myself." That mistrust, and because "it was all-important that there should exist a perfect understanding among the army commanders," led to Sherman's selection of Howard for the position as commanding general of the Army of Tennessee.[17] Or, as Sherman put it in a wartime letter on a different issue, "we must deal with men as we find them and it is not Logans fault that he was a Citizen only three years ago, and looks at all questions from another view than a professional soldier."[18]

There was some plausibility to Sherman's position because of the importance of agreement and mutual confidence among senior commanders. Furthermore, with West

Pointers inevitably dominating both armies' high command echelons due to the need to put them in senior positions from the war's earliest days due to the absence of any plausible alternatives, some degree of inbred self-selection among academy grads was unavoidable. From the checkered records of "political generals," we can perhaps see the benefits of some degree of "ring-knockerism." However, this highlights all the more the failings of the West Point curriculum, which self-consciously set out to train the leadership corps of any future American army, but diverted so much of the average cadet's attention away from either practical military training or a solid foundation in military history and strategy, but instead focused on an overly technical curriculum relevant to only one branch of the army. One Secretary of War, John B. Floyd, justified this approach by declaring that "the great mission of the Academy is to engraft on the mind of the cadet the principles of a thorough scientific military education, and considering the time requisite for this object, it is doubtless impracticable to bestow as much attention upon practical instruction as would be required to turn out perfect adepts in every branch."[19] Floyd would have agreed with the earlier assertion by Erasmus D. Keyes, future Civil War corps commander, that "it has been settled that scientific acquirements are the basis of military knowledge."[20]

In sum, West Pointers preferred one of their own to occupy positions of command responsibility due in large part to what was essentially a prejudice akin to the bonds between college alumni or fraternity brothers, as opposed to a rational appeal to some useful body of knowledge and expertise that West Pointers exclusively possessed, especially with regards to large unit command. At the outset of the war, West Point graduates did have a virtual monopoly on the fundamentals of minor tactics and army administration, but these were all skills that volunteer officers could learn with enough time and effort, and which served as poor predictors of suitability for high command. At times, West Pointer' prejudice for one of their own could remain compatible with productive command climates, as it was in the armies under Grant, Sherman, and Lee, but it could also lead to a host of military and political problems, as can be best seen in McClellan's Army of the Potomac. Individual commanders, not a shared body of substantive knowledge received at West Point set the tone in individual field armies.

West Point's academic curriculum and the common psychological bonds at West Point did not affect Civil War generalship in any sort of significant way, but what did have profound effects, mostly because it provided the rationale for their early prominence in the war, was their virtual monopoly on practical military knowledge at the outset of the Civil War. While antebellum West Point should have focused more on practical military training, cadets did receive a solid foundation in antebellum minor tactics of all arms, and we should not underestimate the importance of this basic tactical training. The miniscule size of the antebellum regular army (a little over 16,000 officers and men on the eve of the Civil War) and the collapse of the state militia system made even the most rudimentary military expertise extremely scarce when open war broke out in April 1861. For all the flaws in the old army's training and institutional structure and the far from uniformly successful generalship of West Point-trained generals, regular army men possessed knowledge and skills that neither the Union nor the Confederacy could do without. This knowledge did not concern itself so much with questions of high strategy, ignored for the most part at the academy, or the engineering knowledge that dominated the academy curriculum, but the most indispensable elements of mid-nineteenth-century military expertise.

How does one keep a field army supplied with the most basic of necessities? How does one move troops from one point to another under conditions of extreme stress? How does one train troops to use their weapons at a high enough level of competence that they are a greater threat to their enemies than their comrades? The historian Richard McMurry's comments on the benefits the Army of Northern Virginia obtained from having a high proportion of officers with Virginia Military Institute and West Point educations applies to both sections: "Men who had been educated and trained at a military school entered Confederate service already knowledgeable about small unit administration, drill, tactics, weapons, and other matters. That knowledge allowed them, from the start, to give their companies, batteries, battalions, and regiments a higher tone, more thorough training, greater confidence, and better discipline than would have been the case if the leaders had had to learn their duties after assuming command."[21]

While the Army of Northern Virginia also could draw on VMI, probably the strongest antebellum military school outside of West Point, the Union had no real equivalent (the Norwich Military Academy perhaps comes closest), and even the other southern military schools had a far less martial character than the federal school on the Hudson. Like West Point, antebellum southern military colleges emphasized the sciences and engineering in their curriculums, but unlike West Point, this education was a preparation for middle class professional careers, as opposed to service in the regular army.[22] Cadets at these institutions did engage in close-order drill and guard duty,[23] while being subject to a disciplinary regime modeled on West Point's military hierarchy, but it was the original federal school's connections with the United States Army that gave it a strongly martial character.

Whatever the academy's real flaws as an institution of professional military education, West Point along with regular army service provided the best available preparation for Civil War high command available to antebellum Americans. While this preparation was deficient and would have proved disastrous in an environment such as continental Europe, with its large standing armies and professional military establishments, in a war amongst Americans who had as a whole seen so little of war, old army veterans became in effect one-eyed princes in a kingdom of the blind. Furthermore, it was not just the familiarity cadets acquired with basic close order drill, but the important habits of mind the West Point experience inculcated in them. In the words of the leading historian of antebellum military professionalization, "exposure to the West Point environment drew cadets into a professional military ethos, causing them to internalize such military values as discipline and regularity, identify with the army as an institution, and, in many cases at least, make a strong personal commitment to military service."[24]

"Discipline and regularity" were perhaps the watchwords of the West Point experience, for better or for worse. The academy could help produce pedantic and militarily problematic officers like Don Carlos Buell or Henry Wager Halleck, but it could also train conscientious officers like Robert E. Lee. Like the service academies now, the institution had only mixed success in preparing officers for command. As Sherman recalled in his memoirs, "at the Academy I was not considered a good soldier, for at no time was I selected for any office, but remained a private throughout the whole four years. Then, as now, neatness in dress and form, with a strict conformity to the rules, were the qualifications required for office, and I suppose I was found not to excel in any of those."[25] In addition to this focus on compulsory routine, the academy's relentless quantification of cadet performance, resulting in the numerical rankings of the order of merit, fed into this larger environment of professional "regularity," all combined with a heavy curricular emphasis on mathematics and engineering. Indeed, Academy administrators claimed that this technical curriculum tended "to exercise and discipline the reasoning facilities," and that cadets will "be always greatly the better for their long continued exercises in a course of investigation and reasoning that excludes, absolutely, all specious and sophistical conclusions."[26]

This emphasis on regularity could have its drawbacks, but it also helped both armies ramp up their logistical and administrative apparatuses to handle the unprecedented (in American history) size of both sections' citizen-soldier armies. The organizational and professional reforms that the United States Army underwent in the decade or so after the close of the War of 1812 went beyond the establishment of the Thayer system at West Point. They included far-reaching reforms in the Army's logistical and administrative apparatus—what the American service called a General Staff, not to be confused with the Prussian *Generalstab*, which had next to no influence on the antebellum American army. The sophisticated and standardized procedures of the reformed staff bureaus, including strict standards of personal accountability, allowed the army to survive on the frontier with limited resources and an execrable transportation network, all while under the eyes of a Jacksonian Congress ideologically predisposed to find corruption and waste.[27]

The importance of this administrative legacy should not be understated. Staff work and logistics have tended to be the ugly stepchild of Civil War history, but it is hard to imagine the rapid military build-up in both sections during the first years of the war without the organizational and administrative experience veterans of the regular army carried into their respective services. In the North, the Quartermaster's Bureau, the most important of the Old Army's staff bureaus, successfully managed a transition to large-scale mobilization.[28] Furthermore, both initial heads of the Confederate Quartermaster and Ordnance Bureaus were also old army veterans from the same bureaus in the Federal service—Abraham C. Myers and Josiah Gorgas.[29] Even in the settled regions of the Confederacy, logistics remained challenging due to the low population density of the theater of operations (compared to Western Europe) and a sparse transportation network. As an invading army entering hostile territory, logistical problems posed a special problem for Federal forces. Even in the eastern theater, where Union forces could sometimes use seaborne transport, logistics presented a real problem, but these problems became especially acute in the western theater, after the initial mid-Tennessee campaigns where Federal forces could use the Mississippi, Tennessee, and Cumberland rivers as secure lines of supply that penetrated the Confederacy's northern frontier. The long term solution Sherman and Grant developed through raiding and mobile armies living off the land would require years of development, but before such innovations could occur, more rudimentary questions of provisioning and supply would need to be established.

Returning to the issue at the heart of this conference, however, while logistical expertise composed a crucial part of why West Pointers were so valuable to both war efforts, cadets learned little about this topic until they became actual serving officers. While they did become acclimated to the bureaucratized routines that allowed any modern supply apparatus to function—one of the crucial innovations of Winfield Scott's important Army Regulations of 1820 was the inclusion of standardized forms—the academy did not devote much attention to the strategic implications of logistical requirements, since it did not focus much on strategy at all. And even in the serving army, logistics remained the domain of the staff bureaus in Washington, which had a contentious relationship with the line army on the frontier.

While I have spent much of this paper criticizing the technical prejudices of the Thayer System, the reality is that whatever its failings in content, Thayer executed with relentless efficiency his model of military education, giving the academy a sense of identity and purpose, while sufficiently immunizing it from political pressure and dissolution. Thayer also deserved credit for persuading the American people that his academy at West Point presented neither a threat to republican liberties, nor a colossal waste of taxpaper money. Indeed, the academy's heavy engineering emphasis was connected to the Army Corps of Engineers' role in internal improvements, and while militarily problematic, it at least provided some political top cover from suspicious Jacksonian congressmen. I would like to make clear, though, that from my own reading of the sources, men like Thayer were dead serious when they argued for the primacy of the scientific and technical disciplines in military education.

Furthermore, while a bright and earnest West Point cadet might receive a vision of professional officership overly preoccupied with engineering, he still imbibed a conception of military leadership that was fundamentally "professional." We need not use here Huntington's famous social science model of professionalism, but simply say that at West Point, a cadet realized that war presented dangers and rigors, which required study and one's full mental energy. In an American that still worshipped at the shrine of the myth of the citizen soldier, and which during the Jacksonian period also believed that society's best leaders came out of democratically elected partisan machines, this trait set West Point graduates apart from their contemporaries. When West Point graduates met their first test in the Mexican War and were then tested again in a more serious way in the Civil War, this starting premise—that political skill in the world of Jacksonian America did not by itself suit one for military command—would give West Point graduates a more realistic starting point than that possessed by most officers drawn from civil life.

Even the daily routines of constabulary duty could provide a crucial introduction to the daily business of military life, and many future Civil War generals also saw a more sustained operational tempo in Mexico. Even at a quiet post on the frontier, an officer could not escape such crucial parts of army administration as accountability of personnel and property, regular inspection of equipment, provisioning, etc. Frontier realities meant that many officers saw service fighting Indians, which in the trans-Mississippi West was hard and grueling service. Some officers even managed to find some time for professional pursuits—for example, after the promulgation of Hardee's new infantry tactics in the

PANEL 1

1850s, one can find commentary on the new manual from an officer posted as far away as San Diego, which was literally on the far side of the continent.[30]

At West Point, cadets received a solid foundation in minor tactics of all arms—the crucial baseline of movement and fire on a Civil War battlefield—and in the Army, they became familiar with the basic routines of military administration and management. When war broke out in 1861, this knowledge put veterans of the regular army far ahead of their civilian peers in military knowledge, and made them essentially indispensable. This thus ensured their historical significance, although the reality remains that from the standpoint of the most effective use of cadet time, West Point's curriculum looks both inefficient and lagging. However, perhaps no generation of men and women ever truly receive an education that fully prepares them for the challenges of uncertain adulthood.

# Notes

1. Tom Cahart, Sacred Ties: From West Point Brothers to Battlefield Rivals: A True Story of the Civil War (Berkley, 2010); Wayne Wei-siang Hsieh, West Pointers and the Civil War: The Old Army in War and Peace (Chapel Hill: University of North Carolina Press, 2009).

2. James L Morrison, Jr., "The Best School in the World": West Point, the Pre-Civil War Years, 1833-1866 (Kent, OH: Kent State University Press), 91, 95-96, 100, 162.

3. Report to Col. J. G. Totten, 7 February 1845, vol. 4, pp. 44-50 (quote on 50), Staff Records, U.S. Military Academy Archives, West Point, NY.

4. Morrison, Best School in the World, 114-15, 120.

5. Morrison., 141-44. Quote on 142-43.

6. William B. Skelton, An American Profession of Arms: The Army Officer Corps, 1784-1861 (Lawrence: University Press of Kansas, 1992), 306.

7. Alexander Macomb to Sylvanus Thayer, August 22, 1822, West Point Thayer Papers, 396-97, Special Collections, U.S. Military Academy Library, West Point, NY.

8. John F. Marszalek, Sherman: A Soldier Passion's for Order (New York: Free Press, 1993), 441.

9. Morrison, Best School in the World, 147-48.

10 Edward Hagerman, The American Civil War and the Origins of Modern Warfare: Ideas, Organization, and Field Command (Bloomington: Indiana University Press, 1988), 6-13, 33; Hsieh, West Pointers and the Civil War, 82.

11. Marszalek, Sherman, 22-28; U Ulysses S. Grant, Memoirs and Selected Letters, Library of America ed. (New York: Literary Classics of the United States, 1990), 31-32.

12. Marszalek, 129.

13. Skelton, American Profession of Arms, 446.

14. Morrison, Best School in the World, 15.

15. Hsieh, West Pointers and the Civil War, 81-82.

16. Douglas Southall Freeman, Lee's Lieutenants: A Study in Command (New York: Charles Scribner's Sons, 1943-1944), 3:200; 2: 419.

17. William Tecumseh Sherman, Memoirs of General W. T. Sherman, Library of America ed. (New York: Literary Classics of the United States, 1990), 559.

18. William T. Sherman to Philemon B. Ewing, April 21, 1864, in Brooks D. Simpson and Jean V. Berlin, Sherman's Civil War: Selected Correspondence of William T. Sherman, 1860-1865 (Chapel Hill: University of North Carolina Press, 1999), 625.

19. John B. Floyd, January 5, 1860, "Instructions for the Board appointed to revise the programme of instruction at the Military Academy…," Board of Officers—Curriculum Revision, January-April 1860, part 2, series 15, 4b, box 1, Records of the Academic Board, U.S. Military Academy Archives, West Point, NY.

20. Minority Report, February 12, 1845, vol. 4, pp. 52-56 (quotation from 55), Staff Records, U.S. Military Academy Archives, West Point, NY.

21. Richard M. McMurry, Two Great Rebel Armies: An Essay in Confederate Military History (Chapel Hill: University of North Carolina Press, 1989), 104.

22. Jennifer R. Green, "Books and Bayonets: Class and Culture in Antebellum Military Academies" (Ph.D. diss., Boston University, 2002), 6-7, 79.

23. Green, 91-92.

24. Skelton, American Profession of Arms, 180.

25. Sherman, Memoirs, 16.

PANEL 1

26. Joseph G. Totten quoted in Skelton, American Profession of Arms, 169-70.

27. On these administrative reforms, see Hsieh, West Pointers and the Civil War, 34-53.

28. Mark R. Wilson, The Business of Civil War: Military Mobilization and the State, 1861-1865 (Baltimore: Johns Hopkins University Press, 2006, 2, 35, 65-71.

29. Richard D. Goff, Confederate Supply (Durham, NC: Duke University Press, 1969), 8-10.

30. Hsieh, West Pointers and the Civil War, 87.

# Day 1, Panel 1: Antebellum Officer Educatiion, 1800-1865

## The Development of Successful Non-professional Officers in the Army of the Tennessee, 1861-1863 by Steven E. Woodworth, Ph.D.
(Transcript of Presentation)

## Moderated by Donald P. Wright, Ph.D.

**Dr. Wright:**

Next we have Dr. Steven Woodworth, who received his doctorate from Rice University in 1987. He is currently a professor of history at Texas Christian University in Fort Worth. He is a prolific author with several important works about the American Civil War, including *Jefferson Davis and His Generals* and *Six Armies in Tennessee*. His topic today is the development of nonprofessional officers in the Army of Tennessee during the American Civil War.

**Dr. Woodworth:**

Thank you. Within the history of the American Civil War, the miserable performances of political generals have became proverbial. The misadventures of Tammany Hall hack Daniel E. Sickles as a Corps commander in the Army of the Potomac at the Battles of Chancellorsville and Gettysburg are almost the stuff of legend. Only slightly less famous are the mishaps of Major General Nathaniel P. Banks at the hands of Stonewall Jackson in the Shenandoah Valley campaign of 1862, and then at the hands of Jackson's attentive student Richard Taylor in the Red River campaign two years later. Benjamin F. Butler may be more famous for coining the term "contrabands," with reference to African Americans, and for his no-nonsense response to expressions of hostility from New Orleans women. But his 1864 Bermuda Hundred campaign was a fiasco. Jefferson Davis may have felt less pressure than did Lincoln to put political aspirants in general's uniforms, but Confederate military history nevertheless offers the spectacle of Virginia governorsformers Virginia governors, two of themthan Confederate Generals Henry A. Wise and John B. Floyd losing West Virginia, in part at least, because each was more intent on seeing the defeat of his political rival in a gray uniform than that of his military foes in blue uniforms. Floyd then featured in a second and even more disastrous debacle for the Confederacy when he and his second-in-command, Tennessee politician-turned-general Gideon J. Pillow, pooled their incompetence to doom Fort Donelson, and then abandoned the trapped garrison to its fate.

In Civil War terms, a political general was a man appointed to general officer rank direct from civilian life. Not because of any military skill or qualifications he might possess, but solely for the political benefits the president hoped would accrue from the mere fact of having him in a uniform with general stars. While it is true that during the course of the war, some West Point graduates with years of experience in the Old Army also proved unsuccessful as generals, the overall record of the political generals is worse. Their blunders were more numerous and/or egregious. The inescapable conclusion, therefore, is that the

PANEL 1

political generals were failures because they were not adequately prepared and because no previous experience of their lives had sifted them as a group and removed those who were hopelessly lacking in aptitude, as West Point and the Old Army experience had done, albeit imperfectly, for the professionals. Yet the Civil War demanded far more generals than the office ranks of the Old Army could reasonably supply, given that a number of the regular officers would remain in their positions within the Regular Army, the regular regiments, and that some would no doubt already have demonstrated to their superiors that they were not adapted for higher rank. Even the number of West Point graduates who had since left the service and were, at the time of the outbreak of the Civil War, occupying positions as railroad company presidents, educators, or clerks in leather goods stores, those of you who are familiar with the biographies of Civil War generals will recognize who those were. This combined number was not sufficient to meet the leadership needs of the mass armies that the Union and Confederacy fielded during the conflict of the 1860s. Given these facts, it was unavoidable that men who had little or no military background in 1861 would rise to the rank of general. Not all of them, not even a majority, were political generals. The rest, that is, the nonprofessionals who were not political generals—were men from civilian life who worked their way up through the ranks to win their stars, and some proved to be highly successful generals.

The Army of the Tennessee, that is, the Union Army, which was formed and saw its early service under Ulysses S. Grant, which fought at Shiloh and Vicksburg, and went on to other successes later in the war. The Army of the Tennessee compiled an especially impressive track record not only in defeating its enemies and achieving its military objectives, but also in finding and developing such gifted military amateurs and making them into successful generals. The record of its nonprofessional generals stands in stark contrast to the dismal performance of political generals in the Civil War, and it is worthwhile considering how this came about. I'm going to look particularly at the cases of two of the relatively successful nonprofessional generals in the Army of the Tennessee.

Ulysses S. Grant was the most important, he was a professional, of course. Ulysses S. Grant was the most important factor in shaping the Army of the Tennessee. He was this army's first commander and he led it for almost two years through some of its hardest battles and most significant victories, including Fort Donelson, Shiloh, and Vicksburg. In a number of ways, the Army of the Tennessee bore Grant's stamp throughout the Civil War. I might say that as the Army of the Potomac was McClellan's army long after McClelland had been sent into retirement, the Army of the Tennessee was Grant's army, and continued to function in the ways that Grant had taught it and shaped it to do, long after Grant had gone on to other things.

One of the most significant of the ways in which Grant shaped the Army of the Tennessee was in the composition of its officer corps, and in particular its successful use of nonprofessional generals. We have no records of Grant ever holding any formal periods of instruction for his subordinate generals, as some Civil War commanders did. One might think here of the Confederate Army of Tennessee, without the definite article there, and of General William J. Hardee, author of the Army's prewar tactics manual, who held regular periods of instruction for the subordinate officers within his army corps in the Army of

Tennessee. We have no record of Grant doing that. Such a practice would have been very much out of character with Grant, since he had little use for tactics books, expressed some doubt as to whether he had ever read Hardee's standard prewar tactics manual. Grant probably had paid very little attention also to the prewar writings of Antoine-Henri Jomini, the most respected military theoretician of that time, at least in the United States Army. Grant had almost certainly never read the works of the famous Prussian philosopher of war of the preceding generation, Carl von Clausewitz, because, as far as we know, Clausewitz had not been translated into English by that time. I'm not aware of any English translation of Clausewitz prior to the Civil War. Grant, like most other American-born Civil War generals, did not know German. So Grant almost certainly had not read Clausewitz. But like Clausewitz, Grant seemed to believe that most knowledge of tactical prescriptions was far less valuable in an officer than having a strong mind, well informed by experience and historical example. Grant had learned much from his own experience in Mexican War, and his observation there of his two great Army commanders, Zachary Taylor and Winfield Scott. During the Civil War, Grant patterned his personal style more after Taylor and his generalship more after Scott. In developing his subordinates, Grant depended on personal example and informal advice, and he used shrewd selection and careful sifting to assure that the officers who advanced to important positions within his army were the best available.

John A. Logan, whom Dr. Hsieh mentioned earlier, was an early case of an officer whom Grant selected and developed into an effective general. Logan was a Democratic politician from Southern Illinois, and his loyalty to the Union had actually been in question during the early weeks of the war. In the summer of 1861, while still a civilian, Logan had demonstrated his loyalty and gained Grant's favorable notice by helping Grant, who was then Colonel of the 21st Illinois Regiment, persuade his troops to reenlist for three-year terms. The personal leadership qualities and motivational ability that Logan displayed in that incident would prove to be among his greatest strengths as a general. Returning to his hometown of Murphysboro, Illinois, Logan recruited a regiment of his own, the 31st Illinois, and was soon a colonel serving under the command of Grant, who by then had made brigadier general. In the November 1861 Battle of Belmont, his first under Grant, Logan may well have been one of the officers who allowed his troops to get out of hand during the mid-battle lull. Those of you who are familiar with the Battle of Belmont know there was an intense initial phase followed by a lull in the captured Confederate camps, during which some of the volunteer officers, whose names we don't necessarily know, but Logan was very possibly one of them, lost control of their troops, who thought the battle was over. Then there was an intense final phase of the battle, in which the Army, with difficulty, recovered from its mid-battle blunders or its blunders during the lull. But during the initial phase of the battle and during the very intense final phase, Logan performed spectacularly well in inspiring and leading his troops. Grant was apparently willing to overlook a beginner's error in an officer who showed as much obvious aptitude as Logan. Grant also seemed to be characterized by a readiness to play the hand that was dealt him, to deal with facts as they were and not as he would wish them to be. This is another startling contrast to some other generals, notably McClellan, who insisted that everything should be perfect, should be as he would wish it to be. Grant took the circumstances that were given

PANEL 1

to him -- including a number of generals who, simply, initially were not qualified for that job, took them where they were and worked with them there.

By the time of the February 1862 Battle of Fort Donelson, Logan was commanding a brigade within Grant's army. He was in the hottest of the fighting there and he did well, holding his ground against superior Confederate numbers at the point of contact as long as was possible, and then making an orderly retreat. During the fighting at Fort Donelson, Logan suffered a severe wound that kept him out of action for several months and caused him to miss the Battle of Shiloh. Logan was back in action in time for all of the Vicksburg campaign, during which he commanded a division and steadily won more and more of Grant's approval and confidence. Logan's corps commander, by the way, was James Birdseye McPherson, who was a West Point professional par excellence. But Logan, like McPherson, was surprised by the unexpected Confederate attack at the May 7 Battle of Raymond, Mississippi during the Vicksburg campaign. But he recovered quickly and performed ably in beating off that attack. At the Battle of Champions Hill nine days later, the decisive battle of the campaign, Logan showed even more of his amazing ability to motivate and inspire troops in the midst of battle. Despite his fiery demeanor in combat, which led some observers to speculate on his possible state of inebriation, Logan committed no serious blunders, and I do not believe that he was drunk at the Battle of Champion Hill. His actions all made good sense. He was very fiery and he had a way of inspiring his troops that really amazed his contemporaries.

By the time of the Vicksburg siege, Logan was clearly Grant's favorite division commander. His unit was called on to do some of the hardest fighting, including the battle for the first Vicksburg crater, the result of an undermining of Confederate defensive works and then their subsequent explosion. When the Confederate stronghold in the Mississippi finally capitulated on July 4th, 1863, Grant gave Logan's division the honor of being the first to march into the town. Between 1861 and 1863, Grant had overseen and cultivated Logan's development from a colonel, devoid of military background, through the ranks of brigadier general and major general of Volunteers, to the point that Logan had become the army's best division commander and was well on his way to becoming, by the end of the war, one of the two or three best nonprofessional generals of the conflict.

Another nonprofessional officer whose development Grant started within the Army of the Tennessee and who also appeared to be on his way to success at higher rank was William H.L. Wallace. A veteran of brief volunteer service as a junior officer in the Mexican War, Wallace had had no formal military training. Not West Point, not anywhere else. He was an Illinois lawyer when the Civil War broke out. He raised a company and, as usually happened when someone raised a company of volunteers for Civil War service, he became the captain of that company, with no further qualifications than that of a successful recruiter. His company became part of the 11th Illinois, and the regiment's other captains elected him its colonel, which is also how it worked in the early days. Within the small, scarcely division-sized command that was to grow into the Army of the Tennessee, Grant was able to interact with his subordinates closely and extensively enough for his example to have a powerful, direct influence on his subordinates. That is, they could watch from day to day how Grant exercised his command. Wallace did not always agree with Grant's actions. Sometimes he didn't think Grant was doing a very good job. But he generally kept any negative opinions to himself or shared them, this is how we know about them, with his wife, in letters to her. She was his confidant and he could share anything with her. As far as we know and as far as we've heard from any of the others around Wallace, that was where those opinions stayed. It was for him and it was for his wife, and he kept quiet about that. But he was obviously watching and thinking a lot about different things that Grant was doing. At the same time, the close association within the small command gave Grant sufficient opportunity to observe his subordinates in various types of situations so that he was able to make excellent selections of those officers who were capable of handling more responsibility. Given enough time and close enough association within the intense atmosphere of active wartime operations, Grant proved to be an almost flawless judge of character and aptitude.

Those of you who are students of American history and can think on to the Grant administration might find this a remarkable statement, because this seems to be the reverse of what we see in President Grant. I actually think that the key is that, for Grant to be a good judge of your character, he has to work with you on a day-to-day basis, closely, for an extended period of time, that is, for at least several months, very closely, preferably more, and in fairly intense circumstances. And in those conditions, Grant seemed to make decisions about personnel that were almost always right. It's interesting that later in the war, after Grant leaves the Army of the Tennessee, he comes east and he has brief interviews with people like Benjamin Butler, who he seems to think he can make into another John Logan. And, again, students of the Civil War will gasp. But you know that it's true. And with others. And we find him making some misjudgments. Apparently an interview of several hours and a few brief associations was not enough for Grant to make a decision. Then he goes on to be president and we find him making a number of bad personnel choices.

Grant advanced Wallace gradually in rank as the erstwhile lawyer learned his craft. Not only did Wallace perform well as a commander, he also, as I mentioned before, showed good judgment in what he said to others within the Army. Wallace did not always understand why Grant took certain actions, but he wisely confided such doubts only in letters to his wife. He kept quiet within the camp until he gained a better grasp of the situation. In doing so, he showed the loyalty that was a very important consideration for Grant and his subordinates. I might add that this, I believe, is a key factor in why Wallace's namesake, at least as pertains to last names, General Lew Wallace, did not advance more rapidly. Some of you are familiar with the story of the Battle of Shiloh, in which Lew Wallace's division was encamped five miles from the battlefield and took, as Grant believed, much too long reaching the battlefield, covering that five-mile march. We know that Wallace took a wrong road and then countermarched and took all day to make that five-mile march that Grant felt that Wallace should have made before noon. Some of the discussion about whether Wallace was to blame or to what extent Lew Wallace, this is not William H.L. Wallace but Lew Wallace, was to blame for this, some of that discussion has turned on whether Lew Wallace was justified in taking the wrong road or whose fault was it or what did his orders really say, and the written orders got lost, and so on. I believe the real reason that Grant subsequently sidelined Lew Wallace and did not promote him any further, did not use him any further

Panel 1

and really shunted him aside, was not so much that Wallace had taken the wrong road early that morning, or mid-morning, actually, by that time, but that once Wallace realized later in the afternoon that he had taken the wrong road, that he was overdue and long-inspected, and that the Army of the Tennessee was in desperate trouble fighting with its back to the river, fighting for its life, Lew Wallace made a march that, while it would be considered good under normal, routine circumstances, would have been considered a very respectable march, was not at all what Grant expected of a situation where your comrades are fighting for their lives with their backs to the wall, so to speak. Grant expected a desperate march out of Lew Wallace during that Battle of Shiloh. He expected Lew Wallace to push on in a hard force march, and what Wallace did was a nice, orderly, decent, respectable march under non-pressured circumstances.

Again, just to interject the contrast here to the kind of general who showed the kind of loyalty that Grant did expect during the Vicksburg campaign, when the Navy's gunboat flotilla was nearly trapped during the Sunflower Creek excursion in another attempt to get around Vicksburg and several of the Navy's valuable gunboats in waters far too narrow for them to operate were nearly trapped and needed infantry support desperately, General William T. Sherman personally led an all-night march to get there, wading through swamps, at the head of his troops. Sherman, when he hears about the problem, actually sets out to gather up his scattered detachments for this relief march by personally going through the swamps in a canoe, gathering these units, getting them together, and marching all night through the swamps. That's the kind of loyalty that Grant expected in his subordinates. When the chips were down, so to speak, to use a cliché, I guess, but when the situation demanded this kind of intense effort and you did not bring it forth, as was the case with Lewis Wallace, Grant would write you off as not the kind of man that he wanted to have in his army, whereas men like W.H.L. Wallace showed that degree of loyalty, and of course Sherman, par excellence. But Sherman was a professional and I'm talking about nonprofessionals. W.H.L. Wallace had, by the time the Battle of Shiloh, risen to brigade command. In fact, at Donelson he had commanded a brigade. Unlike Logan, Wallace had escaped wounds at Donelson, which didn't, in Wallace's personal case, turn out to be an advantage. Because unlike Logan, W.H.L. Wallace was present at Shiloh. He performed well. Moved his division up smartly, got into line where they were needed, performed stellar service, held his section of the line against repeated Confederate attacks, and then, when troops on either flank gave way and retreated, Wallace alertly saw the need to withdraw his own division to a more defensible position. He was in the act of pulling his troops out when he was mortally wounded, and died several days later.

During his relatively brief career in the Army of the Tennessee, Wallace had matured rapidly as an officer and made an important contribution to the army's success. That this could take place within the space of nine months speaks well for Grant's ability to select and cultivate effective officers from the men he had available, most of whom were nonprofessionals. The examples of these two officers are illustrative of Grant's ability to develop men with little or no military training or background into effective officers. The Army of the Tennessee, especially during the early months of its existence, was small enough to allow Grant's example to be effective and to allow Grant to gain a sufficient knowledge of his subordinates to select those who would function well at higher levels of command.

Grant's method of developing these officers was very much a factor of his own overall approach to command, and is remarkably similar to ideas that Carl von Clausewitz had expressed but that Grant had not read. That is, Grant valued in his subordinate commanders a strong mind, and he excelled in identifying those who had a strong mind. Then, also in similarity to Clausewitz, Grant favored example and experience rather than precept and prescription as means of instructing his officers in the business of war. Think of Sherman, or of Sheridan echoing this after the war and saying the best classroom for learning about war is in the camps or the forts or the army and so forth. Finally, Grant valued loyalty and teamwork. No matter how gifted and experienced an officer might be, Grant believed that officer would disrupt the overall function of the Army if he were allowed to engage in backbiting or spread dissension within the officer corps or if he failed to respond as needed in pressure situations. The end result of Grant's approach was developed within the Army of the Tennessee more and better in nonprofessional generals than surfaced in any of the other major armies during the course of the war.

Well, there's much more that I could say, and would be interesting to say, but we can leave that for the question time if folks have interest in it. Thank you for your attention.

## Day 1, Panel 1: Antebellum Officer Education, 1800-1865

### Questions and Answers
(Transcript of Presentation)

## Wayne Wei-siang Hsich, Ph.D.
## Steven E. Woodworth, Ph.D.

## Moderated by Donald P. Wright, Ph.D.

**Dr. Wright:**

Thank you, gentlemen, for the two papers that complemented each other in an excellent way. Let me offer a few comments in the form of several questions, and then we'll turn it over to the rest of the audience for their questions, perhaps, or comments.

First of all, for Dr. Hsieh, as I was listening to your paper, I was thinking about the general purpose for this symposium, as Dr. [William Glenn] Robertson, the Director of CSI, and I were talking with Mr. Kendall Gott, the organizer of the conference. We are trying to link this with what the Army is going through right now, which is sort of a reassessment of its own leader development system, especially in light of the last nine years since 2001. We're trying to figure out the big themes that force change on the leadership development system. Some of the ideas we came up with were doctrinal change, organizational or technological change, geopolitical situations that alter and therefore force the military institutions of the United States to rethink what they are and what they're supposed to do. But also, when you look back, you find the institution itself trying to pin certain values or attributes or competencies on the leadership in order to create the kind of institution that it now needs because of the doctrinal, technical, geopolitical change. In thinking about the antebellum period, specifically with West Point, was there any discussion of particular values, competencies, attributes, anything similar to this, that West Point was supposed to cultivate? Before I let you answer that one, Wayne, one other. To what degree was the curriculum at West Point tied to a particular type of war fighting or particular type of style of war? But I'm thinking of the decisive battle here that comes out of (inaudible) and the Napoleonic experience.

**Dr. Hsieh:**

The engineers have a rationale, and their rationale is that war is a science. If any of you are familiar with Brian Linn's book, *Echo of Battle*, the engineers are the guardians. They believe that the American national defense is basically you build lots of really strong harbor forts, and that's all you need to do, and everything is solved. And West Point's curriculum is very suited to that. West Point graduates are great engineers. They have a great, excellent technical education. West Point was the first engineering school in the United States. Part of that is connected to the perception of war as a science, as a subject to these mathematical principles, especially a country like the United States, which (inaudible) in its military policy. Also, there is a perception that history and English and things like that are useful. I once had a history major at the Naval Academy, one of his engineering professors tried to dissuade him from being a history major and told him, "You can read history on your own. Why do you need to take history classes in college? You can just learn it on your own. You just read it. You don't need a lab and apparatus and stuff like that." So the perception is that war is a science. There's a quote I cut and triage here. There's also a sense that the technical disciplines give a mental discipline and rigor. It prevents these sophistical illusions. It's firm and certain, and that's what you want in officers. That's linked directly to the scientific cast of the curriculum. It does not focus on things like creativity. It does not focus things on flexibility. That's why Sherman has a hard time at West Point. Sherman likes to sort of make trouble. Sherman's sort of a little bit too innovative. The education is very much key to the values. But what's sort of interesting about West Point is that, in this case, one section of the Army, by virtue of its control over the academy, is able to take its concept of what the Army officer corps should look like and then make West Point conform to develop that. There isn't a very strong sense in the army as a whole as to what do we really want out of our officers? You have people like McComb who are opponents to this view but who don't have the same institutional leverage. Is that a good....

**Dr. Wright:**

Thanks very much. A question for Steven, as I was listening to your presentation, I was thinking to myself, ah, this problem of the political general is unique to the American Civil War. And then I remembered my decade of service in the Louisiana Army National Guard. I quickly realized it's not particularly unique to the 19th century. In fact, the Louisiana Guard, when it mobilized for Desert Storm and later on, had some severe problems with officers who were not competent, did not have the right attributes and skills and talents. That's a story that doesn't get told a lot and probably speaks more to what the RC, the Reserve Component, should be doing with its (inaudible) system. So my question for you is, what did the Army learn post-1865, or what insights did it take about the issue of political generalship? Was it just basically in the past? Will we never have to deal with this again? Anybody writing or thinking about it?

**Dr. Woodworth:**

I'm not sure that there was an institutional response. I'm not sure that the nation really learned the lesson about political generals, because you look at the Spanish-American War and you have political generals. Again, men whom you put in a general's uniform, you hope they'll win battles. You don't put the general stars on them because you think they can lead your troops to victory. You do that because having them as generals will secure the support of one or another faction. In the Spanish-American War, it's of course all about reunification of the country, healing the rifts of the Civil War, so you have Joe Wheeler, a former Confederate general, now serving as a general in the United States Army in the Spanish-American War, and entirely for political reasons. Because if we make Joe Wheeler a general, then Southerners who might be in some doubt as to whether this is really their cause, is the American cause our cause? They will know Joe Wheeler is out there so it's OK. So I'm not sure that they did learn that lesson. I think they kind of went right back. I think what had to change eventually was that the American people, I think through the progressive era and a growth of ideas about professionalism, had to learn the idea that for warfare it would be best to have leaders who are professional at leading in wartime, and that we don't have these sort of general-purpose, natural-born leaders of men sort of things.

**Dr. Wright:**

Thank you. Let's open up to the audience. If you have a question, please just make sure you turn on your microphone after I identify you. Sir?

**Audience Member 1:**

I was interested that you brought John Logan forward. As you know, after the war he did a lot of writing on his own and was famous for the volunteer soldiers of America and kind of set himself up as a counterpart and antithesis to Emory Upton, and Emory Upton was kind of epitomizing the professionalism and the West Point tradition. Logan was, contrary to that, attacking the West Point system as manacles on the volunteer solider. Yet Logan was recognized, brought forward, and approved by a West Point grant and was brought into the framework that was thought to be the West Point system. I got kind of a two-part question, one for each of you. Was Logan biting the hand that fed him or were his later views compatible with the views he should have developed in the Civil War? And following on that, this West Point tradition, you mentioned as being superfluous. That is to say, that it didn't hurt but it didn't harm; it was OK. Did you encounter in your research in antebellum period conscious attacks on West Point as being adverse to the purposes of the armies it served?

**Dr. Woodworth:**

With regard to Logan, yes, I would say in part, at least, he was biting the hand that fed him. He learned the trade of war from West Pointers like Grant and Sherman, so a lot of what he knew that made him successful as a general, he learned from Grant and Sherman and other West Pointers. And yes, it was Grant and then also Sherman who had promoted Logan to the positions he enjoyed. But Logan never got over July 22d, 1864, or the immediate aftermath of that time, when James Birdseye McPherson, commander of the Army of the Tennessee, falls in its most desperate battle, the Battle of Atlanta, and Logan takes over and leads the great rally and leads it to victory. And when Logan is flirting with a vice presidential campaign almost 20 years later and he has that great Atlanta Cyclorama painted, it features himself there on the horse, charging in there to lead the rally and save the Union. What happened then, he commanded the army, well, for that day. I think in a desperate battle, your army is in a desperate battle, fighting for its life right now, and it needs to do really hard fighting for the next several hours in a Civil War context, John Logan is the man you want to have in command of your army. But Sherman believed, and Logan's most recent biographer, [Gary Acklebarker], agrees with him, that Logan lacked the administrative ability. Maybe he couldn't fill out those forms or whatever it was. Lacked the administrative ability to be able to run the Army of the Tennessee on a day-to-day basis and keep it functioning well, and so he gave the job to a West Point officer, Oliver Howard. Logan was very bitter about that, remained bitter about that and never really got over it. I think that's at the heart of all of Logan's post-war attacks on West Point.

**Dr. Hsieh:**

PANEL 1

The great irony is Sherman's. Yes, there is criticism. To use the classifications Brian Linn has used, there are heroes in the antebellum army too. And a lot of these heroes, I think, don't leave as much written material, because the officers who don't serve in the seacoast garrisons of the engineers or on staff duty or aren't instructors at West Point, they're Indian fighters. Indian fighters par excellence. They are on the frontier, and for them, I know [Andrew Berdell] has kind of argued, and I think he's right, there is kind of an informal doctrine, there's an informal set of rules and hard-earned practical experience the Frontier Army has for constabulary duties with regards to the Indians. But I think that's an important part of the Army's culture. It's one that leaves fewer written documents and is thus harder to pinpoint and maybe doesn't have the same degree of intellectual abstraction. It's not convenient. It's not like when you go to West Point and you look at academic boards, papers and things like that. But that certainly exists and you see it come up with people like [McComb]. You see it in Sherman, which is ironic because I think Sherman has this West Point prejudice, but Sherman himself, even if you look very early during the Civil War, Sherman is very Uptonian in his insistence on the superiority of West Pointers, but he's also very self-conscious about the importance of practical knowledge. I think it's clear that Sherman never quite drank all the West Point kool-aid. You see that in his time as a cadet. He liked making hash. That seemed to be a higher priority for him. That's the illicit food that, illegal cooking, basically, in the room. Sherman was famous for this. He was famous for that, not for being at the top of his class, which he was not. So I think you definitely have a string in the Army that is suspicious. It happens to be not in control of its main professional institution.

**Dr. Lewis Sorley:**

I'd just like to suggest that it's possible to take a broader view of the influence of Colonel Thayer and the importance of the Thayer system. I'll just cite a small number of areas in which that seems to me to be the case. First is Colonel Thayer's personal example of integrity and devotion to duty. He served a long time as superintendent. The corps cadets in those days were smaller. Every cadet knew Thayer and Thayer knew every cadet intimately. They were aware of his example and it was very important. Secondly, with respect to the curriculum, without regard to the substance of it, Thayer introduced the concept of accountability, daily accountability, as it were for most cadets and most subjects. That was an important part of the training and development of cadets. And thirdly, Thayer, at minimum, laid down the basis for what was later codified as the honor code and the honor system at West Point. All things far more important, it seems to me, than the narrower critique of the content of the curriculum and so on in those days. Would you like to comment?

**Dr. Hsieh:**

Sure. I think it is definitely correct to say that Thayer's legacy, I want to make it clear. Thayer's legacy for me is mixed. I think it's right to say, though, I'm balanced, considering the history of West Point before Thayer and it's utter confusion and chaos that exists there. An utter institutional weakness. It has to be seen as obviously far more positive than negative, because Thayer makes West Point a real institution. Without him, without his influence, they probably would not have survived that early chaotic period after the

War of 1812. Although, of course, he was supported in a very important way by people like Secretary of War Calhoun. One of Thayer's great virtues is his tremendous sense of purpose, and as such he attempts to basically import the (inaudible) technique, and in many ways does that. He looms very large in the history of the academy because, even after his departure. He actually leaves due to a disciplinary dispute with President Jackson, but even after his departure, people are very strongly influenced by his legacy, and it's clear that West Point, under him and his tutelage, sort of benign, conservative regime, for lack of a better term, and I put no pejoratives on that at all. West Point runs very well.

But I do think the content could have certainly been different. History is a great example. Thayer himself believed that things like history were kind of important but, again, something that you could learn yourself. You have examples from, already, the European staff colleges in France and Germany of a greater focus on strategic thinking. And you have figures like Mahan who's extremely widely-read and extremely intelligent, who knew stuff about strategy. But by being bound to a very technical conception of military education, those subjects were in effect crowded out. Mahan even had interesting things to say about Indian warfare. But he was always so wedded to the system he grew up with that he could never find enough time in his capstone class to add very much on that. I think for serving officers, that would have been perhaps useful. The West Point experience was important because it was rigorous and it was demanding and it inspired a certain code of service and dedication in its graduates. But you can be rigorous and demanding and have the curriculum be adjusted better to maybe fit the needs of the service. That would basically be my response. And there are discussions within the academic board. There are discussions within curricular review. And as I said, it's recognized by academic boards. That's why they add the fifth year, because there's a recognition that you need these other subjects. What should have just been done is cut some of the science and engineering out. At the end of the day, it was very hard for people who had grown under the Thayer system to be willing to acquiesce to what they would have seen as a repudiation of his legacy, although arguably it wouldn't have. Which is actually kind of what happened to West Point later. West Point still has a strong technical core, but it's in many ways more flexible than we are in terms of history. There's the military art sequence. We have a one-semester plebe naval history class, or plebes never remember because they're plebes and they have other things to worry about than me. I do think it is still right to say that the curriculum certainly could have been adjusted, especially because there are figures during the period who talk about it.

By the way, the five-year program dies in many ways because it's too long and hard. Mahan himself talks about this. Cadets are too exhausted at the end of the fifth year. It really dies because of the Civil War, but they're already going to get rid of it earlier. That shows why the science and engineering classes should have been drawn down, so you could have still kept it at four years. And the choices then made that, OK, we'll discard the fifth and just keep the strong engineering, technical side.

**Audience Member 3:**

This is for Dr. Hsieh. I enjoyed your paper, by the way. Didn't Mahan run, as an extracurricular activity, a thing he called the Napoleon Club, which exposed a lot of people to at least the strategic and operational level of war under Napoleon?

Panel 1

**Dr. Hsieh:**

We know the club exists. It's never been demonstrated to me with any degree of satisfaction how much effect it has. We know some officers know Jomini. Beauregard is a great example. Halleck is a great example. But what's interesting is some of these professionally-orientated officers don't do that well in the war. I think it's in Sherman's memoirs, there's a great, great line where he talks about talking with Halleck and they talk about the Donelson/Henry campaigns and the line of operation. It's clear you see there the utility of these things. We know Stonewall Jackson read a lot of, was very interested, even as a cadet, in history. But what is the effect of this? There isn't very much strong evidence of that. Grant read novels when he was at West Point, which is sort of the 19th-century equivalent of watching television. Stonewall Jackson's super serious, reading history. Grant, the greater general, is playing video games. That's essentially, you don't have video games back then, so you read novels. Herman Highway and Archer Jones have made a big deal about Jomini. It never struck me as persuasive, because there is not, I don't see evidence of this really having that much of an effect. That's not to say the Napoleon Club is part of that. There is this constellation of officers who read a lot on their own, but again it's so mixed as to the effects. McClellan is very well-read and is very up to speed on European military developments. McClellan ends up being not a very good general, in all honesty, or, as my mentor Gary Gallagher said, "George B. McClellan is a great general everywhere except for the battlefield." Lee is pretty up to speed. Lee knows things about, for example, the French staff system. Serves as a superintendent. So there you have a positive example, but in other places I think the legacy is very ambiguous. I'm very leery of putting too much causal weight on those sorts of things.

**Mr. Rich Kyper:**

Rich Kyper from the Army Counter-Insurgency Center. We can't have a discussion about political generals without talking about John McClernand. You focused on Logan and Wallace, who in a panoply of political generals were pretty low. More nonprofessional soldiers. But then you put the McClernands, Butlers, Banks in an entirely different level of politician. So while you rightly talked about Grant mentoring, for lack of a better word, these nonprofessional soldiers, it was clear that he had a different approach to the Banks, the Butlers, the McClernands of the world, who had achieved significant political status prior to the war. Granted, there were some egos involved with those three. But do you see any difference in Grant's approach to mentoring nonprofessional soldiers versus clear, absolute political appointees during the time you mentioned? And of course what's ironic in all of this is McClernand didn't like Grant, he didn't like West Pointers. Used words like "gall" and "wormwood," referring to them, but his son Edward then graduated from West Point, received a Medal of Honor against the Indians, and retired as a brigadier general. Do you see Grant's approach as being on two different levels to these sorts of political, nonprofessional appointees?

**Dr. Woodworth:**

First, to clarify, I would not define John Logan or W.H.L. Wallace as political generals, because in the context of the Civil War, I define a political general as a man who's appointed direct to general officer rank from civilian life without prior qualification for that, and who's appointed to that position because the president hopes that this man being in the general's uniform will draw the support of some particular constituency within the population. That's not to say that generals didn't sometimes profit from political help, including Grant, including Sherman. That's not to say that other generals didn't have political ambitions, including Logan and possibly others. Maybe even W.H.L. Wallace. McClernand, however, does fit the bill of the political general. He was a major political figure before the war. He absolutely had political aspirations. For him, it was all about politics, and his appointment was about politics. Did Grant treat him differently, then? I would say yes and no. I would say that Grant dealt with McClernand as he did with Logan who were both very similar politically, of course. I think he dealt with McClernand as he did with Logan to the degree that McClernand's different rank allowed that and to the degree that McClernand was teachable to that. I think the ego thing does come in there. After all, McClernand is the man who goes back to Illinois and makes his speech and says, "I thank God that I was born a natural-born soldier, impervious to fear." I think that reflects an ego there that is not going to be very receptive to instruction. I think the contempt for Grant that McClernand shows early on, and quite early on, his desire often expressed to get out from under Grant's command and to be in an independent command. I think this made it difficult for Grant to teach McClernand, difficult to deal with McClernand. And I think that fairly early on in the process, and I'm not totally sure when, I think after Belmont, maybe after Shiloh, I'm not really sure, Grant sees McClernand as a burden that he's going to have to bear. Grant again accepts the situation as it is and he works with it as it is. He recognizes that Lincoln, for reasons of state, has seen necessary to inflict this political general on him. And part of what Grant has to do, as well as suffering the degradations of Mr. Pemberton and Mr. Johnston on the other side, is also to deal with Mr. McClernand on this side, and McClernand's ego. That's not to say that McClernand did not have real talents as a general. He was somewhat a leader of men, actually. But I think Grant, early on, starts to realize that he's just going to have to work with this as a man that he's going to have to put up with and he's going to have to deal with. Try to use him if you can, but not quite the same way he would with Logan and W.H.L. Wallace, whom he can see as protégées, whom he can develop and really make into effective generals.

**Dr. Wright:**

I think we have time for one more question.

**Audience Member 5:**

Dr. Woodworth, you mentioned that Grant built the Army of the Tennessee's officer corps. How much did Henry Halleck either interfere with him or give him a free hand in terms of building that officer corps?

**Dr. Woodworth:**

That's a good question. Halleck certainly interfered with Grant in terms of Grant's operations until Halleck was sent east and got a little education during the summer of 1862 campaign. An education in his own inability, really, to make things happen operationally. And then Halleck backed off and gave Grant a lot more operational freedom after the summer of '62. Prior to that, he certainly was interfering operationally. He had some input in terms of personnel. For example. Halleck sent James B. McPherson, who had been an officer on Halleck's staff, sent him to Grant to serve on Grant's staff before the Donelson campaign, Henry and Donelson campaign, apparently chiefly to serve as Halleck's eyes and ears to make sure that Grant was staying on the wagon vis-à-vis alcohol. It's interesting that after McPherson then sends back his report to Halleck that Grant was indeed remaining abstinent of alcohol, Halleck then spreads the rumor to McClellan that Grant had returned to his former bad habits. Halleck certainly had some input personnel-wise. But again, Grant worked with what he had. He worked with McPherson and he made McPherson into one of his favorite generals. McPherson, of course, was a professional. I would say minimal, but Halleck had some input in terms of personnel, but not a very large amount. To a large degree, Halleck, like Grant, worked with the people and promoted the people that he wanted to promote, as far as I can tell.

**Dr. Wright:**

OK, I think we're out of time. Please join me in a round of applause for our panelists.

## Day 1, Panel 2: Emergence of a Modern Officer Corps, 1866-1905

## The 1891 Infantry Tactics by Perry D. Jamieson, Ph.D.
(Submitted Paper)

Alben Barkley, who was President Harry Truman's vice president, once offered the opinion that the best audience is one that is intelligent, well-educated, and a little drunk. I'm looking to you for two out of three of those qualifications.

Whether the audience, or the speaker, is drunk or sober, a lot can be said about the modern officer corps that emerged in the United States Army between 1865 and 1905. But it can't be stated in twenty minutes. Narrowing the topic, much can be said about the army's thinking about tactics, as just one example of the emergence of a modern officer corps. But *that* can't be covered in 20 minutes, either.

So, given the time available, I am narrowing the topic farther, to the most important single event in the development of US Army tactics during this period: the publication of the 1891 infantry manual.

A board of officers prepared this work to address a problem that had been developing since the Civil War. During that conflict battalions nearly always were volunteer regiments. They typically fought as parts of brigades, in two-line, close-ordered formations that aligned by the soldiers touching elbows. The firepower of Civil War infantrymen armed with rifled muskets and artillerymen with improved field pieces challenged the traditional drill books. Five months after Appomattox, one veteran described what had happened: "The introduction of the rifled Parrott field pieces, and the rifled muskets made a change of tactics absolutely necessary; and the text-books passed into obsoleteness."[1]

After the Civil War Lieutenant Colonel Emory Upton, an intense student of everything from battlefield tactics to military policy, took up the challenge of preparing a new infantry drill book that would address the threat posed by increased firepower. Lieutenant Colonel Upton's main innovation was to introduce a system of "fours," blocks of four men. After hours of training together, these groups of four soldiers could deploy rapidly from marching column into fighting line, and could march by the flank, wheel, or perform other movements before or during contact with an enemy. Faced with more dangerous battlefields, Upton's fundamental answer was that these blocks of four men would create and change formations under fire more quickly than individual infantrymen could.

Upton's second innovation was to permit infantry battalions in some cases to deploy in a single line, rather than the two-line formation. Drawing on his Civil War experience, Upton pointed to the wartime successes won by dismounted cavalrymen armed with repeaters. He believed these examples proved "that one rank of men so armed is nearly, if not quite, equal in offensive or defensive power to two ranks armed with the Springfield musket."[2]

Upton first published his infantry drill book in 1867, at his own expense. A Civil War veteran of all three arms of the service, he also became interested in what 19th century soldiers called an "assimilated" tactics. This was a system of commands and formations that were compatible among the infantry, artillery, and cavalry. Upton and three other officers prepared three "assimilated" manuals, one for each arm of the service, which were authorized by the War Department and published in 1874.[3]

Upton had taken some important steps beyond the Civil War drill books, but the firepower problem he had addressed continued to grow. During the late 19th century, the deadly menace that firepower threatened against advancing infantrymen continued to increase. Breech-loading repeaters, Gatling guns, breech-loading field artillery, sophisticated entrenchments, metallic cartridges, fixed ammunition, smokeless powder, and other technological advances promised to make future battlefields more dangerous.[4]

By the 1880s, the most casual observers were aware of these dramatic improvements in weapons. Many officers recognized that the army would have to move its ideas about tactics beyond the experience of the Civil War and the contributions of Upton. No one was more aware of this than the soldier-scholar Arthur L. Wagner. In his publications and his teaching here at Fort Leavenworth, Wagner pointed to the need for tactical changes. He warned against headlong advances and emphasized the virtue of flexibility. Wagner stressed that attackers must be ready to make flank rather than frontal offensives, to make the best use of cover, and to take advantage of any weakness shown by a defender, such as low morale or faulty deployments.[5] (We will be hearing more about Arthur Wagner's contributions from Dr. Todd Brereton.)

The reform that Wagner and others wanted to see began in January 1888, when Secretary of War William C. Endicott directed that a board of officers study the tactics of each of the three arms of the service. (Again in the interest of time, only the infantry will be considered here.) Lieutenant Colonel John C. Bates, who had been a company officer during the Civil War, chaired this board and 1st Lieutenant John T. French, Jr., of the Fourth Artillery served as its recorder.[6] Six other officers, two from each arm, completed the panel's membership. The best known among the group was Captain Edward S. Godfrey, a highly respected cavalry veteran of the Little Big Horn and other Indian campaigns.[7]

The board began meeting in February 1888, in Washington, D.C. In late March 1889 the panel moved to Fort Leavenworth, so that it would be close to the School of Application for Infantry and Cavalry, which had been established here in 1881. (We will be hearing in our next panel from Dr. Tim Nenninger about the Leavenworth schools during a later period.) The 1889 board of officers could not find enough room on the post, so its members took offices and quarters in the town.[8] They finished their work in December 1890 and the next month sent final drafts of tactical manuals for infantry, cavalry, and artillery to the adjutant general.[9] The Leavenworth manuals survived a review process which was far more bureaucratic than any earlier such works, and were approved in 1891 by Secretary of War Redfield Proctor and President Benjamin Harrison.[10]

The Leavenworth board produced an infantry manual in two parts: a "Close Order" section and an "Extended Order" one. The fundamental idea was that the soldiers would march and maneuver in close order and then would fight in extended, or loose, order. The "Close Order" part of the 1891 manual provided for a group of eight men, a corporal and seven privates, to move in close order while marching during a campaign or maneuvering into battle.[11]

The second part of 1891 manual, the "Extended Order," included the greatest innovations offered by the Leavenworth board. While the "Close Order" provided for a group of eight men, the "Extended Order" clearly labeled these seven privates and a corporal a "squad," introducing the term to the combat tactics of the United States Army. Moreover, this second part of the manual based the battle tactics of the infantry on having these squads fight in loose order. The "Extended Order" section deployed the soldiers as skirmishers, spreading them out to minimize the targets they would present to the destructive firepower of breech-loading repeaters, Gatling guns, and improved artillery.[12] The 1891 manual declared that the "squad is the basis of extended order. . . This instruction, on account of its importance, will be given as soon as the recruits have had a few drills in close order." The *Army and Navy Register* explained this dramatic innovation to its readers in September 1891: "With these tactics the line of battle disappears…The fighting line will consist of a series of squads as skirmishers, the normal number of men in a squad being eight."[13]

In addition to these specific innovations, the work of the Leavenworth board scored another achievement. It represented the United States Army's first true tactical manual, as opposed to drill book. From the Revolutionary War until 1891, all of the officially authorized volumes described formations and they explained how they were to move from one place to another. From the days of Baron von Steuben until Emory Upton, the army had drill books. It did not have tactical manuals: works that would advise officers how to take advantage of terrain, or how to maneuver and engage their troops in order to gain advantages in battle. The army lacked a volume that would instruct combat leaders, as Upton himself had put it, "How to fight." "What we call 'Tactics,'" grumbled one artilleryman in 1887, "no other nation in the world dignifies with that name."[14] Theorists had offered their opinions on this broader subject in many private publications, but the Leavenworth board's volumes were the first official works to give officers true tactical manuals, advising them "How to fight."

Today it might seem obvious that the 1891 manuals offered significant improvements and represented the army's logical next step beyond Upton and his Civil War predecessors. In their own day, they were not universally viewed that way. When word leaked out from Leavenworth about the extended order formations that the board members were developing, critics began to snipe at the infantry manual while it still remained in draft.[15] The criticisms increased after the War Department adopted the new tactics. In 1893 Inspector General Brig. Gen. Joseph C. Breckinridge claimed that most officers found the close-order drill satisfactory, but did not like the extended order formations. The prevailing view, according to General Breckinridge, was that the loose-order tactics required too many leaders: an NCO would accompany every squad, while a battalion retained its traditional number of company officers. Moreover, the new manual gave these junior leaders too much authority and, under the stress of combat, the system would break down in confusion.[16]

Despite Breckinridge's negative views, many officers perceived the benefits of the Leavenworth tactics. In December 1890 the *Army and Navy Register* offered its first assessment of the volume. Its reviewer declared: "In our judgment, the board has done good work and has been guided by sound and safe principals." This officer recognized the new volume's fundamental achievement, its use of squads in open order as the basis of the infantry's battle tactics, and praised this innovation. A later reviewer for the *Register* complimented the Leavenworth board "that in the matter of tactics it has effectually prepared us for war." 1st Lieutenant Lyman W.V. Kennon, an aide to Major General George Crook who shared that general's interest in tactics, also praised the new manual.[17]

Lieutenant Kennon, the *Army and Navy Register*'s reviewers, and many other officers appreciated the achievement of the 1891 infantry tactics. Faced with the danger of increased firepower that threatened attackers, the Leavenworth board of officers had devised a reasonable solution. They gave the United States Army its first tactical manual, as opposed to a drill book, and they introduced the combat squad to the infantry. They allowed small units of soldiers to maneuver in loose order, with as much flexibility and control as possible on battlefields in the era before electronic communications. Their 1891 work on infantry improved on the manuals of the Civil War and of Upton, endured to serve as the army's authorized tactics during the Spanish-American War, and represented a landmark effort.

William A. Ganoe, in his master-work survey of the history of the United States Army, labeled the years after the Civil War the "dark ages."[18] There is no question that the service faced serious problems during this period. Personnel strengths and monetary budgets were low. During Reconstruction, the Army was given a mission that was impossible to accomplish, without angering, disappointing, or even endangering large groups of Americans. In the case of the Indian wars, it was given an assignment without the support of adequate resources or a political consensus. The units of the army were dispersed and isolated. There was no foreign threat compelling enough to jar the president or Congress into addressing any of these problems.

And yet it would be mistaken to think of the post-Civil War years as a backwater in the army's history. During this era, as often during peacetime periods when the service labored with limited resources, it produced forward-looking officers. The army's examination of its infantry tactics provides just one example of how, during the late 1880s and early 1890s, innovative thinkers were moving a great institution toward a new century.

## Notes

1. Veteran, "Change of Tactics," Army and Navy Journal 3 (September 23, 1865), 75.
2. Perry D. Jamieson, "Crossing the Deadly Ground: United States Army Tactics, 1865-1899" (London and Tuscaloosa, Ala., 1994), 9-10.
3. Jamieson, 6, 9.
4. Jamieson, 128. The endnote accompanying this text gives many sources on the improvement of weapons during the late 19th century. Jamieson, 198-199, note 46.
5. Jamieson, 73.
6. Special Orders No. 14, January 18, 1888, Roll 601, Records of the Board on the Revision of Tactics, AGO File 526 AGO 1880, M-689, National Archives, Washington, DC; Francis B. Heitman, "Historical Register and Dictionary of the United States Army," 2 vols. (Washington, DC, 1903), 1:199.
7. Special Orders No. 14, January 14, 1888, and memoranda of the Bates Board to the Adjutant General, December 1, 1890, Roll 601, Records of the Board on the Revision of Tactics; Heitman, "Historical Register," 1:461.
8. "The History of Our Tactics," Army and Navy Journal 25 (February 11, 1888), 570; Special Orders No. 68, March 23, 1889, Roll 602, Records of the Board on the Revision of Tactics; memorandum of the Board on the Revision of Tactics to the Adjutant General, December 1, 1890, Roll 601; Records of the Board on the Revision of Tactics; "The Tactical Board," Army and Navy Journal 26 (April 20, 1889), 685. See also "New Drill Regulations for the Cavalry," Journal of the United States Cavalry Association 3 (1890), 286; "The United States Army," Army and Navy Register 10 (April 6, 1889), 209; Army and Navy Register 10 (July 27, 1889), 365; and Army and Navy Register 11 (October 4, 1890), 633.
9. LTC J.C. Bates to the Adjutant General, December 2, 1890, and January 15, 1891, Roll 601, Records of the Board on the Revision of Tactics.
10. Jamieson, "Crossing the Deadly Ground," 100.
11. Jamieson, 103.
12. Jamieson, 103, 104.
13. United States War Department, Infantry Drill Regulations, United States Army (Washington, DC, 1891), 186; "The New Tactics," Army and Navy Register 12 (September 26, 1891), 609.
14. Emory Upton to William T. Sherman, January 30, 1880, Roll 26, General Correspondence, William T. Sherman Papers, Library of Congress; John P. Wisser, "Practical Instructions in Minor Tactics," Journal of the Military Service Institution of the United States 8 (1887), 130. See also "Nomen," "Army Correspondence: Misuse of the Word 'Tactics,'" Army and Navy Register 9 (June 2, 1888), 349.
15. Thomas H. Ruger to the Adjutant General, July 1, 1891, Roll 601, Records of the Board on the Revision of Tactics; "The Work of the Tactical Board," Army and Navy Journal 28 (November 8, 1890), 166.
16. Annual Reports of the War Department, 1822-1907, M-997, National Archives, Report of the Inspector General, September 28, 1893, Roll 80, 4:719.
17. "The New Drill Regulations," Army and Navy Register 11 (October 11, 1890), 649; untitled, Army and Navy Register 11 (October 18, 1890), 665; L.W.V. Kennon, "The Tactical Board and Its Critics," Army and Navy Register 11 (December 27, 1890), 828-829.
18. William A. Ganoe, "History of the United States Army" (New York, 1942; reprint, 1964), title of Chapter IX, 298.

# Day 1, Panel 2: Emergence of a Modern Officer Corps, 1866-1905

## The 1891 Infantry Tactics by Todd Brereton, Ph.D.

(Transcript of Presentation)

**Dr. Brereton:**

Well it is really a great experience and pleasure and honor for me to be here, particularly at the place that was largely created by Arthur Wagner, this man right here. And so for me, in a way, this has come full circle. I'm his biographer. And now here I am, I'm talking about him at a place where he spent many years, and took lots and lots of work in accomplishing.

Well, let me ask you a rhetorical question that I don't expect an answer to, but feel free to pop in there. What makes a good combat leader, or for that matter, a commander of regiments, brigades, or entire divisions? What is it? What really is leadership? Is it an innate talent that some individuals have and others do not? Can leadership be taught to someone who isn't a natural leader? How can you tell if someone's not a natural leader? Or is leadership simply an academic discipline in which one can learn and internalize a group of discrete abilities?

Now I'm sure most of you know, I did not, having been out of the Army since I was 22 when my father retired. But in today's Army, from what I understand, and it certainly looks this way when you look around for it, in today's Army, leadership is explicitly taught. The United States Military Academy, USMA has a rigorous leadership training program and even offers a major in leadership: "Hey, what's your major?" "Leadership, dude."

ROTC cadets pass through a leaders training course and a leader development and assessment course. The Army has an official leadership doctrine, which is executed by the Center for Army Leadership and TRADOC, which together have, and I quote, "The goal of successfully synchronizing all leadership and leader development policy." This involves in part the integration of core leader competencies, which suggest to me anyway that leadership is considered by the Army to be an abstract concept that has definable qualities.

Now the edifice that is the US Army's leadership doctrine of course took a long time to build. And there was a time when the quality of leadership and its attainment was a matter of fierce debate. The period in question of course is the late 19th Century, particularly the 1880s and 1890s.

In this debate, two opponents faced each other over the Army's post Civil War character. Traditionalists, and I don't have General Ord up there just because I think he's a cranky, old general. He looks great. But again, two opponents faced each other over this issue. Traditionalists, conservatives, mostly Civil War veterans, who, as Dr. Jamieson has pointed out, preferred the close order because it was easy and it was comfortable, and it reminded them of the old days, but traditionalists sought to preserve the doctrine of inspired leadership, which they claimed was a characteristic in American wars, while progressives, the post-Civil War newbies who had come to age in their graduation from

West Point after 1866, '67, thereabouts, the progressives wanted to introduce new methods of training and learning.

For more than 20 years, these diametric sides clashed over innovation and custom. A principal bone of contention was over the preparation of junior officers through the creation of a variety of service schools.

So here we are at the Command and General Staff College. Here we are, at a place where leadership is the core of its curricula. And as you surely know, everything here was created in 1881 by order of William Tecumseh Sherman. The school he established, the Infantry and Cavalry School, became a focal point for tactical and organizational reform, all of it concentrated upon the necessity to educate officers in the art of war.

Between 1886 and 1905, the champion of that idea was Arthur Lockwood Wagner who argued that good combat leaders were made, not born, and they were made through rigorous education and applied military theory and historical knowledge. An 1875 graduate of West Point, where, I should add, he accumulated an astonishing 731 demerits, I don't know what you have to do or how bad you've got to be to amass that many. One other individual had the most. Was it Custer?

**Audience Member:**

Custer had a lot.

**Dr. Brereton:**

He had a lot. I hope he had more than Wagner. I mean, but when you consider, one of the demerits was for having buckets of beer in full view in his dorm room. And he graduated 40th out of 43 in his class in 1875. But from small beginnings, great things grow.

Wagner graduated from West Point in 1875. And he arrived at the Infantry and Cavalry School in 1886, where he quickly established himself as the Army's preeminent authority on tactics, military organization, reconnaissance, and as the Army calls it today, lesson learning. He relentlessly promoted the concept of postgraduate officer education and he demanded that officers should be scholars as well as soldiers. Scores of lieutenants passed through his classes, and many more read his works, all of which infused the Army with his ideas. In many ways, the Fort Leavenworth of today is Arthur Wagner's creation. And it is really difficult to conceive of its present status without his contribution.

In his most important work, Organization & Tactics, published in 1894, Wagner argued, "Our best military lessons must be sought in the history of wars that were fought under conditions most similar to those likely to be encountered by us in the near future." Now to ensure that those lessons were properly understood, Wagner was aided by Eben Swift, who introduced to the Infantry and Cavalry School the so-called applicatory method. Swift took the lessons that Wagner and other instructors taught in the classroom and had students apply them in real-time situations. Student officers utilized the Leavenworth garrison to practice map orientation, reconnaissance, patrolling, and mock combat.

Quoting instructor William C. Carter, Ronald Machoian notes that the result was, "...a happy combination of theory and practice exercise that was the foundation for a new archetype of soldier who can, on the field of battle, with its turmoil and strange scenes, turn theory into practice."

Now while not directly teaching the principles of leadership, Wagner and Swift nonetheless were introducing a new leadership doctrine for the Army which Carol Reardon has called safe leadership, and Harry Ball has termed responsible command. In Wagner's own words, his goal was to create junior officers who could, "...make command decisions based soundly on an appropriate principle of war."

In Organization & Tactics, Wagner added that such an education would, "...furnish a standard from which an officer in action can vary according to the conditions presented, and not leave him altogether without a guide." Wagner's methodology eschewed discrete rules for leadership and command in favor of flexible guidelines based on historical precedent and field practice.

Tim Nenninger remarks that Wagner, "...wanted to immerse officers in the details of a variety of tactical situations where they could draw their own conclusions regarding a proper course to be pursued." Wagner then required mental discipline and reflective capacity from his students, complemented by historical knowledge of a variety of combat situations. Eben Swift's role in the educational process transformed Wagner's academic lessons into applied knowledge. Swift himself argued that, "Principles are best learned by their application, rather than by the abstract study of the principles themselves." "Such an approach," he said, "takes longer than the other methods of study, but its results are more lasting."

The applicatory method was a global course of study which combined academic lessons and strategy, tactics, military organization, military geography and logistics with practical map exercises, tactical rides, and small unit wargaming known at the time as Kriegspiel. Such a comprehensive curriculum, Wagner concluded, provided officers with, "...careful training in the many branches of human knowledge which are now used in every feature of the profession of arms."

Harry Ball calls this a significant accomplishment, which, "...offered systematic, formal command procedures and a means by which officers could be schooled in those procedures." Now, there was certainly plenty of support for the mission of creating a responsible educated officer corps within the Army. But Wagner and Swift were not without their critics. Wagner in particular faced a reactionary backlash to his methods, chiefly from aging Civil War veterans who countered that the leadership expressed between 1861-65 had required no formal education. As Mark Grandstaff notes, "Those elevated from the ranks to commissions did not see the need for military training. They had gained theirs through experience, something that all the book learning in the world could not obviate."

Well, the undoubted exemplar of this argument was James R. Chester, a Scottish immigrant whose personal bravery had propelled him through the ranks in the Civil War from private to captain. His wartime leadership wasn't founded on book learning, and neither was that of hundreds of volunteer officers. "Experience cannot be purchased [hand?]," he argued. "The art of war is a trade to be learned. And actual war is the best school to learn it in." Now Wagner slyly agreed with this sentiment, suggesting that, "If a nation were constantly engaged in hostilities, it could always find qualified military leaders among its veterans." The problem, he added was that, "...such schools of perpetual warfare do not exist," hence the need for peacetime education and training.

Still, Chester's challenge was a potent one. And the question remained; did it make any real difference if an uneducated officer was promoted from the ranks yet made a first class combat leader? Moreover, he asked, could leadership even be taught? He didn't think so. "In battle, men need leaders more than commanders. Leading is unlearnable. The leader must be born to the business. His power is a patent of nobility and he holds it from the ruler of the universe."

In that vein, any of you like that out here? We were talking about egotism earlier. If you need to get something off your chest, now might be the...OK.

In that vein, Chester took a very dim view of educated officers whom he despairingly called kriegspielers. Accordingly, he argued that, "The spirit of command cannot be educated into a man. Education and training can only produce routine officers, organizers, drill masters, disciplinarians, and kriegspielers, but never commanders in the spiritual meaning of the term." So that's what you've been doing here.

Such an officer to Chester was a sham, able merely to make himself heard. The real commander, on the other hand, is felt as well as heard, and must be obeyed. Because of this innate, almost irrational nature of leadership, Chester concluded that, "Appointments to military command should be made with spiritual discernment, lest the minds of the appointees be garnished with all of the professional jargon of the schools."

can imagine, Wagner found arguments like these ludicrous, and he met them with scorn. He noted here in this vein, "It would be interesting, but hardly profitable to speculate upon the probable condition of the art of war if every commander had to learn the art from his own experience. Such an officer would have to be as old as Methuselah, engage in a hundred wars and pass through every grade from private to field marshal."

"Expertise that could be translated into practical application was vital," he urged. But should the Army prefer Chester's method? He argued then, "Let us come out frankly and say that military study is prejudicial to an officer. Let us warn young officers to avoid study and caution them never to put a pen to paper. Then being devoid of all evidence of a studious interest in their profession, they may possibly be recognized as practical men and escape being stigmatized as theorists."

Wagner's colleague, William H. Carter, echoed these sentiments, but was more circumspect. "Purely practical soldiers are apt to formulate false theories," he wrote, "...while theorists are quite apt to make false application of good principles. A happy combination of theory and practice should give the best results." John William De Forest, writing in The Atlantic Monthly, concurred: "The solemn fact is that to know much of the science of war, the cleverest man needs years of study and experience. And other solemn fact is that we had better look for supreme guidance to experts and to experts alone."

As wrongheaded as Chester's criticisms seem today, it is really unfair to judge him too harshly, although it is fun. A critical look at his complaints reveals that he wasn't condemning military education for itself. Rather, he mistakenly believed that education was becoming a substitute for leadership, whose qualities he considered to be spiritual. When describing the attributes of combat leadership, Chester employed the language of mysticism, suggesting that leaders possessed a motive power, an invisible factor, spirit, a mysterious power, moral force. For Chester, it followed that the execution of such talent in battle, which he called genius, was nearly unstoppable. While kriegspielers might be successful, only a commander with genius could truly conquer. It was this native ability that, "...sustains the warrior in battle and gives him victory in the end."

According to Chester, "It is the spirit that fights. It is the spirit that conquers." This notion of inspired leadership so dearly held by officers of the Civil War generation, is uncomfortably similar to the ideas of Ardant du Picq whose theories ultimately led France to the disaster of August, 1914.

Now what Chester called genius Wagner called, "...merely human wisdom applied to human knowledge." Now whatever it was, innate ability or the accumulation of knowledge, it had to be correctly applied when it mattered most. Chester's solution was to await the providential appearance of natural leaders who would then lead the nation to victory. It had, after all, worked in the Civil War, and similar claims were made for the Mexican War, the War of 1812, and the American Revolution.

So should then The United States await the next, more violent and chaotic conflict hopefully expecting natural military leaders to emerge from the din of combat? How many soldiers might die in the meantime? How many blunders would be committed? What if no leaders equal to the task emerged? These were the sort of questions that motivated reformers like Wagner and SwiFort

Chester's response to them was that no gifted leaders would emerge if the nation somehow did not deserve them. He claimed that, "...education and what is called the art of war is not essential to success as a military leader," even as advances in military technology were proving him wrong. Now war was faster and deadlier, and the battlefield more terrifying and sophisticated. Wagner cautioned that there are officers who pose as practice soldiers, in effect to despise all theory. But what would happen if someday they find themselves compromised on want of knowledge, not from want of talent?

Well, Wagner and his reform-minded colleagues understood only too well that the traditional trial and error approach to war in an era of modern weapons was simply indefensible. Secondhand while it might be, the experience of Königgrätz and Sedan had taught them that.

But still the question, what should be learned? Wagner didn't deny the existence of natural leaders. He knew they were around. You could see them in military history. Chester believed that such individuals controlled the spirits of their men silently, mysteriously, magnetically, which was all fine, but what then? What did a real captain do with that? Certainly there was aptitude for leadership, but in combat, that alone was an insufficient, perhaps even dangerous attribute. Talent, even genius was all to the good, but it had to be properly developed before it could be applied.

The first necessity then was to understand leadership in context. For Wagner, that meant understanding how it was expressed. Wagner's perception of the development of leadership and command skills was strongly historical in nature. He wanted to learn from what others did. All of his significant books and many of his articles stressed the need to learn from military history and to take conceptual, but not specific lessons from military success and failure. When Wagner expounded upon infantry, cavalry, and artillery tactics, he based his observations on battle and campaign histories which provided guidance, but not strict instructions on what to do in combat. His aim, he suggested, was to select the best established theories of European tactical authorities, to illustrate them by a reference to events in our own military history, and to apply them to the touchstone of American practice in war.

In the ninth edition of The Service of Security and Information, Wagner's second book, and the ninth edition came out in 1900. In that edition of The Service of Security and Information, Wagner observed that, "American experience in the Spanish-American War had evolved nothing radically new." Yet, he continued, the campaigns had, "...afforded some valuable illustrations of the application of old principles to new conditions."

So what about those conditions? Writing about this in 1889, Wagner asserted that, "In no profession, trade, or calling have the discoveries and inventions of modern science received a more extended application than in the art of war. As a result, the officers of the present day require a greater degree of professional and scientific preparation than ever known before in the history of war."

Although Wagner himself had never experienced combat, he knew enough from studying the art of war that in battle, "...conditions vary in nearly every respect. No two battles are fought in the same way. And the mostly carefully matured plans have to be quickly altered to meet new and unforeseen circumstances." It was the unpredictability of war that hastened Wagner to emphasize training, practice, and historical knowledge as a means to prepare men for it. Skeptic though he was, James Chester was inclined to agree. He admitted that even for a military genius, "...such training is necessary to his full professional equipment."

Such training, its attainment, discernment, and application is the proper legacy for Arthur L. Wagner, and the school he helped to build. Indispensable in his day and revered in ours, Wagner, in a real sense, was the intellectual father of military thought and leadership education in The United States Army. Referring in 1889 to the work of the Infantry and Cavalry School, Wagner hoped that, "It is not too extravagant to believe that the time will come when the seed planted at Fort Leavenworth will have grown into a great tree." Look at it now. Thank you very much.

# Day 1, Panel 2: Emergence of a Modern Officer Corps, 1865-1905

## Questions and Answers
(Transcript of Presentation)

## Perry D. Jamieson, Ph.D.
## Todd Brereton, Ph.D.

## Moderated by Curtis King, Ph.D.

**Dr. King:**

Thank you very much. I appreciate both presentations, excellent. Rarely does a moderator get lucky enough to have presentations so closely connected, physically of course with Arthur Wagner, but just conceptually the idea of changing the way you educate officers, the way you change doctrine and tactics. Both fascinating presentations.

metimes moderators, you know, exercise a privilege of first question. I have some, but I'm going to hold back. I'll open to the audience. I did want to make one comment, a note here. Early, Dr. Brereton, in your presentation, can you tell if someone is not a natural born leader? Having seen many OERs in my day, I think a lot of us assume that you can do that. How accurate that may be, I'm not sure. So I'll leave that comment alone. Questions from the audience, please.

**Question 1:**

I was interested in your discussion of the natural born leader, the instinctive leader, and kind of Chester's whole, you know, lineup. And it seems to me like he's envisioning or talking about the regimental commander or the Teddy Roosevelt or somebody out in front, you know, with a, you know, waving the sword. But of course to get things done in the Army, there's a hierarchy of leadership. And in particular, there's non-commissioned leadership.

Did anything that Chester envisioned or that Wagner, on the opposite side, spoke of speak to developing that non-commissioned officer level? And when you've had a chance to answer it, I'd like, Todd, I was hoping that we could hear something from Jamie about crossing the middle ground. Because you had some very definite roles for the NCO to play in the literature you were speaking to.

**Dr. Brereton:**

Well, Chester had very decided views on the lower ranks. And he did not view them very favorably. And one of the particular incidents brought up in passing by Jamie's presentation was that he despised what was known at the time, as a result of the extended order, he despised what was called individualism in combat

And the idea that ordinary soldiers, or even NCOs would be able to control a squad, much less a platoon was a radically wrong idea. Power and command rested only in the hands of officers. And officers commanded; NCOs and enlisted men followed. And they followed as a result of inspired command of the natural abilities of those captains and above. I don't know how many lieutenants fought during the Civil War. But he did not trust ordinary soldiers to be able to think for themselves on the battlefield, to be able to assess a combat situation and say, "That's where I need to go, but this is where I'm here. And there's an obstacle in my way. How do I and my teammates approach that and maneuver around it to strike the enemy?" He simply did not fathom that ordinary soldiers would be able to think that kind of problem through. They had to be led.

**Question 2:**

Did he have any practical military experience?

**Dr. Brereton:**

Oh yes. He started as a private in the Civil War and rose all the way through the ranks to captain. He covered himself in glory, if I'm not mistaken, at the Battle of Kearneysville and won a battlefield promotion there, and went on through the ranks, so quite a remarkable soldier in many ways. And it's a shame that there's not more known about him.

**Dr. Jamieson:**

I did brush up against this, but I never really addressed it in my paper, so thanks for a helpful question. I quoted General Brackenridge, who was Inspector General at the time, as saying that he thought a lot of. He thought most officers were critical of this idea of NCO leadership, critical of the 1891 IDRs. But there's a kind of code working here. What I quoted was, he says, "A lot of these officers say, this will create too many leaders," that in other words, you'll have NCOs with this new responsibility. They will become leaders, but will also still have of course the traditional battalion leadership. Well that's, of course, a kind of code for saying, "We don't need these NCO leaders," where today we would say, not only is this inevitable, it's a good thing.

**Question 3:**

Prior to the Civil War, we have Army doctrine expressed in terms of the Army regulations and drill manuals. Dr. Jamieson has talked about the resistance to even a rudimentary tactics manual. Arthur Wagner's books on theory were essentially privately published. Could each of you talk about the factors that inhibited the development of real tactical doctrine, real operational doctrine in the late 19th century Army?

**Dr. Brereton:**

Well, I personally, and Jamie would know better than I on this because he's written so much on it, but I don't get the impression that has yet promulgated as official. There certainly is unofficial doctrine, principally through the works that Wagner wrote and used as textbooks at the Infantry and Cavalry School. But, you know, I don't know about the artillery school. I don't know about any other post schools. Certainly the War College, when it was established in the early 1900s, had its own curriculum.

But as far as, this is how the Army fights and, you know, a doctrine espoused by an organization like today's TRADOC, that doesn't come around until Pershing really starts getting after it during World War I, between, you know, Pershing in March and, how will the Army fight?

**Dr. Jamieson:**

Yeah, in the field of tactics, and of course there are other areas you could consider, you can answer the question from the basis of looking at other fields. But in tactics, the point I'm making is that essentially from colonial times through even Upton, although Upton was more sophisticated than Civil War works, the idea is to tell the men what position to get into. It's to describe formations. And then it's to tell them how to move, how to march and how to maneuver in battle.

So I'm identifying that as really a drill book, that this really isn't tactics. It doesn't advise a combat officer, as Upton put it very succinctly, how to fight. Now you can argue there's implied within Hardee's tactics or Casey's tactics a larger tactic. There is in fact a larger tactics implied here. If you line these men up in close order formations, regiments in two-line formations, brigades in two-line formations, and a few hundred yards between one brigade and another as a division advances, of course there is an implied tactics there. And certain things are liable to happen or not happen.

But to address this as really a tactical manual, I would argue it just isn't there until 1891. And then I think Todd is right, that even what we read in 1891 is sort of how to take, we would regard as just kind of common-sensical. And we would hope some Civil War and Mexican American War officers and others generations earlier would have already recognized this, how to take advantage of ground and other obvious common-sensical things.

I kind of foot-stomp it because there it is in print in 1891. And you won't find it in Upton, Hardee, or Casey. But I think Todd is right; it doesn't really come to fruition (overlapping dialogue) until the new Army period.

**Queston 4:**

A favorite topic is one you've both addressed, to whether leaders are born or made. You could argue, I think, that the existence of the entire Army school system represents the conviction, or at least the hope that they could be made. This morning, General Brown pointed out that at the lower echelons, command can be directly applied. Whereas if you get, I think you said beyond battalion, John, it has to be largely indirectly applied. So I'm wondering if either of you in your research has formed any views as to whether that higher level leadership might require a different and maybe more spiritual qualities that perhaps fall into the realm of born, not made.

**Dr. Brereton:**

Yeah. I don't know. I don't think Wagner ever really went there, to be honest with you. He did want majors and more senior officers to attend the new War College, which he also taught at. It was, I think, co commandant for two years before he died in 1905. And that's one of the great tragedies is that he died so really young. He was about my age when he died, and that's a scary thing to think about.

But as far as the spiritual component and trying to develop and nurture that, whatever it is. Although Wagner, as I mentioned, recognized that there were such things as natural leaders, he, I think that his impression would have been or his conviction would have been to train them in certain techniques and sufficient academic knowledge with applied applications so that their natural ability would enable them to better incorporate those ideas, doctrines, and historical knowledge into combat, into leading other men.

**Dr. Jamieson:**

I think the only thing I could add to that or I would add to that would be that I think in the late 19th century Army, a lot of officers are looking to and appreciating senior officers who we would say mentor them. In the old Army, professor Woodworth, Steve Woodworth mentioned this morning, Grant patterned himself in appearance and command style on Taylor, but in operational terms, on Scott. Officers have probably always done this, learned from senior officers. But they weren't looking to these people, I don't think, to mentor them. But I think this is another part of the story, emerging officer corps in the late 19th century, Upton clearly is mentored by Sherman. So this is, I think, another emerging role for senior leaders.

**Mr. Ben King:**

Hi, Ben King from headquarters, TRADOC. Aren't we talking here about really a revolution in the concept of leadership? You know, as General Brown discussed this morning, like, 18th century, Frederick the Great wants the guy that's not too bright and not too ambitious. And there are a lot of Civil War leaders who were that way, whether political or not. But what their purpose was, to be on their horse, to provide inspiration for the men and attract bullets. And when he said, "Follow me," they were going to follow him, because he provided that positive example.

However, by the end of the Civil War and into the late 19th century, you have a revolution in weaponry. You have revolution in tactics. And so you have to have a revolution, maybe I'm overusing the word, in the concept of leadership. And isn't that what we're talking about? Because it's almost like, and this is maybe a little stretching it, it's the armies in the early 18th century when all of a sudden you have to have a non-commissioned officer if to do nothing else than beat these guys back into ranks when they want to run away. You have to have somebody at the lowest possible level that understands the tactics, understands the battle, and needs to provide that very low level of leadership.

So it seems to me that we're having that same kind of revolution in the end of the 19th century, where leadership is no longer being on your horse and providing inspiration for the men in the line, linear tactics. You have to have somebody that understands the tactics. And you have to have somebody that understands, I hate to use this word, doctrine, I'll explain in a minute, and understands the drill so the unit can be successful in combat.

And so I think that we're talking about, you know, really apples and oranges, the apples being what happened in the Civil War, and the oranges as what happened later in Upton's manuals and the manual of 1891. And I'll just make a comment on doctrines.

Our first major doctrinal piece did not occur until the field service regulations of 1905. And one of the problems we had in developing doctrine is the fact that we did not have the units to do it. And if you read the manual, it basically says, you know, division is consisted of so many regiments. And later on, the regiments could be partially militia regiments. But we really did not have enough units to make an entire division. So we couldn't practice it. We couldn't experiment with it. And even the large maneuvers of 1904 in Manassas, which took, like, something, 26,000 men, we still couldn't get a grip on it, because we did not have those permanent units. And I think that's one of the problems we have in the late 19th century. We just don't have the kinds of units we needed to develop that intellectual organization.

**Dr. Brereton:**

It's my impression that during Wagner's day, there really was no sense of a concept of leadership in the way certainly that we understand it today. And my impression really is that Wagner and his colleagues on either side of this debate really saw this as a command issue, rather than necessarily a leadership issue that could be inculcated in junior officers and expressed on the battlefield and improved. So frequently, in the writing of certainly reformers in the Journal of the United States Military Institution, JMSI, Journal of the Military Service Institution, the assumption, generally speaking, is that commanders will lead, that they will know how to lead, and that with the proper tools, they can lead.

But as far as an actual leadership doctrine, no, I don't see it. Although men like Chester certainly talk about it in the terms that you mentioned.

**Question 5:**

I'd just like to make a comment, partly about that and about leaders and senior leaders. I think the context of the 19th century Army, where you have the demographic hump that you mentioned, you have Civil War veterans on one side, and then a new generation of lieutenants coming in that are going to serve 20 years as lieutenants, junior captains through this kind of thing, creates an uncertainty, you know, creates a division in the Army.

I suggest, too, the other reference to the fact that you go from one to two company posts, to by the end of the century, maybe a whole regiment on a post, if you're lucky, kind of thing changes the demographics. And all this creates an uncertainty as to what is war. And what is the future of the war? And what is the role of the Regular Army in that war? And therefore, what is the role of the regular officer in that war, kind of problem.

As a biography of John Schofield, he generally looked at leaders as an intellectual exercise, that the training of leaders was self-training, that an officer didn't have the intellectual energy to go study things, then you were going to have serious problems. Not that he didn't believe in the value of Leavenworth, and not that he didn't believe in the value of the practical school at Fort Riley. As a matter of fact, he was the defender of the practical school at Fort Riley.

But he also was the guy that says, in the absence of consensus, in the absence of certainty, then we'll use the military service institution and its articles and people presenting papers among peers. I'll create lyceums to have officers present papers and senior officers mentor the junior officers to these things. And that finally you can see in how he does business. Even in promotion boards, he says, "No, I'm not going to say that the Arthur Wagner manual is going to be the standard for the promotion boards. Since there is no manual, we're going to leave it to the judgment of the senior officers to ask pertinent and relevant questions to the junior officers about what constitutes promotion." So in a sense, it is the sheer uncertainty that says, "OK, self education is the most important characteristic of a leader."

**Dr. Brereton:**

I'd just respond. I'd say that what I've seen in the history of the Army's tactics gives kind of a case study example of the larger point you're making. I think in revolutionary days, we thought we'd brought one of the international experts over here from Europe and he taught General Washington's troops the drill. So the tactical problem is solved. And then we had Scott's tactics. The problem is solved. Casey and Hardee, the problem is solved. Upton, the problem is solved.

What I see in the late 19th century Army for the first time is an awareness that we may take our best shot at this, but finally we're up against a battlefield so dangerous that a lot of us are willing to say, "We're not really sure we've solved this." You know? You may study this a long time and there may just be no way to get around this, that this firepower we're moving against is too much for us.

So I think your theme of uncertainty is a good one. It's certainly reflected in the Army's attitude about tactics. I see a definite change in the late 19th century. I don't see officers, the Mexican War, Civil War era musing about this the way they do in the late 19th century.

**Dr. Jamieson:**

Arthur Wagner's goal, practically for the Army as a whole was to move it away from non-military engagements like strike breaking and fighting Indians, garrisoning posts, defending harbors, things of this nature, and to return it to its core mission, which was to fight war. Well, if we are going to fight war, we are going to have to know how to fight war. And in order to do so effectively and successfully, then we're going to have to have certain tools. And those tools are going to have to be taken largely from those people who we may wind up fighting in an increasingly dangerous age. I've been told by some individuals that, you know, well really, all Army reform in the late 1800s occurred in a vacuum because it didn't matter.

Well, you can say that now. I mean, hindsight is golden. They certainly did not know this. And the reformers of the Army certainly wanted to move the Army away from those non-military tasks to, what's an Army for? If we're going to have it, then we should train it appropriately.

**Question 6:**

One of you all mentioned the Spanish-American War. I think it was you, Dr. Brereton. And I'm curious about these other case studies that were available, at least by 1905, which is the South African case study and the Manchurian case study, which are closely being examined by European counterparts. So did The United States Army, anybody in the US send observers to either the Boer War or the Russo-Japanese War? And perhaps in the next panel, this will come out. And if they didn't, that'd be interesting to know. And why didn't they? Did they learn, take any insights from these?

**Dr. Brereton:**

I really don't know, frankly, to be honest. I'm ignorant on that. But I can tell you that Chester wrote about the South African War and came to the conclusion that extended order, the open order, individualism could not work. We have to have close order ranks to fight these battles, in order to develop the volume of fire that is necessary. And despite the fact that, you know, all of these...You know, by the 1890s, you've got rows of soldiers behind fortifications shooting repeating arms. So no, I haven't seen that.

**Dr. Jamieson:**

The only thing I've seen is American officers primarily looking at the Spanish-American, their own Spanish-American War influence. And it's the same questions. Are we going to have aimed individual fire? Or is volley fire better than aimed individual fire? Are we ever going to be able to have direct artillery fire? You know? Is the bayonet finally dead? You know, the same kind of arguments were going on in the late 1860s and '70s based on Civil War experience. There's the same kind of argument back and forth after 1898, that as Todd put it, you have sort of two schools. You have a Wagner school and a Chester school. And you pick whatever question you want, the bayonet, saber, whatever, this kind of thing. It's not resolved anymore by the Spanish War than it was resolved by the Civil War.

**Dr. Brereton:**

Now, Wagner was in Cuba and later Puerto Rico. And think it's in 1899, he did publish a report on the Spanish-American War. In that, in a very, very slim volume, he came to the conclusion that everything that he had said in, you know, The Service of Security & Information and in Organization & Tactics, and in some other articles that he had read, everything that he had written had come true, that the effect of smokeless powder was not going to be a big deal, that the extended order was right, that it could, despite the dispersion of the fighting line, that those soldiers armed with repeating rifles would be able to overwhelm a well organized defense behind fortifications, that the artillery needed to be indirectly observed, all of these things. And he makes these notices in this book, you know, one, two, three, four, you know, and goes right through the list of all of the improvements in weapons and tactics and whatnot, and how they all combine, and how he was right all along.

**Dr. Schifferle:**

Pete Schifferle, School of Advanced Military Studies. The answer to the Boer War is, I'm not sure. I think probably not a very robust observer group, if any, probably because of the nature of the war being, one, fought by the British. The US had kind of a love/hate relationship with the British Army at the turn of the century. But it was also a mostly guerrilla war and probably a little dangerous for an observer to go to the Boer War, considering the nature of the fight.

The Japanese, Russo-Japanese War was very heavily observed by US officers. Some of the most famous officers of the period ended up as observers over there. Primarily I think not so much the Russian, they were observers usually on the Japanese side. And I think it was because of the fear of the great yellow peril, that Japan was considered, even in 1904/1905, Japan was considered a future threat from across the Pacific. Interestingly enough, in the '20s and '30s, a goodly number of the student papers written at Leavenworth were written on the Russo Japanese War. Even with the experience of the AAF behind them, they were still looking at the 1904/1905 experience as an exemplar of how Asiatics fight, for example, given the language of the time.

**Dr. Brereton:**

One of the conclusions, I have read some of the articles by individuals who wrote about the Russo-Japanese War in JMSI. And some of the conclusions are, yes indeed, the closed order, double rank can work if you just throw enough men at your objectives.

**Dr. Schifferele:**

Yeah. There was a lot of concern from my memory of the reports back that very much a case of uncertainty about how to win, that they saw the Russians doing certain things that should have worked and didn't. They saw the Japanese doing things that should not have worked, and worked, and basically came back with quick rapid fire artillery, indirect fire artillery, machine guns, barbed wire, stabilized front warfare, so to speak, but were not exactly sure how to turn it into an effective offensive.

**Question 7:**

In late 19th century, matter of fact, it took until 1914 for the Command General Staff College to translate the two volumes of Balch's tactics. And I was wondering, was there any influence from things like that, or any foreign thing? Because Balch goes into a great deal of detail, especially on automatic weapons and things. And obviously he did not understand how devastating a machine gun was. But nonetheless, he recommends, you know, platoon of machine guns per… So did he have any influence, or that sort of thing have any (overlapping dialogue; inaudible) --

**Dr. Brereton:**

He did read Balch. I understand that Wagner could read German. He also read Clausewitz, and he incorporated both of them in Organization & Tactics. The closest that Wagner got to a machine gun of course was a gatling gun which he saw in action in Cuba.

**Question 8:**

I would like to address a question to both gentlemen, maybe from somewhat different angle. Preface this by saying I'm interested in this question or influenced by the fact that Combat Studies Institute will be doing some activities with TRADOC in the coming week, which is a bureaucratic, not in a negative sense, but a bureaucratic organization dealing with doctrine, leadership obviously. We know that.

But the key is, we're looking at people like Wagner and maybe Upton to a degree, or other reformers. We're studying here mostly are—Almost exclusively we're looking at combat leadership. But they have to exercise a certain leadership to get reforms through. Can you comment on their ability to fight against the naysayers, to get a large—it's not nearly a large as we are today, but, bureaucracy to make drastic changes if possible? The new regulations, 1891, how much fight was there? And how much effort, leadership did it take to just win over, to get through? So both gentlemen, if you could comment.

**Dr. Jamieson:**

That's a helpful question in my case, because again, I brushed against this, but I didn't, in the time I had here today, think it would be helpful to spend a lot of time on it. So thanks for coming back to that.

I mentioned in passing that the drill books before this, in an earlier period—and they were drill books—will be adopted by the Army much more readily and much more simply. If Secretary of War Jefferson Davis thinks Hardee's tactics are good enough, they're good enough. And that's pretty much the end of the matter. What we see with the 1891 IDR, I mentioned, was by far and away, much more bureaucratic review process. Today, by our standards, this would be the first work of this kind that was staffed, that generals were busy, and they'd only have time to read this. So junior officers would read this first. And the 1891 works were staffed, as I recall, through all three (inaudible) certainly I'm certain to say through the infantry.

And so ultimately, as I mentioned, they're signed off on by the Secretary of War and the President of The United States. But I'm pretty confident that President Harrison didn't spend a lot of time reviewing all this. It's interesting, because it tells us something about the history of the Army. The Army's becoming much more bureaucratic.

**Dr. Brereton:**

Wagner certainly had a role in the 1891 IDR. He was a consultant. He was at Fort Leavenworth teaching in the Infantry and Cavalry School at the time, although I have really no idea. I haven't seen what exactly his role was in the formation of that. Maybe you've found out. But if you have, please let me know. But as far as getting his actual reforms implemented, of course none of those really came to pass until the root reforms, and the creation of a general staff and the War College and many other things that many reformers, including Wagner, wanted to achieve and had been unable to for any number of reasons, mostly because of the bureau system of the Army, you know, simply would not let them.

But to the degree that Wagner was able to get anything accomplished, it was primarily, if you don't mind my saying, through nagging. He wrote and wrote and wrote. And he wrote letters to people. He wrote books. He wrote his articles, which were, in some cases, vituperative, against those who opposed him, Chester being one in particular. Another, what's his name...? I want to say Edward [Wisser?]. I can't remember the fellow's name. But Wagner just whined a lot.

He also cultivated friends. And this was the Army of that time where you really, in some cases, an officer like Wagner, who had no combat experience, he rose through the ranks on the strength of his intellectual and academic abilities alone, Wagner needed patrons. And so he went to men like Adna Chaffee and J. Franklin Bell, and cultivated their ability to cut through the red tape and to get things done for him that could not otherwise have gotten done.

**Dr. King:**

I know from the staff ride perspective, because I work on the staff ride team, that it took even Swift to really execute what Wagner had conceived of.

**Dr. Brereton:**

Well, there's also the fact that Wagner died young. He died right when all of his reforms had come to fruition. And then he croaked.

**Dr. King:**

We have time for a few more questions. Yes, please?

**Dr. Hsieh:**

Yeah, Wayne Hsieh, US Naval Academy. You mentioned sort of Wagner, and you see this trend let's say with Upton too, a desire to get the Army away from strike breaking, from fighting Indians and insurgents. But I was thinking, you know, Brian Linn's characterization of, in a lot of ways, that the Army is sort of willfully ignoring what its actual imperial constabulary mission is, especially after the Spanish-American War. I mean, that's what the Army ends up actually having to do.

And I think it's fair to say, as I read it, Linn comes down pretty hard on the Army. I just wanted to get what your—I mean, do you think that's a fair criticism? I mean, is this the Army insisting on just fighting wars it wants to fight, not these messy, imperial policing measures which unfortunately it's stuck with? Or is there a rationale that's really given that's defensible, that, you know, institutions like Leavenworth shouldn't have to worry about that, that's not necessary and not appropriate?

**Dr. Brereton:**

Well, to some degree, I look at the early creation of Infantry and Cavalry School as giving those reform-minded officers something to do. Many of these officers did not want to be on the frontier. Wagner hated his work with the 6th Infantry during the Nez Perce campaign and up in Fort Robinson, way the hell up there in North Dakota. But many of these reformers despised the kind of work that they were doing, but also understood that that's all we've got.

So what they became engaged in really was this famous search for a mission, which has been written on in a number of fora for that period. And they were looking for something to do. They needed somewhere else to go, and they also, men like Wagner, Swift, some others need to come to mind at the moment, but don't. But they understood what an Army was for. They didn't see their Army doing what they thought an Army should be doing. It's not that they anticipated overseas combat or even war with a foreign aggressor. But there was also the possibility, well, you know, England can still get here, and the Germans are building a big fleet. Did you know, by the way, that, you know, Chile had a larger navy than that of The United States Navy in the 1870s, up 'til the early 1880s? So there's that whole point of, what are we doing here? We want to go from here to there, and we need to push the Army to seeing our point of view.

**Dr. Hsieh:**

Let me just ask a follow-up. I mean, you bring up the Navy. And this is kind of an interesting point, because, you know, my department recently had an interesting paper seminar. And Bob Love, who's actually a Naval historian, is really of the position that the Navy really doesn't have an opponent of late 19th Century. A lot of these "Mohanian" reforms are really the products of professional self-aggrandizement, to put it bluntly. Right? I mean, you know, how much of it is, you know, and the Army looking for a mission, but did it arguably already have a mission and just was trying to ignore it? You know, that its civilian political masters (overlapping dialogue) were….

**Dr. Brereton:**

The difference between the Army and the Navy of course is that the Navy builds things. I mean, they build these big, hulking steel monsters. And that looks good and it gives The United States prestige. We're beginning to expand globally. We're taking Hawaii. We're taking, what is it, Guam and got to have a two ocean fleet, and all of these things. And it's glamorous to do this. I mean, it's also a great source of patronage. Particularly in the Navy Department, you got all of those contracts and things of this nature. It really looks good. But what does the Army have? They've got horses and mules. They don't even have the Krag-Jorgensen yet. I mean, for heaven's sake. You can't spend any money on the Army. But you can sure as hell spend money on the Navy.

**Dr. Jamieson:**

I think it is fair to say, these Army thinkers in the 1880s and '90s who were interested in some of these questions are, for the most part, overwhelmingly for the most part, assuming a conventional war. What they're interested in, what the 1891 IDR assumes of course is a European opponent. And so what they come up with is fine for the war with Spain. It's fine for the Philippine War at first. And then when the war becomes a non-conventional war, I think in fairness to them, we have to say they do go back to their Indian fighting experience and some other things. And there are some interesting connections there. Well, to fight the Philippine War, after it becomes a guerilla war, wouldn't it be a good idea to have some Native help? You know? We used Indian scouts to, we had native warriors help us find and fight our opponents, the Apaches and on the Plains. And there are some of those kinds of connections and drawing on earlier experience. But I think the basis of your question is factually right, that in the '80s and '90s, the overwhelming interest was in, let's think about what it would be like if we had to fight a large conventional war.

PANEL 2

**Dr. Nenninger:**

Tim Nenninger, National Archives. Particularly after 1900, when Leavenworth reopens, in terms of the curriculum, they're really not looking at what's going on in the Philippines in terms of the military art courses. They're really looking at big battles, European style. The models they're studying, as often as not, are the Franco-Prussian War. But in some of the subsidiary courses in the curriculum, including military law, of which there's a military government component, at the time, they taught foreign languages, at least on occasion. Most of the students took Spanish. And some of the other subsidiary courses, there was a sense that some of this is going to be immediately practical when I get assigned with my regiment to the Philippines. But the larger focus in the military art courses completely ignored that, completely ignored, you know, the Indian fighting experience. I think it was a response to the overall changing nature of military organization and military technology at the time, not any problem that would be on the immediate horizon on most of the student officers.

**Dr. Connelly:**

I want to make a comment about the bureaucracy there. The US Army of the 19th century was an incredibly decentralized institution. You know? I said before the Civil War, you have the unifying idea of the Army regulations, you know? You know, that's one of the few unifying things. To a certain extent, West Point creates a values agenda for the rest of the officer corps. But it's very decentralized. And it truly is, doctrine is the opinion of the senior officer present, you know? And it could be the first lieutenant, you know, that's running the operation.

So that one of the things that becomes significant about the 1891 thing is, is yes, it was intentionally bureaucratic. It is taking a thing that had been done before, boards, right, putting together a board to try to take all these disparate elements of the Army and all these opinionated general officers who were essentially peers and colonels and majors, you know, because many of these majors are as old and has as much Civil War experience as the colonels and the generals, taking this army of almost near peers and trying to beat out an answer, trying to come to some sort of conclusion. So the very fact that it is bureaucratic, the very fact that it's disputatious, you know, and it goes back and forth is reflecting that reality of an Army that has no institutions of authority, if you will.

**Dr. King:**

I think we're towards the end of our time. Do you have any comments about that last (overlapping dialogue) remark?

**Dr. Brereton:**

No. Thank you all, very helpful questions.

# Day 1, Panel 3: Changing Leadership for a Changing World Role, 1906-1939

## The Leavenworth Schools, Professional Military Education, and Reform in the Old Army, 1900-1917 by Tim Nenniger, Ph.D.

(Submitted Paper)

The period from the end of the Indian Wars to World War I saw the evolution of the U.S. Army from a 25,000 man frontier constabulary to a modern professionally led force with 2 million men fighting in a coalition war in Europe. This also was a period of developing professionalism in the officer corps, creation of professional military education schools, and nascent efforts to foster reforms that would improve the quality of Army life and organization. It was also a period when the roles and missions of the U.S. Army were rapidly changing, when technological and organizational changes were affecting the art of war, and when qualities of knowledge and experience were evolving for individual officers to be considered true professionals.

A number of professional military education institutions had their genesis in this period. The Artillery School at Fortress Monroe, which reopened in 1867 after closure during the Civil War and taught the technical aspects of artillery, by the 1880s also examined "the general progress of military science." In 1891, to provide basic instruction for junior lieutenants and a more general forum for professional discussion, John M. Schofield, Commanding General of the Army, ordered creation of lyceums (later known as "garrison schools" or "post schools") at all posts housing troops of the line. The last decades of the 19th century also saw creation of the Engineer School of Application at Washington Barracks, the School of Submarine Defense at Fort Totten, and in 1887 the School of Application for Cavalry and Light Artillery at Fort Riley.[1] But there was no professional military education system, no connection between the schools, no progression from one level to another. Moreover, there was no system of selection for attendance which was largely in the hands of individual unit commanders, who often did not send their most competent officers.

Leavenworth was arguably the most significant of these schools at this time. In 1881 William T. Sherman, Commanding General of the Army, established the School of Application for Cavalry and Infantry at Fort Leavenworth. Modeled on the existing school for artillery officers at Fort Monroe, Leavenworth was to provide young infantry and cavalry lieutenants with a practical course in small unit tactics and administration. By the mid-1890s the school had broadened and deepened its curriculum, attracted good officers as faculty and students, and largely overcome its early reputation as a "kindergarten." The basis of the Leavenworth system was the "applicatory method," practical problem solving as a means of learning tactics. It had been introduced at the school by Captains Arthur L. Wagner and Eben Swift, two of the Army's acknowledged intellectuals of that period. Leavenworth closed in 1898 on the outbreak of the war with Spain.

It reopened in 1902 as the General Service and Staff College, a one-year remedial course for newly commissioned lieutenants; it graduated two classes. (Over 1000 officers, with little previous military education or training, had been commissioned during the Army's expansion in the wake of the Spanish-American War and Philippine Insurrection.) But after a fundamental reorganization in 1904 Leavenworth became two one-year schools with only the best graduates of the first year advancing to the second. The first year course, titled the Infantry and Cavalry School (after 1907 the Army School of the Line), encompassed military engineering, foreign languages, military law, and especially military art. During the first year students practiced troop leading of mixed tactical units up to division in size. At the second year Army Staff College military art predominated, with emphasis on general staff duties, logistics, and operational control of units as large as an army corps.

Also during this period there was growing recognition that if military art did not have an "intellectual" content, it was at least a field that required study, contemplation, and practice from its practitioners if they wanted to be considered professionals. Articles on tactics in professional journals, books on recent military campaigns, and translations of similar works from foreign military writers proliferated at this time, with such stalwart Leavenworth instructors as Wagner, Swift, Matthew F. Steele, John F. Morrison, and Arthur L. Conger among the most prolific officer-authors. Their participation in these activities largely contributed significantly to the growing reputation of Leavenworth as an intellectual center of the Army, where matters of tactics, operations, and doctrine were not only learned but, within limits, debated.[2]

In order to improve military art instruction at Leavenworth, in the early 1890s Swift introduced a technique adapted from the German Army of analyzing and solving tactical problems. It required students systematically to follow a series of steps to solve a problem and to prepare written orders that would make the solution clear. What began at Leavenworth as a means of instruction, however, evolved to become the "five paragraph field order," which by the time of World War I was the standardized form used by the U.S. Army to convey operations instructions on the battlefield. Whether ordering the advance of an infantry company or a field army, the process, the analytic technique and sequence, and form were the same: (Paragraph 1) general situation; (Paragraph 2) objective; (Paragraph 3) disposition of troops and tasks assigned component parts of the command; (Paragraph 4) logistic instructions; (Paragraph 5) communications instructions.[3] Another activity in which Leavenworth staff and instructors became involved was the preparation and dissemination of *Field Service Regulations*, which became the military "bible" by which the army in the field organized, trained, and operated. It contained in essence the Army's description of the nature of combat and became its doctrinal statement on how to fight. In 1905 Captain Joseph T. Dickman of the General Staff, but a recent Leavenworth tactics instructor, translated and adapted German Army regulations to the U.S. Army's needs. The value of such a manual to the course of instruction then being followed at the Infantry and Cavalry School and the Army Staff College was clear; at a minimum it would serve as a measuring rod against which students could be measured in graded tactical problems. Consequently, Leavenworth staff became intimately involved in preparing the several subsequent revisions, which in part were an effort to "Americanize" editions of *Field Service Regulations* (published 1908, 1910, and 1914) that were issued prior to World War I.[4] The reputation of Leavenworth as an intellectual center of the Army, the essence of the five paragraph operations order, and the involvement of Leavenworth staff and faculty in preparing the Army's capstone doctrinal manuals continue to this day.

The development of professional military education was a central element in the series of reforms initiated by senior War Department leaders, both civilian and military, particularly during the period Elihu Root was Secretary of War (1899 to 1903). Russell Weigley nicely captures Root's overall focus: "Reserves, planning, and command were the essentials of a better Army."[5] Improving the preofessional qualifications of individual officers was an important ingredient in insuring the success of all three areas. Root and William H. Carter, his principal military adviser, tried to establish a *system* of Army education where before only several independent, basically unrelated Army schools existed.[6] They attempted to use military education as a means to further aspects of their reform program, namely creating a trained body of officers to man the newly created War Department General Staff, to improve the professional attainments of militia officers which was part of the overall effort to link the separate state militias more closely with the Federal government.

Between the Spanish-American War and World War I, the postgraduate military education system inaugurated by Secretary Root seemingly was more successful than other elements of his reform program—efforts to strengthen War Department administration and improve the nation's military reserve system. During that period Army schools encouraged a heightened awareness of the intellectual content of military art among the professional officer corps, which in turn led to improved individual expertise, particularly in the realm of conducting combat operations with large units. But in many of its particulars, the postgraduate school system did not develop as Root had wanted. Who went to the schools, at what point in their careers, and why they went, had a marked impact on the reputation and broader influence of the post graduate schools. Who did not go and why were also significant. An examination of the students at the schools at Fort Leavenworth, will indicate how Root's system, once established, functioned and will reveal some shortcomings which limited its intended effect.

The best graduates from lower level institutions, garrison and branch schools, were to go to Leavenworth for combined arms training. For many officers, Leavenworth was their first experience away from their own branch. The best graduates from Leavenworth, in turn, were to go on to the Army War College, the apex of the Army school system. For these reasons, Leavenworth was central to how effectively the entire system functioned.

A major element of Root's reform program was to increase subordination of the state militias (the National Guard) to federal, essentially Regular Army, control. Although the Dick Act, passed by Congress in 1903, did not go as far in that direction as Root would have liked, it did authorize the federal government to mobilize state National Guard units to repel invasion and maintain internal order. The Act further recognized the organized militia as the country's first-line military reserve. In return for this recognition, the militia of each state had to meet minimum federal standards of efficiency. The Regular Army became responsible for assuring these standards were met and for providing weapons, equipment, and instruction to state units.[7]

As one means to foster cooperation, as well as to raise standards, the Dick Act authorized militia officers, on the recommendation of their state governors and with the approval of the President, to attend Army schools. Implicit was the mutual benefit of Regular and militia officers undergoing instruction together and to serve as a means to break down mutual hostility. Thus in the wake of the Dick Act, the prospect of militia attendance at Army schools, particularly Leavenworth, had a generally favorable reception.[8]

Early in 1903 Secretary Root ordered his staff to draft a detailed plan to enroll militia officers in Army schools, thereby fulfilling Section 16 of the Dick Act. The response from the organized militia was enthusiastic, with state governors initially recommending 89 officers for appointment to the service schools. But authorities on the newly created General Staff and at Leavenworth, which was the school all parties assumed most of the militia officers wanted to attend, had reservations. First, there were insufficient quarters at Fort Leavenworth to accommodate more than a handful of militia. Additionally, many Regular officers were skeptical that militia officers could materially benefit from the Leavenworth course without any prior military schooling; a qualification most lacked. Further, the Regulars doubted the militiamen understood what would be expected of them. As one staff study reported "…many of these militia officers have expressed a desire to go these schools without an appreciation of the real nature of the requirements of student officers…"[9]

Because of the limited capacity of the Leavenworth schools and questions about the qualifications of potential students from the militia, the War Department modified the original plans regarding attendance. State governors had to screen carefully, by means of written examinations if possible, all militia officers they recommended to the War Department. Because of lack of quarters, bachelors were preferred and no militia officer could bring his wife or other dependents. Most importantly, the authorities at Leavenworth would administer an entrance examination to any militia officer who had not graduated from one of the Regular Army garrison or branch schools, as would have most of the Regulars in attendance. The result was about as predicted by General Bell, the Leavenworth commandant after he had convinced the General Staff of the necessity of these changes: "I don't suppose it is possible we will have any militia officers next year, but if we do it will be few of them."[10]

In late September 1904 the first group of militia officers, only four, arrived at Fort Leavenworth for examination prior to admission to the Infantry and Cavalry School. As many Regulars had predicted, they all failed. Not only did they lack knowledge of basic military subjects, they knew "nothing about geometry, trigonometry, or algebra," all required for military engineering courses. Despite his persistent skepticism about the wisdom of admitting militia to Leavenworth under any circumstances, General Bell did not want to humiliate the individuals involved. He also worried about fostering good relations between the militia and Regular Army only a year after passage of the Dick Act. Consequently, Bell had the four officers admitted to the garrison school at Fort Leavenworth to pursue a specially designed course of study that would qualify them for the Infantry and Cavalry School the following year. All four officers concurred in Bell's plan, although only two actually completed the course and entered Leavenworth the next year.[11]

Despite his accommodation with the militiamen, when the question of militia attendance once again arose in 1905, Bell declared: "I honestly don't believe there is a man in the militia in the United States, who has had no instruction in post schools, who can pass the examination for admission here, and there are devilish few of them who could take the course successfully if they come here." But four of the five militia officers assigned to the class entering the Infantry and Cavalry School in August 1905 did pass the qualifying examination. An instructor described one of them as a "cracker-jack" who would make many of his Regular Army classmates "hustle" in competition. Another observer, more optimistic than General Bell, believed the education of militia officers in the service schools to be "an interesting experiment." He thought that although it had potential to end in disappointment, it could become a valuable feature of American military policy. The answer to that proposition was soon at hand.[12]

In June 1906 the Infantry and Cavalry School class, which included the four militia officers admitted to Leavenworth in August 1905, graduated. One of the militiamen, Capt. W.O. Selkirk of the Texas National Guard, had performed quite well. His class standing in the first year course, 19 of 50, qualified him as a "distinguished graduate" eligible to continue for a second year of instruction at the Army Staff College. He also did well at that institution the following year. But Selkirk was very intelligent and unusually diligent in his studies. Unfortunately, he was unique. The other three militia officers in the class of 1906 graduated near the bottom—45th, 47th, and 48th of 50. These officers at the bottom of the class all failed one or more subjects over the course of the year and had to be reexamined in those subjects in order to qualify for graduation. Moreover, one of the three, Lieutenant Charles N. Akeley of the Massachusetts Volunteer Militia, made a number acrimonious charges against Regular Army instructors who he considered prejudiced against the militia. His conduct, believed by some to be characteristic of neither an officer nor a gentleman, and the defensive response by Leavenworth authorities hardened attitudes on both sides. The experience did little to engender cooperation between the Regular Army and militia that joint attendance at Army schools was supposed to foster. Yet it did much to reinforce the skepticism among the Regulars about the professional ability of the guardsmen, while confirming the belief among the guardsmen that the Regulars were indeed prejudiced against them. Despite Root's grand plans, only four militia officers graduated from the Infantry and Cavalry School at Leavenworth between the Spanish-American War and World War I, all with the class of 1906, and only one, Selkirk, went on to the Army Staff College.[13]

The unhappy experience of the class of 1906 essentially ended the "interesting experiment" of militia officers attending Leavenworth. It did not completely deter all from trying to gain admission, however; several in subsequent years tried but failed the admission examination. Neither did it end all efforts by which the militia might benefit from the Leavenworth experience. For instance, the Academic Board at Leavenworth rated all graduates on their suitability as inspectors and instructors with state militia units. A number of graduates in subsequent assignments performed such duty. In addition, many recent graduates immediately after leaving Leavenworth served on temporary duty as umpires, observers, and instructors at at militia maneuvers and summer training camps. Some Leavenworth faculty also assisted state units with instruction at their officer training schools; John F. Morrison, best know of the service school instructors of this period, was in particular demand. On at least one occasion Leavenworth held a three-month course to prepare 22 Regular officers for duty with the militia. Interestingly, there was a continuing perception among some militia officials that despite the acrimony surrounding the class of 1906, something positive was happening at Leavenworth from which they could learn and benefit. As a New York officer put it in 1914: "We would like to have the spirit of Leavenworth among our officers." This was difficult to accomplish, however, without actually attending the school. Root had a good idea. It simply did not work out as he had planned.[14]

If the Army educational system was one means for the Regular Army to reach out and improve the militia, Secretary Root also saw it as the principal mechanism for improving the Regular Army officer corps itself. The selection procedures for each school and the progression of the most qualified graduates from one Army school to the next highest level were critical to the effective functioning of Root's scheme. The order establishing the system stated:

Especial attention will be paid to the records made by individuals at each step of this progressive course, in order that those most deserving shall be given further opportunity for perfecting themselves in the profession of arms, and that the Nation may have at all times at its disposal a highly trained body of officers and may know who they are.

Root wanted to assure that all students a particular level had a common base of knowledge or similar military experience. This was particularly important at the higher level schools, namely Leavenworth and the Army War College, from whose graduates Root and Carter, expected those selected for the War Department General Staff would come. In several respects implementation of the system again fell short of expectations.[15]

Army regulations required regimental commanders to select "the most promising lieutenants and captains" from among the best graduates of their garrison schools to attend the Infantry and Cavalry School. But shortly after the 1904 reorganization of the Leavenworth course, one officer wanting to attend the Infantry and Cavalry School complained of his regimental commander: "It is as I feared. He does not want to send any Captains to the school, basing his decision on the grounds that captains and graduates of West Point do not need this detail and none but officers from the ranks or civil life should be sent." If all regimental commanders made selections of that basis, Leavenworth would again become a "kindergarten," the place for the "regimental idiot," and the entire system of Army postgraduate education would be endangered. The best officers would not have an opportunity to attend Leavenworth, and thus would not be selected for the Army War College or for service on the General Staff. General Bell, at that time commandant at Leavenworth, wanted regimental commanders to abide by the regulations and threatened to return to their regiments any unqualified officers sent to the schools.[16]

When some colonels recommended "poor material" for the next Infantry and Cavalry School class, Bell carried out his threat and refused to accept them. Well placed friends in the War Department backed his action. As a result and because students in the class of 1904-5 informed officers in their regiments of the situation, in most regiments selections procedures improved. A few units even used competitive examinations to determine their representatives. Leavenworth and War Department officials were intent on straightening out those colonels who ignored the regulations on selection, for as one officer on the General Staff put it: "That once done, we will get the cream of the whole Army into the school."[17]

It had occurred to some that as the Leavenworth curriculum improved and became more advanced, lieutenants and junior captains would receive less immediate benefit from the course than would senior captains and field officers. As company and battalion commanders, the "seniors" were better able to apply what they had learned in leading, instructing, and training their troops than were lieutenants. Moreover, few lieutenants would be serving as General Staff officers. One recent graduate wrote in 1906: "Get a lot of the captains and you will have men that can do something. Some few old moss backs will not go under any conditions but get a good percentage of graduates in a regiment and the influence of the moss backs will be nil."[18]

Despite some objection from the "moss backs," from 1904 to 1916 most Leavenworth students were captains. The War Department changed regulations in 1907 to permit only captains and majors to attend the first year school. In 1912, however, the so-called "Manchu Law" limited the number of years officers could spend away from their regiments on detached service, such as was required to attend Leavenworth, the War College, or serve on the General Staff. Because this reduced the number of eligible captains and majors available to attend the first year School of the Line, fifteen lieutenants were admitted to the 1913-14 class. The three remaining classes before World War I, however, again included only majors and captains. Largely as result of these admissions policies, Leavenworth had a much greater effect upon captains than upon field grades. Between 1905 and 1916, 432 Regular Army officers graduated from the Infantry and Cavalry School/School of the Line. (The size of the Army officer corps throughout that time was about 4000.) Of that total 307 were captains, 83 first lieutenants, 27 second lieutenants, and only 15 were majors, or field grade officers.

Regulations required infantry, cavalry, and field artillery regiments in the continental United States annually to submit to the War Department the names of two officers eligible (having served five years) and willing to attend Leavenworth. The Chief Signal Officer, the Chief of Engineers, and the Chief of Coast Artillery, each could nominate one or two officers from their branches. From this group of nominees the War Department General Staff selected the first year classes at Leavenworth, which averaged 36 students. Because admission to the second year Army Staff College was, with a few exceptions, limited to honor and distinguished graduates of the first year course, the second year classes were much smaller, averaging 21 students, predominately infantry and cavalry captains.

There were factors besides regulations that determined whether an officer attended Leavenworth. On at least three occasions the marital status of the prospective students determined size of classes. Married officers could not be admitted to the school unless there were sufficient quarters available for them and their families. The requirements of regiments detailed for overseas service and after 1912 provisions of the Manchu Law, limiting time an officer could serve on "detached service," kept other individuals away. Commanders of regiments soon destined for the Philippines usually discouraged their officers from seeking the detail. Other commanders, who believed too many officers from their units were already on detached service, did the same.[19]

Not all officers who were eligible wanted to attend the schools. For them the professional advantage did not outweigh the effort required to graduate. Attacks on the Leavenworth system discouraged some potential applicants. In 1907 a regimental commander warned that the schools' reputation of putting a premium on "liberal memorizing" made it difficult to get qualified officers from his unit to attend. Because previous graduates were so critical of the school, George C. Marshall was the only officer in the 30th Infantry who applied in 1906. The next year not a single captain in the 5th Cavalry was "enthusiastic" about the detail. Fear of not making the Staff College class kept other away. Some officers believed that failing to graduate high in the first year course hurt a reputation more than not going to Leavenworth at all.[20]

Laziness overcame ambition to keep others from applying. The effect of years of boredom and routine in the garrison army led a cavalry officer, who did not want to go to the school, to describe his intellectual condition as "semi-fossilized." Numerous other officers, believing they could not physically stand the stress of the academically rigorous first year at the schools, declined the detail for reasons of health and age. Rumors of broken health, nervous breakdowns, severe eye strain, and even suicides, had enough basis in fact to deter the less enthusiastic. Still other eligible officers procrastinated. Concerned that they were unprepared, they requested the detail "sometime in the future" after individual study improved their professional knowledge. Few who passed up the detail were later give a second opportunity to go.[21]

But generally most eligible officers were interested in attending the schools. The difficulty was to get them to commit to attend in a particular year. In 1907 the Adjutant General polled regimental commanders to determine the number of officers interested in attending Leavenworth during the next five years. Replies from forty-four regiments indicated only two regiments had no one interested, five had only one officer interested, and the other thirty-seven had several who wanted to go. In 1910 the Adjutant General received 325 affirmative and only 150 negative responses to a similar question put to eligible captains. But when the Adjutant General tried to get commitments for the 1910-11 academic year, only thirteen officers in the twenty-three regiments polled showed any interest. The situation in the 4th Infantry was typical: "Neither Captains Dorey or Coleman desire detail this year. Captain Coleman would take it if he cannot get in next year. I have not been informed by any Captain who wants it."[22]

Among officers who did go, personal motivation was most important for securing the detail. As one put it: "I also saw that the science of tactics consisted of something more than 'fours right' and 'fours left,' and that there were other problems to solve before I could consider myself efficient. It was necessary for me to have some aid to accomplish the task so I decided to try and get the detail to go to Fort Leavenworth." Leavenworth's reputation as the "intellectual center of the Army" attracted others. Billy Mitchell desired an assignment to the post for some time before becoming commander of the experimental signal company associated with the Signal School at the post. Later, he sought and obtained detail to the School of the Line and became the first Signal Corps officer to attend the Staff College. For most officers, assignment to the schools was a very individual matter; as one said, it seemed to be the "best thing for me at the time." Many saw potential career benefits from successful completion of the course, particularly when more senior officers encouraged them. A Line School graduate frankly stated: "I fully understood the advantages the school present to an ambitious officer."[23]

"Connections" were sometimes as important for getting an appointment to Leavenworth as ability. General Bell, as commandant and subsequently as Army Chief of Staff (1906-1910), frequently played a role in selecting students. Although he criticized others for trying to use influence to get a detail to the schools, Bell himself played the game and was susceptible to pressure. When one student, whose father had already successfully influenced his selection for the School of the Line, tried for another school detail, Bell opposed his appointment because of the previous pressure. Bell's aide assured the officer; "General Bell is too big a man to allow any personal feelings…to influence him in his official action." Yet at the bottom of the office copy of that letter, Bell had scribbled: "He'll never enter if it depends on my recommendation. J.F.B." Regulations and ability aside, friends in the right places did no hurt when seeking admission to Leavenworth.[24]

For the most part, officers attending Leavenworth in the years before World War I were mature professionals with more than average career motivation. Initially the schools probably appealed more to younger officers who saw it as a means of quickly attaining career goals. Eventually older officers "saw the light," wanted "to get into the game in earnest and for that reason [went] to the schools as a preliminary step."[25]

But importantly, many perceived it as only a preliminary step. They assumed that good performance, as indicated by high class standing, at Leavenworth would lead in turn to selection for the Army War College and possibly duty on the General Staff. Root and Carter clearly has assumed such a progression when planning the postgraduate education system from 1899 to 1903. Almost immediately following the 1904 reorganization to a two-tier institution, the Infantry and Cavalry School/School of the Line and the Army Staff College, Leavenworth began graduating small annual classes of skilled, highly motivated officers. Arguably Leavenworth graduates were the best equipped officers in the Army to fill important command and staff positions in the War Department and in the field. But many officers at that time believed Leavenworth graduates were not getting an adequate opportunity to compete for such positions. In particular, Leavenworth graduates were not going to the Army War College or serving on the General Staff in anywhere near the numbers they should have been had Root and Carter's progressive system been adhered to closely. Indeed, some thought that many selected for those institutions were relatively untrained, if not unqualified.[26]

Between 1904 and 1917, 251 Army officers attended the War College. Only forty-five were products of the post-Root reform Leavenworth schools. And eight of that number had graduated so low in the first year course that they did not qualify for the second year Staff College course. For such officers to go to the War College was an obvious perversion of the progressive features of the school system planned by Root and Carter. Of the remaining War College students, fifty had graduated from the much more elementary pre-Spanish-American War Leavenworth, while the vast majority, 156 officers, were not graduates of any advanced postgraduate institution. Similarly, 202 officers served on the War Department General Staff from 1904 to 1916; but only twenty were post-Root reform Leavenworth graduates. Again, most of those on the General Staff, 112 officers, had no postgraduate military education at all. Age and lack of seniority were the principal factors inhibiting the regular progression of qualified Leavenworth graduates to the War College, then to the General Staff. Few field grade officers went to Leavenworth, where most students during this period were captains and lieutenants. The newly created General Staff had an immediate need for field grade officers and senior captains to perform its multi-faceted duties. It could not wait for the post-1903 Leavenworth graduates to mature and become eligible for assignment. Consequently, more senior officers, without the knowledge or experience Leavenworth should have provided, went to the War College to prepare for duty on the General Staff.

In 1908 Brigadier General W.W. Wotherspoon, the President of the War College, complained to Major John F. Morrison, senior Military Art instructor at Leavenworth, that all War College students should first have gone through Leavenworth. Wotherspoon observed that the few Leavenworth graduates who did progress to the War College invariably performed much better than those who had not gone to Leavenworth. Because Wotherspoon had recently reoriented the War College course, he was especially aware of these shortcomings. Under its original president, Brigadier General Tasker Bliss, the War College in effect operated as an adjunct to the War Department General Staff, with neither an established curriculum nor a specified length to the course. Bliss assigned students independent studies on a range of organizational, strategic, and political-military topics. When he became president, Wotherspoon changed that, establishing a course of study that stressed the strategic employment of large forces in field operations and geo-political planning. Wotherspoon recently had brought Major Eben Swift to the War College from Leavenworth, where he had been assistant commandant, to introduce the applicatory instructional techniques used at Leavenworth to the War College. As a result, students had to know the techniques for preparing an estimate of the situation, systematic issuance of operations orders, and tactical map study. As Wotherspoon pointed out, previously many War College students lacked such skills.[27]

Equally important, Wotherspoon wanted to establish the principle that Leavenworth graduation was required for attendance at the War College in order to prevent "sisters, cousins, and aunts from using their influence…to get their friends [or relatives] into what they consider a position of ease and comfort." Too many recent War College students had not been "up to the mark," according to Wotherspoon. Their sole motivation for attending was that they had wives with money and social ambition who wanted to have an "opportunity to shine in Washington." Those shortcomings made uniform instruction at the War College difficult. In addition, well-prepared War College students with a Leavenworth background were held back by simplified instruction done for their less-prepared classmates. And he wanted a means to assure that each War College student had the Leavenworth "seal upon him."[28]

Wotherspoon, therefore, recommended that selected field grade officers, likely to be sent to the War College but who because of age or seniority were not graduates of the post-1904 Leavenworth, be sent there for an intense but abbreviated course in military art. Authorities at Leavenworth, particularly Morrison, and at the War Department, including then Army Chief of Staff J. Franklin Bell, enthusiastically supported the proposal. Morrsion saw an opportunity to spread Leavenworth doctrine and influence. Bell had long asserted that Root's military education system would not succeed unless senior officers supported it. Wotherspoon's suggestion seemed to offer several interrelated benefits. For six weeks in 1908 and for three months each winter from 1911 to 1916, the War Department sent field grade officers to Leavenworth for the special course; just over one hundred attended, with about half of each special class subsequently going on to the War College. Although Leavenworth, the War College, and the field grade officers in attendance, all benefited from the special course, more junior officers who had submitted to the rigors of the one or two year regular Leavenworth course were not so impressed. They labeled it the "get rich quick" course.[29]

Between 1903 and World War I the postgraduate military education system did not entirely function as planned by Root and Carter. The failure to sustain militia officer attendance at Leavenworth and the perceived need to create a special class for field officers, both clear indications of shortcomings of the system, suggest that for those attempting to reform the Army getting the human equation correct was often the most difficult problem to solve. Neither officers who were potential students at the Leavenworth schools, nor more senior officers commanding regiments or supervising staff sections in the War Department completely accepted the potential of, or in some cases even the necessity for, a professionally educated officer corps. Success in that regard did not come until after World War I, when, then Army Chief of Staff, John J. Pershing again reformed Army professional military education, establishing clear entrance requirements; requiring graduation from branch schools in order to progress to the Leavenworth General Service Schools, and graduation from Leavenworth prior to admission to the Army War College, and selection for the General Staff. Pershing eventually brought to fruition the system that Root and Carter had planned.

## Notes

1. Timothy K. Nenninger, "Early Army Professional Military Education System," in William E. Simons (ed.), Professional Military Education in the United States: A Historical Dictionary (Westport, Conn.: Greenwood Press, 2000), 121-124.

2. Timothy K. Nenninger, *The Leavenworth Schools and the Old Army: Education, Professionalism, and the Officer Corps of the United States Army, 1881-1918* (Westport, Conn.: Greenwood Press, 1978), especially 34-50.

3. Ibid., 45-48; John McAuley Palmer, *Washington, Linclon, and Wilson: Three War Leaders* (Garden City, New York: Doubleday, Doran and Company Inc.: 1930), 294-99.

4. Nenninger, Leavenworth Schools, 127-28; Edgar F. Raines, "Major General J. Franklin Bell and Military Reform: The Chief of Staff Years, 1906-1910" PhD Dissertation, University of Wisconsin, 1976, 470-80.

5. Russell F. Weigley, *The History of the United States Army* (New York: Macmillan, 1967), 315.

6. Good discussions of the "Root reforms" include William Harding Carter, "Creation of the American General Staff: Personal Narrative," in 2d Sess., 69th Cong., Hearings before the House Military Affairs Committee, *The National Defense* (Washington: GPO, 1927), 507-517; Ronald G. Machoian, *William Harding Carter and the American Army: A Soldier's Story* (Norman: University of Oklahoma Press, 2006), 98-198; William R. Roberts, "Loyalty and Expertise: The Transformation of the Ninereenth Century American General Staff and the Creation of the Modern Army," PhD dissertation, Johns Hopkins University, 1980, 208-268.

7. "An Act To Promote the Efficiency of the Militia," Appendix F to 1903 Annual Report, in *Five Years of the War Department: 1899-1903: As Shown in the Annual Reports of the Secretary of War* (Washington: GPO, 1904), 490.

8. See the 1901 Secretary of War Annual Report, which among other benefits refers to "instruction by and with" Regular Army officers; in Five Years of the War Department, 162-63 and 167-68.

9. Report of LtCol. James Parker (Assistant The Adjutant General), May 30, 1903; MajGen. S.B.M. Young, 2d Ind. To Parker's report, June 10, 1903; Secretary of War to The Adjutant General [TAG], June 25, 1903, all in AGO 487284; Memo for the Third Division War Department General Staff [WDGS], April 15, 1904, AGO 1086586; Memo Report 136, Third Division WDGS, August 15, 1904, AGO 915980, Adjutant General's Document File, 1890-1917, Record Group 94, National Archives [hereafter AGO..., RG 94].

10. BrigGen. J.F. Bell to TAG, January 27, 1905, File 537; Bell (in D.C.) to Maj. W.W. Wotherspoon (at L.), May 14, 1904, Miscellaneous File; Bell (at L.) to Wotherspoon (in D.C.), October 14, 1904, Misc. File; all Army Service Schools Document File, 1901-1918, RG 393 [A.S.S. File..., RG 393].

11. Bell to LtGen. Adna R. Chaffee, October 5, 1904, Misc. File, A.S.S. File, RG 393; Bell to TAG, October 8, 1904, AGO 1146007, RG 94.

12. Bell to Wootherspoon, April 14, 1905, Misc. File; Col. C.B. Hall to Bell (in Paris), August 25, 1905, File 685, A.S.S. File, RG 393; Annual Report of the Inspector General, *Secretary of War Annual Reports, 1905* (Washington: GPO, 1905), 450.

13. Maj. Eben Swift to Wootherspoon, June 28, 1906; Wootherspoon report on militia discrimination, June 29, 1906; Bell to TAG, July 6, 1906, AGO 1146007, RG 94.

14. Capt. H.F. Elsasser to Congressman C.O. Lobeck, August 22, 1913; Chief of Militia Affairs Division, 2d ind. to Elsasser to Lobeck, August 27, 1913, AGO 2071594, RG 94;

Commandant Army Service Schools, *Annual Report, 1911* (Fort Leavenworth: Army Service Schools Press, 1911), 12; File 4037, A.S.S. File, RG 393, contains several requests for Morrison as an instructor; LtCol. R.F. Malton to Secretary Army Service Schools, September 29, 1914, File 8220, A.S.S. File, RG 393.

15. War Department General Order 155, November 27, 1901; Carter, "Creation of the American General Staff: Personal Narrative," *The National Defense*, 507-17.

16. Capt. F.J. Koster to Col. A.L. Wagner, February 17, 1905; Wagner to Bell, March 3, 1905; Bell to TAG, March 18, 1905; File 537, A.S.S. File, RG 393.

17. BrigGen. W.W. Wootherspoon to Bell, July 10, 1905, Misc. File, A.S.S. File, RG 393.

18. Capt. R.F. Walton to Secretary Army Service Schools, September 10, 1906, File 5341, A.S.S. File, RG 393.

19. Commandant to TAG, September 2, 1911; TAG to Commandant, April 3, 1912; Commandant to TAG, July 8, 1915, File 537, A.S. S. File, RG 393.

20. Col. H.A. Greene to TAG, February 14, 1907, AGO 1203201/X, RG 94; Notes on transcript of interview of Forrest C. Pogue with George C. Marshall, April 4, 1957, in author's possession; Adjutant 5th Cavalry to Capt. George VanHorn Moseley, April 13, 1907, Scrapbook (1889-1911), Moseley Papers, Library of Congress; Capt. G.W. Moss to Adjutant 15th Cavalry, January 17, 1910, AGO 1624501/7, RG 94.

21. Capt. H.F. Reuthers to Moseley, August 15, 1908, Scrapbook, Moseley Papers, LC.

22. The surveys of the regiments are in AGO 1203021 and AG) 1566073, RG 94; Commanding Officer 4th Infantry to TAG, August 14, 1910, AGO 1566073, RG 94.

23. Lt. G.A. Wieczorek to Secretary Army Service Schools, May 19, 1905, File 2076, A.S.S. File, RG 393; Alfred E. Hurley, *Billy Mitchell: Crusader for Airpower* (New York: Franklin Watts, Inc., 1964), 10-13; author interview with Col. Fay W. Brabson (USA, Ret.), January 10, 1970, Walter Reed Army Hospital, D.C.; Capt. A.U. Falkner to Adjutant 1st Field Artillery, January 21, 1910, AGO 162449/2, RG 94.

24. Bell to Koster, July 20, 1905, File 3924; Secretary Army Service Schools to Lt. C.A. Dougherty, May 1, 1909, and Bell's note on letter received from Dougherty, File 4427; Bell to Lt. C.F. Busseche, May 17, 1905, A.S.S. File, RG 393.

25. Pogue interview with Marshall, April 4, 1957; Secretary Army Service Schools to Capt. C.D. Rhodes, March 29, 1911, File 2094, A.S.S. File, RG 393.

26. For an example of the criticism of the qualifications of those selected for the General Staff, see the statement of John McAuley Palmer, in *The National Defense*, 341-56.

27. Harry P. Ball, *Of Responsible Command: A History of the Army War College* (Carlisle Barracks, Pa.: Army War College Alumni Association, 1983), 105-43.

28. Wotherspoon to Morrison, March 30, 1908, File 943-a22, Army War College Miscellaneous Correspondence, 1903-10, RG 165.

29. The "get rich quick" course is discussed in detail in Nenninger, *The Leavenworth Schools and the Old Army*: 121-25; in this I mistakenly attributed the original idea for the short course to Morrison, but subsequently discovered the Wotherspoon letter (March 30, 1908) in which he clearly spells out to Morrison the need for remedial action.

# Day 1, Panel 3: Changing Leadership for a Changing World Role, 1906-1939

## So Rigorously Trained and Educated: Leader Development in the US Army, 1919 to 1939 by Peter J. Schifferle, Ph.D.

(Submitted Paper)

**Author Note:**

Material for this paper was drawn from America's School for War: Fort Leavenworth, Officer Education, and Victory in World War II by Peter J. Schifferle (c) 2010 by the University Press of Kansas. Used by permission of the publisher.

> The World War has made of the Army a great school. We are all of us its instructors. We receive instruction in subject matter and take courses in methods of instruction that we may pass our knowledge on to others most efficiently. Indeed, is it not a fair premise to say that in time of peace the major part of the work of the armed forces is instruction? To this end the appropriations are made, to this end all the organization is accomplished and administered—that men may be instructed to battle proficiency.
>
> Major Frederick Pond, Pennsylvania National Guard, "Supervision of Instruction," *Infantry Journal*, January 1930

The development of leaders in the interwar Army was significantly different than the situation faced by the Army in the second decade of the 21st Century. A different legal basis for the readiness of the Army, the grudging acceptance of this new statute by the officer corps, the stagnant, but equitable, promotion system, a dissimilar training system, and a general disregard for teaching leadership or command at the officer education system are all noteworthy differences. However, the structure of the officer education system was nearly identical to today's schooling arrangement. The differences, though, were greater than the similarities.

### Preparedness and an Impecunious Army

General Pershing conceived the next war as a war of the entire nation, not of just the regular army. In his address to the 1920 graduating class of the General Staff College, Pershing declared:

> It would seem pertinent to emphasize the great importance of general staff instruction and its bearing upon the future war efficiency of the army. Indeed, we should say upon the war efficiency of the country, for it is the nation with all its resources including the army that makes war.[1]

Pershing, and Congress, and to some extent, the American people, understood that, if war came again, the entire resources of the nation would be required to fight and win. But, without immediate enemies, with no perceived current threat to the national existence, the maintenance of a large force was politically impossible, indeed not even desired by anyone in authority. The maintenance of a large, regular force in time of peace would have been

Panel 1

unique in American history, and was not contemplated for long by Congress. The lesson of the World War—that it took the mobilization of the entire nation—presented Congress with a new requirement for national security in the immediate post-Armistice period. The new policy that resulted was, in the words of Allan Millet and Peter Maslowski, "A reasonable response to the risks of the 1920s."[2]

The National Defense Act of June 4, 1920 established a novel military policy for the United States. This act, a result of a vibrant debate in 1919 and early 1920, conceived of the military as a preparatory force, and established the expansion base for a war of national mobilization, not for a force ready for immediate combat. This concept, a small regular army designed as a school house for both the National Guard and a large reserve force, and consisting of an unusually large proportion of commissioned officers, did not match the perception of some regulars, but was the appropriate military policy for the nation.[3]

Given the spirit of the times, Congress proceeded to under-fund the Army it had designed. Although the 1920s were a time of national economic prosperity, they were not years of affluence for the army. Concerns over seemingly petty financial issues were reflected in the professional journals. The June 1923 edition of *Infantry Journal* included a note from the Chief of Infantry that asked the readers to:

Look about the orderly room. Our eye rests on the typewriter, among other things. You know how hard it is to get a typewriter repaired, or to get a new ribbon for it. Has the machine been oiled and cleaned every week as required by regulation? If the ribbon is a bit worse for wear, i.e., makes a weak impression—has it been turned over? Think of what it means when all the orderly rooms in the Infantry want a new ribbon.[4]

Hardly the concerns that should have forced the major general in charge of the infantry branch to write an article for his professional journal, but indicative of the lack of resources the army struggled with throughout the interwar period.

The central core of the army, the officer corps, survived these two decades of scarce resources and the failure of all efforts to generate universal military training or peacetime conscription. Officers found refuge from the problems of typewriter ribbons in the mundane life of the Army—troop duty in dusty little posts scattered around the country, occasional more challenging assignments to China, the Philippines, Hawaii or Panama, and repetitive assignments as either students or instructors with the newly refashioned officer education system and in support of the National Guard or the Reserves.[5] In 1929, as reported in *Infantry Journal,* nearly half of the infantry field grade officers and captains were assigned as instructors or students in the officer education system. Of these officers, one in ten was at a branch school, one in twenty at Leavenworth or the War College, and more than half were teaching ROTC, the Reserves or the National Guard.[6]

These mundane daily activities of the army, including the education of the officer corps, were themselves not necessarily vulnerable to budget cuts or Congressional mandate, if sufficiently protected by the senior officers of the Army. The senior officers, unable to change the portions of the Army that required extensive resources, chose to change, and maintain, those things within their purview— including the army educational system.[7]

## Acceptance of the New Army

Two related factors led to the eventual acceptance of the new role of teacher and student as the norm for professional officers. One was the continued declarations by General Pershing of the need for a new form of professionalism in the officer corps. In an Army War College graduation speech published in *Field Artillery Journal* in 1923, he called on the graduates of the Army War College to develop "a breadth of vision essential to the efficient Army officer of today." He continued;

> In no other army is it so imperative that the officers of the permanent establishment be highly perfected specialists, prepared to serve as instructors and leaders for the citizen forces which are to fight our wars. The one-time role of a regular army officer has passed with the Indian Campaigns and the acquirement of colonial possessions. Our mission today is definite, yet so broad that few, if any, have been able to grasp the possibilities of new fields opened up by the military policy now on the statute book.... There are officers, fortunately in constantly diminishing numbers, who cannot turn their minds from concentration on a diminutive regular army, successfully, and gallantly fighting the country's battles as in Cuba and the Philippines, or serving at isolated stations along the Mexican Border. Those days have not entirely passed away, and probably never will pass, but they are now of secondary importance in the general scheme of National Defense.[8]

The other voice was that of Congress, ready to spend sufficient funds for officer education, but not to maintain a large ready force.

This change in the profession generated a spirited debate in the professional journals. *Cavalry Journal* led with an editorial in its October 1921 edition entitled "The Task of Teaching." Calling on its readers to embrace that "we have entered upon a large field that may be characterized as 'teaching duty,'" and to understand that, in time of peace, this was not only necessary, but natural for Army professionals. That the editor felt compelled to write "Reduction Must Not Effect Cavalry Spirit" for his very next editorial comment was emblematic of the shift in the profession from duty with units to education.[9] The debate had been stimulated by an article in *Infantry Journal* in May 1921 by Major Bernard Lentz, a frequent contributor to the journals in the 1920s. He asked, "Who is Going to Soldier When Everybody is Going to School?" His answer was a cautionary note to the army that the soul of the profession had to continue to be troop duty.[10] Elbridge Colby, another prolific contributor, responded, explaining that Lentz's critique reflected a misunderstanding of the purpose of the officer education system. The system was designed to not just begin the education of officers, but also to require them to continue self-development for their entire careers. The in-house schooling was not to replace either self-study or the experiences of troop duty, but to enhance both.[11]

Major Lentz returned to the discussion, this time in a 1932 article entitled "The Applicatory Method." Lentz, although still critical of the lack of proper teaching skills, and methods, at Army schools, was now much more accepting of the need for officer education. Where earlier he had called for a reduction in the length and number of courses, now he simply called for optimizing the educational experience through high quality educational methods.[12] He wrote, "The schools have been worth all the money and all the efforts we have expended," and, writing of his earlier article condemning excessive officer education, "'fools who came to scoff, stayed to pray' now aptly describes the change of sentiment that has taken place"[13]

The funding of the officer education system permitted the construction of large school facilities at Fort Benning in the 1920s for the infantry and at Fort Sill in the 1930s for the field artillery. Usually overlooked by historians of the period, the relatively large investment of funds in the officer education system was an essential part of the competence of the US Army in World War II. Although it is difficult to precisely determine the amount of resources expended on the Army schools in the interwar period, given the nature of the published financial records, it is clear the schools consumed a significant proportion of the available resources. Fort Benning, created towards the very end of the World War, for example, consumed more than a million dollars in the construction of the school facilities for the Infantry School.[14] After the war, new construction at Fort Benning for the Infantry School consumed some 12 million dollars in the 1920s, and at Fort Sill, nearly 10 million dollars were spent during the Depression.[15] A major construction project had been completed in 1916 at Fort Leavenworth, so there was no comparable expenditure of funds for the Command and General Staff School in the period.[16] Nearly half of all regular army officers were assigned to various school duties, and with pay accounting for 40 percent of the annual Army expenditures, the schools consumed a sizable proportion of officer pay funds through the period.[17] Although the operating expenses of the schools were minimal, averaging less than $100,000 for all schools annually, the investment was in construction and personnel, and these were considerable.[18]

**Promotion's Very Slow**

The 1920 National Defense Act did pose some serious challenges for the officer corps, including stagnant promotions, poor training opportunities with troop units, and, despite relatively robust experimentation, little procurement of new equipment for the ground forces. The almost stagnant system of promotions in the 1920s and 193s was a major crisis for the leaders of the Army, and had some effect on the sense of professionalism of the officers themselves. This stagnation was generated by an artifact of the World War—a 'hump' in the officer corps' promotion list. The accession of thousands of officers through rapid commissioning after April 1917 generated a large population of junior officers who remained in service through World War II. From a strength of 5,960 regular army officers in April 1917, the commissioned strength of the Army reached some 203,786 by the Armistice.[19]

As explained in official War Department testimony before the House of Representatives Committee on Military Affairs;

The dominant feature of our present personnel is an abnormal group of about 5,800 officers, considerably more than half of the present promotion list, who were inducted into the service between November, 1916 and November, 1918, and who therefore, vary in length of commissioned service by less than two years…. The great bulk of them fall within narrow age limits. Under normal conditions the entry into service, and consequently, the difference in length of commissioned service, of this large group of officers would have been spread over a period of about 20 years, and they would be similarly graded by age. Practically all of our difficulties are due to the existence of this "hump" in our personnel.[20]

This hump of officers was 55.4 percent of the total number of commissioned officers in 1926, and would still be there, like the pig in a python, upon the outbreak of World War II.[21] Despite various studies and proposals for reducing the hump, and thus accelerating the stagnant promotions, only the onset of Protective Mobilization in 1940 solved the problem, with its attendant increase in promotion possibilities, at least in temporary rank.

The effect of the hump and the National Defense Act upon promotions was intense. Although efforts were made to have promotions occur to "first lieutenant at three years of service, to captain, ten years; to major, seventeen years; to lieutenant colonel, twenty-two years; and to colonel, twenty-eight years," this was not achieved for the officers in the hump.[22] As told in many of the memoirs and biographies of the officers of the interwar Army, promotions were exceedingly slow for the officers in or "behind" the hump. Promotions, when they occurred in accordance with the statute, occurred by strict seniority. The promotion system in the interwar period was based on a classification system of officer evaluation reports. Under this system, officers were designated by their superiors as either Class A officers, qualified for promotion in due course; or as Class B officers, officers who should be removed from service for any and all reasons. The Class B category was used rarely, and officers categorized in Class B could appeal their categorization all the way to the White House. As a result, although the officer corps population usually exceeded 12,000 in the period, only 350 officers were eliminated from the service under this classification system from 1920 to 1937.[23] Officers were always promoted to the next grade, by seniority, unless they had been separated from the service under a Class B Board.[24]

Selection by quality, or by merit, was extremely controversial in the interwar army, and never became a matter of course. In the words of 'Agrippa II' in a 1939 article, promotion by selection "just does not work equitably and satisfactorily to all concerned." Promotion by seniority had one great advantage—everyone was treated the same. The only promotion that was considered influenced by "who you knew" as opposed to "what you knew" was promotion to general officer. With only 68 general officers authorized by statute from an officer corps of almost 9,000, and with mandatory retirement for age at age 64, the chance of making general for someone in the hump, was, in peacetime, remote indeed. The 'Agrippa' article pointed out that in the hump, officers would be retired for chronological age while still majors and lieutenant colonels, leaving a great gap in senior officers by 1949.[25]

Many other authors joined in this debate which raged from 1921 through 1940. Part of the initial debate was the proposal of a single, Army-wide, list for promotion. After passage of the National Defense Act of 1920, the Army formed a board of officers, who created, from June 1920 to January 1921, in strict accord with the statute, the single promotion list for all Army officers. In an effort to educate its readers, *Infantry Journal* published two very informative and detailed articles about the statute and the board proceedings.[26] The editor felt so strongly about the 'One List' issue that he wrote that it was necessary for national defense—without it, training of draftees for the next war would be very difficult.[27] Eventually accepted by the Army officer corps over complaints by some branches, who thought they were being slighted, the single list remained the law through the period. The majority of the debate continued to be about the hump. Completely unresolved by several efforts to accelerate attrition, offer early retirement, and other proposals, the hump slowly ground forward with each passing year, gradually having small numbers of officers promoted to the next grade by pure seniority, off the single list. It was, at least, impartial.

In addition to slow promotions for officers in or chronologically "behind" the hump, there existed a perception that officers who had served in France would receive preferential promotions. This perception on the part of many officers who had not served in France in 1917 or 1918 was moderated by the huge numbers of officers who had not had the opportunity, yet remained in service. On the day of the Armistice, slightly more than half of the mobilized army had been shipped to France.[28] The percentage of regular army officers who deployed to France was even less than that of the overall army, since a disproportionate number remained as part of the training and mobilization establishment. Many junior officers, as well as the majority of field grade officers (the grades of major, lieutenant colonel and colonel) had remained in the continental United States, preparing the remaining divisions for deployment in late 1918 and throughout 1919.[29] Examples of the attitudes of these officers, and their desire to learn from those who did deploy, and their awareness of having "missed the war" are related in their memoirs. Many reported that they made every effort to join the American Expeditionary Force (AEF), usually without success, and they understood that they "hadn't gotten into" World War I.[30]

Assessing the proportion of officers who served in the AEF would have mitigated some of their concern. Of the class of 1915 from West Point, 102 of the class of 164 (62 percent) were sent overseas by Armistice, but only fifty-six (34 percent) served in actual combat duties in France. Sixty-two (38 percent) of the class were never sent overseas.[31] This assessment was corroborated by Brigadier General Lytle Brown, Director War Plans Division, War Department General Staff, who wrote in a December 14, 1918 memorandum, that military instruction in the post-war army should begin with the "nearly 60 percent of the regular officers who had not had service in France.[32]

**The Officer Education System**

Future combat realities were the prime, indeed usually only, subject of the officer education system. After World War I, the army officer corps understood that competency in the craft was largely a matter of skill in handling large formations in both stable defensive and mobile offensive operations. They also appreciated their sense of obligation for preparedness, for basic competence, especially in a society where the desire to never again fight a major war rapidly deteriorated to an article of faith of "never again."

Immediately after the World War, senior officers, both in the AEF and in the War Department, discussed re-establishing the officer education system disrupted by mobilization. A group of officers met in Treves (Trier) Germany in the spring of 1919, and began a series of conversations, orders, boards and meetings that established a new and comprehensive officer education system.[33] This system remained intact through protective mobilization in 1939-1940, and itself became the basis for a hugely expanded officer education and training system for the World War II mobilization. On the eve of that conflict, at least one observer saw the system of officer education to be the very foundation of Army officer professionalism, with every officer fully schooled in multiple courses. In the words of Major John H. Burns, "It is doubtful if any professional group are so rigorously trained and educated as the American officer."[34]

In the busy days of demobilization and transfer of many officers back from the AEF, the War Department General Staff circulated a seventy page comprehensive draft plan for re-establishing the schools on March 8, 1919.[35] It recommended a comprehensive system of officer and soldier education, from pre-commissioning through colonel-level instruction. Included in this plan were discussions of West Point education, of company grade officer education at division schools, branch instruction for officers and some noncommissioned officers at Special Service Schools, usually with a course for lieutenants and a more advanced course for captains and majors, and two General Service Schools, one school of the line for general staff officer education for duty with large units and a General Staff College for education in War Department-level general staff duties.[36] The Special Service branch schools and the two-stage General Staff education would be adopted and remain the hallmarks of officer education for the next two decades.[37]

Critical to the post World War development of programs of instruction were the lessons of the AEF, including the value of staff processes and the absolute requirement for a general staff system to cope with the new realities of modern war. George C. Marshall wrote to the Commandant of the Army War College in 1920;

"My observation of the General Staff work in France, particularly at G.H.Q. and in the First Army, and my recent experience at the War Department in connection with Army reorganization, has caused me to feel that one of the most serious troubles in our General Staffs have been the failure to follow the proper procedure in determining a policy or plan."[38] Marshall continued "we would do well if we could obtain examples of this character of General Staff work" for use as instruction aids.[39]

General McAndrew, commandant of the War College, distributed copies of this letter to his faculty.[40]

In the post-World War era, the War Department took several steps towards harmonizing the officer education system. These War Department efforts usually took the form of officer boards, convened to investigate certain challenges and recommend solutions to the Chief of Staff. The first board ordered to investigate the school system after its initial post World War establishment was the McGlachlin Board, convened in February 1922.[41] The board, charged by Pershing to investigate the entire school system with a view towards decreasing the expenditures for the programs, making the system as efficient as possible in an era of decreasing resources, and improving instruction for the National Guard and Reserves, traveled to every Army school in the country and met with representatives of every chief of branch in Washington. A later board, chaired by Colonel Fiske, convened in Washington in late July 1922. The Fiske Board made recommendations which delineated the border between the Army War College and the Command and General Staff School as the line between armies and above, which would be taught at the War College, and corps and divisions, which would be taught at Leavenworth.[42]

After the various boards had made their recommendations the outline of the school system remained intact for the next fifteen years. Officers, the majority of them commissioned in peacetime from West Point, would attend a branch basic course, normally eight months in length, within the first several years of their active duty. Later, if selected by their branch, they would attend a branch "advanced course." Still later, if selected by their branch, officers would attend the school at Fort Leavenworth, focusing studies on the Army division and corps in combat operations. After the most selective screening, a few officers would then attend the Army War College, the last step in officer education, where studies were at the Army, Theater, and War Department levels.

The mission of the Army War College changed in the interwar period from advanced general staff training, primarily under the leadership of Major General James W. McAndrew, to education for command while Brigadier General Edward F. McGlachlin, Jr., was Commandant and then to preparation for war and conduct of war under the command of Major General William D. Connor.[43] Instruction, under Connor, became a series of large-scale problem solving exercises, with the students divided into committees. Each student committee was responsible for a significant contemporary military problem. After a month of study and research, each committee prepared a staff study, briefed the entire War College class on the problem and their recommended solution, and received the benefit of a student and faculty critique.[44] Although there were frequent lectures by visiting experts and dignitaries, the students only infrequently were taught in classrooms. The War College was less an academic institution and more a problem-solving extension of the War Department, to whom it reported. The students were expected to learn, but that learning occurred in extensive problem solving, usually of real-world problems given to the War College by the General Staff.[45]

By July 1925, the mission of the schools at Leavenworth was established by issuance of Army Regulation 350-5—a mission that remained intact for the next twenty years. The Leavenworth School was ordered to;

Prepare officers for command and general staff duty by training them in the following:

1. The combined use of all arms in the division and in the army corps.

2. The proper functions of commanders of divisions, army corps, and corps areas and the techniques of exercising command.

3. The proper functions of general staff officers of divisions, army corps, and corps areas and the technique of general staff concepts.[46]

The critical role of combining the arms of divisions and corps, of commanding these formations, and of serving as the general staffs of these formations, was Leavenworth's and no other institution of the interwar Army. Despite efforts at training, maneuvers and Command Post Exercises, and despite a growing and robust sense of professionalism, officers in the interwar period had to rely on the education system for preparation in division and corps operations.

### The Untaught Curriculum—Command and Leadership

At Leavenworth in the interwar period, the school leadership frequently discussed the question of whether to provide an education for commanders or staff officers. These discussions usually began because of either external or internal criticism that the school was over-emphasizing staff skills and paying insufficient attention to the skills required of senior commanders. The consistent response was a conflation of the two sets of skills, usually worded in an argument that general officers must know the skills required of their subordinate general staff officers, and those general staff officers of divisions, corps and armies required the knowledge and skills of the generals commanding these formations to be effective general staff officers.

One example is the discussion in the 1922 *Annual Report* by Brigadier General Hanson Ely, school commandant. Reacting to apparent external criticism, General Ely endorsed the comments by the Assistant Commandant, Colonel Drum, and the Director of the General Staff School, Colonel Willey Howell, that the "command phase of the instruction here has been strongly emphasized." However, he continued that the faculty "realized that all commanders to be fully efficient must have detailed knowledge of staff work and that all staff officers to be fully efficient must have intimate knowledge of the commander's viewpoint."[47]

In the same year's report, in response to an "impression [which] seems to exist that these schools are primarily intended for training officers in general staff duties," Colonel Hugh Drum, Assistant Commandant, concurred with General Ely's commented. Drum wrote "it is our conviction that the efficient commander must know general staff work and the efficient general staff officer must know and have the commander's viewpoint." Any distinction between command and staff education, or capabilities, according to Drum, "does not rest on theoretical knowledge or training, but, rather, on personal qualities and mainly on the factors of experience, judgment, personality, leadership, determination and aggressiveness. However, the fundamental training should be the same for both classes of officers."[48]

Colonel Willey Howell, Director, General Staff School, continued this discussion in his report that same year. Howell stated that the "ability to command" is based three elements, the "physical, the psychological, and the professional. Some of these may be acquired in a school; some may not." Howell agreed entirely with the inherent requirement to educate both future commanders and future staff officers in the same manner. He reported;

But so far as any school can be concerned in the development and furtherance of the growth of military leadership, there can be no practical difference between the training required for command and that required for general staff duty, since the fundamental difference between the two is not one of professional qualification but one of personality and there is little a school is able to do in respect to the development of personality in mature men.[49]

These arguments also found fertile ground in the professional journals. Perhaps most evocative of the debate was an exchange in *Infantry Journal* in 1935 and 1936. Begun by 'Mercutio' in the "Cerebrations" column in May-June 1936 with a call for making the bottom 10 percent of the school classes into senior commanders, since only they had "men who think and who think along original lines," and the typical officer in the 90 percent category was a "slide-rule tactician, a mechanical brain-master, a canned commander," the response was spirited.[50] Another author, 'Singlebars' responded with a critique of

'Mercutio.' This time, the argument was that commanders needed to be intelligent, and the bottom 10 percent of 'Mercutio's' Canned Commanders had;

> Forgot[en] the mission. The mission of the student is to get an "s." [satisfactory rating] The mission of the school is to teach the right dope. Let the student learn, let the teacher teach. If you don't like it, do it anyway, because that's the system and that's the way to get high command. If you're so smart that you know a better solution than the school's old obvious solution, you'll know it in time of war...intellectual capacity is essential for high command and in direct proportion to the highness of the command....Commanders must have mental and physical force. Foch called it 'habit of command.'[51]

These authors did not seem to draw any distinctions between future commanders learning the art of war and future senior staff officers learning the art of war. Both appear to have required mental and physical energy, and both required knowledge of the "brick and mortar of battle." The debate in the journals, or rather, the lack of debate, reflected in two articles on the role of command and staff, one written in 1920, the other in 1940. In the first article, Major R. M. Johnston wrote "Our Army at the present day is in even greater danger than the German that the Command may become unduly subordinated to the Staff. Both functions are essential and complimentary; they both call for an improved system of Staff training and of high military studies."[52] Twenty years later, 'General Gripe' wrote:

> No one can deny that the Command and General Staff School does a fine job of teaching men how to analyze a military situation, appreciate the value of terrain, make reasonably sound decisions, get out a complete order and in doing so, act either as a commander or as one of his G's. It teaches the relation between the command and staff by showing how the command gets out a directive for a movement and how the staff amplifies this directive into detailed order.[53] Command and staff were combined, because they were complimentary skills, not antithetical approaches to the "brick and mortar of battle."

Analysis of the class schedule for the two-year course, 1934-1936, shows, rather starkly, that staff work predominated. Of all courses taught in these two years, listed on the schedule by fifty different types, ranging from equitation to legal principles, only one course was devoted to leadership. The course in leadership, taught in the first year, encompassed five hours of 2,211 class hours in two years.[54] Although leadership as a discussion point was raised in other classes, a review of the course material, the faculty instructions, and student comments all support the assessment that leadership was not a subject taught at Leavenworth. The Army senior leaders in the interwar years either believed that officers with more than twenty years of service knew how to be leaders already, or leadership was innate character, and could not be trained.

Discussions of staff skills dominated the academic courses. A course entitled "Strategy" focused on issues more appropriate to a staff officer than a commander. In 1929-1930, the Strategy course discussed the campaigns of Napoleon, the American Civil War, and the Russo-Japanese War. An analysis of the discussion material reveals that the students assessed and evaluated logistics and administration much more frequently than issues of leadership. Even when required to discuss the decisions of the historical commanders, they were required to discuss their problem solving "objectives" rather than their leadership or command influence.[55]

The 1923 edition of the *Field Service Regulations* also conflated the skills of the commander and of the general staff. Addressing the role of the commander, this manual discussed the estimate of the situation in terms identical to those taught at Leavenworth:

> In estimating a situation, the commander considers his mission as set forth in the orders and instructions under which he is acting, or as deduced by him from his knowledge of the situation, all available information of the enemy… conditions affecting his own command…and the terrain, weather, climate, morale, and other factors in so far as they affect the particular military situation. He then compares the various plans of action open to him and decides upon the one that will best enable him to accomplish his mission.
>
> In general, it is the function of the staff to elaborate the details necessary to carry the decision into effect.[56]

However, on the next page of the manual, the duties of the staff are expanded to include all of the duties of the commander identified in his estimate of the situation. In particular, the duties of the chief of staff, the officer in charge of the formation general staff, enumerated "powers of supervision, coordination, and control in the commander's name are coextensive with this responsibility and are exercised to the extent that he [the Chief of Staff] deems necessary to its discharge." The role of the staff was to serve as an extension of the commander, primarily in the areas of control, supervision, and coordination. Limits to the staff's power were established only to the extent that those limits would not imperil accomplishment of the mission, and according to doctrine, the Chief of the Staff, not the commander, determined those limits.[57] This blend of the duties of commander and staff, while it could be problematic if personalities clashed, could also be an effective form of teamwork in a division or a corps.

The Leavenworth texts made some clear distinctions between the responsibility of command and the duties of the general staff. According to the 1923 "Command, Staff and Tactics" text, the commander was "a leader of men." His authority was his "lawful exercises over subordinates by virtue of his rank or assignment." His duty was to "produce individual or collective military action or non-action on the part of subordinates, regardless of the will of the latter." The staff were "the personnel who help the commander in the exercise of the functions of command by professional aid and assistance."[58]

Students at Leavenworth would learn the functions of commanders and staff simultaneously in the interwar period, in part because the doctrine required intimate integrated knowledge of the staff functions by the commander, and of the commander's requirements by the staff officers. Leadership, the very essence of command, was not taught in the courseware, since the faculty believed command an innate skill, certainly not educable in forty-year old professional officers.

Panel 1

**Training**

Unit training in the interwar period was not up to the professional standards of the officer corps. Many officers criticized the lack of resources available for unit training and many methods were discussed to optimize what resources were available.[59] However, at the end of these two decades, the standard of training for field units in the regular army was woeful. The standard for National Guard units was even lower. Most evocative was a piece in the February 1926 edition of *Infantry* in which the author awakens from a dream of effective training to face another morning of training his battalion with "a total of four or five squads available for instruction! Oh, hell!"[60]

Despite recommendations to make the most of training under the resource constraints of the period, many officers complained about the lack of resources, particularly soldiers, to train. Leading these complaints, by the 1930s, was the voice of Major General Douglas MacArthur. As Chief of Staff from 1930 through 1935, MacArthur advocated for additional funding, but to little effect. The Army's budgets never allowed for anything other than skeletonized units, despite relatively robust expenditures for the Air Service and officer education.

Calls for additional resources were frequent in the interwar journals, but so were observations that the economies of the National Defense Act, and subsequent minimal appropriations, were the proper policy for the United States, if perhaps carried to an unfortunate extreme of parsimony. As the president of the Reserve Officer's Association wrote, in a 1926 edition of *The Infantry Journal*;

The essence of the National Defense Act is that it brings the expense within reasonable limits by eliminating all those things which can be done within a reasonable time after the declaration of war and provides for obtaining and having in readiness only those things that take a long time to obtain and prepare.[61]

One of the rare bright spots for unit training in the interwar period was the occasional large unit maneuvers and command post exercises conducted on an annual basis for some units. Although criticized in the journals as being generally unrealistic, these maneuvers did offer training opportunities for the officers assigned, and for the readers of the professional journals, where the results of maneuvers were frequently published. Maneuver reports began soon after the end of the war in Europe, initially about the training of the American occupation forces in Germany.[62] In 1924, Major Adna R. Chaffee reported on the 1923 maneuvers of the First Cavalry Division in a very detailed and lengthy report. Conducted in the vicinity of Marfa, Texas, on land "roughly that of the land area of the state of Rhode Island," the maneuver included road and rail movement, both horse drawn and motorized, of the entire 1st Cavalry Division. Using radios for communication, the division deployed distances in excess of 200 miles to the training area. Upon arrival, umpires oversaw the two-sided maneuvers, which included eight days of force-on-force maneuver.[63] Maneuvers like this one continued throughout the interwar period, usually at the division level, but occasionally involving smaller organizations.[64]

Many of these events introduced to the participating officers, and subsequent journal readers, many of the issues involved with long distance troop movements, command and control over significant distances, and forming cohesive organizations from a polyglot group of smaller organizations. For example, the First Army concentration, which occurred from August 17 to 31, 1935, formed units from two corps area commands and five different divisions into a coherent training effort focused on "combined field exercises, training in logistics, and testing active units of the Regular Army as to rapid concentration." Colonel Conrad Lanza, author of this report, one of the more prolific authors in the period, concluded that the maneuvers demonstrated both the need to update training regulations and that motor equipped units would "make circles around foot troops." He recommended, as did most observers, that more maneuvers, with larger units, and more appropriated funds, should be conducted to improve the training level of the entire force.[65]

Command Post Exercises were also conducted in the period, but reported on less frequently than maneuvers. Designed to provide training for unit staffs, without the expense involved with large unit maneuvers, these exercises were held frequently, including National Guard units and officers of the Organized Reserves.[66] That these exercises were useful as a training program for modern war is demonstrated by the critique of Command post Exercises raised by General H. S. Hawkins, a frequent contributor to *The Cavalry Journal*.[67] Hawkins complained that the army had "gone wild over command post exercises." He believed that all such exercises were based on the trench warfare system taught to the AEF by the French, and that the "we have continued to use this method ever since our 'successful' campaign in France." Declaring that commanders must get away from the telephone and go to see for themselves what is happening, Hawkins appeared to forget his article was about exercises that did not involve troops or terrain.[68]

A special category of Army officer experience, neither experiment, nor maneuver, nor command post exercise, but a large scale practice run for mobilization, was the Army's involvement in the Civilian Conservation Corps. Involving huge numbers of young men, organized into camps by Army officers and soldiers, this experience was an important adjunct to the other professional events of the late interwar period. Numerous articles explained to the readers how to conduct camp administration, how to lead large groups of young men using the character of military leadership without the stick of legal authority, and how to publicize the Civilian Conservation Corp experience for the good of the Army.[69]

Significant time spent in officer education, limited troop unit training, some degree of overseas duty, and nearly non-existent promotions were the reality of the interwar army. The same reality developed a profound sense of professional dedication amongst the officers who either experienced the Great War, heard about it in the officer's mess, or came of age as young officers in the 1920s and 1930s. This sense of professionalism, dedication to duty, and awareness of the need for individual preparation, coupled with a national defense policy that made nothing else possible until crisis, generated the "wonder" of the World War II victory.[70] Many historians believe the National Defense Act of 1920, and the appropriations in the 1920s and 1930s left America woefully unprepared for the next world war.[71] However, within the Army officer corps, a new sense of purpose, and a new idea of how officer competency was created altered how the American officer corps itself gained and maintained its professional competence.

Panel 1

## Notes

1. "Address of General Pershing," "Addresses Delivered at the Graduating Exercises, General Staff College, June 29, 1920," MHI, AWCCA, 1919-1920, Box Curriculum 1919-1920, Volume VI: Special Course Volume VIII Field Exercises, 3. Also see Allan R. Millett, The General: Robert L. Bullard and Officership in the United States Army, 1881-1925, (Westport, CT: Greenwood Press, 1975), for the discussion of post-war National Defense policy on 439-449.

2. Kreidberg and Henry, *Military Mobilization*, 377-380; Allan R. Millett and Peter Maslowski, *For the Common Defense: A Military History of the United States of America*, (NY: Macmillan, 1984), 363-372, quote from 363.

3. Summerall Testimony to House Committee on Military Affairs, December 16, 1926, printed in "Promotion and Retirement," *Report of Secretary of War on Promotion and Retirement in Pursuance of the Provisions of Section 4 of the Act* Approved July 2, 1926, 69th Congress., 2d sess., 1926, (GPO, 1926), 307.

4. Notes from the Chief of Infantry, *Infantry* 22, no. 6 (June 1923): 680-681.

5. See Edward M. Coffman, *The Regulars: The American Army, 1898-1941*, (Cambridge: Belknap Press of Harvard University, 2004).

6. Of 2,307 regular infantry colonels, lieutenant colonels, majors and captains on active duty, 622 (27 percent) served in units, 319 (14 percent) served overseas, ninety-one (4 percent) served on the staffs in Washington, D.C., and 1125 (49 percent) served in some capacity in the Army education system. 262 (11 percent) served at the Infantry and Tank Schools, 101 (4 percent) at Fort Leavenworth, sixty-two (2 percent) at the Army War College, and, by far the largest numbers, a total of 647 (28 percent) served with the Reserve Officer Training Corps detachments, 281 (12 percent), the National Guard, 198 (9 percent), or the Army Reserve, 168 (7 percent). Notes from the Chief of Infantry, "Duties of Infantry Officers," *IJ* 34, no. 1, (January 1929): 80.

7. See Millett, *Bullard*, 439-442. Also, see Cooke, *Pershing and His Generals*, Chapter 10.

8. Current Field Artillery Notes, "General Pershing on the United States Army," *FAJ* 13, no. 4, (July-August 1923): 360-362.

9. Editorial Comment, "The Task of Teaching," *Cavalry Journal* 30, no. 125, (October 1921): 416-418. *Cavalry Journal* hereafter cited as *CJ*.

10. Major Bernard Lenz (sic), Infantry, "Who is Going to Soldier When Everybody is Going to School?" *IJ* 18, no. 5, (May 1921): 441-443. A filler piece on the closing page of this article was a reprint from Harper's Weekly entitled "The Reduced Army."

11. Captain Elbridge Colby, Infantry, "The School of the Officer," in Varied Ground, *IJ* 19, no. 3, (September 1921): 327-328.

12. Major Bernard Lentz, "The Applicatory Method," *IJ* 19, no. 6, (December 1921): 604-609, quotes are from 355.

13 Lieutenant Colonel Bernard Lentz, Infantry, "A Decade of Army Schools," *IJ* 39, no. 5, (September-October 1932): 355-357.

14. *Report of the Secretary of War to the President, 1921*, (GPO, 1921), Table 1.

15. Lieutenant Colonel A. B. Warfield, Q.M.C., "Fort Benning, the Home of the Infantry School,' *IJ* 33, no. 1, (June 1928): 573-580; Major Edwin P. Parker, Jr., Field Artillery, "New Construction at Fort Sill," *FAJ* 24, no. 1, (January-February 1934): 5-14.

16. See Elvid Hunt, *History of Fort Leavenworth, 1827 – 1937*, second edition brought up to date by Walter E. Laurence. (CGSSP, 1937), 261, 269.

17. Of 2,307 Regular infantry colonels, lieutenant colonels, majors and captains on active duty, 622 (27 percent) served in units, 319 (14 percent) served overseas, ninety-one (4 percent) served on the staffs in Washington, D.C., and 1125 (49 percent) served in some capacity in the Army education system. Numbers and percentages from Notes from the Chief of Infantry, "Duties of Infantry Officers," *IJ* 34, no. 1, (January 1929): 80.

18. The $100,000 figure was for 1922. Report of the Secretary of War to the President, (GPO, 1922), Table 1.

19. Title of this section taken from "Benny Havens," a West Point song written in 1838, available on http://www.west-point.org/greimanj/west_point/songs/bennyhavens.htm. Accessed 16 June 2007. *Promotion and Retirement,* 306-307. Kreidberg and Henry, *Military Mobilization,* 221, 247.

20. *Promotion and Retirement,* 2.

21. *Promotion and Retirement,* 23-24 and 31.

22. *Promotion and Retirement,* 8.

23. Edward M. Coffman and Peter F. Herrly, "The American Army Regular Officer Corps Between the World Wars," *Armed Forces and Society* 4, no. 1 (November 1977): 58.

24. A very useful summary, and interpretation, of the 'hump' from the perspective of June 30, 1938 is 'Agrippa II,' "Promotion," *CJ* 48, no. 3, (May-June 1939): 200-203. Quote is from 202.

25. Agrippa II, "Promotion," 202-203.

26. Captain Thomas Marshall Spaulding, "The Creation of the Single List." *IJ* 17, no. 2, (August 1920): 132-141 and Major Thomas Marshall Spaulding, Coast Artillery Corps, "The Promotion List," *IJ* 18, no. 4, (April 1921): 356-361.

27. See Colonel G. V. S. Quackenbush, Infantry, "One List for Promotion," *IJ* 16, no. 1, (July 1919): 17-18. Editor's comment is on 18.

28. Troops in the United States and its overseas possessions numbered 1,679,000 (some 46 percent of the total), while troops deployed to France numbered 1,944,000, with some 10,000 at sea enroute to France. Kreidberg and Henry, *Military Mobilization,* 307.

29. By November 11, 1918, only 36 percent of all officers listed in the official Army Register were or had been assigned to the AEF. US War Department, The Adjutant General's Office, *Army Directory, November 1, 1918.* (GPO, 1918).

30. See, for example, Chynoweth, *Bellamy Park,* 84 and 115; and Kenneth S. Davis, *Soldier of Democracy: A Biography of Dwight Eisenhower,* (Garden City, NY: Doubleday, Doran & Co., 1945), 178.

31. Omar N. Bradley and Clay Blair, *A General's Life: An Autobiography,* (NY: Simon and Schuster, 1983), Chapter 5, page 680, note 10.

32. Brigadier General Lytle Brown, Director War Plans Division, War Department General Staff, "Memorandum for the Chief of Staff, Subject: Occupancy of quarters by officers not on duty at the Army Service Schools, Fort Leavenworth," December 14, 1918, NAII, RG 165, Box No. 13, Folder 58, Army Service School, 1.

33. Major General James McAndrew, "Introductory Remarks bys the Commandant," "Addresses Delivered at the Graduating Exercises, General Staff College, June 29, 1920," MHI, AWCCA, Box Curriculum 1919-1920, Volume VI: Special Course Volume VIII Field Exercises, 1.

34. Major John H. Burns, "The American Professional Soldier," *IJ* 47, no. 5 (September-October 1940): 418-423. Quote from 422.

35. "Memorandum to accompany proposed revision of Article XIV. Compilation of Orders – embracing the subject of Military Education," Office of the Chief of Staff, War Plans

Division. Cover letter dated March 8, 1919, signed by George F. Baltzell, Colonel, General Staff, War Department Office of the Chief of Staff. NAII RG 407, Box 808, folder 352 (10-13-19) to (10-4-18).

36. "Memorandum - Military Education," 1-3.

37. Brigadire General Lytle Brown, "Memorandum for the Chief of Staff, Subject: Occupancy of quarters by officers not on duty at the Army Service Schools, Fort Leavenworth," December 14, 1918, NAII RG 165, Box No. 13, Folder 58, Army Service School.

38. Letter, George C. Marshall, Washington, D.C., July 9, 1920 to Major General James W. McAndrew reproduced in Bland, *Soldierly Spirit*, 195-196. Letter available in MHI, AWCCA, Box 003 062.1 1.34, Letter, George C, Marshall to Major General McAndrew, July 9, 1920, with marginal note in pencil requiring copies to be furnished to directors at the War College.

39. Bland, *Soldierly Spirit*, 197.

40. Bland, *Soldierly Spirit*, 197. Corroborated in "Notes of Conference of Directors General Staff College, July 12, 1920," MHI, AWCCA, Box 003, 062.1 1.34.

41. A very useful summary of the McGlachlin and Fiske Boards, and a précis of student selection criteria for the Leavenworth Schools and the Army War College are found in "Memorandum for the Chief of Coast Artillery, Subject: Operation of the School System with Special Reference to the Coast Artillery Corps, December 28, 1931." Located in NAII RG165, WDGS G-1 (Personnel) Numerical File 1921-1942, 12311-12675, Box No. 85, Folder 12585-12600. Both Boards are also addressed in Ball, *Responsible Command*, 180-186 and 194-195.

42. U. S. War Department, "Special Orders No. 175, July 28, 1922," and "Letter of Instructions for Board, August 16, 1922" paragraph 2 and 3. Documents found in NAII RG 407, Bulky Packages, 352.01 (9-5-22) (1) Pro. B/O Record Board of Officers, Package No. 1066. Hereafter cited as Fiske Report. The service schools, each run by their own branches, were required, according to the board's recommendations, to "train competent leaders of [each branch's] units and provide instructors for the Regular Army, National Guard, Organized Reserves, R.O.T.C. and C.M.T.C." Fiske Report, 5, 12, and 15. There also existed, for a brief period, an Educational Advisory Board, but it was ineffectual. Educational Advisory Board, "Report, 22 October 1924." NAII RG 407, Box 806, Folder 352 (11-3-24) to (10-30-24). This appears to have been the only formal meeting of this Board. See discussions for the 1925 EAB in NAII RG 407, Box 806, Folder 352 (7-28-25) to (11-24-24); for the on-again-off-again EAB of 1926, see RG 407, Box 808, folder 352.01 (10-13-25) to (6-26-25). For the 1927 EAB, see RG 407, Box 2045, which contains the records of the June 20, 1927 Corps Area and Division Commander's Conference.

43. The role of these commandants, and others as well, is told by George S. Pappas, *Prudens Futuri: The U. S. Army War College, 1901 – 1967* (Carlisle Barracks, PA: The Alumni Association of the US Army War College, 1967), 89-129.

44. Much higher quality analysis than Pappas is Ball, *Of Responsible Command*, 210-214.

45. Ball, *Responsible Command*, 212-213.

46. US War Department, "Army Regulations, No. 350-5, Military Education," Washington, D.C., July 1925, 8.

47. *AR*, 1921-1922, 16.

48. *AR*, Assistant Commandant, 1921-1922, 23-24.

49. Director, General Staff School, *AR*, 1921-1922, 49-50.

50. "Mercutio,' "Canned Commanders," in Cerebrations column, *IJ* 42, no. 3 (May-June 1935): 269.

51. 'Singlebars,' "Canned Commanders – Continued," Cerebrations column, *IJ* 43, no. 1 (January-February 1936): 74-75.

52 Major R. M. Johnston, Historical Section, G.H.Q., AEF, "Staff and Command," *IJ* 16, no. 1 (July 1919): 88-92. Quote from 92.

53. 'General Gripe,' "Wishful Thinking," *CJ* 49, no. 4 (July-August 1940): 349-359. Quote is form 349.

54. CGSS, "Summary of Schedule (By Courses)," (CGSSP, n.d.), CARL Archives, typescript located in files for CGSS, 1935-1936, "Schedules." Also see CGSS, *Index to School Problems, Series 1919-1920 to 1932-1933*, (CGSSP, 1933), *passim*; *Course Schedules* for 1928-1929; 1929-1930; 1934-1935; and 1935-1936, located in the CARL archives. The quantification done from this source is supported by Dastrup, who, although using a different categorization, states that in 1938-1939, "practical work accounted for 744 out of 1073 scheduled hours for the (single) year," Boyd L. Dastrup, *The US Army Command and General Staff College: A Centennial History*, (Manhattan, KS: Sunflower University Press, n.d., c. 1982), 76.

55. Examples drawn from analysis of conferences ST 203, 205, 207, 211, 214 and 215 in CGSS, *1929-1930, Second Year Course Conferences: Command, Staff and Logistics; Strategy; Military History; Field Engineering; Military Intelligence; Methods of Training; Military Geography; Political Economy*, (CGSSP, 1930), 196-234.

56. *FSR, 1923*, 4.

57. *FSR, 1923*, 5.

58. GSS, *Command, Staff and Tactics*, special edition, (GSSP, 1923), 22-24.

59. Lieutenant Colonel J. E. Lewis, Field Artillery, and 1st Lieutenant Champlin F. Buck, Field Artillery, "An Additional Training Medium," *FAJ* 27, no. 4, (July-August 1937): 302-304.

60. Among many examples, see Major L. D. Davis, Infantry, "What Strength Units?" *IJ* 26, no. 3, (March 1925): 247-251; Captain Richard M. Sandusky, Infantry, "Skeletonized Drill," *IJ* 28, no. 4 (April 1926): 406-409; Colonel P. L. Miles, Infantry, "Training of Peace Strength Units," *IJ* 35, no. 4, (October 1929): 336-339; and the satirical piece by Major Ralph E. Jones, Infantry, "These Recent Factors," *IJ* 28, no. 2, (February 1926): 148-151, in which the author awakens from a dream of effective training. "Oh, hell!" quote is on 151.

61 Brigadier General John Ross Delafield, Ordnance Reserve, "National Defense of the United States," *IJ* 28, no. 2, (February 1926); 145-146. Quote is from last paragraph on 126.

62 Major C. B. Hodges, General Staff, "Fall Maneuvers, 1921: American Forces in Germany," *IJ* 19, no. 6, (December 1921): 620-625.

63 Major Adna R. Chaffee, General Staff Corps, "The Maneuvers of the First Cavalry Division, September-October 1923," *CJ* 33, no. 135, (April 1934): 133-162.

64 Brigadier General H. B. Fiske, "Maneuvers of the Second Division," *IJ* 31, no. 3, (September 1927): 225-235; Major George S. Patton, Jr., Cavalry, "The 1929 Cavalry Division Maneuvers," *CJ* 39, no. 158, (January 1929): 7-15; "The Cavalry Maneuvers at Fort Riley, Kansas 1934," *CJ* 43, no. 184, (July-August 1934): 5-14; and Major James T. Duke, Cavalry, G.S.C., "Third Army Maneuvers, Fort Bliss, Texas," *CJ* 47, no. 6, (November-December 1938): 528-535.

65. Colonel Conrad H. Lanza, "The First Army Maneuvers," *FAJ* 25, no. 6, (November-December 1935): 540-565. Quotes are from 541 and 565. Conclusions are on 565. See Lieutenant Colonel John S. Wood, Field Artillery, "Maneuvers and the Umpire System," *CJ* 48, no. 3, (May-June 1939): 208-209 and Hanson W. Baldwin, "Maneuvers Reveal Deficiencies," *CJ* 48, no. 5, (September-October 1939): 390-391.

66. Examples of reports on CPXs include The Regular Army Infantry, "1st Division Command Post Training," *IJ* 34, no. 4, (April 1929); 429-430; The Organized Reserves, "The Command Post Exercises," *Infantry* 34, no. 2, (February 1929): 214-215; Colonel W. K. Naylor, Infantry, "Command Post Exercises," *IJ* 36, no. 1, (January 1930): 83-85; Colonel Arthur S.

Conklin, General Staff Corps, "III Corps Area Command Post Exercise, Fort George G. Meade – 5-19 July, 1930," *IJ* 37, no. 3, (September 1930); 237-242; Colonel Conrad H. Lanza, Field Artillery, "The First Army CPX," *FAJ* 27, no. 6, (November-December 1937): 405-414.

67. See below for more articles by Brigadier General (retired) Hawkins, and for a brief description of his service in the World War as Chief of Staff of the 35th Division during its disastrous experiences in the Meuse-Argonne.

68. Brigadier General H. S. Hawkins, "Command Post Exercises," *IJ* 35, no. 4, (October 1929): 339-345, quotes are from 340 and 342.

69. For a few examples, see Major John J. Bohn, Cavalry, "The Civilian Conservation Corps," *CJ* 42, no. 178, (July-August 1933): 41-42; Corporal George Chancellor, 1st Cavalry (Mecz), "The C.C.C. at Fort Knox, Kentucky," *CJ* 42, no. 178, (July-August 1933): 36; Colonel Duncan K. Major, Jr., "Yes, Sir, the Army Can!" *IJ* 40, no. 4, (July-August 1933): 283-288; Representative James W. Wadsworth, New York, "The Army Gets the Job," *IJ* 40, no. 4, (July-August 1933): 292-293; Captain Leo Donovan, 12th Infantry, "The Establishment of the First Civilian Conservation Camp," *IJ* 40, no. 4, (July-August 1933); 245-249; and Captain George A. Hunt, 16th Infantry, "Army Publicity Objectives in Connection with the C.C.C." *IJ* 40, no. 5, (September-October 1933): 330.

70. The most recent, and in some respects, the most comprehensive discussion of this issue is in Coffman's *The Regulars,* Chapter 7, "The Army in Limbo." For the professionalism and competence of Regular Army officers, see the works of Keith Bonn, Peter Mansoor, and John Sloan Brown, among others.

71. See, as a single example, Abrahamson, *America Arms*, 186.

# Panel 3, Day 1: Changing Leadership for a Changing World Role, 1906-1939

## Questions & Answers
(Transcript of Presentation)

## Dr. Tim Nenninger, Ph.D.
## Dr. Peter Schifferle, Ph.D.

## Moderated by Dr. Rick Herrera, Ph.D.

**Dr. Herrera:**

Gentlemen, thank you for two very good presentations. Ladies and gentlemen, rather than hearing from me, let's hear from you. Yes?

**Audience Member 1:**

Dr. Schifferle, it seems to me a conclusion one can draw from your presentation is that the Leavenworth model in the interwar period is exactly the wrong kind of model we should be looking for today.

**Dr. Schifferle:**

Yes and no. The yes part, in other words, it is the wrong model, is we have a different (inaudible) system. We have a different form of an army. It's not expansible. In fact, we're now beginninsg to think that we could not expand it if we wanted to expand it. And the form of the threat is also questionable. The focus on a European threat, which brought US Army in the Pacific to some kind of issues in 1941, '42, now we're faced with the globalization of that kind of threat. We're not exactly sure what the post-Iraq, post-Afghanistan threat is going to be. But corps do what corps do and divisions do what divisions do. I would argue that what we ought to teach here is what divisions and corps do, are there any questions. And we have lost that focus. We have turned the Leavenworth school into a, well, OK, everybody's good idea instruction base. And we teach too much at too little depth to really serve our majors well. I think that's been true since at least 1983, when General (inaudible) did his staff study, which resulted in the production of SAMS, to be a school where only division and corps operations are taught. So it's kind of yes and no.

**Audience Member 2:**

Would you then posit that we need a joint school that is in the hierarchy or progression in schools, then?

**Dr. Schifferle:**

I think reinforced and more rigorous jaws would be appropriate. There's been a lot of discussion and monographs written about how far down you have to teach joint. I think part of that question is how far down do you have to teach joint and to what level of rigor, length of time spent teaching joint, do you have to teach joint. I think the first question we

PANEL 1

should ask, since this is an Army school, (inaudible) one. Because this is an Army school, we should ask, what do we have to teach Army majors to be in their last really tactical and operational school they're going to attend?

**Dr. Herrera:**

Yes? Would you go ahead and press the button?

**Audience Member 3:**

If I could (inaudible). Your opening quote was, "Which war, which rank." Now that we've kind of transformed a little bit and we are brigade-centric, I think that makes an add-on to it. What is our focus as we're developing leaders?

**Dr. Schifferle:**

Well, to be blunt, that depends if you believe the bumper stickers. For a brigade-centric Army, we certainly are keeping division and corps headquarters employed. Brigade-centric in the '20s and '30s was taught at Fort Benning, Fort Riley. Taught at the branch schools. I wonder where we're teaching brigade operations today. And are we teaching enough brigade operations wherever it is we're teaching brigade operations? I'm not certain we know what the transformed brigade really ought to be educated at. I think it's a very good question.

**Audience Member 4:**

I had a follow-on to your comment on your observation that divisions and corps are continuing to operate and continuing to be deployed. That is true. But I think you'll find they're very different in nature than their previous nature in that headquarters are cellular, they're scaled down. They don't have the overhead built into them intrinsically. They don't inherently have the logistical structure of the previous divisions. The logistical assets that used to be associated with a division and most of the combat support assets really have been farmed down to the brigade. As far as your observation on whether or not brigade operations are being taught and where they should be taught, if it's not being taught here, I'm concerned. This would seem to be the place, because the brigade is now the operational chip on the board. But that's an observation. A question I was going to ask to both of you was that coming through your conversation, I ended up with a little bit of a negative feeling about our, I believe you represented your feelings of what Leavenworth had accomplished and where we're going and what we're doing in a bit of a negative light. I'm wondering how we square that with a comment by Chief of Staff J. Lawton Collins and others who were World War II veterans and came out of it and said World War II was won in the Army school system, because this very tiny cadre of senior officers, or professional officers, or officers that hadn't experience at all, did in fact successfully pull together an 18 million-man Army and deploy it and succeed in combat. I'm wondering was Collins wrong in giving as much credence as he did to the Army schools?

**Dr. Herrera:**

Tim, would you start out with addressing that so we can do it chronologically?

## Dr. Nenninger:

I don't think Collins was wrong. I read Pete's book a couple of months ago. I certainly got the impression from "America's School for War" that, while not everything they taught during the interwar period was relevant to what they did between 1941-1945, without the Leavenworth experience we would have been a lot further behind. I remember a quote from General Quesada, who was an Air Corps officer who attended Leavenworth in the late '30s. He was quite positive about his experience at the schools, which was unusual because a lot of the Air Corps officers that went weren't so positive, partly because they weren't getting the tactical school experience from Maxwell in the Leavenworth curriculum. One of Quesada's criticisms wasn't really a criticism at all. He said, "We just couldn't anticipate the scale of operations we were dealing with, the distances we were dealing with, in a multi-theater war. It's not what we learned wasn't applicable. It's what we didn't anticipate that we weren't taught." I think that's probably the dilemma in any kind of educational experience, certainly in PME. You can't always anticipate what the future will bring.

## Dr. Schifferle:

I think I gave you the wrong impression if I gave you the impression that Leavenworth was not responsible for the victory. I think Leavenworth was the only place the victory was enshrined, if you will. That we would not have been able to have competent corps and division commanders without Leavenworth. I began my dissertation, which has a dim resemblance to the book, I began my dissertation with the thought that I would investigate the staff officers of the US Army as having come from Ford Motor Company and General Motors and General Electric. I thought the Army had to rely on outside educated officers, managers, in order to succeed, because we didn't have that much throughput from the Army school system. I was right and I was wrong. Every general staff officer of every division and corps that I surveyed in the ETO was on active duty in 1938. They were all professionals. But the Leavenworth graduates were only the commanders, the deputy commanders, the commanders of artillery, and the occasional chief of staff at the division level. Every general staff officer was not a Leavenworth graduate. I think what happened is that the commanders trained their staff officers to be staff officers based upon what they had learned at Leavenworth. Because there was really no place in the Army, in the '20s and '30s, to learn those skills except at Leavenworth.

## Audience Member 4:

Didn't Leavenworth run kind of a crash program during the course of the mobilization wherein the division staff were brought here and trained? So although the division staff officers weren't Leavenworth graduates in the sense of the two-year course, they benefited from the Leavenworth faculty having taught them for a month or so?

## Dr. Schifferle:

Yes. Two photographs on the cover of my book. One photograph is [Omar Bradley] with the staff of the 82d Infantry Division and the other photograph is a large classroom in World War II. In World War II, we graduated something approaching 19,000 graduates from Leavenworth. Some of those graduates were in the new division course, but we only cycled through about a third of the divisions. It was too late in the cycle for the active

PANEL 1

divisions and the initial National Guard divisions, so we caught the tail end of the National Guard and all the active divisions, and then we stopped the program. About two-thirds of the divisions. That was a three or four-week course, but it was focused specifically on those divisions' challenges. It included some discussion of training. It was about an hour and a half at the commandant's house about how you should train your division once you go back to it.

**Audience Member 5:**

I still subscribe to *Army Times*. If the impressions I gained from reading that publication are correct, we seem to have a very formalized and robust system of senior mentors now for fairly senior commanders. These are apparently senior retired officers who are brought on, maybe in a continuing relationship even with one given commander. Could the panelists comment on the extent to which that supplements or takes the place of the deficiencies in the kind of education that you were talking about a little earlier? Contemporaneously.

**Dr. Schifferle:**

I'm not really sure I'm qualified to talk on that. Our students at SAMS go out to become, effectively, the general staff officers of divisions and corps. We now have graduates at every rank from four stars down. But I have not really engaged the more senior of those in a conversation about their mentorship by more senior officers still. I really don't think I'm qualified to talk about that.

**Dr. Nenninger:**

I think a lot of interest in military mentorship comes from General Eisenhower's nice little memoir called *At Ease*. The accolades that he gives to Fox Conner as being his mentor when they served together in Panama. I must say, perhaps it's my historical roots, but I'm a little bit skeptical, because there are other stories in *At Ease* that are not necessarily entirely accurate either. The one source that we have for Fox Conner being a mentor of Eisenhower is Eisenhower's *At Ease*. I'm unaware of other sources that speak to that question, which isn't to entirely say that it's wrong. It's just that I've yet seen a whole lot of other corroborating evidence. There were several other stories in *At Ease* which are very interesting, including Eisenhower saying how Fox Conner rigged things so he could get to Leavenworth, because he was on the outs with the Chief of Infantry, who, as Pete describes, the branches were the ones that set up the lineup of who they were going to recommend to the schools. Eisenhower says that Fox Conner told him to take an appointment in the Adjutant General's department so that the Chief of Infantry wouldn't have any say in the process of Eisenhower going to the school. It's completely untrue. I can find you the documentation in the National Archives where, from the get-go, Eisenhower is on the list for the Chief of Infantry, and although he did serve as a recruiting officer briefly under the Adjutant General, he was not on the Adjutant General's list for Leavenworth. I'm a little bit skeptical of one-source stories like mentorship of Fox Conner and Eisenhower.

**Dr. Schifferle:**

One of the things I wanted to research when I began the process was what is usually referred to as General Marshall's desire to fix Leavenworth when he became Chief of Staff. That, I think, is in the bucket of apocryphal stories. Because General Marshall had an opportunity to name the commandant. He named General Lesley McNair to become the commandant. They had an office call in Marshall's office. McNair came here and there was basically an exchange of about three letters between McNair and Marshall for the entire period of McNair being in charge of Leavenworth, and they basically consisted of, "Keep doing what you're doing. You're doing a great job." So then I went to, OK, what did McNair do when he was commandant? And basically he did the same thing as previous commandants had done: taught division and corps operations, are there any questions? He surveyed the students. The students said get rid of the horses. He got rid of the horses. But other than that, he kept doing what he was doing. George C. Marshall was happy with that.

**Audience Member 6:**

This is a question mostly for Dr. Schifferle, but Tim, you can add to this if you think you have something that is appropriate. Peter, you mentioned that, and I quote, "Arthur Wagner kind of lost."

**Dr. Schifferle:**

Based on your presentation, yeah.

**Audience Member 6:**

It's not that I take that personally.

**Dr. Schifferle:**

No fisticuffs yet, please.

**Audience Member 6:**

My question is, what happened to the reform impulse that was so strong during the late Gilded Age and even the very, very early Progressive Era? The intellectual ferment, the debate over which way are we going to go? Are we going to go left, are we going to go left, are we going to have this, are we going to have that? Why did it go away, or did it?

**Dr. Schifferle:**

I think that's a great question, because it allows me to get into some areas that are in the book but not in the presentation. The inaugural faculty issue, the fact that, I can't remember. I think there were 14 or 18 instructors at Leavenworth in 1919. All 14 or 18 came directly from the AEF. It wasn't just that that imposed an AEF-focused World War I-style of warfare solution set. It was that, from the inaugural faculty, every senior member of the faculty except for two or three for the whole period were drawn from that inaugural faculty. A major on the inaugural faculty will come back as a colonel in charge of a program. A colonel in the inaugural faculty will come back as a brigadier general in charge of the school. So the lock on the intellectual system was of that inaugural faculty. But they were in general agreement about the nature of the challenge in World War I. Incompetent staff officers. And they knew that Leavenworth was the training school for staff officers, therefore they should train competent staff officers. But the literature of the period, the journals of the period, are just alive. I wish our journals were like those journals now. The journals of the period infantry cavalry and field artillery are just alive with intellectual, artistic, creative ferment about the nature of the officer corps, the nature of education, how do you deal with civilian conservation corps camps, who's our next threat, what's the war going to look like, the motorization mechanization armor warfare tanks. It's just a live with all of that. So the intellectual ferment is there. It's not in the schools, per se, but it's in the literature that students and instructors are writing for in the journals.

**Audience Member 6:**

So then do you assume or can you demonstrate that that ferment from the diff journals, did that filter into the instructors at Leavenworth? Is that ultimately inculcated into the lessons to students at Leavenworth?

**Dr. Schifferle:**

Yes, whether it's a direct lift from the journals or it's a lift from the experimentation that we were doing. By 1937, there was a student text entitled "The Mechanized Division Tentative." So 1937, long before anybody's ever really thought about a panzer division, we're teaching basically an armored division here at Fort Leavenworth as part of the course. And we had been dealing with mechanized brigades in the curriculum, in the exercises, since, I believe, '26. I think in mid-'20s, this was our first exercise where they put officers in the role of the German right hand army during the execution of the so-called Schlieffen Plan. They have them go through it the way it was done in 1914, and then the next day they bring the students in and they say, "OK, now what would you do if you were a mechanized force?" That's going on in 1925 or '26.

**Audience Member 7:**

This is a question for both of you. Dr. Nenninger started among the earliest of the root reforms, which was the creation of the post schools. Dr. Schifferle then talks about the Leavenworth system being built on the existence of all armed branch schools at the infantry school and the armor school. To what extent is the creation of the branch schools one of the greatest unsung professional military education developments of this period?

**Dr. Schifferle:**

The books need to be written. There's books on the posts. There's books on the branches. But I am not aware of monographs on each of the schools with the same kind of holistic appreciation to take it from formation through the end of World War II. I just don't think they're there yet.

**Dr. Nenninger:**

I agree.

## Day 2: Featured Speaker:

## History Strengthens by General (R) Gordon Sullivan
(Transcript of Presentation)

**Mr. Ken Gott:**

Ladies and gentlemen, our featured speaker today is General (Retired) Gordon Sullivan. When I was a young lieutenant, he was the Chief of Staff in the Army and we all looked up to him with adoration and was just an incredible man. General Sullivan is currently the President and the Chief Operating Officer of the Association of the United States Army, headquartered in Arlington, Virginia. Since assuming the presidency in 1998, General Sullivan has overseen the transformation of the Association into a dynamic, 100,000-plus individual and 500-plus sustaining member organization that represents soldiers' families in the defense industries. For those of you in service or retired, you are very familiar with the good things that AUSA does.

Born in Boston, Massachusetts and raised in Quincy, he was commissioned a 2d Lieutenant of Armor and awarded a Bachelor of Arts degree in history from Norwich University in 1959. He holds a Master of Arts degree in political science from the University of New Hampshire. His professional military education includes the United States Army Armor School basic course and advanced courses, the Command and General Staff College and the Army War College.

General Sullivan retired from the United States Army on 31 July, 1995 after more than 36 years of active service. He culminated his service in uniform as a 32d Chief of Staff. He is a co-author with Michael V. Harper of Hope Is Not a Method, published by Random House in 1996, which chronicles the enormous challenges encountered in transforming the post-Cold War Army through the lens of proven leadership principles and a commitment to shared values. He is Chairman of the Board of Trustees at Norwich University and the Marshall Legacy Institute, and was formerly a director on the boards of Newell Rubbermaid, Shell Corporation, Institute of Defense Analyses and General Dynamics.

General Sullivan is married to the former Gay Loftus of Quincy, Massachusetts. They currently reside in Alexandria, Virginia. He has three children and three grandchildren. He is an avid reader, amateur historian and active sailor and sport fishing enthusiast. Ladies and gentlemen, please welcome General (Retired)s) Gordon Sullivan.

**GEN Sullivan:**

Well it's nice to be with all of you. General MacFarland, nice to be with you. John, good to see you. Many friends, colleagues from days past. It's always great to come to Fort Leavenworth. Two of those children by the way, two of those grandchildren have roots here in Leavenworth, Kansas, having, being really part of the Davis family from Leavenworth which has been here since the 1800s. So I still have roots here in Leavenworth, in addition to a real love for this school and what happens here at Fort Leavenworth. I had many fond memories about my days here, some of which we were just discussing, days hunting and just being here. Participating in a triathlon when I was the Deputy Commandant and as you know, some of you may know, one of the events of a triathlon is a swim. It seemed like a good idea to swim in the duck pond since it was there. Two years later the medics decided that that wasn't such a good idea since every goose from Toronto to wherever was camped out in that thing, and I remember looking up when we were standing there in our suits and the numbers on our arms and Mark Hertling was standing beside me and I think he was the captain of the West Point swimming team, and I quickly found out what that meant but we didn't know any better so I think it's been changed though if there still is such a thing as a triathlon out here.

Okay, so anyway it's nice to be with all of you. I've got some thoughts which I want to give you, some of which, a lot of which you know and I'm not going to bore with what an amateur historian may know about the origins of this place and so forth. Is Tim here? Yeah, right there. Dr. Nenninger is here. God forbid, I mean he's one of the living experts on what happened here back in the 1800s. So I'm going to give you my views about life and Army leader development, and I think it rests on three pillars and I think those pillars are still talked about, that is in the individual; the individual has a role in his or her own education and development, and the institution, places like Leavenworth and Fort Knox and Fort Benning always had a major role. And last but not least, and equally as profound, the units of assignment. TRADOC has certainly since the '70s, since it's inception, been instrumental in the melding of these three into a powerful triumvirate, and I think that while the system sometimes operates at reduced efficiency because of operational needs, that is reduced student output and student flow, the fact of the matter is that this triumvirate of the school, the individual and the units of assignments is very important. Now I never intend to say much more about that but suffice it to say, I think looking forward that the TRADOC schooling system and the situation that the United States Army finds itself in because of what happened back in the '70s is in better shape today with its non-commissioned officer education system, its officer education system, warrant officer education system, than we were in 1973 and '75. However you may feel about input and output on the schooling system, and people receiving constructive credit and so forth and shortened courses the fact of the matter is the structure is here upon which to build going forward.

I get that question a lot by the way; I just returned from Schofield Barracks. I was with the 25th Division, and while they actually feel very positive about their accomplishments, and many of them are going back for their third or fourth tours and the next rotation, one of the questions on their mind is, are we in as bad a shape as you were in '73, '74, and '75? And the answer to that is a resounding no. It's not the same Army. In my view, it's a much stronger Army with much greater depth because of the schooling system and the way in which the Army approached the education and training and development of our young people, and I believe that system is still here and it certainly needs and it will receive attention, but there is a reason to believe that all leaders who are responsible for the Army education system know this and are working hard to respond to increasing demands as our forces return from certainly Iraq and Afghanistan, which remains a question. New York Times this morning is full of that; we're now going to get a complete inside look into what Bob Woodward found out about how so-and-so thought so-and-so was a jerk and blah blah blah. But the fact of the matter is we still don't know how that's going to turn out.

Now just as I don't intend to dig into the guts of the Army leader development system, I'm not going to give you any tutorials on the historical record of the development of the Army education system. Tim Nenninger, as I mentioned, and Glenn Robertson by the way, and many of you in this room, are much more versed in that subject than I am and if I started to get into it, you'd laugh me out of the room. I do know that Eben Swift's, I do know of his work by the way, I wonder sometimes and I actually did when I was a Chief, ask a question, is it time to take a look at the five paragraph field order? Well that brought everybody, it's kind of like, okay, Chief, great, let's move. You know, how about if we worry about something else. So agreed, agreed. We did and that was the first and last time I mentioned that, however I'm not sure where we are today frankly. I don't know and that's just kind of out there. But Eben Swift, as you know, is fundamental. He was a very catalytic person for the Army and his applied method has been used here at Leavenworth forever and I think it's probably one of the more powerful aspects of this education system and it has been. As he said in 1908 in the opening of the War College, "Armies in fact have been more efficient than ever before in the history of the world. Although they have been trained in times of peace, their efficiency is due principally to the improved methods in which the leadership of troops has been studied and learned," and he was talking about in the schoolhouse and looking at battles and so forth and the staff ride and so forth. And Swift is an important character in the history of the Army. Certainly the lyceum at Agawam, while interesting, has little application today when we're not regimental-based in our home station training. But Glenn and I were just talking on the way in about just quickly mentioning the virtual staff ride and I believe some of the virtual staff ride techniques which are being developed will be applicable to colonels and so forth with their people and that will be very important going forward.

Now...the applied method is in fact the intellectual bedrock of this institution, as is the historical record. I looked at the tables as I was coming in here and I think back to my time here as a Deputy Commandant, that table is about three times the size as anything that was here then. What's happened here is enormous and it's a result of dedicated people who appreciate the history of the United States Army and they understand the role that it plays in the development of our officers, non-commissioned officers and soldiers. It's this appreciation to which I will speak and I'll begin noting that our history as an Army, as an institution combined with operational, tactical and historical records and first person accounts of sacrifice is or should be the well from which everyone who considers themselves a professional drinks. Sadly in my view, and my career is probably testament to that, the appreciation of the role of history and the developmental process and as an aid for serving leaders has really waxed and waned during my professional life. Thankfully after Vietnam a revitalized history program was created and staff rides at the Combat Studies Institute, Leavenworth papers, Military History Institute, School of Advanced Military Studies, all were based on a in-depth look at the history of the Army. The 230-year history thereabouts of our Army is what it is. It's what it is. And while we from our present vantage point might choose to wonder why such-and-such was done or not done, the fact of the matter is it was done. And why was it done? What was the context in which it was done and can we learn from that? Eisenhower and Robert Murphy in North Africa. Very complicated, very complicated relationship. By the way, reading Murphy's book is pretty interesting when it comes to thinking about general officers operating in an alliance and operating closely with the State Department. There's some things to learn. What I learned was when Eisenhower showed up in Gibraltar after that horrible trip coming out of England, he was standing there in the bunker smoking a cigarette, reached in his pocket and pulled out six coins, one from each of the six Allies who would invade North Africa. By the way, not a bad technique. Of all you can say about Eisenhower, he was focused; he had six coins in his pocket representing each of his allies and it probably wasn't lost on those who worked for him that this gent really means business. And he did. And he did. Not a bad insight. Kind of trivial, but you know what? In that business at the top, things like that work.

I applaud the energy which has been devoted to this conference. I'm coming here next week, not here, but I'm coming to Kansas City to talk to General Dempsey's senior leadership conference and I note that it's starting off with a visit to the National Museum of World War I. Any conference conducted by a four-star general which will take the time to go to this museum with his leaders indicates it's a perfect manifestation of how he feels about history and the development of our people. That is not a throwaway event. It's very significant. And I think you all know that; I'm not telling you anything you don't know about how four-stars operate but that tells you a lot about him and how the Army feels about our history.

The question I will try to answer is how to create professional Army leaders with a lifelong appreciation of our heritage so that in their contributory years, they can take strength through the application of both doctrinal concepts and understand the technological characteristics of equipment, and understand the well spring from which the courage of their troops flows. This was, has always been a challenge and it will continue to be a challenge; that is to create professional leaders who appreciate the fact that history, a reading of history and an understanding of history, is very important. Now I'm not here to suggest I know what truth is, even with a small T. I'm just like most people, kind of trying to do my best as I go through life. You're the experts; many of you are the experts and you can draw judgments about these programs better than I. I just want to reflect on how hard it is to keep history in the vanguard of leader development and how difficult it is, if not only to keep it in the curriculum but to keep it vibrant, relevant and interesting. Taught by qualified and experienced faculty who can stimulate young people, young officers and non-commissioned officers, to read their history. Now I was commissioned in 1959 as was mentioned. I came into the Army having been influenced by General Ernie Harmon, Major General Ernie Harmon of...World War II and World War I; he was actually a mounted calvaryman in World War I with the 2d Calvary Regiment. One of the few mounted US units other than the artillery. Well I don't want to get into that; let's just say the Calvary unit. There weren't many mounted calvary units in the expeditionary force and he was a troop commander. I was influenced by him and the retired officers and non-commissioned officers who surrounded him up at Norwich. And we all felt their presence. I mean these were good soldiers, highly decorated and as you might expect, friends of his, colleagues of his that he had a lot of respect for.

So I graduated and went down to Fort Hood, Texas, the 2d Armored Division, which was really not a division; it was a sham. I quickly found that out when I arrived. We were actually training troops. It was an advanced individual training operation. I was in the First Battalion 66th Armor; at the time my battalion commander was a Big Red One veteran and all of the company commanders were Korean War veterans, some of them actually were for one reason or another happened to be World War II veterans. You know what, other than going to the bar, one never talked about history. The 66th Armor carried lineage from World War I, World War II; had been in Germany. The division gyroed back to Hood. You know, the battalion commander was a Big Red One veteran; certainly he must have had something to say but he never said it. We didn't know anything about the way, the second World War or the Korean War, which was [actually] only over for six years; it's kind of strange. It was like it never existed so lo and behold I was assigned to the 1st Calvary Division next and it was in the western corridor in Korea and it was like, okay, well here you are. I mean the 1st Calvary Division, one of the most highly decorated divisions in the United States Army for its service in the Pacific in World War II, the Korean War and I went to another tank battalion with five tank companies because it was a Pentomic Division, and we didn't talk about it.

Now you have to ask yourself...we were getting rid of the pinks and greens and going to Army green. Modern Army green. That transformation said a lot about the Army's sense of history. The Army turned its back on its history. Modern Army green, Pentomic Divisions, Army and Defense Command, atomic cannons, one of which is perched up on the rim-rock out at Junction City between Manhattan and Junction City. Honest John Rockets, Red Stone missiles. I looked out of the Quonset hut and there was a Davy Crockett. Was that it, the Davy Crockett, the football on the end of a stick? I mean by this Quonset hut, I mean it was kind of like out of body experience. You know, the symbol was, look you guys aren't going to be doing what you used to do; we're changing it and all of that is past. So we didn't talk about our history; it was like it wasn't important.

Now I know you all look at the errors of history much differently than when we change uniforms but it certainly appeared that we were going from one Army, forgetting about all of that which had gone before, and moving in to a new era. You know, I am the quintessential Cold Warrior by the way. I was in the Army when the Wall went up and when it came down so when I look at my experience in the Army, I probably look at it differently than some of the historians do. The pre-Vietnam Army that I joined, which might be a way of categorizing it, might be a lot better than the Army that came out of Vietnam but it didn't make the most of its leaders and the most of its potential for training all of us and developing us. Now I understand the next war. I learned this probably in Fort Knox, maybe even before I came in the Army, that the next war isn't going to be like the last one. Okay, I got that. I'm not sure, by the way, that that's so hard to understand. North Africa wasn't like Italy in World War II and it certainly wasn't like southern France or northern Europe . It wasn't like the Philippines or whatever, or the islands in the Pacific. And by the way, Iraq is not like Afghanistan; we were just talking about that right outside. It's completely different and it's not the same. It's not the same terrain, obviously, and the issues are different and the people in the Army have to understand that and they do. J. Lawton Collins, 25th Infantry, Guadalcanal, and he winds up taking corps ashore at Normandy in 1944. And he did it. By the way there's others who didn't, which I don't need to go into, who couldn't make the transition, but interesting enough, I'm not sure that couldn't make the transition is the judgment; it might be that the ones who should have listened wouldn't listen to him because he hadn't been one of them in North Africa, Italy, southern France. You decide. You're the experts. Not me. You decide.

So anyway in every case, leaders had to figure out how to make things happen with combined arms operations, operating with allies. And they learned how to lead citizen soldiers which was an art unto itself, which John's famous book has told us about. They formed and led competent staffs and they work with the Navy, Air Force, Marine Corp and our allies in productive ways. It wasn't easy by the way just because Eisenhower was walking around with six coins in his pocket. Didn't quite get it. He had to do something about it. But they learned to plan, execute and drill down in their battles in ways that men such as Arthur Conger, who was Colonel Arthur Conger, who was involved with the development of this place; Eben Swift and a fellow by the name of John Bigelow who was a captain writing about probably what is the most in-depth look at Chancellorsville as a teaching tool, what he developed. And they were the ones, actually Bigelow, probably and Cottington. They were some of the bedrocks from which Glenn developed his staff rides.

Now I would just say as an aside, I've been on staff rides with John Marsh when he was the Secretary of the Army; General Carl Vuono who would get us up on a Saturday morning, it was pouring rain, and we still went. It actually rains in war too so we got that. I mean we got that message, which we actually understood that before we went but at any rate, it's sort of like General Dempsey doing what he's doing. We went out together and we listened to him or we listened to Mr. Marsh and it was and is important, and I still go on staff rides, probably three or four a year and it's a way for me to stay linked with my, with our, profession.

So from my point of view, lots of things that were strong in the pre-Vietnam Army were weakened, you know, some of them were weakened by the Vietnam experience. But the study of history wasn't one of them because it wasn't there to begin with. It had to be revitalized by people such as you in this room and there are some people who participated in that. We sacrificed our history on the altar of "modernity". Frankly, at least from this guy's perspective, we didn't talk about it; it was like it didn't exist. I never had anyone stand up, well there is an Army flag but the battle streamers aren't on it, and point at the battle streamers and say, look here, look here, this is your Army; this is the Army you are a part of. And you need to feel proud about that and you carry those streamers. It's kind of like the picture I just saw of the West Point "Duty, Honor, Country" speech by MacArthur. And often the clouds, often the clouds are who? Well Grant, Pershing, infantrymen, so forth, young lieutenants, young captains; it's kind of there. And that's the, I believe, the kind of environment we are trying to create or we should be trying to create so that people who are professionals call themselves professionals think of their history in that way.

The dedicated leaders that put us on track to rebuild the Army understood the importance of teaching history to leaders. Back in the days before CSI was founded, General DePuy decreed that all Leavenworth students would take three tactics electives. The evolution of combined arms warfare was one of them and plenty of the other offerings had a good dose of historical case studies. There was still a need to study thermal nuclear warfare but there was a healthy appreciation for history and our leader development programs and some of it at the heart of it was values. Some of it was working on values. An appreciation that had faded about 1940 and didn't really return until about '73, '75 in there. But in those early days, the emphasis was on tactical matters and the Army did little to use its history to develop improved strategic and operational capabilities in its senior leaders and I don't want to get into the development of *FM105* and how what was handed off to General Starry and so forth. Just suffice it to say that history was not necessarily, well some, World War II history was but at the tactical level.

By the time I came to Leavenworth as the Deputy Commandant in 1987, the Combat Studies Institute was going strong. Denny Frashe, Colonel Denny Frasche was in charge. Was sort of in charge, that's hard to say down at Combat Studies Institute who's in charge; I know Glenn is but things kind of happen. Roger Spiller was there and others. I don't think Roger Cirillo was there at the time. Now I believe that in those days this appreciation of our history flourished. And I believe we sustained this level of excellence beyond the end of the Cold War and as I've said many times, the history of the United States Army has given me strength throughout my—the latter phases of my time in the Army. It means something to me and I want to share some thoughts with you. These are kind of personal insights and I've spend a lot of time thinking about this. I was, I don't know, it feels like a hundred years ago I was asked to do this, make these remarks. It's not that long ago; it's about six or seven months, I think moved around a little bit. So I've had time to think about this.

I sent a woman around the Army when I became the chief and she's an academic and an observer. She has a couple of Ph.D.s, one of which in evolutionary biology, and she's a quantum physicist and so forth. She had written a book called Leadership in the New Science, name is Meg Wheatley, and the special ops guys were pretty into her at the time and they gave me the book, said, you ought to read this book, chief. So I did and essentially the basis, the foundation upon which the book is based is that living organisms modify themselves, I'm not going to teach you evolution, but they modify themselves based on stress and, you know, those that can modify themselves survive. So I got it. Okay, so I said, got a hold of her, talked to her for about a couple of hours, said, okay, what are you doing? You got a few weeks, go around the Army. We paid the bill, gave her a guy named Eli Rosner who was a major at the time; said, Eli, take her around the Army, bring her back and have her tell me what she found. So she walks into the room and we sit down at the round table and she said, sir, I can give it to you real short. You guys don't know what you know. So I probed her a little bit and really what she was saying was what I think might be readily apparent to all of you. The US Army has done so much that it's possible to overlook what we have done because there's no way for us in our daily lives to necessarily retrieve it so that we can contemplate. Now I understand all about Ernie May and thinking in time and the danger of going down this line of reasoning. But the Army has done a lot and there are a lot of insights that people at all levels can use; this is how so-and-so wrestled with that problem.

Okay, now along that vein, and I told Bob [Sorley] this some time ago, and some of you may even have heard me say this. Every morning when I was in Washington, I would leave the house at some ungodly hour with my dog, Minnie, and she and I would go out and she'd schlep for chipmunks and I'd kind of get my head screwed on for the day and we would walk the perimeter so to speak. But at leaving Quarters One, I would walk by the miniature portraits of every Commanding General of the United States Army from Washington on and every Chief of Staff. By the way, you ought to try that some time. It's pretty daunting to walk by those pictures because there are some real giants and needless to say, it's humbling but it was also a source of inspiration and as I would go by if I was wrestling with a problem, I would see someone there that would cause me to want to understand how that person, Marshall, for instance. You know, the famous 1939 operation when Poland gets invaded by the Wehrmacht, you know, when I had time I had no money; now I have, you know all about that. But how did he do it? How did he do what he did and how did he make the points he needed to make to generate the resources that he needed? So Marshall was important; his days at [Fort] Benning and many other things and his struggles with the president and the Allies, you know, Marshall said no to North Africa, no to Italy. I mean he was actually no, no, no and then all of a sudden, you know, he wants to go in in '42, all of which you know, and by the way he stuck with it. Character counts. Character counts. He stayed at his position, stuck with it and served this country proudly, and with honor. There's a real lesson there. I mean he said no many times, which may be, according to his son, it's one reason, according to Eisenhower's son, and there's another source on the same subject said, that may be one reason Eisenhower became the Supreme Allied Commander and not Marshall. But I don't want to get into that because I don't know enough it to draw that conclusion.

Okay, so at any rate, one of the things I thought about and Chris Gable with his book Louisiana Maneuvers, it all happened to come together at the same time. Louisiana Maneuvers became a touchstone for me as I tried to organize ourselves to get things done while I was the Chief. General Abrams, of course his picture is there and General Abrams lives in Quarters One because it was where he essentially died, and obviously a very important figure to any of us who fought in Vietnam. What I thought about it actually it was not when I saw his picture, the portrait there, it was actually not what he did in World War II which I knew. Everybody that was an Armor officer knew that. By the way, we're doing away with the 37th Armor; I guess we're sacrificing that for some, somebody's got some notion somewhere in this hierarchy about what unit should stay and which should go. Hello out there in America or in America's Army. So anyway, that's going on and I understood all of that and I understood what he did, you know, throughout his career but what really resonated with me was him in the officer corps in the Army when he was the Chief of Staff because we were in bad shape and his steady guiding hand was critical to the rebuilding of the United States Army. And we owe him a real debt of gratitude and people can learn a lot from what he did. One of the most famous episodes was actually something that just came up recently. I had mentioned to General Caslen one night at a casual dinner that in my memory, there was some sort of a oh, I don't know what you would call it; I don't want to overplay it, but the students at Leavenworth were very up in arms about the war in Vietnam, about how it ended and how things went and the values and so forth and how things worked in the divisions. General Cushman, Lieutenant General Cushman, who was the Commandant at the time, set up some seminars. We had a conference on the "Ethos of the Army" or something like that and somehow some generals in Washington were sent out to participate. These were all Vietnam generals, Vietnam era generals, general officers. And they came and the students actually asked them tough questions. And they told them, look, you know, somebody said, well this kind of stuff went on, you know, packets of medals. Everybody got a Distinguished Service Cross and so forth and so on, and they said, no they didn't and apparently some major said, well it did, sir, and it happened in your division. Boom, boom, boom, and sort of outlined it. Well General Abrams hears about this because somebody went in and whined to him about how they were scuffed up out here so Abrams was coming out to give a speech anyway and he apparently didn't say anything in the speech. He told them what he wanted to tell him and then he took Q & A. And I think he , I didn't know him personally but I think he really knew exactly what he was doing; then he had this Q & A and in that people asked some of the same questions to him. Probably more respectfully to him than they did, I would suspect. And when he went back to the airport, he told General Cushman, I think the young majors are great; they are doing good. Okay. Caring, caring, leadership. There's a real lesson there. There's a real lesson there for people who will be in leadership positions as we phase out of these wars, to listen, listen carefully and to understand the concerns, and I believe that the system is such and the leaders today are such that that comes second nature because of what happened then. But those kind of insights are important. What about Malin Craig? Malin Craig set things up, he set the stage for Marshall. Now who pays any attention to Malin Craig? I know everybody pays attention to MacArthur but how about [John L.] Hines? Hines is the same one up there beating up on the Congress, beating up on the president. Hey, listen, we're too small; you are sacrificing our readiness for other things. MacArthur said one of the worst things that ever happened was the CCC [Civilian Conservation Corps]. Now it may be a great thing for the country but it wasn't for the Army; he made sure he said that because he gave away all kinds of property and so forth and so on.

I sometimes wonder, although I've never gone into it, the role of J. Lawton Collins, Omar Bradley and even Ike after the war and what happened in June of '50. I'll let others get into all of that but all of these giants, for me, because a source of inspiration and intellectual strength, as did obviously the chiefs I knew personally. In fact, my days as the chief were actually deeply involved, not only with many forward looking things but the history of our Army and the relationship of senior leaders with Allied leaders, diplomats and politicians became my life; it became my life. And I knew who to turn to. I would turn to Hal Nelson and Bill [William A.] Stofft and others, but you can't afford not to have an appreciation for the history of the United States Army. And I did know who to turn to to ask for help and by the way, sometimes I ask them to come with me to battlefields. I didn't know why I wanted to go to the battlefield but they would ask me, well what are you worried about? What are you doing? And I'd tell them so they would take me someplace and we'd walk over these battlefields, Chancellorsville, Spotsylvania down into the Wilderness where it's hard to think about anything but trees. How the hell did they get in here? But, you know, Gettysburg, Antietam and it became a way of revitalizing my soul to get back to the history of the United States Army because by the way, it dawned on me the first time I testified that, okay, well, geez I don't know that I, you know, go up on Capitol Hill to get beat up over some obscure issue. Well I said to myself, well how would you have liked to have been Grant, Sherman, or Sheridan to go up and testify before John Gordon? That's John

Gordon of Georgia, not my grandfather. That's, you know, remember Old John and I'm up there begging for money from the southern senators for the US Army. Okay, so I said, well if they could do that, I can do what I got to do so off I went.

I don't want to bore you anymore with my journey but I will tell you a little story. I was in Saratoga last Saturday night speaking to the Army National Guard of New York. Famous outfit, needless to say. The Zouaves at Antietam, you know, the firefighters and you all know about that history. So anyway I talked to them, pumped them up a little bit about what they did in Iraq and Afghanistan. Performed magnificently, one of the iconic pictures of the war in Afghanistan is a Chinook with its rear landing wheels on a hot house up in some god forsaken valley in Afghanistan. I mean it's a huge feat of airmanship and very courageous, so I talked about that with them. So I left Saratoga Springs early on Sunday morning to drive up to Norwich to Northfield and I crossed into Vermont at Whitehall, which is actually was called Skenesborough in the 1700s; that happens to be the name he listed as the home of the United States Navy and I'll tell you why in a minute. But as I was crossing the river, I was thinking about these remarks and as I looked out you go right from the river valley to the mountains of Vermont and what do I think about? I don't think about scenery; I think about terrain. How would I move up this valley? How would I do this? How would I get across this river? And then I see the sign "Skenesborough-Whitehall." That happens to be where Benedict Arnold built the tin gondolas, the gunboats, which he used to keep the British away from Ticonderoga and Saratoga and the Hudson River the first time they made the attempt, so he delayed them for a year. It dawned on me that scenery is terrain and the history is like that MacArthur picture to me. It's like the mural at West Point. You can not be a senior leader in the United States Army and not have an appreciation for all of this which has gone before us. It's a transcendent thought; it's a transcendent thing that happens and I believe what you people do here at the Combat Studies Institute and what happens at Leavenworth and other places, and what happens in the units when the commanders walk the grounds of Leavenworth and stand in front of the peach orchard and ask their officers where was Lee? This was the main attack, where was he? Not to make a value judgment of where he was but to understand the calculus Lee used not to be with Longstreet but to be with his two inexperienced corps commanders. That's a hypothesis, by the way; I have no idea why he was where he was. But the imponderables are worth thinking about with your officers and non-commissioned officers, and I think senior leaders and the school house are where the lessons are learned. And I can tell you when I first came in the Army, that was not the case. And I will never forget that I was a captain in 1964 enrolled in the Armor Officer Career Course; there were 12 of us, one of whom was Andy O'Meara; Bill Carpenter, Don Smart. These were all men who were commissioned about, in '59, '58. Each of us had been in Vietnam as advisors and do you think anybody at Fort Knox gave two hoots and a holler about the 12 of us in the back of the room? No way. No way, we were irrelevant. This is '64, '65. We're irrelevant to people who had been training in Europe who could say "Ulm", with the proper, you know, diction and so forth and so on; we didn't know anything about Ulm or Friedberg or all of that. What we knew about, what I knew about was Moon So Ni [sp?], the 1st Calvary Division and a fake 2d Armored Division, that's what I knew. Hey, what's Sullivan, what do these guys know? Well, you know, we graduated in '65 and by '70, you know the rest of the story, many of them had been, some of them killed, wounded, severely wounded and so forth and so on. I can tell you gents, without an appreciation for the history of the United States Army, what we have done and what we will do, we have real problems. We have real problems.

So what is my recommendation? Well my recommendation is to continue to do what you're doing and not lean farther forward in the foxhole and shoot faster and so forth and so on but just encourage the dialogue between people who have been in Iraq and Afghanistan, and the good and the bad, and get the good and the bad out and I know you're doing that. Robust lessons learned program, CALL [Center for Army Lesson Learned], Company Command dot com, all of that is going on. Articles for publication, it's going on all the time. Revitalize staff rides; encourage the commanders to do staff rides, real, virtual and constructive. Unit histories, unit events, company battalion brigade and divisions. I must say this 37th Armor, I just heard about that, that's troublesome and it is troublesome that we tend to gloss over the experiences of men in combat, men and women in combat by changing all the time. The 172d out of Alaska. One day it's in Alaska, the next day it's the 172d. We had men and women fighting and dying in that outfit and they want to keep it. God they sent a group of wives, I think, down to talk to somebody about it and lo and behold we wake up and there's something else. Things count, symbols count; it counts to have a Big Red One on your shoulder or a 1st Cavalry patch or 101st, 82nd, 3d Infantry Rock of the Marne. These things are intangible sources of strength. I mean after all, the troopers of the 7th Calvary said that to each other in the Ardennes. We were beaten once before, we won't be beaten again. It works. It works. Dining ins, dining outs, you know.

Look, people want to be like Mike. If my battalion commander or if my squadron commander, my brigade commander and division commander is talking about this stuff, guess what? Officers want it, young officers want to emulate them. In 1981, Major General Walt Ulmer stood up at a gathering of officers and wives in Hanau, at Fliegerhorst and he said something which frankly, is one of the most important things any officer ever said to me. To the group. He didn't say it to me. He quoted the Sherman letter, March 18, '64, which went to Grant. Sherman wrote Grant a letter. Grant is in Culpepper, Sherman's down in Memphis. So Sherman says, get out of Washington; come out here, the war's going to be won out here. There was probably some truth in that but Grant obviously didn't go. Wasn't going to go for many reasons. Then down in the letter he says, throughout the war you have always been in my mind. I have always known if I were in trouble and you were still alive, you would come to my assistance. How profound. I'll tell you, I have taken that to heart ever since. I got that from Walt Ulmer in a smoky place in Hanau, Germany, a social event and I have never forgotten it. I believe that thought is what motivates soldiers, sailors, airmen and Marines and members of the Coast Guard to do what we do on battlefields all over the world. When the CG says it, huge legitimacy. Do not let anyone tell you the Army is anti-intellectual. It's not true. What is true, in my mind, is that the Army, the United States Army is action oriented. Action oriented. Ideas are critical. Innovation is critical. Brains count. Brains and courage. There is no substitute for brains. But brains must be leavened with experience, plain old common sense, love of soldiering. Read Mike Malone. You want to read about love of soldiering, read him. I'm at Schofield Barracks, what do I think of? The screen doors closing, breaking starch, Brasso, Kiwi shoe polish, sweat. That's what I think of. Mike Malone made us think about that again. Long rides in buses across Georgia. Why we love the Army; why it's a part of our life, and I believe reading and thinking those thoughts requires brains and character, and you build resilient minds, adaptive and creative minds and resilient, courageous soldiers by your programs here at Fort Leavenworth. And you ought to feel good about it and gear up for the future because it's on us. And my reading suggests to me that in spite of what the politicians might like, we are in for the long haul in the United States Army, in the Marine Corps and the special operating forces because people who operate on the ground, in my view, are the strategic weapon for the 21st century.

That's what I have to tell you troops. I love the Army. I'm proud to say I'm an American soldier. And I know it's going to sound strange for a Norwich guy to say this but the older I get, the more I feel as if somehow I am a member of a profession...that is characterized by the phrase, "The long gray line." There's a long line of us and you may not think about yourself in that way if you are not a West Point graduate but you really are part of this long gray line of men and women who have served America. Thanks a lot to all of you.

## Day 2: Featured Speaker

## Questions and Answers
## General (R) Gordon Sullivan

**John:**

Sir, thanks for a fascinating speech. One of your emphases upon history, I think, that thrills all of us. One of the most striking examples of the use of history that I'm familiar with is your LAM Task Force, your Modern Louisiana Maneuvers and could you share with us a little bit about your thought processes and the historical precedent that you were emulating and the extent to which history influenced your decision to transition the Army by the virtue of that mechanism.

**GEN Sullivan:**

Yeah. That's a great question. I obviously knew, I knew a couple of things. First of all, the General Vuono and I was the ops and then the vice so I was involved in this but it was him who drove it, created the physical. He created the plans to do the physical downsizing of the Army. You know, we dropped 500,000 in a relatively short period of time and we wanted to maintain continuity with the past as much as we could. We worked very hard to treat people with dignity and respect, those who were staying and those who were leaving, because those who were staying had to know that the ones who left were taken care of and were not just dumped like Vietnam, and we wanted to do all of that. So I became the chief, you know, he told me the day before I took over on the 19th of June of '91, which was the day before I sat at his desk and he said, Sully, I don't want to say tears were rolling down his face but it was pretty emotional. I'm going to make it sound like it wasn't but it was. He said, "It's different here than it is there and you'll find that out tomorrow". Well I did. It was different. It was different waking up the next day.

Okay, so I struggled to find a way to exercise what I think is one of my strengths, my leadership. I had to find a way to talk about a future for the Army and to operationalize that so that people might understand it that there is in spite of this downsizing, which was unsettling to the Army, that there was a way ahead. And I couldn't quite come up with the device which I needed. And about that time, Chris's book was published. I mean I knew about the Louisiana Maneuvers but I mean I knew about it and I knew about the, you know, the tank destroyer and how we shouldn't have done it but the maneuvers themselves said, well, tank destroyers are pretty good. All of that, I knew that but the book came and then I really got into it and I said to myself, this is it. This is it, because it will give me a way to think about the future with the laser and the digital communications and digital processing and focal plane array and blah blah blah, all of this stuff, which was very embryonic at the time, although based on digits. But it sounded sterile to talk about digits. And I felt that I had to have a way that those who knew the Army could say, okay, we understand what the guy is doing. I'm not completely sure that everybody did but, you know, since I was the senior officer present, that's the way it went. A piece of the action was this tank destroyer thing. I believe they probably wouldn't have bought the tank destroyer if they had some of the simulators and simulations that were here so they could have it run it over and over again and said, woah, wait a minute; this is not going to do it. And I thought that the experiments that we could do were actually more sophisticated than what they had and what they had was Louisiana and Mississippi and that kind of stuff, and that we could do it in a different way. But still do it and get into the head of the Army that there was a future out here. You know, first job of the chief is to keep hope alive. Frankly, there was a lot of that, and I think sometimes people have felt, well the guy was a cheerleader and so forth and so on but I felt and I still do feel that when you're redistributing ammo on the fire base, you're not giving everybody the harsh reality of what this really means. You know, they don't expect you to be walking around saying, well, okay, I got this from Sullivan over here, you know, I took it off him who's dead and I'm giving it to you, you know. What you expect is, okay, we're going to get out of this thing and this is what we're going to do to get out of here. And that's what I thought I had to do as the leader; I did not look at myself as just some mythical figure up in the Pentagon. It was my war. Did I want to be out in Whereverland? Yeah, sure, that's what I really wanted to do and I never thought I would be the chief. And I said, okay, that's what I'm asked to do, that's what I'll do. And I was honored to do it but I figured I had to treat it as my war and think of it that way and the Louisiana Maneuvers was a way to do that.

I said I have to have a way to talk about the future. So we'll do the experiments and I could exercise whatever talents I had as a leader through it. You know, it wasn't different times and so forth, you know, thinking in time , the purists would say, well he overdrew it or this or that. Task Force Smiths became a mantra; somebody wrote an article about that. This guy sounds like a Buddhist. Well by the way we have never failed. The US Army, in spite of all of that, has never failed the country since so...yes?

**Henry Gold:**

I don't have a question, I have a statement and I want to thank you for what you said today about soldiering being a love affair. I want to thank General Brown for personalizing an intellectual exercise that was punctuated by his personal involvement, an affair of the heart. I was very pleased to discover that Bob Sorley's title of his talk today, which I just discovered yesterday, is called "Soldering as an Affair of the Heart." That has motivated me through my entire life and I want to thank you. Those three distinguished gentlemen for sharing my feelings. Thank you.

**GEN Sullivan:**

Yeah. Yeah, it's, I think at some point in your journey as a soldier you make the swap. You just, it just happens. I tried to think about when it did, I can't. I don't know when it happened but it does. And you can not think about your life anymore as just one person; you're a part of this huge organization and it is an affair of the heart. I mean why would somebody who's 73 years old on a beautiful sunny day in northern New England think of what he's looking at as anything other than scenery? I'm thinking about actually climbing those hills. How would I have soldiers do it? That's more than this. It's this. Who else, anybody else?

**Audience Member 1:**

Sir, I got a question and it's a little bit off topic so I apologize but I've been in a lot of correspondence with (inaudible) at this center about the proper role for a retired general and what are the limits?

**GEN Sullivan:**

Well, you know, I pride myself on an interesting position because I run the Association of the US Army, so sometimes my opinions are contrary to that of the Pentagon, like pay, healthcare, so forth and so on, so but I have an institutional reason to say what I say and I know it may be, oh, parsing. But I think that, you know, for obvious reasons I think it's okay. I think, and there may be somebody who disagrees with that but I think that some of what we heard was off the ranch. I don't think that some of what we heard was what we would expect of a retired general. I think as Rick [Swain], nice to see you, Rick, I see you there under that moustache; I didn't recognize you initially, he wrote a very interesting piece on all of that. I think it was beyond what one would expect and this constant drum beat by a couple of them is somewhat troublesome. Distinguished officers in their own right, and I can't quite figure it out. And I think that this critiquing of senior leaders in uniform and second guessing and so forth for general officers is over the line. And constant appearing on TV as the world's living expert about events which you might even not even understand, I think is frankly beyond the pale too. I don't like it. I don't like it. I'm not sure frankly how they can rationalize some of what they've said. General Vessey said once, take advantage of a perfect opportunity to keep your mouth shut. (pause) I don't know what are they saying about it? Since this is a dialogue, what's West Point saying about it?

**Dr. Sorley:**

Well I was talking to…do you know Don Slander?

**GEN Sullivan:**

Don Slander, yeah, hell yeah.

**Dr. Sorley:**

(inaudible)

**GEN Sullivan:**

He can't. It doesn't work. You're coming in weak and distorted, Bob which is a great Armor expression when—

**Dr. Sorley:**

Broken and stupid is the other one. But, yeah, thanks. Of course this would be the one that doesn't work, but what they are saying, sir, out there is that how you are really bound not to say anything that will damage the institution in any way. If you are, attain the title of a professional, you are a steward of that profession for the rest of your life essentially and once you take off your uniform, you still have an obligation to those that are still in it not to in any way harm it. So I guess it's the do no harm rule.

**GEN Sullivan:**

I can tell you, that is a much more elegant expression of it than what I was stumbling through. I believe the most important thing to be able to say to anybody is, I'm an American soldier and proud of it. And to think that someone, some senior general would critique someone who he probably had a role in creating...I mean I don't get it. I don't get it. That's my way of thinking about it. I just don't get it. And I don't like it, and I don't think it should happen. And Rick, I mean his paper, have you read his paper? It's a very good paper. I mean we're still on the payroll in a crass sense but it's more important that it transcends money. That's not to say you might not have an opinion about something but, you can have your opinions but it just depends on how you talk about your opinions and where you talk about them.

**Dr. Sorley:**

And what was the, of course the context of this is if you disagree with the policy, there are those who say, well General (inaudible), you don't get to contradict judicial policy. And there's the school of thought that says, well, who has a more informed opinion about how the policy translates into operations than the retired general officers? So that is a positive attribution to the public discourse. To have an actual expert opinion and not self-appointed pundits and self-appointed experts who spend 72 hours on the ground and therefore know all there is to know.

**GEN Sullivan:**

Well some of those who are doing it are those expert opinions. I can tell you the week after I walked out of the Pentagon, I didn't know what was going on. I'm in the Pentagon a lot and I talk to people a lot. I don't think I'm a, I mean I understand the broad outlines of what's going on in Afghanistan and what happened in Iraq but it's vicarious. I did not use Marshall, that business about Marshall and saying to the President of the United States and our British Allies, I don't think we should go to North Africa; I view Italy as a sideshow and in a sense, you know, you could argue that it was although in another sense. There's two sides to that coin and then of course his desire to invade the continent in '42...but he gave his opinion and he didn't go to the Washington Post or the New York Times and say, well I told the President this. He kept his mouth shut. Colin Powell, by the way has any stage he wants and people pay him tons of money to be on any stage that he wants, and he doesn't have anything. He doesn't critique anybody; he goes along. And you know the example I give to people at Carlyle? The question has never come up here. It's normally Carlyle. General Shinseki said what he said in the course of his duty. He was asked three or four times and he finally gave an answer. He was obliged to do that, give me your personal opinion. When he retired is when you see the mark of the man. He was offered tons of money to write a book for political reasons and he didn't do it. Character counts. Character counts and I believe most officers can process what I just said. Character counts.

**Mr. Gott:**

Sir, our time has ended for this panel. I'd like to introduce the Director of the Combat Studies Institute, Dr. William Glenn Robertson who would like to say a few words, sir.

**Dr. Robertson:**

General Sullivan, we thank you for those most inspiring words. I heard last night that we had made a great faux pas in that we had not gotten you a copy of our latest publication on the current conflict in Afghanistan, A Different Kind of War, done by our Contemporary Operation Studies team. So on behalf of General MacFarland, the LD&E community, Combat Studies Institute and the Combined Arms Center, I'd like to present you with this copy of "A Different Kind of War."

**GEN Sullivan:**

Thanks a lot. Thanks a lot. Thank you. Thanks. It means more to me to get it this way than to get it some other way so thanks a lot. Thank you.

# Day 2, Panel 4: Conventional and Unconventional Challenges of the Cold War, 1945-1975

## Soldiering as an Affair of the Heart by Lewis Sorley, Ph.D.
(Transcript of Presentation)

**Mr. Ramsey:**

OK, we'll begin now with the next panel. Panel number four today will deal with conventional and unconventional challenges of the Cold War, 1945-1975. We have two former soldiers and practicing historians. I happen to know them both from a previous life and have the greatest respect for both of them. We'll have Dr. Sorley first and he'll give his presentation, and then we'll have Dr. Gole.

Dr. Lewis Sorley was a graduate of the Military Academy. He was experienced in armoring armored cavalry units. He also worked with the CIA. He taught at the Military Academy and the Army War College, and he received his Ph.D. from Johns Hopkins University. He's written numerous books; among them are biographies of Creighton Abrams, General Howard K. Johnson, and General Brown mentioned his well received book *A Better War*, which deals with Vietnam. I just want to mention that he's done three edited works, one of which CSI published last year, a two volume study called *Press On: The Selected Works of General Donn A. Starry*. Dr. Sorley's presentation today is titled *Soldiering as an Affair of the Heart*. Now, Dr. Sorley.

**Dr. Sorley:**

Well, you know the old saying in Vaudeville, never follow the dog act. But I have to tell you, I am honored to follow my friend Gordon Sullivan, and I told him outside that I have heard him speak many times and I have never been more moved than I was this morning. If that was not straight from the heart about what it means to be a soldier, then I'm never going to hear anything like that. It's also a good lead-in to what my good friend Henry Gole and I want to talk about. Everybody who stood up here practically has said something about what it means to come back to Fort Leavenworth, and I'm going to follow in that mode.

I came here at the age of four. My father was a student officer, and we lived in the Beehive. The Beehive in those days was a residential building, full of kids and dogs and bicycles and a great place to live. And I think this is the earliest thing I can remember on my own, as compared to, you know, what you hear your parents talk about, and it was the Stable Sergeant who came on Saturday morning with ponies, and we stood at the curb with a nickel in our mitten, and Corporal then Isaac Harris, a Buffalo soldier, long OD (olive drab) overcoat with rows of brass buttons, came with the reins of ponies in his hand, and we gave him the nickel and he put us on the pony and took us once around the Beehive, which if you're four looks like a pretty long trip. And I thought about him for many years, and I was talking about him once when my sister was visiting and was at my dinner table, and she said, "Oh, Bob, I think you have a picture of him in your baby book." I don't know if they have baby books anymore; I haven't looked at mine in 25 years, but I ran down in the basement and got it, and sure enough, there's a picture of Corporal Harris with the reins of three ponies in his hand. On the left pony is Buzzy Glinch, age four, later my classmate at West Point; on center pony is me; and on the other pony, we haven't figured out who that kid was yet, but I hope we can someday. Anyhow, you know that they closed the Beehive as a residence and later rehabbed it and reopened it as a gaming center, so I asked Leavenworth if they would accept a gift from me, and they said they would, so we had this blown up and nicely framed, and if you go in the foyer, you don't even have to have the clearance to go inside, just go in the foyer of the now Beehive Gaming Center or whatever, you'll see this picture of Corporal Isaac Harris, nicknamed Horse because of the ponies. And I learned about him, I kept tracking down more and more about him. I learned about him from General Truscott's great memoir, *The Twilight of the United States Cavalry*, and to my delight I learned that he didn't just get the nickels we kids gave him but that at Christmastime the fathers gave him some real money. And so he's commemorated there, and I think the plaque says something like this: "In memory of Corporal Isaac 'Horse' Harris, whose Saturday morning pony rides brought joy to a generation of Army kids." So that's my early Leavenworth recollection, and I love to come back here, especially since I got a little short shrift. The Army, in its wisdom, sent me to the Naval Command and Staff School, and that was fun but not as, I would've loved to have been here, too. I wish I could've done both.

I want to say something about John Brown, who got this conference off to such a wonderful start, and I told him last night at dinner that I was delighted that every succeeding speaker had found some reason to make reference to the remarks that John began with, and John mentioned an experience in his early service when he took command of a tank platoon and had some very inadequate subordinates there, and he's such a gentleman that he didn't rat me out as the battalion commander at that time, but that was me. (laughter) And John, I'm very sorry I wasn't able to do more for you then, but that's what we had! But you handled it, you handled it really well, and I've always been proud of you. And I will say this, too, since General Sullivan gave us such an eloquent testimonial not only to the utility but to the power of historical example and historical recollections, the Army in Europe at that time, we're talking very early 1970s, was really in a terrible state. It was short of everything there was to be short of, and the soldiers that we had were, a lot of them anyhow, had been enlisted or drafted. They had served a tour in Vietnam, and then they were within months, literally, of being eligible for discharge, but to keep our NATO numbers up instead of sending them home or putting them somewhere in the States they sent them in Germany, maybe three, four months to serve. And they didn't want to be there, of course; what they wanted to be was out of the Army and home, and frankly I didn't blame them. In an effort to motivate these young soldiers I tried to learn all I could about the history of that battalion because it was a direct lineal descendent of the battalion Colonel Abrams had had in World War II, the 37th Tank Battalion, and, in fact, this battalion, 2d Battalion, 37th Armor, was directly descended from B Company of the 37th Tank Battalion that had been commanded by a great soldier named Jimmy Leach, a later Chief of Armor Branch. So, you know, I went to Bastone and learned all I could about that. I wrote a little three or four page history of the battalion, had that mimeographed, passed that around, gave little talks on this and that and the other thing to the officers and the sergeants and the soldiers, and I wish I could tell you that that had a big effect but frankly I don't think I influenced anybody very much, in large part because we were turning over about a quarter of the outfit every 90 days, because, you know, these youngsters would finish their three, four months, and then they'd go home and be discharged. And it wasn't just us, it was pretty much that's the way it was in Germany in those days. But the one, I'll say, saving grace is that in the process of that I influenced myself considerably, so much so that when I later looked around and I didn't see anybody telling what I thought was the great story of Creighton Abrams, not only in World War II but thereafter, and eventually I thought I would try to do that myself. So anyway, John, I'm very proud of what you've accomplished since then, and I wish I could've gotten you off to a happier start, but that's the way it was!

**John Brown:**

That was only momentary. The next day was much better. (laughter)

**Dr. Sorley:**

I also wanted to thank you for explaining something to me that I've wondered about for a long time. You showed the acumen for leadership, and then, you know, loyalty and all those things, and I had always wondered why they had their seven things, and why they had two of them were two words instead of having nice, clean one word for each one, and I think I now understand. They didn't put just 'courage', they put 'personal courage' so they could have something started with a P, so thank you, thanks for explaining that to me! I've wondered about that for years. And I would like to give myself a little credit, also: I once invented an acronym, a very useful acronym. As cadets we were, of course, taught the principles of war, and we were supposed to be able to regurgitate those on command, and so I invented the following acronym: MANEUVER US MOOSES. (laughter) So 'maneuver' is one of them, of course, U is unity of command, S is one of their three S's. You can make it whatever, maybe simplicity, and then you go on, mass objective and so on spells MOOSES. Well, everybody can remember MANEUVER US MOOSES, so a lot of my classmates are very proud of me for that, and so now I'll consider myself a connoisseur of acronyms, thanks to you.

I really enjoyed yesterday, and I would characterize what we talked about yesterday maybe as dealing primarily with institutional approaches to leadership and the teaching of leadership, and so today I would like to talk about an individual approach to leadership and the teaching of leadership, and maybe you could look at those as two ends of a spectrum. You know, General Sullivan talked about the school and the unit and the self study as the three pillars of education, not only in these fields but, I think he'd agree, in all professional fields. So no big surprise to anybody here, at least anybody who knows me, I would like to talk about Creighton Abrams, and I want to talk about some of the examples of his leading by example at various levels, and then maybe draw from that some analysis of the quality of, qualities of leadership he exemplified and what that had to do with the concept and teaching of leadership during the years that he served.

You know, yesterday we played around a little bit with the age old question of whether leaders are born or made, and I think the respectable middle ground is that there are some of each, and maybe you could argue also that no matter whether they're made you can

PANEL 4

maybe improve on what they start with, and I suggested that the whole premise of our school system is that yes, leaders can be made, or at least improved. And I believe that, or I wouldn't be here. So I hope that you will agree with that, too.

A soldier who was with Abrams in World War II, Lieutenant Colonel, then Abrams Commanding Officer of 37th Tank Battalion later said, "Colonel Abrams never talked much about leadership, he just exampled it," and I thought that was a nice formulation. Abrams was commissioned in the Cavalry in 1936 when he graduated from West Point, and he was assigned a troop duty in the famous 7th Cavalry, in those days, of course, still the horse cavalry. And as almost everyone here knows, I'm sure the Depression era Army was a very austere organization, and the unit that Abrams joined, like many, perhaps most in those days, was, interesting to me, short-handed in soldiers but up to strength in horses. Now, I'm not sure why, but what that meant was, you know, horses can't just lie around. They have to be exercised, and so the way they would do this is they would go out, a soldier would ride one horse and he'd have two on leads, so he'd exercise three horses on one go round, and they were out doing this one day, they're moving across the desert near Fort Bliss. Abrams was at the head of the column and one of the soldiers with him was a new private who was named Sanford, and Sanford was having a little trouble with his horses. So he started around one side of a sand dune with the horse he was riding, and those he was leading decided to go around the other side. Brief tug of war, inevitably, of course, lost by Sanford with the result that he ended up being pulled out of his saddle and dragged across a sand dune, which, of course, was covered with mesquite and cactus, and this roughed up poor Sanford no little bit. I'm telling you this because Abrams is a brand new officer. You know, he's been through West Point, and that's about it, and he used this mishap to apply what I later learned was a technique he used throughout his career, and that was to make an example of somebody he thought was doing a good job. So when the troops had gotten back to stable and they looked after the horses, Abrams lined his soldiers up, and he said to them, "You men can take Private Sanford here as an example." They pulled him right off his horse, but by God, he didn't let loose of his lead horses. Sanford told me 40 years later this had a tremendous effect on him. "There I stood," he said, "with my ass full of mesquite and cactus stickers but just proud as hell." (laughter) Well, more to the point, it had an impact on all those other soldiers. Here's a lieutenant, a brand new lieutenant and a brand new private, and he's holding this guy up as an example. And I could give you a number of other cases of that, but I think that was a wonderful technique.

Even in those early days of his service Abrams demonstrated another quality that he would later describe as an essential attribute of successful leadership, and I happen to agree with this so I'm going to quote it to you, too: you have to like soldiers. And often he would, in illustrating this point, he would recall an occasion, again at Bliss when he's a brand new officer, when he is the Duty Officer. And late one evening some soldiers who had been on pass in town, El Paso, and had enjoyed themselves quite a bit, came back to post with a couple of alligators that they had borrowed from the El Paso Zoo. (laughter) This is going to be trouble. They put these alligators in the basement of one of the barracks and tossed in a couple of smoke bombs and locked the door and pulled the fire alarm. Well, before long the Post Fire Department arrives, and, of course, so does the Duty Officer, Lieutenant Abrams, and the Fire Department arrives. They've been chopping down the doors with their axes and hosing down the premises, and Abrams described this later with some relish. He said, "The Fire Department came in and they knocked down the doors and they got in there with their hoses and the alligators and the smoke, and," he says, "it was really a mess." And he added, "Of course, you can't authorize that kind of thing," but you could hear the smile in his voice when he said it. No real harm was done. I guess the alligators made it back; I don't know that. But Abrams enjoyed soldiers, and he had a lot of stories to tell about them, and many times those stories were at his own expense. I'll just ad lib one very briefly because it'll illustrate that aspect of it.

Abrams is later commanding the great 2d Armored Cavalry Regiment, and down in one of the squadrons a master sergeant is court marshaled for some offense, and he is busted all the way down to private first class, and he had considerable service, and Abrams reviews this and he concludes that that's too harsh, and so he amends that to only one grade reduction and he takes the sergeant into his headquarters, you know, regimental level headquarters, and he has him in and he gives him a heart to heart talk, and he decides to put him in charge of the post theater. And he says, "Now sergeant, I'm giving you another chance. Go and make a better life for your family." This is about, let's say, the 20th of December. On Christmas Eve the sergeant absconds with the proceeds of the theater and never seen since. (laughter) Abrams tells that story on himself. I rather like that. I know some general officers who probably never admit anything went wrong on their watch.

The young officers, Abrams and Bruce Palmer, Jr. and others of their ilk in these late 1930s units, they understood that they were in the last days of the horse cavalry. There were many things they found valuable there, and yet as World War II approached and a newly forming mechanized corps came along, lots of them volunteered for service with that, Abrams among them and Bruce Palmer and others, and so before long, 27 years old, just six years out of West Point, Abrams took command of a tank battalion, and he trained them hard. In training preparatory to going overseas on the gunnery range Abrams or one of his battalion staff officers would ride on the back deck of the tank to observe how the crew performed and what they did on the gunnery range, and they'd coach and critique. Well, some of the company commanders came to Abrams and they said that it made them nervous to have a staff officer riding the back deck of their tank. "Well," Abrams said, "if that makes them nervous, what are they going to do when the Germans start shooting at them?" And so that was the end of that complaint. And Abrams set some fairly demanding standards for how quickly you had to get off the first round and get a first round hit, how quickly you had to get off the second round. Before long, the company commanders are back. They say the standards are too tough, it's impossible to do that in the time that Abrams said, specified. So Abrams gets some members of his battalion staff and he forms them into a little impromptu tank crew and they do a couple dry runs, and then they go out with him as a tank commander and they go through the gunnery course and show how it could indeed be done within the parameters that he had established. And so that was the end of the complaints on that front. And that's the way it went.

The battalion that Abrams took into combat, 37th Tank Battalion, had as its motto "Courage conquers," and I'm going to say if ever a unit lived up to its motto it was this one. I once gave a talk based entirely on unit mottos and what they revealed about Army

Panel 4

values, and I had a lot of fun putting that together, but John and I later served in the unit and wore the crest that said "Courage conquers," and I was always very proud about that. And when they got into combat, staff officers at higher levels, division and corps, later revealed that, and they would set their radios to Abrams' frequency just to be entertained by his hard driving brand of leadership. Said a tank driver from his battalion, "I can recall during our tank battles Abe was right alongside of our tank, giving orders to my tank commander and having a ball, shooting tanks like the rest of the boys. He would mix in wherever the toughest battle was. It made us feel more like fighting harder when you could see a great man like Abe right alongside of you." As the conflict neared its end the 4th Armored Division's commander wrote, "The brilliant combat record of Lieutenant Colonel Creighton Abrams constitutes one of the sagas of this war." His command was the first to cross the Moselle River, he led the advance which resulted in the relief of Bastogne, and his was the first element in Third Army to reach the Rhine. In the process Abrams won two distinguished service crosses, two Silver Stars and a battlefield promotion to Colonel, but he gave the credit to his soldiers, writing near the war's end to his wife Julie to say, "I have traveled in gallant company."

Now, I would like to say that despite these impressive battlefield accomplishments, what continues to move me most about Abrams as a combat leader is how his men remembered him. "I have fond memories of the kind of man Abrams was," said one of his maintenance sergeants. "He never made things more difficult and unhappy than they were, as did some of the officers of far less rank." A tank commander said, "I remember his big smile and hard handshake when I got my Silver Star." And another, "When he smiled, his smile was complete." Remembered a radio operator who wrote to Abrams many years later, "I have never forgotten your strong sense of values and magnetic feeling of leadership. I still respect you as a soldier and love you as a fine human being. I teach children to grow up to be like General Abrams." I ask you to imagine being a commander in combat, and tough combat and continuous combat, and inspiring that kind of admiration. His reconnaissance sergeant, who I got to know quite well and was with Abrams all the way, spoke of his essential modesty. "He was," he said, "no changed from a captain to a colonel." Said another, writing to Julie Abrams after her husband's death, "Abe had a tremendous effect on me when we and the world were young. His strength of character and kindness he was wont to show to civilian soldiers, such as myself, is a memory I cherish. The time I spent in his command I consider to be the most fortunate period of my life." And said another, a company commander, "I consider that Abe was one of the major forces influencing my life. I often think about him, even today." This was many years after Abrams' death. "His memory has never left me." A lieutenant from one of the division's armored infantry battalions, later a lieutenant general, this is Dewitt Smith, for whom I served at the War College, said, "As a very senior officer, Abrams seemed much the same," as he had known him in World War II, "a little older, of course, a little chunkier, perhaps more reserved, but the essential qualities remained unchanged: moral courage to go with the physical courage of another day; dignity; strength; a sense of humor; philosophical; total integrity; and great wisdom. Above all, integrity and wisdom." "Character counts," General Sullivan told us.

Shortly after the end of World War II Abrams was back in Europe and in command of another tank battalion, this one called the 63d, the only tank battalion in the European theater in these early days of the Occupation Army. He wasn't too happy with that at first. His outlook was he'd commanded a tank battalion when it counted, in combat, but he soon found out that commanding one in post World War II Europe was a lot more challenging than commanding one in Germany, where all you really had to worry about was the enemy. But he pitched into it the way he pitched in to everything else. He had an Adjutant. Some of you will know the name, Hazard, who later became a colonel. Hazard was the S1, the S2, the S4, the S everything basically, because the other staff officers were not too sharp. Abrams would take officers out of the companies if he didn't think they were performing too well, and he'd put them on his staff where he could sort of help them along. So Saturday mornings, we worked until noon on Saturdays in those days, Saturday morning Abrams would come in and he'd say to Hazard, "Well, what are we going to be dissatisfied with this morning?" And Hazard said, he came in with his overcoat on and his helmet on, and he looked like he was going to Bastogne, but he's going out to inspect the companies. But in the process of setting high standards and being exacting in insisting that they be met, Abrams also, and this is crucially important, I think, made it fun and challenging and exciting. There was a young lieutenant in that battalion that later became a general officer who told me that he didn't go on leave for two years. Why? "I was afraid I'd miss something," he said.

Over the years, from what I've told you now what I'm about to tell will come as no surprise, I'm sure, over the years Abrams emphasized the overwhelming importance of the soldier. "People are not in the Army," he said over and over again, "People are the Army." And often elaborating he would add, "By people I do not mean personnel. I do not mean in strength. I do not mean MOSs. I do not mean files. I do not mean any such categories that deal with people as a commodity. I mean living, breathing, serving human beings. They have spirit and will, and they have strengths and weaknesses, and they have names and faces. Whatever is accomplished," he said, "is accomplished with people. They are the heart of our preparedness, and this preparedness as a nation and as an Army depends upon the spirit of our soldiers. Without it we cannot succeed."

A closely related matter was tradition, and again, Abrams was passionate on the topic. "Tradition is important for an Army, for our Army," he told members of the Old Guard. "It gives us pride in ourselves and our abilities, it helps us set great standards, it instills faith in ourselves and in the country, and," he added, "management cannot do this. Efficiency isn't the only requirement. We need to form links with the past, a past that gives us real pride, deep pride." Senior civilian officials of the Army were among those influenced by the Abrams example, especially as they moved up into the higher ranks. One of these was Paul Ignatius, who was then an Assistant Secretary of the Army. When he was new in his job he made his first trip to visit the Army in Europe. Abrams was then commanding the 3d Armored Division, one stop on the Ignatius itinerary. The unit was in training at Grafenwöhr. As Abrams took Ignatius around to visit various companies and platoons, said Ignatius later, "General Abe never intruded himself between me and the immediate unit commander. They would arrive at a unit, land the helicopter, and General Abrams would disappear, and I must say," continued Ignatius, "that I did not find in subsequent visits an officer in all of the services who was willing to do that. He wasn't there, standing there listening to what they were saying or coaching them in their answers, and I felt that this was an indication of the confidence he had in his people, and really the confidence he had in himself."

The first time Abrams went to this chapel serving the 3d Armored Division Headquarters after taking command of the Division, he found that they had no choir, so the next Sunday he showed up in choir robe with hymnal and processed down the aisle right behind the chaplain, a choir of one. Next Sunday, full choir, full chapel. Everyone wanted to see Abrams in a choir robe following the chaplain down the aisle, result of his example.

Like most senior officers, as Abrams went around the division visiting various elements he often met soldiers he had served with on earlier occasions. One of those in the 3d Armored Division was Sergeant Love, a platoon sergeant. I've spent much effort trying to find Sergeant Love but never succeeded, I'm sorry to say. Abrams said to Love, "Well, how are the troops that you've been getting in?" And Sergeant Love told him, "They were great," he said. One was a young man who wanted to be a tank driver, but to have a driver's license you had to be a high school graduate, so Love had enrolled this young soldier in a GED program, and sometimes on the weekend he'd stop by the house and Mrs. Love would help him with the math. Another newly assigned soldier had been very homesick, said Love. He was about the age of Love's oldest son, and so they'd have him over to the house for dinner every week or so, and the two boys became friends, and that helped a lot with the homesickness, and so on, stories illustrating that Love knew and cared about every soldier entrusted to his leadership. When Abrams got back to his headquarters that evening he was talking with the division sergeant major, I mean, excuse me, Judge Advocate, and he said to his top lawyer, "If we had more Sergeants like Sergeant Love, you'd be out of a job."

Later Abrams would go back to Europe and command V Corps, next higher level up from 3d Armored Division, and he had 3d Armored Division as one of the divisions under his command then, and demonstrated that despite being elevated to that level he still focused on the soldier. So during the course of a winter maneuver he happened on a young trooper who, if you've been to Europe this will resonate for you, inexperienced in operating on the high crowned roads that were now icy and wet, had managed to slide his tank off the road and into a deep ditch. Abrams stopped his Jeep and he went over to talk to the tank driver. "Having trouble, son?", he asked. "Yes, sir," said the soldier disconsolately. "Here, let me show you how," said Abrams. With that he took the youngster's place in the driver's seat, gunned the engine up to such a pitch that the crowd which had gathered thought the transmission would surely be ripped out of the hull, and Abrams neatly popped the tank right out of the ditch and up on a road. "There," he said, "see how it's done?" "Yes, sir," said the tank driver. "Think you can do it?", said Abrams. "Yes, sir." "Good," said Abrams, and with that he reversed the tank back into the ditch, climbed out, got in his Jeep, and without another word or backward glance drove away. (laughter)

Now, I've been giving you anecdotes about exampling leadership, as one young soldier once said about it, but as he became more seniored, just as we saw General Sullivan here today, Abrams also, of course, was asked to talk about leadership, and there were some few points that he came back to again and again, and many had to do with the essential elements of principled leadership. "Nobody on the face of the Earth can take honesty away from anybody," he said. "If you're going to lose it, you've got to give it up yourself." He had these sayings that, you know, the people picked up and repeated around, and so one of those dealt with what I'll say, I'll call essential modesty. He often said, "There's no end to what can be accomplished if you don't care who gets the credit." His wife Julie told me he got that from General Marshall, which I would like to believe is the case. That's a nice lineage. Asked another time to speak about leadership, Abrams stressed his conviction that leadership in our Army involved service. "What the country needs, what the country expects: it is," he stressed, "beyond material compensation. Nobody can buy it and nobody can sell it. It has to come from the heart." And thus, one of his favorite sayings, "Soldiering is an affair of the heart."

When he was invited to West Point to talk to cadets of the First Class about leadership, Abrams told them, "What you are about to come into this summer," when they graduate and were commissioned, "is a kind of service which in my opinion is what the country needs and, to a large degree, what the country expects. You cannot be compensated or reimbursed for it in a material way. There isn't a salary that is adequate for what is needed and expected. What the country needs and expects from you as leaders just isn't for sale anywhere in the world. Nobody can buy it and nobody can sell it. It has to come from the heart." Like most senior officers, Abrams frequently had occasion to testify before some element of the Congress. A famous anecdote concerns an occasion when, as Vice Chief of Staff, he was a witness at hearings on the proposed Army budget, and, you know, they go from one topic to the next to the next, and so someone asked him whether the Army needed a new handgun to replace the Model 1911 caliber 45 pistol that was then still in use. "Well," responded Abrams, evaluating the 45, "it all depends on the circumstances. In a crowded elevator there's no finer weapon." (laughter) And I've seen the transcript, and they move on to the next item. And I see the hook is coming here, so I'll move quickly now.

Years later, still on the Congress for a minute, in a tribute to Abrams after his death, a Senator McIntyre recalled those occasions when Abrams had been a witness. "In the veritable sea of uniforms, faces, and voices that flows before the Committee each year," said the Senator, "his voice stood out. His voice, unlike some, was not loud, not overbearing, not pompous, not righteous, not indignant, not demanding. No, his voice was quiet. His thoughts were personal and candid. He spoke modestly with force and meaning." I submit that that, too, was an example of leadership by example. Abrams spent, as I'm sure you know, five years in Vietnam, the last four as commander of American forces there, and during that time our forces were being drawn down. I believe, and there are good historians here; try me on this, I believe Abrams may be the only example of the commander of an expeditionary force who sent his Army home before himself. And so as these units went, Abrams would go and talk to them, units that sometimes had been there for years on end, and he told them goodbye and he thanked them for what they had done. An example was the 1st Infantry Division, in which he said, "In a changing world, changing times, and changing attitudes, the 1st Infantry Division represents a constancy of those essential virtues of mankind: humility, courage, devotion, and sacrifice. The world has changed a lot," he said, "but this division continues to serve as it had in the beginning, and I choose to feel that this is part of the cement and the rock and the steel that holds our great country together." And then, I've heard the recording, a husky voice, husky with emotion, he closed

## Panel 4

by quoting back to them the division's own great motto, "No mission too difficult, no sacrifice too great, duty first."

Finally, it was time for Abrams himself to say goodbye, and on the last night in Vietnam, speaking to fellow officers in the command mess, Abrams told them this: "The longer I serve, the more convinced I become that the single most important attribute of the professional officer is integrity." As you know, Abrams went on to be Chief of Staff of the Army, and to put it on the road to recovery after the long ordeal of Vietnam. Abrams died after just under two years in office, after which General Jack Vessey, former Chairman of the Joint Chiefs of Staff, said this: "When Americans watched the stunning success of our armed forces in Desert Storm, they were watching the Abrams vision in action. The modern equipment, the effective air support, the use of the Reserve components, and, most important of all, the advanced training which taught our people how to stay alive on the battlefield were all seeds planted by Abe."

I'm going to skip ahead now because I don't want to use more time than I should. I'll just say this: I interviewed probably 5 or 600 people over the course of a number of years in working on the Abrams story. Since he died before he retired they weren't able to do the usual end of career interviews at the Military History Institute that they do with senior officers. Lieutenant General Dewitt Smith was the commandant then, he's the one I quoted about the younger Abrams and the older Abrams, so he cranked up a special oral history program called The Creighton Abrams story, and pairs of student officers went around and interviewed people. Over time 55 different people were interviewed, including General Abrams' widow and his sister and people who served with him at every level of command, and different, you know, groups of students would do this as one year would end and another year would start and so on, and over time they realized that they were only getting very positive stuff and they were getting worried that they would be criticized that they had just done a puff job, so they began to tell their interviewers, the people they were interviewing, interviewees, this and ask them, you know, "Isn't there anything on the other side?" And they got to George Patton, the younger, who had known Abrams very well, including from the 63d Tank Battalion post World War II. And Patton says, "Oh yeah, hell yes." He said, "Abe had his faults just like any of us, but not very goddamn many of them," and that's all he would tell them. (laughter) And so, you know, I tried in the books that I have written about him to say the things that I thought I had deduced, and one of them was you wouldn't want to encounter him very early in the morning. He got off to a rough, you know, sort of a rough bear start, and he did drink a lot and enjoyed it, and people liked to drink with him. Nobody would ever say that it had adversely expected his performance of duty, and I haven't found any examples where I thought I could say that it had, and that was about it. You know, that was about all that I could find.

When he died, as I said, General Smith was the commandant at War College, and he had a monument erected there. If you've been to Carlisle Barracks I'm sure you've seen it; it's just a chunk of rock, really, and it's just right outside the main entrance so every student will see it every day when he or she leaves the college, and has on it these few words of Abrams' own: "There must be," he said, "within our Army a sense of purpose and a dedication to that purpose. There must be a willingness to march a little farther, to carry a heavier load, to step out into the darkness and the unknown for the safety and well being of others." Even now, 40 years later, I think that is his message to us from beyond the grave.

I've been talking about leadership by example and the teaching of leadership by example. I know that not all of us can be Creighton Abrams or be like Creighton Abrams, but what I think we can do is learn from and be inspired by the example of someone like Creighton Abrams, and in that most magnificent of all Army recruiting slogans, do our dead level best to be all that we can be. Thanks very much. (applause)

**Mr. Ramsey:**

Thank you, Dr. Sorley. Our next presenter is Dr. Gole. Henry spent a lot of time overseas. He was an infantryman in Korea. He served two tours in Vietnam as a Special Forces officer. He also taught at the Military Academy and the War College. He has a degree, a Ph.D. from Temple University. He's written several books, and one of the latest one has to do with General DePuy, and his presentation today is *Leadership: DePuy, Slim, and You*. Now, Henry.

# Day 2, Panel 4: Conventional and Unconventional Challenges of the Cold War, 1945-1975

## Soldiering as an Affair of the Heart Leadership: DePuy, Slim, and You by Henry Gole, Ph.D.

(Transcript of Presentation)

**Dr. Gole:**

Thank you, Bob. First, thanks to the organizers for keeping this on track, well conceived. Interesting to me that General Brown's remarks, General Sullivan's remarks—which I hadn't heard, obviously, I had no idea what Bob was going to say—have all emphasized the unit dimension, which happens to be the thing about military service that matters the very most to me. I'm happy to see a lot of, not a lot, a few old, familiar faces, and some new ones. I'm pleased to share this session with Bob Sorley. Besides being a gentleman and a scholar and an old friend, who I first met in the archives of the Military History Institute, I don't know if he remembers that; that was our initial meeting, at Military History Institute in the old building, in the old attic, and he was plowing through some stuff for Abrams, and I was working on a book having to do with more plans. I've known him since then, and I think I can say without fear of contradiction that no one knows the officers who rose to the top of the tree, the Four Stars, the Three Stars, in the period from the '60s through the '70s, '80s, and probably until this day. Most recently he's produced the book, edited the book on General Starry, which got a very, very intelligent and positive review in the latest [edition of] *Parameters* by Greg Fontenot.

As I thought about today I thought I'd take a very small bite of a very big apple called leadership, and I conceived of this as my advice to aspiring young leaders, not a company of academics, in which connection, by the way, I felt sad to look around and to listen to this very powerful commentary by former Chiefs of Staff of the US Army and there are only 30 or 40 people in the room. I was almost wounded at that. But that is not my business. My advice to the aspiring leader is called *Leadership: DePuy, Slim, and You.* Every American recruit in basic training takes about one or two days before he pronounces on the subject of leadership. The polite form of his expression of disapproval typically includes "fowled up" or words to that effect, alliterative words to that effect. He and almost everyone else are prepared to speak on the topic of leadership. Apparently, personal experience and individual genius permits us to do that. Additionally, we can find whatever we want in a cookbook by Caesar, Alexander, Genghis Khan, Napoleon, or some other great captain, simply turn to the right page and get on with it, and if we're too lazy to read the cookbooks there are legions of experts prepared to consult and conduct seminars at your place or offsite, dispensing wisdom via PowerPoint presentations on organizational effectiveness, management, and leadership. Shake a tree and the latest theories and current buzzwords fall like leaves in the tree in the fall in the wind in Pennsylvania. Or you can hire a motivational speaker whose charisma will have us crossing the line of departure on time while smiling and singing *Onward, Christian Soldiers*. In brief, there's no shortage of gurus out there.

Panel 4

The opinion comes to us from staff colleges, business schools, academic disciplines, and from people who famously succeeded as leaders, but despite all that help here we are today still trying to get it right.

I think I'm here because the gray beard and a few books I wrote, one on DePuy. I'll be happy to tell you about DePuy. Be comforted in the knowledge that as I reflected on what I might say today that could possibly be of use in cultivating leaders, the words of my favorite poets came to mind, among them Alexander Pope who wrote *Fools Rush in Where Angels Fear to Tread*. I'll try not to be foolish. My remarks will not satisfy those raised in our Chicken Little's Military subculture who find the sky falling every day, the sky is always falling, those who believe that if something is worth doing that it's worth overdoing, and that we need to pull up plants every day to check the roots to see how well the plant is growing. We are a very impatient subculture. Some of what I learned about DePuy in my research leaped out as insights into his leadership, note the emphasis on "his leadership." Not all of the insights are of particular use to you and to me. Here are several: Be born smart as hell. DePuy was. Be raised in the 1930s in the upper Middle West, with values like hard work, honesty, respect for others, a deep sense of responsibilities, values in consonance with that time. DePuy was. To learn how this all works, tune into the Prairie Home Companion, where all the women are strong, all the men are good looking, and all the children are above average. Be a 2d lieutenant six months before a big war, and advance in grade as the Army increases by a factor of about eight in a few years. Be successful as an infantry battalion commander in combat. Pin on your Distinguished Service Cross, three Silver Stars, two Purple Hearts, serve as a division G3, be recruited by George Patton to be his aide, and do all of that by the time you're 25 years of age. Obviously, we can't all do what DePuy did. We can't all be like Mike, as General Sullivan said.

Toward the end of an interview with General Paul Gorman several years ago I told him that my research was leading me to conclude that DePuy, more than anyone else, fixed my broken Army in the post-Vietnam period. I asked if Gorman agreed. He did so without reservation or qualification. I put the same proposition to General Donn Starry. He paused, thought it over, and pronounced from Olympus with his usual precision, "I can accept that statement." Starry and Gorman played a major part in fixing my Army. Either of these enormously talented four star generals could've claimed credit for themselves for fixing that Army. They did not make that claim, though I would give them much credit for it. Gorman further stated that without DePuy it might've taken a generation to fix the Army. With DePuy's leadership it began when DePuy kicked the hornet's nest in the mid 1970s. Are you checking your bestsellers list, "kick the hornet's nest?" I thought that was a nice term.

The next question I asked Gorman was as logical as it was simple-minded: "What leadership traits might we identify in DePuy that made him effective, some clues he might pass on to young aspiring leaders?" Norman said it would be a mistake to mimic DePuy; he was unique. That was the point of my cryptic description of DePuy's personality, boyhood, and early experiences. Gorman was warning us not to try to make imitation DePuys out of our officers; it wouldn't work. Few of us have his combination of intelligence, focus, intensity, and once he decided on a course of action, ruthlessness. He was also lucid in explaining abstract concepts and detailed programs. In brief, he got more than his share of talent. I think DePuy's son got the essence of the man exactly right, as we discussed aspects of the father's personality. He called his father an autonomous man. Most of us need a pat on the back from time to time, but General DePuy didn't seem to need that. We like the approval of our peers. That didn't seem to be terribly important to him. In his professional life, General DePuy was subject to his own rules, but I want to be very clear about this: he was not a difficult subordinate. In fact, he was the very model of loyalty. And as a boss, he was scrupulous in examining all aspects of an issue and in listening very carefully to the talent that he assembled around him. However, once convinced that he hade taken the right course of action he was supremely confident and persuasive in execution. Some saw this as arrogance. He was unique, and I would tell the prospective young leader, "So are you." Gorman's observations about DePue reminded me of something Field Marshal Sir William Slim said in a presentation here at Fort Leavenworth on 8 April 1952. He said, "Command is an intensely personal affair." He was addressing command of an Army or an Army group, but he made it clear that he thought what he said applied to command at any level. It has to be exercised by each man in his own way.

He ended his talk emphasizing, "Be yourselves, because no imitation is ever a masterpiece." I commend the May 1990 issue of Military review to you for Slim's distilled wisdom in just ten pages called *Higher Command in War*. That issue also contains several other excellent articles on command, May 1990. For an extended lesson on leadership, read Slim's *Defeat Into Victory*, possibly the best World War II General's book. He began by saying, he begins his book by saying the very four best commands are a platoon, a battalion, a division, an army. How's that for setting the hook? I had to ask why those and not some others. Clever rascal, he starts that way.

See what George MacDonald Fraser has to say about Slim in his memoir of World War II, *Quartered Safe Out Here*. See what John Masters says about Slim in his personal narrative, *The Road Past Mandalay*. His soldiers loved the man for his honest and unpretentious good sense, what we used to call in the Brown Shoe Army "old shoe." It's entirely likely that you will forget what I say and you will misplace the notes that you take at this symposium. Don't worry, they'll turn up when you put in for your TDY or for your next PCS, but do yourself a favor: read Slim, Masters, and Fraser as they look at the same Burma campaign through the eyes of a rifleman, a middle grade professional officer, and the commanding general. They are fuel for your ruminations about leadership and good for your soul.

I think Slim and Gorman are absolutely right by all means: be yourself. Pearl handled pistols work for some generals. So does toting an M1 rifle or hanging hand grenades on one's chest. Thespian rhetoric served at least one famous general very well, and shouting is probably still in fashion. My friends and I as young officers noted with irony, "When in doubt yell and shout," but the Prussian officer's model rings true: Sein Stap Sein [sic], literally, "Be rather than appear to be." Perhaps better, "Essence not appearance" is a better rendering in English. Of course, this is the very opposite of cultivating an image. It means being true to yourself. But most of us prefer a human model, leadership personified, to theoretical constructs or laundry lists of principles or cardinal virtues. I'll highlight some formative experiences that shaped DePuy, and with a great deal of caution I'll leave you aspects of the man to consider in your own self-analysis, major or lieutenant colonel.

DePuy learned early in his career how not to train and how not to lead. Commissioned from ROTC in 1941, he participated in wasted training opportunities in the United States that continued in England where he noted that the terrain wasn't very different in England than from what it was in Normandy. Poor training was compounded by mostly inept leaders at all levels. He was taught extended order, a skirmish line, an assault technique that was a bad idea in 1863 and did not improve with age. Paying the butcher's bill in Normandy was no doubt in part due to close combat with a very skilled enemy, but DePuy saw American lives wasted as a result of inadequate training and poor leadership. Those early lessons made a deep and permanent impression on him. His 90th Infantry Division stumbled so badly it was almost disbanded by Omar Bradley after the Normandy experience. Then, according to DePuy and other senior leaders, including Patton and Eisenhower, it became a very good division. The transformation was bought with American blood as the rapidly expanded US Army sought combat leaders at all levels. At the division and regiment level the solution was to relieve commanders until the right men were found. DePuy credits his third in a succession of division commanders in a very short period of time, Raymond D. McLean, with saving the division. Colonel George Bitman Barth did the same for the 357th Infantry after his predecessors had failed. Barth remained DePuy's model of a great troop leader for the entirety of DePuy's life.

Barth succeeded a man DePuy described as "a horse's ass of the worst order," "a goddamned fool, a disaster." DePuy had a way with words. By the way, he really rarely used profanity or blasphemy, but this was a special case. The sixth was otherwise at battalion. There the junior officers in their twenties who were good at war stepped up to battalion command. Brave and skilled battalion commander Major Ed Hamilton, much admired by DePuy, said that in the period 5-12 July 1944, "I lost five company commanders, two killed, three wounded, one week." Hamilton himself lost an eye in battle in September. DePuy said that in the first six weeks of the Battle of Normandy his division lost 100% of his soldiers and 150% of his officers. In the rifle companies, that translates to losses between 200-400%. I teach at the War College in the springtime, I teach an elective, and I and my students always marvel at the sheer numbers of people killed and wounded in both the First and Second World War, which is almost out of our imagination as contemporary soldiers.

Those losses in Europe, the Second World War, compared with the worst of the last few months of World War I. Twenty of the 61 divisions in the European theater of operations had a personnel turnover rate of 100% or higher. The 90th, with 196%, was sixth on the list of infantry divisions. At the officer corps in Czechoslovakia, marking the end of war on 8 May 1945, the first time that all of the officers of the 357th had assembled since their days in England, an artillery battalion commander who was present made this observation: "There wasn't a single company commander who left England who is still present. Only the service company commanders hadn't changed." Memories of losses that he attributed to poor training and leadership shaped DePuy's behavior for the rest of his professional life. "My regiment simply did not perform, notwithstanding the heroic efforts and tragic losses among the lower ranking officers and the bewildered troops. The value system of the 90th Division did not identify and eliminate officers before they had done their grizzly work." He would not allow that to happen on his watch. DePuy's regimental commander at the end of the war, John Mason, said that DePuy was "by far the best combat battalion commander and natural leader of men I have known." DePuy found his calling in close combat.

The leaders who fought in Normandy and were still standing in May of 1945 were very good. Some people are very good at war. DePuy was such a person. Not all of us are. DePuy took lessons from his combat experience. He got rid of leaders who did not have his complete confidence. They didn't have to screw up, they just lacked his complete confidence and he would fire people. That was particularly evident in his command of a division, and he gave responsibility to young tigers who showed initiative, energy, and smarts. That is evident in his later leadership of a large and complex organization. There is a personal component constant in DePuy's behavior. It was most often called focus or intensity.

Due to time constraints we skip over some interesting stories: his CIA detail during the Korean War; his attitude about military professional schools, he didn't think much of them; a second opportunity to command an infantry battalion; affection for the British; battle group command; permanent fascination with tactics; staff jobs in Washington; and his private life. We can return to those topics in the Q&A if you'd like, but for now let's go to Vietnam.

From 1964-1966 DePuy served as MACV J3 in Saigon where he enjoyed General Westmoreland's complete confidence, and he served once again with his old friend from World War II, Richard G. Stillwell. As a brigadier general in a relaxed and contemplative moment with a trusted assistant, he described how he would do things in the best of all possible worlds. He scoured the Army to find the 12 brightest and most articulate majors in the Army and put them in 12 cubicles without portfolio, no S1, S2, S3, S4. As issues arose that he needed, and he needed a staff study, a position paper, or an answer for the boss, he'd distribute to the problem to the right major with basic guidance saying, "Now you run with the ball and tell me what to do in 5,000 words or less." Later, in the Pentagon from 1969-73, he organized just such a collection of young and creative self-starters in the grade of lieutenant colonel in a studies group led by a colonel. They were regarded by some in the building as unguided missiles. I happened to be in the building at the time, by the way, but they enjoyed DePuy's protection. As he prepared to take command of TRADOC, he told then Lieutenant Colonel Max Thurman to go to the Personnel Office and get the 20 brightest colonels you can find, the 20 brightest lieutenant colonels, and the 20 brightest majors. "Then," he said, "we can run the other 100,000 in the command."

As TRADOC commander he again tasked an ad hoc cell of his bright young guys to write the early drafts of the 1960s, the 1976 FM100-5. Historian Richard Swain—present with us at the conference but he's AWOL right now, for which I'll take him to task—says that the reaction to DePuy's version of that FM produced a decade of doctrinal debate that was the richest professional dialogue in the US Army's history, and he ranks DePuy with Marshall as a master trainer. I think he's probably right. I also think that the germ of the notion of small ad hoc cells to address critical issues came from what he saw in the bright young tigers in combat in 1944, 1945, and it was refined as he matured and took on great responsibilities in our very large and complex organizations. In brief, the most creative people may not be the most senior people. Some people perform routine tasks superbly, but for special jobs you want to get special people, and he was not particularly attentive to the grade of the people who got the job done for him.

DePuy commanded the Big Red One [1st Infantry Division] from '66-67. His relief of subordinate commanders got him a lot of attention in Washington and in trouble with Army Chief of Staff Harold K. Johnson. So did his prodigious use of artillery, particularly harassment and interdiction fires, that is, unobserved fires. As a consequence, upon his departure from Vietnam DePuy did not get the job at Fort Benning that he wanted; he wanted to run the Infantry School and train young infantry officers. In fact, Johnson didn't know what to do with him and didn't have a job for DePuy in his Army. At this point, Westmoreland intervened by telling Wheeler, Chairman of JCS, that DePuy was available for assignment to the JCS staff, thus, in Westmoreland's own word, thus saving Bill DePuy's career. By taking him out of the chain of command of the Army, JCS staff job.

It was my intent to make two major points about DePuy's leadership, both of which stem from his formative World War II experience, his relief of subordinates in combat, and his inclination to go with bright and energetic young officers, even of the highest staff levels. He prepared his bureaucratic battlefields as carefully as he prepared his battlefields in 1944 and '45 and in Vietnam in 1966, 1967. I did not dwell on his political skills, his power of persuasion, or another aspect of his leadership, perhaps chief among them, a degree of intensity and focus on the business and hand that actually frightened people. That returns us to Gorman's observation: DePuy was unique. It would be unwise to imitate him. He also emulated Slim's admonition to "be yourself." It's equally unwise to think you must pack a pearl handled pistol. Not all of us can go to the top of the heap. Some of us will have that happy combination of experience, training, and the right genes, and don't forget pure luck. DePuy was lucky that Westmoreland was in a position to intervene, recommend him to Wheeler in 1967. So far, World War II luminaries would've retired as anonymous lieutenant colonels without the big buildup of that big war. That point recalls the toast in the British Officer's mess regarding advancement and greed. "Here's to a bloody campaign and a sickly season."

It should be very obvious that there's no template for leadership that can be taken off the shelf and be applied to your current command issues. Marshall, MacArthur, Eisenhower, Bradley, Patton were very, very different men. Leadership seems to be like happiness in the sense that both are byproducts of what one does, not an objective. Slim doesn't put it exactly that way, but he does advise that we trust our professional leadership experience, the military schools, and the accident of our individual uniqueness. This is not very far from theory and practice applied. My personal bias is to add: read, read, read, and don't omit fiction from your reading list. Thank you. (applause).

**Mr. Ramsey:**

Thank you both very much for some very interesting comments. We are open now for questions.

## Day 2, Panel 4: Conventional and Unconventional Challenges of the Cold War, 1945-1975

### Questions and Answers

(Transcript of Presentation)

### Lewis Sorley, Ph.D.
### Henry Gole, Ph.D.

### Moderated by Mr. Robert Ramsey

**Rich Kuyper:**

Henry, about DePuy. I'm Rich Kuyper, Army Counterinsurgency Center. Those of us who were lieutenants and captains in the late '60s, knowing we were going to Vietnam and be platoon leaders or infantry company commanders, knew two things about the 1st [Infantry] Division. One was the DePuy Fort, and the other was the word you used about DePuy himself, and that was 'ruthless'. There as a concern among some of us that we would end up in the 1st Division either under DePuy or under leaders who were emulating this ruthless reputation that he had. Fortunately I did not. My concern about the stories that we hear about DePuy and carrying around spare company commanders and battalion commanders in his helicopter, I think about my experience as an infantry company commander. The first battalion commander, we'd come back from an operation and he would take us, you know, when I'd come back, shower, eat, meet him literally under a tree and a couple of chairs, and we would talk about the operation. It was a mentoring, learning, critiquing, advising, helping, developing attitude that that particular battalion commander had, and I think it helped me and I felt comfortable, you know, because sometimes I really did screw the pooch on operations, but he didn't hold it against me. It was to take that and development. The second one was, to use a technical term, an asshole who did not do that, had no interest in developing subordinates. Tell him that you screwed up and you were gone. So there was this stark contrast, and the more I learned about DePuy the more I came to equate him to the second guy from the leadership perspective. Now, forget FM 100-5 and all of that. And the more I learned about him the more I thought, "What a great example of somebody I do not want to be like." So I get a little uncomfortable sometimes when we don't necessary lionize DePuy but we don't focus on what Bob talked about, as treating soldiers as human beings and taking young officers and helping them develop. And I've always viewed DePuy very negatively because it seemed to me that was his approach: no development, but only ruthlessness.

**Dr. Gole:**

Needless to say, DePuy was a highly contentious figure at the time, and to this day. In the book I tried to be balanced. He was so offensive to so many people at the time that one future lieutenant general, when a major told me that he was going to contact, he attended, he was on DePuy's staff in a secondary position as an Assistant 3, a G3, and he said he was going to blow the whistle on DePuy to the Department of the Army IG because of DePuy's abuse particularly of staff officers. DePuy would hop in a plane and spend a day on the battlefield, come back, and his deputy went out and did the same thing. They would have firsthand experiences and see what was going on. They'd sit down, have a drink, chat, and then go in for a brief. The briefers didn't know as much as the principals, and they were continually, regularly abused by the commanding general and deputy, his assistant divisions commander. So it is true that he was one tough SOB. There's no question about that. I'm not going to try to legitimize it, but those numbers that I recited from World War II, the bloodbath, convinced him that as a commander if he suspected that Captain Smith or particularly Lieutenant Colonel Jones couldn't cut it, he would relieve them. He didn't have to have cause. Department of the Army became well aware of this, too. The staff of the Army, as Bob would tell us, became keenly aware of this. As a matter of fact, they started to dilute the price of relief by DePuy, like it wasn't the same as relief by anybody else. There were second chances.

For example, I read through, as you probably know, I don't mention the names in the book; there's no reason to defame people, but he relieved about 13 people, most of them rate of lieutenant colonel, some commanders, some staff officers, but most of them commanders. There was an incident in which an artillery battalion commander was relieved. He was on that list that I was aware of, but most of these people are long dead. I was already a captain and a major in that war. These fellows were lieutenant colonels and commanded battalions, so most of them are no longer living. I ran down one and I called him down in Alabama from Pennsylvania, and I said, "My name is Henry Gole. I'm writing a book about General DePuy and I'd like to get some information about him." The guy at the other end said, "I don't have anything good to say about him." I said, "Sir, I'm not looking for something good to say about him, I'm looking for something true to say about him. May I have your permission to call you in 24 hours? Will you have time to think about the good or bad things? I called him back the next day. He was on the ground when there was a screw up. Wasn't his screw up. He was the nearest artillery battalion commander. He was told to get in the chopper and straighten that out, so he went out and straightened it out. When he returned, he was relieved by his DIVARTY commander, and the person in question said, "I was relieved because if my DIVARTY commander didn't relieve me DePuy would've relieved him." This was an interesting story. I called Donn Starry, and in the course of the conversation the first go around I asked him about relief questions, and he said, "There was a guy, can't think of his name. He was screwed by DePuy. He was an artillery man, and later on he commanded very well in a different corps area." I got back to Starry and I said, "I just spoke to Colonel X," and he said, "Yeah, that's the guy!" He was called Skeeter. "That was Skeeter so-and-so." So it's absolutely true that DePuy was cruel, merciless in relieving people.

At the same time, there were company commanders and battalion commanders who had an absolute affection for him. There was some development or cultivation of these people in their eyes, not very visible, because he felt, and his difference with General Johnson, who didn't have a job for him when DePuy was to leave Vietnam, his difference was this question, I believe General Johnson thought it was unreasonable, and he said, "I don't have enough lieutenant clonels to keep the 1st Infantry Division in battalion commanders." And so, and DePuy, as General Johnson spent Christmas of '66 with the Big Red One, and it was there that there was a confrontation between DePuy and General Johnson, guess what? General Johnson won. DePuy did not get the assignment that he wanted to command at Fort Benning.

There were others later. Now, you were talking about the division command and combat. I could take this story to later staff situations, but General Sid Barry said of DePuy, in combat in Vietnam he was very confident. Later, he behaved as though he was a borderline case of arrogance. I don't know if I've sufficiently addressed your question.

**Unknown male:**

If you will permit me, I would like to relate a personal anecdote with General DePuy that I had as a captain in headquarters TRADOC.

**Dr. Gole:**

I was looking for the... Where were you three or four years ago when I needed you?

**Unknown male:**

Hiding! (laughter) In 1975 I was assigned as a law and order officer for headquarters TRADOC, and one of my duties was to close the personnel control facilities, the deserter processing centers. As the Vietnam War had already run down we were getting fewer and fewer deserters and we were closing these facilities. And the following year, '76, I was told the commanding general wanted to see me concerning the closure of the personnel control facilities, and I was the "subject matter expert" on it. So I went to DePuy's office with a colonel who was the XO of DCSPER, and I don't remember his name. I'd have to look on the manning chart, but we walked in the general's office. He kind of looked in my direction, greeted the colonel. We sat on the sofa. And the colonel proceeded to give him all kinds of wrong information, including calling them personnel confinement facilities, which they weren't, and a bunch of other stuff. And the general thanked him and sort of looked in my direction. I felt that I was kind of translucent, being only a captain in DePuy's presence, and I left. And it really made me wonder about DePuy from that point on, because there I was, the so-called subject matter expert in that one particular thing, and he never even asked me a question.

Now, from a career and personal point of view I was glad because as this colonel was telling him all this wrong information, I was literally saying, "Please, God, don't let the general, you know, ask me a question," because I wasn't about to say, "Well, what the colonel told you was just, you know, inaccurate," but I wasn't going to bring it up, but I do because of all the comments made. There was certainly nothing godlike about him, and I think he had a tendency not to listen to company grade officers. I think his confidence was in field grades and in higher, and whether you were an SME or not, it was the rank that he was listening to and that was it. And that's just my impression, and that's....

**Dr. Gole:**

Yeah. Of course, I don't challenge what you said for a moment, but I will cite some things that I was told by, for example, General Paul Gorman on this subject of a star system and listening, to whom he listened. As a matter of fact, he didn't listen at TRADOC, he didn't listen very seriously to some generals. Paul Gorman told me that consistent with what I said about DePuy way back when he was a brigadier, said, "Give me, you know, those majors," and he did that again and again and until the day he retired. The boathouse gang at TRADOC was such a collection of rather junior guys, but rather junior meaning majors, lieutenant colonels. I don't know if there were any captains in that bunch.

But Gorman told me everyone knew who was on the good guy list and who wasn't, who was the first team and who wasn't, and Gorman said it had to be demoralizing to those officers who were not on the hotshot list. Break, Pentagon, earlier, studies group, lieutenant, mostly lieutenant colonels, some majors, six or eight of them under the supervision of the colonel, protected by DePuy, Friday. In the good old days before the sanctimonious SOBs took over, DePuy would periodically stick his head into this studies group where Colonel Segal apparently had a bottle of Scotch and some makings for a martini, feet up, PM, five, six, chat. And DePuy would loosen his collar and be one of the boys and chat, to the point someone said "So-and-so isn't carrying his weight" or something like that, and DePuy said, "Oh, just a minute, just a minute. Be gentle. Be kind," is what he said, "be kind." He said, "You know, we have people in this building—this building's filled with people who went where we sent them in World War II. They went where we sent them in Korea. They went to Vietnam, and they'll do their daily salute and do whatever we tell them to, and they're ordinary types. They should be treated with a great deal of consideration." What he was saying was there are fast movers, and when I want something really done that's why I turn to guys like you, but don't be critical, usually of older men, don't be critical of those guys. They're ready to do their duty, but they're ordinary types, and he would assign, those are my words, 'ordinary types', and he would assign them routine tasks rather than the golden boy tasks. That's what I learned about him.

**Mr. Ramsey:**

Sure, yes, one more question. Yes, sir.

**Unknown male:**

We've heard two very different leaders described, or at least I have the impression, and I was wondering if I could turn to Bob and ask him to comment on DePuy, and perhaps also since Abrams. There must have been some kind of an overlap there. Did Abrams have an opinion on DePuy. I mean, he was much senior to him, but....

**Dr. Sorley:**

Ten days ago I turned in the manuscript of my Westmoreland biography, which I've been at work on for several years. Earlier, as you know, I wrote a biography for L.K. Johnson when he was, who has already been mentioned here in connection with his interactions with DePuy. I think when General Abrams came back to be Chief of Staff of the Army he was not favorably disposed toward General DePuy, but he changed his views considerably, largely because of the positive aspects of DePuy's capabilities that were demonstrated to him primarily in the context of planning for reorganization of the Army that led to the breakup of Continental Army Command and, as you know, the development of Forces Command and TRADOC. I know a lot about General DePuy, and I consider him one of the most complex biographical subjects I can imagine. I think Henry showed great courage in taking it on. I know some things about him that are very good, and some others that are very bad. Some of those have been brought out here, especially by your comments, which I thought were very insightful.

When General [Westmoreland] took command of the forces in Vietnam DePuy was the J3, as Henry mentioned, and it's very clearly that primarily DePuy and secondarily Stillwell were the authors of the strategy of attrition and the search and destroy tactics that Westmoreland employed, and after the war was over, to his great credit in my opinion, General DePuy said forthrightly and without trying to make any excuses, and in writing in military publications, "We were wrong. We were wrong in our assessment of the enemy and his staying power, we were wrong to think we could, by killing enough of the enemy, dissuade him from further aggression, and it is now clear that the approach we took never had any chance of success." He said those things in writing. I consider that very courageous, and by way of contrast, General Westmoreland could never bring himself to make that same admission. I'd just say that.

**Dr. Gole:**

May I just make one point about what Bob said? Some of what DePuy's behavior as division commander can be explained by the situation and the location of three corps, the distance between Saigon and the Cambodian border, and the fact that the enemy had owned the real estate between Saigon and the border, particularly along the border, which wasn't very clear anyway, and DePuy was convinced that local ragtag regional forces, various kinds of indigenous military organizations couldn't handle it. The enemy was sending the first team in his direction, not far from Saigon, and he thought it was necessary to use American main force elements against enemy main force elements because of the situation in three corps and the border and what had existed the previous decade in the VC buildup of infrastructure, and so he thought he didn't have much choice. He had to go get them first or nothing good was going to happen. Of course, you may remember at this time in the war an enemy tactic would be to move into a big town or a small city, take over for a very short period of time, punish in the cruelest way the local authorities, and then vacate the premises, and, of course, that memory didn't go away with the VC troops who were moving away. It would be remembered that you better play ball with the indigenous people and not play ball with the Americans. So that's just a partial explanation of the heavy handed behavior of DePuy with his division at that time and place.

**Mr. Ramsey:**

OK. Thank you both for your comments and your presentations. Thank you very much.

# Day 2, Panel 5: Rebirth of the US Army, 1976-2001

## Thoughts in Spring on Professional Identity by Richard Swain, Ph.D.
(Submitted Paper)

## Moderated by MAJ(P) Clay Mountcastle

Mac Coffman, who could not be here this year because he is recovering from ankle surgery, began his classic social history of the Army with the words: "The Old Army is the army that existed before the last war."[1] By that reckoning, I have belonged to several armies. I joined the local Army Reserve at the age of 17, in 1961. The Berlin Wall went up that year. It was my first realization that I might actually be required to do more than attend six months active duty for training, weekend drills in Palatka, Florida, and summer training at Fort Eustis or Fort Story, Virginia.

The transportation company, with which I spent four months of active duty for training that summer and autumn, had a first sergeant who had been a captain in World War II and I remember one Korean War veteran. That was my first Army. I decided to become an officer; I applied to and was accepted by West Point. I entered before the U.S. commitment to Vietnam was particularly serious. When Captain Roger Donlon received his Medal of Honor, I was in Germany on summer training. Germany was glorious that August.

I graduated from the Military Academy with the class of 1966. As an active duty officer I was a member of the Post Vietnam Army, the pre-Gulf War Army it became, and the post Gulf War army that followed. Since then, I have been a camp follower, gradually losing touch with the Army in any meaningful way except for continuing, if distant admiration and gratitude. This paper concerns itself with leaders of post war armies, looking for new identities.

In the spring of the year, ever since 1947, distinguished gentlemen, leaders of the U.S. and U.K. armies, transit the Atlantic to speak at their ally's institutions of professional education in honor of the long ties between our two nations and of Kermit Roosevelt, T.R.'s son. The younger Roosevelt served in both armies, in the first and second world wars. The speeches vary in quality and focus. My suspicion is the Americans benefit most from the exchange and it has always struck me as an irony that, so far as I have been able to discover, while there is a repository, albeit incomplete, of British speeches here at CGSC, there is no central collection of the American Roosevelt lectures. The Army War College lists a folder of twelve.

The speakers are, as I say, a distinguished lot. The first was Albert Wedemeyer. He was followed by, among others, Maxwell Taylor, Lawton Collins, Al Gruenther, Anthony McAuliffe, James Gavin, Andrew Goodpaster, Ted Conway, Richard Stillwell, Bill DePuy, Bruce Palmer, Bernard Rogers, Edward Myer, John Vessey, and Glenn Otis. These are just some names taken, more or less at random, reading down the list. I looked for General DePuy's Kermit Roosevelt Speech unsuccessfully when I compiled the collection of his papers issued by CSI upon the occasion of his death. Henry Gole does not refer to it, so I assume he had no more success locating it. I have had copies of General Starry's and General Richardson's speeches for some years. I found General Davidson's on line at MHI at Carlisle, and, with the help of Lieutenant General Mark Hertling, I managed to obtain copies of General Fred Franks'.

This spring General Martin Dempsey was the U.S. Kermit Roosevelt speaker.[2] Dempsey applauded his hosts for addressing the erosion of strategic thinking, which he took as a shared phenomenon, and offered the observation that the U.S. and U.K. militaries both find themselves challenged by "a lack of intellectual and institutional clarity about the enduring nature of war, distinctive in important ways," he observed, "from the changing character of warfare." An "important subplot" he went on, "is the erosion in leader development in general."[3]

Dempsey went on to offer that there would be no shortage of work for military forces. Armed conflict will continue; natural disasters and economic turmoil as well. "We will," he said, "be surprised by the pace of change in technology, how it proliferates, who will use it, and for what purposes."[4] Rather than claim that technology will solve all our problems, like the futurists of the nineties and the early Bush administration, Dempsey offered the conclusion that technology "has leveled the pitch between us and our potential enemies, creating a far more competitive security environment.[5] It makes surprise more likely and hence puts a greater premium on leaders who are resilient and adaptive."[6]

Dempsey's concern then involved accounting for, and avoiding, what he calls "the failure of imagination." "The military profession in particular," he said, "demands imagination: the ability to discern the weak signals of impending change from a vast array of events and data."[7] His primary focus, then, was on avoiding what he sees as failures of the past in the overvaluing of the benefits of technology and, in particular, neglecting to account for the creativity of the other, the opposing human enemy who, as Clausewitz reminds us, is a constant companion in warfare.

Elaborating on his theme of a failure in imagination, Dempsey condemned in florid terms the unfulfilled promises of the Revolution in Military Affairs, characterizing its champions as "apostles of knowledge dominance and worshipers at the altar of stand-off precision strike."[8] He chose for scorn, particularly, an idea associated with former Chief of Staff, General Ric Shinseki, the notion of the 'quality of firsts'.[9]

Our imagination failed, Dempsey said, because we did not account for the imagination of the enemy. "They adapted their strengths to our weaknesses. They dispersed among the population and in difficult terrain. They decentralized and leveraged commercial technology to empower their networks. They syndicated with criminal, religious and political groups to suit their common interests."[10] One is reminded, in this jeremiad (understandable from the former commander of the 1st Armored Division in the early dark days in Baghdad) of an old, vaguely remembered cartoon of a muddy Marine surrounded by the debris of the war in Korea, asking plaintively, "Where the hell are the push-buttons?"

It struck me that it might be useful to go back and look at other Kermit Roosevelt Speeches to see what they might contain of interest to the incumbent TRADOC Commander.

Now a disclaimer is called for. Aside from the differences in personality of the respective speakers, the conditions governing their appearance were dramatically different. Generals Davidson, Starry and Richardson possessed the important advantage denied Generals Franks and Dempsey of a clear threat against which to build and plan, and well known ground on which to fight, if it ever came to that. Of course, the army they envisioned never did meet the enemy it was designed to fight. Instead, that Army, and its joint and allied partners, overran the Iraqi forces occupying Kuwait in 1990-'91, justifying in four days the long investment in post-Vietnam recovery. That single fact in no way discounts their efforts or concerns.

General Davidson spoke to the British National Defense College on or near the very day the South Vietnam collapsed.[11] His speech, focused on the role of U.S. forces in Europe, seems to have been aimed at American ears as much as the British allies. It recounted the history and fluctuations of the U.S. commitment to Europe since 1945. Davidson observed that U.S. forces had drawn down from the 1961 Berlin Wall high of 278,975, to around 190,000. During the same period, while the U.S. was distracted in Southeast Asia, the Soviet forces had increased 30%, added 2,000 additional tanks, improved their air force and turned their navy into a global, blue water fleet.[12] Davidson observed as well the lessons of the 1973 Arab-Israeli War, in which, he said the Israelis had lost three divisions worth of tanks in 18 days.[13]

Davidson's argument to his British audience was that the danger of Soviet aggression was real and that the U.S. and its allies had to confront the question, whether "the West, by the quality and number of men and weapons in its conventional forces, reflect the <u>will</u> and <u>intent</u> to defend its society."[14] He warned his British audience of post-Vietnam U.S. Congressional opposition to maintaining current U.S. deployments and quoted Secretary of Defense James Schlesinger arguing for their necessity. He concluded, saying:

Certainly, we would have chosen a more propitious time to be challenged—a time when problems at home and the problems of our allies would not distract us from our duties. But history is a cruel and impartial judge…it will not reward us for the challenge, but only for the response.[15]

By the time Donn Starry delivered his Roosevelt lectures, the Reagan military build-up was underway and the Army was bringing the new generation of fighting equipment on line. Recruiting standards were raised and the Army instituted administrative discharge provisions that facilitated removing much of the human dead wood accumulated in the previous ten years. Although General Starry was Commander in Chief of U.S. Readiness Command in 1982, he used the occasion of his appearances at The Royal Military College of Sciences, Shrivenham, the National Defence College, Latimer, and the Army Staff College, then at Camberly, to introduce the British Army to the concepts of Air Land Battle, which he had brought into army doctrine while commander of Training and Doctrine Command.

Starry, who had been one of the prime movers of the Army's recovery after Vietnam, had begun his part of the work reviving the Army in conditions of severe post war stress.[16] Carter budgets were stringent. The active Army was over-structured at 16 divisions and unable to meet its recruiting and retention goals as it shifted from a conscript force to volunteer manning. General William DePuy's 1976 tactical doctrine was dogmatic and ill-received but it got the Army into the field and onto the ranges. Gradually discipline and a sense of purpose were restored.[17]

Much of General Starry's presentation of the NATO Airland Battlefield seems dated today, in absence of a first class armored enemy across the way. Two of his Roosevelt speeches, though, retain interest in respect to their timeless considerations of the requirements of war.

The first is the speech on leadership presented to the Cadets at the Royal Military Academy, Sandhurst.[18] Starry offered five observations. First he addressed the human content of battle leadership:

"Leadership," he said, "is the ability to harness the courage of human beings into concerted action in a most dangerous and complex undertaking." Second, he continued, "Leaders must learn to identify complex situations in advance, to find logical answers, and to prescribe regular drills that their units can use to cope with those complex situations… Thirdly, to win, leaders must think…leaders must be trained to think[:] think ahead, think correctly, logically, quickly, precisely, with creativeness and imagination about the complex situations they can expect to encounter." Fourthly, because leaders cannot be everywhere, they must ensure their subordinates know what to do until the leader can arrive to direct them. And fifth, and finally, he observed that, "in battle, the only thing that can be expected is the unexpected…we must train our officers and men for it…"[19]

In light of General Dempsey's interest in the nature of the profession, it is also worth recounting what Starry had to say about the importance of leaders modeling certain values. The first was professional competence, made up of "a superior sense of disciplined professional responsibility…[and] willingness to sacrifice." It includes, he said, "developing the ability to infuse the young men and women you lead with those values."[20] Secondly," Starry went on, "the professional military reflects a commitment…to the unit of which you are part, and to the men and women you lead…the commitment is to something larger than yourself—there is no room for careerism." Thirdly, he added, "the military profession must hold in high merit the virtue of candor—the willingness and ability to discern and tell the objective truth." And finally, he said, "there is courage…courage is not the absence of fear…Courage is the willingness to admit and the ability to control fear."

Starry allowed that while he commanded the 11th Armored Cavalry Regiment in Vietnam he interviewed every incoming officer. Among the questions he asked, one was whether or not the new leader was afraid. He got, he said, some strange answers to the question.[21] He closed by reminding the British cadets of the essence of their calling: "Never forget," he said, "you are the leaders—the few who must provide the inspiration to do well what has to be done in those brief, highly incandescent moments of history when everything comes together, all at once, demanding a solution."[22]

To the Royal College of Defense Studies, Starry gave a speech on "Strategic Imperatives—Towards the Year 2000."[23] Still resonant in our day, he offered that the most critical need was for "a fully coordinated policy framework in which all elements of national power…are combined as integral parts of a coherent strategy." He led a tour de horizon of the challenges of the day and offered five guidelines for a "rational framework for military action in pursuit of national goals:"

1. First, if military forces are to be employed, it is imperative that it be decided early on what is to be done.

2. Secondly, whatever may be the course of action on which we embark, it must be decided whether or not sufficient forces are or can be made available to accomplish the mission.

3. Thirdly, can available deployment means move the forces to the right place in time to accomplish the mission?

4. Fourthly, can the forces deployed be sustained after they're employed?

5. Finally, having satisfied one commitment with whatever forces, deployment means, [and] sustainment resources may be required, there may be a need to respond to other commitments as well. Can that be done?[24]

To these he added a follow-on observation, that "no public official in a democratic society today can afford to ignore taking into account the political, economic, social and military environment in which his actions are viewed and his programs put into effect."[25] Two years later, General Richardson, whose central role in the recovery of the post war Army was both substantial and remains to be documented, confined himself to discussing the importance, purpose and limited focus of professional education; a topic that those of us privileged to attend his recent induction to the CGSC Hall of Fame understand clearly still excites his interest, his passions, and his critical judgments.[26]

In 1992, General Fred Franks, was making something of a victory tour with his principal ally when he delivered his lectures. A year before he had commanded the U.S. Army VII Corps in Southern Iraq and Kuwait. One of the divisions under his tactical control was the British 1st Armoured Division, commanded by then Major General Rupert Smith. Franks awarded some British soldiers their campaign ribbons and joked with the veterans of that war that he had come looking for missing U.S. Army cots, for which, he said, British officers had developed quite a fondness.

Like General Starry, Franks varied his remarks according to his audiences, though all his talks were about the balance between the intellectual and emotional content of soldiering. Like General Richardson, he published the heart of his lectures in *Military Review*, first in an essay titled "Matters of the Mind and the Heart,"[27] which he tied to a Staff College lecture given a month after the Kermit Roosevelt journey, and later in a valedictory article published in 1993, "Battle Command: A Commander's Perspective."[28]

In contrast to General Starry, for whom Franks had served as executive officer, the commander of VII Corps in Dessert Storm found himself confronted with the post Cold War build-down without the appearance of a single dominant foe on which to orient. In fact, Franks' VII Corps had been deactivated immediately at the end of the Gulf War. Both the British and U.S. Armies were in the process of undergoing deep reductions in force, about 25%, according to Franks.

PANEL 5

As the Army built down, Training and Doctrine Command drew in and Franks and the new Army Chief of Staff, Gordon Sullivan, focused *both* on maintaining the balance of the existing force—"No time outs!", General Sullivan said—and developing the concepts that would enable the Army to realize the promise of the communication and precision fires technologies, the potential of which had been revealed in the recent Gulf War. To that end Sullivan sent the Gulf War divisions back to the National Training Center and created an experimental organization called the Louisiana Maneuvers, after the World War II mobilization exercises.

Sullivan gave Fred Franks and TRADOC the task of mapping the future. Absent a definable threat, combat developers began talking about capability-based rather than threat-based force structures. It was an approach which, progressively divorced from the human dimension offered by history, perhaps, contributed to overlooking the importance of the adaptive abilities of potential foes.

The theme of Franks' lectures, like Dempsey's, was preparing leaders and the institution to confront change while retaining a combat edge.[29] There was concern that the Army would lose focus on its preparation for combat while it dealt with the rapid changes bearing down on it. General Sullivan referred over and over again to the example of Lieutenant Colonel Brad Smith's task force in Korea. Franks repeated the story in his lectures. "No more Task Force Smiths!" was the battle cry for continued emphasis on the primary mission, what General Dempsey said recently was the one task in which the Army must never fail, employing lethal force in the service of the nation.[30]

Franks warned against being bogged down in short-term change and missing the future. He believed, he said, "you can't roll up your sleeves and wring your hands at the same time." It was necessary to look ahead. "What a shame it would be if about ten years from now," he said, "we look back on a period of relative stability for our military and say what we forgot to do was look ahead."[31]

In his Roosevelt speeches, Franks proposed concentrating on two themes, the interaction between doctrine and technology, and the evolution of the nature of conflict. From his experience in the Gulf War, Franks had concluded that AirLand Battle had risen to a new level, one where simultaneous attack throughout the depths of the enemy forces had become a reality.

Franks pointed to history for warning examples. He observed the long failure to adapt to the conditions of tactical lethality created by rifled musketry and he balanced this view with the difficulty contemporary observers must have had looking at early prototypes of armored vehicles and seeing the possibility of massive, coordinated or synchronized armored maneuver. Franks' answer, driven in part by the need to pay for retaining combat forces by reducing the size of the institutional side of the Army, was creation of focused Battle Labs, not to theorize but to experiment, to tinker, he said, to use simulations and exercises to see where emerging technology might take us.

Franks quoted Martin van Creveld's *Transformation of War* (Free Press, 1991), which asserted that war was abolishing itself. Franks surveyed the recent spate of deployments and doubted it. He quoted as well Sir John Hackett who said, "The function of the profession of arms is the ordered application of force in the resolution of social problems."[32] Franks asked "What social problems may we asked to resolve? What's next?...I don't think," he said, "we ought to lose sight of the fact that our nations will call on us again. Where and when I don't know." And, he challenged his audiences to help think through that question.[33]

He spoke in the end about the unchanging "Matters of the Heart"—The soul and spirit of the military. He talked generally about what he called the T-words: Training, Teamwork and Trust. Speaking to British Soldiers, he drew on British examples of courage in battle and command, and he concluded reading a short note of thanks from the mother of one of his VII Corps Soldiers. "I believe," she wrote, "the excellent training my son received, and the teamwork involved throughout DESERT STORM, kept my son alive. My son has been telling me that you all are the best, and seeing is believing."[34]

So what is to make of all this?

In a recent You Tube reflection on the Army Profession, General Dempsey argues the Army has a need to reflect on the nature of the Profession of Arms and to have "a discourse…a discussion within our ranks…about what it is that makes us a profession, and then encourage the self-examination to help us understand whether we are living up to it."[35] Part of such a discourse is looking back to where the Army has come from, how its members have met previous challenges, and led transitions, to redefine themselves as a *relevant* profession of arms.

All of the Kermit Roosevelt speakers I have addressed here were confronted by the need to recenter the force and redefine its identity in light of new developments, strategic and technological. General Davidson stood at the end of a failed war when he gave his Roosevelt speech. He didn't know how the future would turn out, but he pointed to the direction the Atlantic alliance would have to go to meet the increasingly obvious Soviet challenge, and he appears to have been alerting the British allies not only to the common threat but to the need to mobilize his own nation's Congress to the common necessities.

When General Davidson spoke, General Starry was, or was about to become, the Commandant of the Armor Center, where he would contribute to the conceptual revitalization of the broken Army, even as budgets and force limits made it seem doubtful that the necessary forces could be created to realize the vision. By the time Starry was TRADOC commander, for reasons largely beyond his influence and certainly beyond his control, the potential to realize and improve on that early vision had come into being. When resources again became available, the Army had identified its requirements and desired formations and was prepared to synchronize the integration of ideas and resources, with a force growing increasingly professional in its self-identification and behavior. General Richardson's role in all of these developments, as ADCSOPS, as CAC Commander, DCSOPS and TRADOC commander, was significant and is neglected here only because his own reflections are recent enough at the Staff College not to warrant repetition.

General Franks' question, about the imperative of looking ahead ten years and using the time wisely, defines the task that confronted them all. General Davidson's observation that it is the quality of the response not the convenience of the challenge, which will be judged, remains true. As both Dempsey and Franks warned, the signals of change are weak and misleading. General Franks pointed out to me, recently, "What I was trying to do was structure the Army so we could ask the right questions…then let the generation who would have to execute the answers go find those answers."[36] Something must be left to the generation that actually confronts the emergent problem on the ground. Imagination is applied most critically in real-time.

General Dempsey's clear criticism is that after the first Gulf War, the Army did not look ahead well enough, institutionally. It did not develop in its leadership the conceptual agility to respond to unanticipated changes, to reframe understanding rapidly, when the system no longer responded as expected. Imagination failed. Faith in technology, confidence, perhaps, in the old successful conventional combat identity, led to complacency and, when tested, the imaginative and conceptual tools of Army leaders did not reflect the imaginative agility to read the fluid situation and make the necessary transitions in timely fashion.

If General Dempsey is correct about the failure of imagination, and there are certainly those who will dispute the specific content and locus of failure, then the remedy must be found in recreation of the educational system which was so much a part of Starry's, Richardson's, and Franks' legacy to the Army. For imagination in uncertainty comes from searching curiosity, openness to new ideas, rigorous, critical, collaborative learning, and a fundamental understanding of the reciprocal nature of conflict. In that respect, it is interesting to observe a perceptive forecast by a 1988 graduate of the Command and General Staff College. This particular major offered that:

> If the professional officer goes to war today, he will probably fight for a nation with an obvious aversion to war. He will probably fight in a less-than-total-war environment for very limited and vaguely-defined political objectives. He will probably fight an adversary who will meet him on the field of battle with the fanaticism of a religious crusade. Such circumstances will surely test his concept of Duty.[37]

The major was one Martin E. Dempsey…now the TRADOC Commander.

## Notes

1. Edward M. Coffman, *The Old Army: A Portrait of the American Army in Peacetime, 1784-1898* (New York and Oxford: Oxford University Press, 1986), vii.

2. Martin E. Dempsey, Kermit Roosevelt Lecture; "A Campaign of Learning: Avoiding the Failure of Imagination," *The RUSI Journal* 155: 3, (June/July 2010) 6-9.

3. Dempsey, 6.

4. Dempsey.

5. See candidate Bush's 1999 Citadel speech: http://www.citadel.edu/pao/addresses/pres_bush.html, (accessed 30 August 2010).

6. Dempsey, "A Campaign of Learning: Avoiding the Failure of Imagination," 6.

7. Dempsey, 5-6.

8. Dempsey, 7.

9. "At the tactical level, Objective Force Units will *see first, understand first, act first and finish decisively as the means to tactical success.*" United States Army White Paper, Concepts for the Objective Force, [n.d.], page 6. On line at http://www.army.mil/features/WhitePaper/ObjectiveForceWhitePaper.pdf, (accessed 30 August 2010). See the 2003 critique of the Army White Paper by then Lieutenant Colonel H. R. McMaster, CRACK IN THE FOUNDATION: Defense Transformation and the Underlying Assumption of Dominant Knowledge in Future War. U.S. Army War College, Center for Strategic Leadership, November 2003, Volume S03-03. On line at http://www.af.mil/au/awc/awcgate/army-usawc/mcmaster_foundation.pdf, (accessed 30 August 2010).

10. Dempsey, "A Campaign of Learning: Avoiding the Failure of Imagination," 7-8.

11. On 30 April 1975. Davidson's series of appearances were from 27 April to 7 May.

12. General Michael Davidson, Remarks for the Kermit Roosevelt Lectures, England, 27 April to 7 May 1975. 355.

13. Davidson, 358.

14. Davidson, 356.

15. Davidson, 363.

16. See General Donn A. Starry, "The Profession of Arms in America," in *Encyclopedia of the American Military; Studies of the History, Traditions, Policies, Institutions, and Roles of the Armed Forces in War and Peace,* John E. Jessup and Louise B. Ketz, eds, Vol. 1 (New York: Charles 'Scribner's Sons, 1994), 467-503. Roger Spiller, "In the Shadow of the Dragon: Doctrine and the U.S. Army after Vietnam", Chapter 9 of In Roger J. Spiller, *In the School of War* (Lincoln, Nebraska: Bison Books, University of Nebraska Press, 2010), 220-257. (Essay first appeared in the RUSI Journal.) Richard M. Swain, "Filling the Void: The Operational Art and the U.S. Army," Chapter 8 of The Operational Art: Developments in Theories of War, B. J. C. McKercher and Michael A. Hennessy, eds (Westport, CN: Praeger, 1996) 147-172.

17. Department of the Army, Center for Military History, Information Paper, SUBJECT: Breaking the Army, 1965-1980," written by Dr. [William A.] Donnelly/202-685-2251, dated 29 August 2007.

18. Titled "The Leadership Challenge" and delivered on 7 May 1982. Transcript in possession of author.

19. "The Leadership Challenge," 26.

20. "The Leadership Challenge," 28.

21. "The Leadership Challenge," 28-29.

22. "The Leadership Challenge," 29

23. Delivered on 11 May 1982. Transcript in possession of author.

24. Delivered, 35-36.

25. Delivered, 36.

26. The author has a copy of General Richardson's speech presented at the Royal Military College of Science, Shrivenham, 22 May 1984. The paper was published as General William R. Richardson, "Kermit Roosevelt Lecture: Officer Training and Education", *Military Review* (October 1984), 22-34.

27. General Frederick M. Franks, "Matters of the Mind and the Heart," *Military Review* (March 1993), 2-10.

28. General Frederick M. Franks, Jr., "Battle Command: A Commander's Perspective" (Military Review, May-June 1996), 4-25.

29. General Franks' lectures were gathered in a pamphlet, 1992 Kermit Roosevelt Lecture Series. A copy was provided the author by the TRADOC History Office through the good officers of Lieutenant General Mark Hertling, formerly General Franks' executive officer.

30. Dempsey, "The Army Profession", June 2010, YouTube.com.

31. General Frederick M. Franks, Jr., Kermit Roosevelt Lecture Series, "Soldiering: A Matter of the Mind and the Heart", Joint Services Defence College [UK], 14 May 1992, 3.

32. Sir John Winthrop Hackett, *The Profession of Arms* (Department of the Army, Officers Call, CMH Pub 70-18, Facsimile Reprint of 1962 Lees Knowles Lectures given at Trinity College Cambridge, by Lt.-General Sir John Winthrop Hackett, 1986, 1988, 1990), 3. There are other printings of these speeches. The LondonTimes published them as a pamphlet in 1983. General Hackett made some interesting comments on how the U.S. came to reprint his essay in the old *Encounter* (January 1986), 75-76.

33. General Frederick M. Franks, Jr., Kermit Roosevelt Lecture Series. "Soldiering: A Matter of the Mind and the Heart,:" Royal Military College of Science, Shrivenham, 13 May 1992, 18-19.

34. Franks, 25. The quotation was the closing of all the presentations.

35. Dempsey, "The Army Profession", June 2010, YouTube.com.

36. E-mail from General (Ret) Frederick M. Franks to the author, Monday September 13, 2010.

37. Martin E. Dempsey, Duty: Understanding the Most Sublime Military Virtue. A thesis presented to the Faculty of the U.S. Army Command and General Staff College in partial fulfillment of the requirements for the degree, MASTER OF MILITARY ART AND SCIENCES. Fort Leavenworth, KS, 1988.

# Day 2, Panel 5: Rebirth of the US Army, 1976-2001

## Presentation by James Carafano, Ph.D.
(Transcript of Presentation)

## Moderated by MAJ(P) Clay Mountcastle

**MAJ(P) Mountcastle:**

I will proceed with Dr. Carafano's talk, and then we'll go into the Q&A session on the completion of his talk.

Dr. James Carafano is also a career Army officer in field artillery, so we have our fair share of field artillerymen here today. And is the assistant director of the Heritage Foundation's Kathryn and Shelby Cullom Davis Institute for International Studies, and is Senior Research Fellow for Defense and Homeland Security Issues. He also earned his stripes in the classroom at USMA, teaching at West Point, and is currently a visiting professor at the National Defense University in Georgetown University. He's the author of numerous books, the latest of which is *Private Sector, Public Wars: Contractors in Combat—Iraq, Afghanistan, and Future Conflicts*. Dr. Carafano.

**Dr. Carafano:**

So, like, I am so excited to be here. First of all, I feel right at home. I'm very used to the fact that when people hear I'm going to talk, they run out of the building. But, even more importantly, this gives me an opportunity, because I mostly deal with kind of contemporary things. But to really be an ambassador and advocate for a way of looking at military history, which I think is absolutely essential and critical and vital to our discipline. And not just to our discipline, but I really believe in serving our profession. And the argument is, is that the kind of military history that we read, need to be writing today, is really at the center of the starburst of economic and political and business and the history of popular culture and science and military. That the fruitful and important history to understand our profession and understand leadership in our profession has to be written by integrating all those perspectives.

Now, that's not to make an argument for new military history, which I'm not. I was a fan of the Annales School, giving voice to the voiceless, I think that's OK. But quite honestly, the way that kind of social history has developed in the military history discipline has been pretty disappointing. I mean, mostly, it's really come about articulating political and stakeholder and social agendas in history hasn't really informed, I don't think, military history all too terribly well, and it's been more of a mirror for how people see the world than really kind of informative. I think, you know, the histories that John Dower's written kind of actually taken to a dead end, as military historians.

But, I would argue that you cannot write really good 20th century military history without this interdisciplinary perspective, because I think there's a really important cycle that we see there, which is, and particularly important when you look at leadership and

PANEL 5

command issues. And it's this, is that that we have this cycle of developing ideas and concepts, intellectual and business constructs in the private sector, and then when we mobilize for war and we adapt to meet all the new changes of a new kind of war, and we suck people in to do that, and we suck ideas in to do that, we transform the military. And those ideas come into the military and they are themselves transformed, and then when we send veterans back out into the private sector, we flush that back out and we change the rest of society as well. And this cycle goes on and on, whether you want to talk about the impact of things like scientific management, and Taylor's writing had that eventually came in and shaped the military for World War I, or how our ideas about middle management shaped how we fought World War II. But I think this cycle is important and I think it's profound. Sometimes it has very positive effects, both on the civil society side and the military side, sometimes it comes through rather awkwardly. But I think it's really critically important, and I think it nowhere has greater and more important and more vital implications than understanding the narrative of the US Army in the 1960s and 1970s and 1980s, and what happened to our profession, and why.

There's this great myth that somehow the problem of the US Military in the 1970s was a problem of the profession. That somehow it was the ethics or the culture or the values or the brains of military service, which really accounted for the failures in Vietnam and the failures of performance in Vietnam. You know, I think this narrative is unbelievably unsupportable, even on the most superficial level. And you can just look back, now historically, at some of the kind of shining things that we put out to prove that. One of my favorite ones was "Zero Defects." We all remember Zero Defects, right? This was the management techniques, drive all the mistakes out of the thing. Zero Defects was a very innocuous civilian military—excuse me, civilian management practice. We imported it, much like we always import these things into, just like we imported Taylor and other management business concepts into the military. Of course, like many things, the Army inartfully integrated it, because you can't necessarily port business leadership concepts just directly into the military and do it smartly. So we had things, like, for example, everybody had to sign a Zero Defects card. To swear that they would make sure that there were no defects. Now, this was then later resurrected as this was the root of all evil, because we had body counts, and bad leadership, and everything, because we had this risk-averse leadership and all this and everything. That's never been studied, never been—and on the face, it's kind of insupportable. We did Six Sigma in the 1990s, right? Six Sigma's just the modern version of Zero Defects. I don't remember anybody running around the military saying that Six Sigma destroyed the culture of the US Military.

There was an enormous debate about leadership versus management. Whether you needed leaders or managers. Again, this was a very innocuous kind of—well, not innocuous. This was a really inane debate that was kind of stupid. If you actually look at modern business leadership writing, they really say, well, leadership and management, you know, it's not one or the other. You have to have both skills. But again, nobody went back and historically looked at this to say, was there really something to this debate. And you could also look at the Military Reform Movement, which I think has been woefully understudied. The Military Reform was opinion without analysis. You had all these great military arguments for military reform based on a bunch of opinions. I mean, there was nothing analytical or substantive behind those things. So, and this all famously culminated, and we're in the right place, right? With, of course, the famous leadership study down at Leavenworth, where they surveyed the students and they said, oh, our leaders are corrupt and valueless and broken and all the rest of this stuff and everything. And everybody looked and said oh god, it must be true. Nobody said, well, it's just a bunch of majors griping. This is really—and where is the real analytical study of this, study that puts it in its context, to see this is really telling us something about the culture and profession of the military, or is it just a bunch of guys spouting off.

So, I mean, I think this narrative is so incredibly unsupportable and inane. I offer just three observations that anybody ought to be able to make in 15 seconds to say that this historical narrative is just stupid and unsupportable. Maybe there's nothing wrong with the US Military profession in the 1960s or 1970s, and maybe resurrecting the profession was not the root of the resurrection improvement in the 1980s.

The first one is like, who did the resurrecting? Who were these guys? And many of them had been mentioned today. If you look at the cadre of leaders who set the foundation for the rebuilding in the 1980s, and some of them led the rebuilding in the 1980s, who are these guys? Well, a lot of them were World War II veterans. They're the Greatest Generation. So how could they have gone from being the Greatest Generation to, like, boobs? And so, you could have just go on with the names, and we talked about some of them. DePuy. Abrams. And then there were names we didn't mention, like Dutch Kerwin. Now, Dutch Kerwin started fighting in North Africa at 26, 27 years old. He organized the artillery fires to the breakout at Anzio. Fought his way, all the way into France. Was Chief of Staff for Abrams and Westmoreland both, and then Vice Chief of Staff. I mean, these guys are all over the military in the '70s and '80s. They were the ones doing the rebuilding. So they couldn't have gone from being the Greatest Generation to not the Greatest Generation. Obviously, somewhere, when the 1960s broke out, they didn't check their culture and their values and professionalism at the door. And then go back and get them out of the closet after the Vietnam War was over.

I think the second problem is if you look at who actually did the rebuilding of the military in the 1980s, last time I checked, they were all veterans of Vietnam. Right? So, you go down the list of the Reimers and the Sullivans and the Vuonos and the Cavazos and the Ulmers and the Franks, so, they didn't get some kind of magic pill in 1980 that turned them from weak-kneed risk-averse leaderless, cultureless, valueless guys, and all of a sudden they got their "mojo" back. So that's unsupportable.

And I think the third thing is, and this is where I really fault us as a profession. With very few exceptions, people like Bob Sorley, who had the audacity to write that there actually may have been people during Vietnam who weren't idiots, like Abrams and Harold K. Johnson, but mostly, nobody went looking in the record for signs of a vibrant US Army professionalism in the 1960s. Or signs of culture or value. And I think the truth is if we had mined there, we'd find a lot very easily. When I was at West Point, one of the projects I worked on was there was a really interesting project that was run by the History Department in the 1960s called the Adventure Board. This was run by Tom Griess. And Tom said, you know, a lot of our graduates are doing great things out there. The cadets don't know anything about that. This is before Facebook. So, this was the Facebook of the 1960s. Something probably you guys have never heard of, it's called "mail." So Tom had a letter writing campaign where they wrote to graduates and former professors and other people in Vietnam, they said write us back on your experiences so we can share them with the cadets. And they posted these letters, and they did illustrations on it. Some of you remember Bob Carson Barsky, who was the cartographer forever at West Point, died a few years ago. He did up displays and all this. It was very popular while around. Then, when the war winded down, they just kind of grabbed all this stuff up and they threw it in a closet and they forgot about it, and when I heard about it, I actually went looking for it. They told me it had been thrown away, and I went—I was walking down the hall one day, and I don't know if any of you guys remember Colonel Dillard, I forget his first name. Scott Dillard, right. Who said that? You've been in Scott's office then, right? OK, so you know where this story is going. Scott Dillard was the world's biggest rat pack. His office looked like the last scene from *Raiders of the Lost Ark*. And so I go to Colonel Dillard, I said, "Oh my god, I just talked to the janitor guy, he said they threw all these things away." He says, "I think they're in my office." So I think I saw them sitting out at the trash bin, I thought that might be interesting, I might want to look at that somebody. And so we go into his office, and buried in the back of his office is these boxes of these letters. And so we drug them out, and we cataloged them, and we put them in the library. But the point is if you read those letters from young junior officers and lieutenants and captains and some majors, you could have changed the date and the name, and they could have been somebody writing from the Meuse-Argonne, or some guy writing from Anzio, or Bougainville, and, they just read like every other. They were honorable letters, there were people who were proud of what they were doing, people that, and granted, they were writing back to cadets, right? But still, you could tell that a lot of these letters were just genuinely honest. And I don't think that's a hard thing to find. I think if we went back and we looked at professionalism in the 1960s, we would find a military whose values and cultures were every bit as resilient and strong as they were in the '40s and in the '50s and in the '80s.

Now, it doesn't mean I think that Army leadership was in this great condition, because I do think there was a significant, and great, and enduring flaw in Army leadership, and it is this. And that is the intellectual capacity of military leaders to adjust to divergent ways of war. I think there is a weakness in the military leadership in the US Army, and I think it hinges on professional education, how we do professional education. I think if you look at the post-Cold War period, there were three big changes. One was the advent of new technology and computers and the information, all that, and quite honestly, the Army didn't do too bad there. We kind of got that one. I think we have to credit Sullivan and Reimer and Shinseki with not missing that. I mean, the other two were expeditionary warfare, which we totally missed. I remember back when we started doing the post-Cold War stuff and we were doing our experiments, and somebody said, "Well, what are we going to do about the deployment phase?" And General Hartzog said, "Aw, we don't have time to worry about that." Right? And so we jumped into fighting the war. And of course, the expeditionary piece was huge. And we spent almost no time on that, 'til we ran into things like Kosovo, and other theaters where the Army found trouble getting in deployment, and of course, the third piece was addressing irregular warfare despite the vast amount of experience we had among our junior leaders in Vietnam, the Army was totally unprepared for that as well.

So, why is that? Why did we do relatively well in the professional development front, but on this intellectual front, this capacity to adjust the military thinking to different ways of war, why did we fare, I think, far less well? Despite the fact that we did such a great job of rebuilding the military in the 1980s, and I would cite three things.

The first was the promotion system. Again, this was something, again, another thing we borrowed from the business sector, the idea that good, smart people, you don't want to lose them, so you want to get them up in the ranks, you want to give them leadership, you want to get them up faster. So the Army developed a system of early below the zone promotions. So one of the problems of below the zone promotions is we literally started deciding when people were captains, whether they're going to be generals or not. Because we were putting people on a fast track when we were captains, and the way the system worked is, quite honestly, unless the guy committed some major crime or something, he just stayed on the fast track, because nobody would take him off, until he became a general. And as you get into the more senior level of promotion, you basically have, when you get into the boards, who are people promoting in boards? Well, they're promoting people that they think are going to be the best leaders. And we all know who the best leaders are going to be, right? That's very easy. It's the people that look like me, think like me, sound like me, talk like me. So the tendencies to promote people who fit the paradigm, and as long as the paradigm was very narrow, doing kind of things closer, mirror the Fulda Gap, the Army was great. But when the paradigm really broadened, and you need leaders looking at very, very divergent cases, then you found, I think, as a whole, with exceptions, the intellectual community of the Army, the leadership was limited. Limited, in part, because of the promotion system that created like that looks a lot like that.

I think the second problem that hurt the Army a great deal was the way we downsized at the end of the Cold War. And there were two problems there. One was that commands disappeared overnight. And so you had several year groups who went from having, like, a hundred opportunities to command, to maybe, like, ten. And of course, in the Army promotion system, if you didn't command, you didn't get promoted. You didn't get to senior service school. So I think there was a whole further narrowing the intellectual variety is, boy, when you're narrowing it down, you can only get a few guys. The like of the like are really the ones that get through.

And then, of course, we had this early out option. We said everybody can take early out. And who are the kinds of people who took early out? This is, again, a practice we borrowed from business. As a matter of fact, Lockheed Martin had just done one of these things, and Lockheed Martin had just rediscovered what the Army rediscovered, is the people that take the early out, they're not necessarily the ones you want to leave. A lot of them are maybe some of your most talented and creative people who are frustrated in the system, and rather than stick it out, they just take the money and run. So I think the combination between the rapid depression of commands and creating opportunities for some of the best and brightest, and even some of the best and quirkiest, to kind of walk out the door, people took advantage of that.

PANEL 5

Then the third place I would really place fault is our senior military, professional military education. Which really, in my mind, ossified in the wake of World War II. Where we're sending leaders to learn how to be strategic thinkers about a week before they retire. So we're sending people who are in their mid and late '40s to really their capstone intellectual experience. First of all, I don't know about you, but I think by the time a brain gets to about 45 years old, it's untrainable. So, I think intellectually, you're not really very adaptive. They're very little time for you to practice that skill. There's very little opportunity for you to practice that skill, and I think in a sense, that really put the Army thinking on hold, the fact that we really weren't cultivating very strategic thinking at very, very junior levels.

You know, I would contrast the model that we had in the '70s and the '80s, which, and maybe we can debate this. But to me, one of the most fruitful and productive errors of leadership and intellectual development in the US Military was the interwar years between World War I and World War II. And my argument is the bad news is, nobody got promoted. The good news was nobody got promoted. And so, in an environment like that, where you didn't get promoted, but you also didn't get kicked out either. In a sense, you could do whatever the heck you wanted to. And we had a lot of military leaders who made a lot of interesting choices, and they could, because they weren't going to pay a price for that. So you had people like Eisenhower went and worked in the Philippines. You had Stilwell, who's going, running off, and Maxwell Taylor going to language school in Japan. So you didn't have this kind of ossification or this very narrowness of thinking and experience. You actually had, for the US Army, one of the more wide and varied levels of experience. Then you jump into World War II, and then what happens is we get into World War II, and we find ourselves doing all kinds of things in all kinds of places in the world that we never thought about doing. So we're doing amphibious operations in the Pacific. We're storming the Siegfried Line. And it's almost like that scene from *Mission: Impossible*, at the beginning of the old TV series, where he pulls out the portfolio and he says, "Where can I find the right guy for the right job?" And miraculously, in World War II, there was a pretty big list. You could find a Stilwell. You could find a Patton. You could find a logistician. You could find guys who are gurus. You could find guys with quirky experiences and backgrounds that would fit the needs of a unique situation that you hadn't anticipated in a way, I would argue, that you don't find when you walk into the aftermath of the invasion of Iraq or in Afghanistan. The bench, you could find some of those guys, but the bench is just not as deep, because you didn't let them develop and mature and grow and gain that variety of opportunity of experience as junior officers. So you couldn't deal with the unanticipated.

So why do I raise this? Well, I think there's a debate here. Whether we're going to continue in the long war, or whether we're going to go into the next interwar period, in the generation ahead. And I think there's good news and bad news there, and I'll just close on this.

So, the good news is, we now have Army leadership from the highest levels from the very most junior levels who have enormous operational experience, right? These guys have way more combat time than maybe any other army in the history of the Army. And it's all kinds of things in lots of different environments. That's a great body to build on.

So, what's the bad news? Well, the bad news is operational experience untempered by intellect isn't necessarily the most helpful thing in the world. There's a great story, which is after World War II, they sent everybody to Leavenworth. Big help, right? After you fought the war, we send you to school to learn how to fight war. But they went anyway, right? Because they didn't have anything else to do. We had the school curriculum and we had the school solution. So we do a tactical problem, and the instructor would present the school solution, whereupon all the World War II combat vets would stand up and just groan and, "Oh my god, that is so stupid." "Oh my god, we would never do that." "Oh my god, that is *so* stupid. *Oh my god.*" And then the Pacific guys would stand up and they go, "Oh, you're right, that is so stupid. But you European guys, you don't know what the hell you're talking about. This is the way you *really* do it." And the point is, they were very smart and intuitive, but from their own operational perspective. So having operational experience is great, but unless you can grow that operational experience and learn how to adopt that to a variety of experience, is not very useful. And you need education to do that. So, I think having a generation of combat leaders is actually almost dangerous, because they're going to think is the answer is what they did in the whatever valley, and they have to learn that that's just one kind of war and one kind of experience, and they have to learn how to take that personal experience and use that to develop the intuitive judgment and insight to adapt that to other kinds of warfare and other experiences. So that's problem number one.

Problem number two is this advantage is temporal. They don't stay around forever. And so, the space between one combat generation and the next, you don't know if that's World War II and Korea, or Vietnam and Desert Storm. So that advantage of combat experience is a temporal, ephemeral thing that goes away over time.

The third thing is downsizing. I don't think another downsizing is out of the question. Nobody can predict the future. But if you talk to Army leadership or you talk to everybody in DoD, the mantra is no money, no this, no that. It's only a question of time 'til they start thinning out the ranks. And the question's how do they downsize. Do we do it again, where we let the best and the brightest walk away. There's some very interesting research on that about whether the best and brightest and staying, and how they're staying, and if they really are the best and the brightest. But I think that creates an enormous challenge for the military. A lot of this is what do you do after they save Berlin? If you've been a 2d lieutenant, and you've commanded on a forward operations base, right, and you are the warrior king, and then the war's over, and now you're a 2d lieutenant, and you're getting yelled at by the captain because all the Humvees or whatever they have now, MRAPs aren't lined up, right, you're thinking, "This sucks. I'm going to go do something else." And so, a lot of times you have trouble keeping a combat generation engaged in their profession, because it's just boring.

And then the final thing is, I think, the professional military education system. I think we are broken, in the sense that we are not keeping up with the rest of the planet. Almost every other major profession has their capstone formal professional educational experience when they're in their early 20s or early 30s. Only the military waits until you're dead, before they actually send you to senior service school. And as much as I love our war colleges, I think they are too narrow to give us the range of leaders and thinkers that we're going to need in the future, and I do think we need a diversity of professional military education experience, and I think we need it much earlier in people's careers. And I think without that, we risk losing all the creativity and innovation and imagination that we've gained in the last years trying to adjust to this long war.

Well thank you, and I appreciate it. Over to you.

# Day 2, Panel 5: Rebirth of the US Army, 1976-2001

## Questions and Answers

(Transcript of Presentation)

## Richard Swain, Ph.D.
## James Carafano, Ph.D.

## Moderated by MAJ(P) Clay Mountcastle

**MAJ(P) Mountcastle:**

OK. And one of the other reasons I was excited to sign up to be a moderator is that I knew at least I could pose my question and not run out of time, because I get to take moderator's privilege and throw it out there first. But, and this question is something I've been thinking about for a bit of time, and it's directed to both members of the panel. Jim, it might fit in a little bit more with what you presented with us now, but certainly, offered to both of you. Clearly over the past eight years or so, we've heard building criticism of the post-Vietnam Army, and particularly the leadership in the post-Vietnam Army, in that it was not keen to pay attention to the lessons of Vietnam. It was too quick to put the lessons of Vietnam behind it and blaze ahead and not look back. However, when those opinions are expressed, I don't see a lot of what-ifs added to that, as to how, had the Army leadership chosen to do that, how that might have affected the rebuilding the process that everybody was so happy with when it finally seemed to work and get the Army to where it was by 1990, and if we're going to look at victory in the Persian Gulf as kind of this capstone to the rebuilding phase, some might argue that, but would we have had the same rebuilding process if the Army leadership had chosen to dwell on those lessons of Vietnam more like the critics would like to have seen, or would we not have had the same Army that we arrived in the Persian Gulf with in 1990, had we chosen to do that?

**Dr. Carafano:**

Yeah, I would say the Army didn't have a choice. First of all, the attitude, not just of the White House, but of the senior members in Congress and the nation as a whole is "Never again, we're not going to do this anymore." So if the Army went into Congress and said I want to spend all this money on sustaining irregular warfare as a mission, everybody would have said, "OK, you're not going to get any money." And the second point was the funding in the post-military was bare bones. It didn't leave a lot—you had to make hard choices, and the Army's hard choice was the enemy that was still in front, and that was the Fulda Gap. So I'm not really sure the Army had many choices, but I think we potentially could be in a situation, again, where the Army is faced with exactly the same choice. And the decision this time may be, "OK, great, we're going to do irregular warfare. We just don't do the conventional warfare anymore." That's the debate we have now. And either way, they're both bad choices, right? Because the enemy's going to do whatever we don't. So if we do irregular warfare, then they'll just beat us conventionally, or vice versa. I don't know how you could be a great power and not do windows, and play baseball and softball and soccer.

**Dr. Swain:**

I agree with the basic premise, which to me, the error, first of all, I don't think you had another choice, for the same reasons. I think the error is that the Army wants to be a one-trick pony, and I don't think that's an option. It's not a true statement that the Army completely abandoned irregular warfare to the extent that the Special Operations people claim that as their jurisdiction and their particular field of expertise. That clearly was inadequate when we ended up in Iraq. I always tell everybody, we wouldn't have had the insurgency problem in Iraq if Dave Perkins couldn't have gotten to Baghdad with a conventional attack, and we've tended to forget that in the intervening nine years. But I think the thing I agree with most is you can't—there's the business about we don't do windows, and you ain't going to get it in the world we live in. We're going to have to be more versatile. Or you're going to have to be more versatile, I won't. (laughter)

**Dr. Carafano:**

Just one quick follow up. I think we should kill the other great myth, which was the answer, which is a great soldier could do anything. So when you talked about irregular warfare, the answer you got was, "Well, we have great soldiers. If they can fight the Battle of the Fulda Gap, they can adapt to anything." And what's proven is that's not true. Great soldiers can do anything. It may take you three or four years and several thousand casualties, and you pay a pretty high strategic price for that. But this notion is, if you build a good disciplined well-organized educated force, that they're going to adjust to radically different kinds of warfare effortlessly, that's just not—I don't think there's any evidence for that.

**Dr. Schifferle:**

I generally agree with the perspective that you both have. But there is a question that we've kind of glossed over both yesterday and today, which is educate what? And the discussion of good soldiers do everything well, or a multi-purpose force, general purpose force versus a constabulary force and an MCO force, but in the officer education realm, are there not common issues that are common to command and control leadership, logistics, sustainment, those kinds of things that probably would fill up all available time and all OES, where the environment in which you're doing those things was only, if you will, the background of the instruction?

**Dr. Swain:**

I think that—I'm not sure exactly how to take that on, except to say that first of all, education doesn't just take place in the schoolhouse. The notion, I happened, my own pet theory right now is I think about General Dempsey's question, is if you watch his tape, he says a very interesting thing. And that is that emulation is what makes someone a professional. That doesn't happen in the schoolhouse. My own view is that you're training for the mass of the Army if you teach sound tactical principles, you can do it in multiple scenarios that'll get what you need, the privates know how to do. The difficulty is having, really, in my mind, the field-grade officers with a sufficient range of possibilities that they can shift from one to another as the circumstances require. And I just, I think, my own opinion is, you can do a judicious curriculum in this college that'll give you that range of skills. I don't see it running out.

Now, just to be critical and controversial, if you want to dispose of a curriculum to teach a technique for a year, you're going to get the results of people skilled in a technique and don't have any idea why that technique is there.

**Dr. Carafano:**

I guess I'd like to confine my comments to talking about the strategic leaders, and not the people that generally who you talk to, is the ones we have to be generous to. So, I think there are three essential leadership skills, and coincidentally, I think, actually, military history and history in general is an extremely valuable tool for all three. And one of the reasons why I've really been disappointed at the semi-demise of military history in general. The first one is the one we've always talked about, traditionally, which is critical thinking skills. How do you think critically about a problem, which I think SAMS does a great job of that. The second one is the why do you think what you think skill, which is why do you believe what you believe? Why do you hold these assumptions? Why do you address problems this way? I think that's an equally valuable and important skill, to understand how to question your own assumption, we do some of this now with red teaming for example. So why do you think what you think. And the third one, which I do think we are arguably, maybe a little neglectful of as a society, is, who are you? In other words, do you understand who you are, as an American? Your cultural values, your social values. What makes an American uniquely an American? And why is that important to you, and why should you care about that? So I would say those are the three core essential intellectual skills that I would like the system to impart to our senior leaders.

**MAJ(P) Mountcastle:**

Of course. A follow up.

**Dr. Schifferle:**

The interwar period had two distinct differences, at least two distinct differences, in addition to the ones that you mentioned, to the contemporary educational environment. The first one was that—and nobody got promoted until everybody got promoted is true. The corollary of that is that the only efficiency reports that really mattered were the school efficiency reports. That students assessed by instructors who themselves were assessed as students, brought to the Army the ability to assess individual skills. Not so much unit performance, but individual skills. So I'd like to toss that out here and say, should we move in that direction? And I think I would add a fourth to your list of three, which is self-confidence. The ability to know that you can do certain tasks under pressure and get a go, gives the officer a sense of confidence once they graduate, and that may go a long way towards explaining how we were able to cope with global war in World War II.

**Dr. Carafano:**

Yeah, just on your point about evaluation, I think that's right. You can have all these great and weird, quirky skillsets, but if nobody knows you had them, they don't do you much good. One of the values of the interwar Army was that it was so small, is everybody knew everybody and knew their strengths and weaknesses, and apparently for [Lloyd] Fredendall, apparently everybody thought he was a great guy. And of course, now it's a bigger military, and you've got the Reserve and the National Guard piece. So, I wouldn't say the interwar system, right, would work terribly well as a model now. But the dynamic of, again, I mean, the problem is, is you got to have this place for these quirky, weird, strange thinkers, right? Who don't fit the mold and look like everybody else, until one day you discover, oh my god, I need that guy. Or girl. And so you have to have a way to keep them in, and flourish them, and develop them as leaders, and not lose them, because you might need them someday.

**Audience Member 1:**

I'd like to follow up on, and solicit from both of you, comments on, particularly your observation that we educate folks too late, that you go to the Army War College and then you die. (laughter) And so, the timing isn't right. It seems to be that that's a very critical aspect of the Army educational process, or of any educational process, is trying to get the timing right so that the person has a sufficient frame of reference to understand what it is they're dealing with, and the problems that you're training them towards have sufficient currency that things will still be fresh in their mind when they get to them. And yesterday, we were talking about 19th century educational paradigms, and essentially, you got your education up front. And then everything else you learned on the job. And by the time you got to the end of it, you're woefully undereducated, because you hadn't kept pace. You mentioned, with some admiration, how doctors and lawyers do it, but doctors and lawyers, at least all the ones I know or are related to have a different problem. They get out of step. They get out of currency. They lose the warm afterglow of having been recently educated, and they have to go to great lengths and great pains to kind of catch up. And a doctor who's been out of medical school for 40 years is almost hopeless, unless he's been re-educated in a period of time. So, two part question is, how do you get the timing right, because our whole evolution has been towards this process of having sufficient penny packets of education that you spread them out in time in such a matter that they're useful when they're needed, and also a corollary question is, in particular with respect to your observation of going to the War College and then dying, how does SAMS fit into that paradigm, because SAMS, of course, trains you to do some pretty ethereal high level stuff at a very early point in your career.

**Dr. Carafano:**

So I think that you characterized the Army education model perfectly when you said basically it's just-in-time education. We give somebody the education they need for the assignment directly before the assignment. So first, I would say is like ten years operational experience—and I agree with you, is the best educational paradigm is the one where you have both a combination of operational real-world experience combined with that academic experience. That's why a lot of times, I used to, before a recession, suggest to my kids when they graduate, go get some life experience before you go back to graduate school, so you know what the heck, why you're doing this, right? So I would say ten years of operational experience would be more than enough for anybody to have a good foundation that they should be able to assimilate a graduate level education and see what really has meaning for them. If it's a good graduate level education, as part of their professionalism, it should instill in them the notion of a lifetime of learning. The notion that they need to be constant learners over their profession, and that they're going to have to seek out opportunities to do that. And I think that would take care of itself.

**Dr. Swain:**

I don't believe you die after the War College. I'm not a beneficiary of the Army War College, I came to SAMS as a War College fellow, and I was telling somebody the other day the great benefit of the fellowship took place for me when we went to PACOM. We did a global trip. And what happened at PACOM was having grown up in the notion of AirLand Battle is the paradigm of how wars are fought. I'll never forget sitting in the PACAF Auditorium while the Commander of the Pacific Air Forces talked about how air power would be employed in an oceanic theater. And it was a completely different paradigm. And it all made sense. But I never thought about putting tanker lines up as the critical thing that an Air Force general would worry about. So I think that, in my particular case, I found it a real perspective change. I remember, I think we can make way too much of the notion of turning out a "Jedi" from the Army War College, and I'm reminded of the young German officer who was counseled by being told that the emperor had one strategist, and he wasn't it. Most of the people I have seen being strategists were being military bureaucrats moving paper, and the skill they had to have was moving paper. It seems to me that the trick is identifying the paper movers who understand what the paper's all about, and moving them forward. And I'm not sure that happens in the War College. I like it when Huba Wass de Czege designed SAMS, I think there was a real elegance to the notion that it was a three year course. The first year was to lay the foundation in CGSC. The second year was what you learned in SAMS, and the third year was a year of actually going out and practicing what you had done theoretically, and Huba's notion was always that it took all of those experiences to produce a, quote, "SAMS officer." And so, my own view is that's about the right model, and where the War College graduate becomes a real strategist is when he gets into a job that requires strategic thinking, and he either succeeds in applying what he's learned, or he learned how to play golf at Carlisle. So, I'm not nearly as worried about it. I'll throw in one other thought. I had a discussion with Mike Steele once, who's really a smart guy, and knows a lot of stuff I don't know. And I was wringing my hands about—my generation came out of Vietnam, and it was expected that you got a graduate degree. I mean, you just had to do that. You know, throw me in that briar patch. But I mean, it was really an expectation until 1987. And all of a sudden, the Army went to muddy boots. And my whole explanation of this was oh, the Army rejected intellectualism. And Mike Steele said no they didn't, they ran out of Majors. There's a correlation between the fore structure and the availability of opportunities to educate. When Donn Starry founded CAS3, and truncated the career course, it wasn't because he thought it was a better idea. It was the only idea the personnel guys could sustain.

So, we have got to learn how to manage a TTS, what is it, TTHS, is that what, yeah. We got to learn how to manage that account as part of the Army, or we're never going to get the structure right. Yeah. I mean, you know, we're liable to look at what's going on now with people that don't come to, you know, we got the structure, but we're not moving the people through it.

**Dr. Carafano:**

Yeah, Pete and I saw that when we taught at West Point. West Point's a very interesting case, and you can track the history of the Academy of when it's considered a career killer for officers to teach there, and when it's considered a gold star, and it has nothing to do with the job, it just has to do with the amount of available officers. So when Pete and I got recruited to go teach, being at West Point was a really plum assignment. By the time we left, it was a career killer. And in Pete's case, it's true.

**Dr. Schifferle:**

I was thinking about this. I think we're about to tell the Army, or to have the Army tell its officers, who wants to get out? If the inevitable occurs, and we draw down to eight or six or some number less than ten. A reminder that in 1920 or so, we asked the Army officers who were going to be eliminated, who wants to stay? And we had promotion panels, selection panels, and tests, and exam. A very rigorous system to make sure that, of the 20,000 or so you're going to kick out, that we're going to be keep the best 5.

**Dr. Swain:**

Well, remember the '90s. The absurdity of the '90s --

**Dr. Schifferle:**

Oh, I do.

**Dr. Swain:**

For me, the first thing we did was bribe people to get out, and then complain because they did.

**Dr. Carafano:**

Pete, I know somebody else had a point, but I just wanted to follow up. Wasn't it a conscious decision to overstaff the officer corps?

**Dr. Schifferle:**

Yes. There was about a 3 to 1 ratio compared to what it was before 1917 and what it was after 1920. We had a conscious decision, and it was primarily because of the National Defense Act of 1920, required 50-plus percent of the officers to serve in educational institutions as instructors or students. So if you were going to have a field force of nine active divisions, you needed those nine active divisions worth of officers. But we needed another two times officers to serve as TTHS account for students, instructors, and then the inevitable staff hogs that are laying around. It was a conscious decision to do exactly that.

**Audience Member 2:**

Dr. Swain mentioned the problem that General Dempsey identified was the failure of imagination. So I want to ask Dr. Swain, how do we develop and educate imagination, and Dr. Carafano, how do we tap and employ imaginative officers?

**Dr. Swain:**

Well, I, of course, convinced that history is the only way to produce imaginative officers, simply by the virtue of the variety that good history gives you of context and contingency. You train for it by, you know, there's a wonderful story of Lawton Collins, in his autobiography, talks about, when he was training in the division staff, he would take them out with one mission, he kept changing the circumstances on them to require them to adapt to it until that became the norm. I mean, that's about all I can offer on that.

**Dr. Carafano:**

That's a great question. I mean, I think the first question is the discussion Pete and I were talking about, what are the critic, obviously, I think that if you have critical thinking skills and the ability to know why you know what you know, understand how do you do critical analysis, and you understand foundationally who you are, that provides the intellectual component foundation of officers who can deal who can manage generally. But your second question's really interesting. Of course, it's easy now, because we have an operational environment, it's very easy to have, for us people to be imaginative, right? Because they just get plenty of opportunity to practice that. What happens when you walk into an interwar period, right, how do you be imaginative then? That's the really interesting question, because nobody's just interested in counting plates in the mess hall. So one way you can let them practice that is through the diversity of their educational experience. And the other way you practice that is you let people go do interesting things. Maybe necessarily outside the line unit. Which, again, poses a big problem, because if you've downsized, you've got very little resources, you know, that has to be a very conscious decision, like they made in the 1920s to say okay, we understand, we're not going to have enough money to do anything. What are we really going to do? You know what? We're going to invest in intellectual capital. We're going to save the people first. We're going to keep the brains, and sacrifice everything else. So you need a leadership that's going make that decision that, not that I'm in favor of downsizing, I fully believe we ought to fully fund the military, and we shouldn't be facing this thing. But if the Army is faced with that, that would only be retained through a conscious decision that you could say, okay, I'm going to let this guy for a year with industry. But if you take your officer corps back to the bare bones you need to keep the operational force afloat, that ain't going to happen. So you're going to lose that ability to do imaginative, creative types of challenges for people.

**Rick Astore:**

I'm from the Center of Military History. To follow up on that a little bit. Perhaps a fourth one of your critical elements that we need to teach more on is the question, who are they¬? As in, not just who are we, but who are the other people in the world that we need to know more about. And I would think that that experience would only come from advanced degrees and outside experience. Again, with the size of the officer corps remaining steady, you have to get that experience somehow, and if you're not actively deployed there, you're going to have to go through a very elaborate educational system to learn about other cultures, and I think the Army still gives lip service to "other cultural training." You know, six weeks of language training. Is not the same as learning deeply about a variety of cultures around the world. So, I think that may be a fourth critical element.

PANEL 5

**Dr. Carafano:**

Yeah, I think you have to be careful on the "who are they" problem, right? Because it's the world. So the notion of are you going to make somebody converse into every culture, everywhere in the world? That's a bit unrealistic. And so are you going to pick your shots, and maybe you'll get your shots exactly wrong, so now we make everybody learn Arabic, and so if we wind up fighting in Venezuela, will be kind of, so, and I'm also very kind of, I'm really skeptical of the Lawrence of Arabia model, that every officer needs to be the Lawrence of Arabia kind of guy, right? So, I think you develop creative officers, and they learn how to adapt to an environment. So I think it would be very good for people to have a cultural experience, like, okay I lived for two years in Japan. Not necessarily that you live for two years in Japan, two years in Morocco, two years everything else. And the other thing is we have to be, we have to recognize that human brains are human brains. Not everybody wants to be a math major, not everybody wants to live in Japan. And if you want to maintain a breadth and diversity in your workforce, you've got to allow some kind of flexibility and career development, and people love to play to their strengths, right? And so, in a sense, some people are going to want to be rocket scientists. And some people are going to want to be Lawrence of Arabia. And you have to decide if you want to create a human capital program that allows for that kind of diversity, and allows people the opportunity to kind of develop intellectually where they feel really strong. And it's a bet, right? It may turn out you don't need a guy who really knows about Japan. But then again, it may turn out that you really do. So, I, as much as, I think, ironically, as much as we talk about human capital, and as important as it is and everything, I think on this intellectual thing is really kind of a blind spot for the Army. If you think about what's going on now, we're investing an awful lot in human capital in terms of thinking about problems of sustained combat, wounded warriors, and all that kind of stuff. But the kind of things we're talking about, as much as I'd love to hear General Dempsey talking about that, and other initiatives and stuff, I think as a whole, the Army, I don't see people really thinking about the intellectual capital piece in a way that's going to get the Army 30 or 40 years down the road. And the Army in the interwar years, they made one good decision. But they just got enough of it right that they had a very good cadre of senior, wound up with a very good cadre of senior leaders that saved the nation during World War II. So, if you get just a little bit of this right.

**Audience Member 4:**

This is kind of a long question. But, I hear this "rebirth" of the Army and all this stuff, and I'm wondering if we aren't looking at this era, '70s, '80s, through rose-colored glasses. If you look at the Army doctrine, the '76's is active defense, and then we have AirLand Battle in the '82, '86 FM 100-5. And it's kind of returned to the comfort zone. It's the hi-diddle-diddle armor, armor heavy philosophy. And yet, look at what's happening in the world. We have Grenada. We have Panama. We have Somalia. All this is light infantry stuff that needs to be deployed very rapidly, and our major doctrinal publication doesn't cover it. All the officers and a lot of the units are going to National Training Center, practicing AirLand Battle, and we don't have AirLand Battle until '91 in the First Gulf War, and if I may bring up just one thing about that, you have General Scales, in his film, Certain

Victory, talking about all of the Army's problems are solved now, and then a few months later, what do you have? You have Somalia. So...

**Dr. Swain:**

I'm not going to be responsible for General Scales.

**Audience Member 4:**

But if you look at it overall through the '70s and the '80s, the education and training we're giving our leaders doesn't match what's going on in the world.

**Dr. Swain:**

But what was going on to me, the fallacy in that argument is the notion that what was going on in the world constituted the main problem. And it didn't constitute the main problem. There was no existential problem in Grenada. The Grenada was something we could do because we were big and powerful and full of hubris. But I don't see where it would have been, I don't see where the alternative would have been useful, to focus Army doctrine on dealing with Grenada. You know, you could send the Mississippi National Guard down there with broomsticks if you had to.

**Audience Member 4:**

Okay, I'm not saying "focus." But we had doctrine that was terribly focused on the operational level war in Europe, and yet, if you look at the 1968 that we rejected, it talks about an Army that's deployed around the world. It talks about allies, NATO, counter-insurgency warfare. It covers what we call "the full spectrum of war." And we don't get to anybody talking about the full spectrum of war until kinda sorta the FM 100 of 1993.

**Dr. Swain:**

And that seems to me to be the argument relevant to today, and I'll give you an example. General Dempsey, right now, one of his principal things as TRADOC Commander to sell is this new idea of mission command. Or mission orders, or whatever the right euphemism is. Interestingly enough, in 2003, FM 6-0 adopted mission command as the Army standard for command. Now, that's only useful if you know FM 6-0 is there. I agree with you, I like the '68 manual. But how many people in '76 knew about the '68 manual? It wasn't rejected, nobody knew it was there.

**Audience Member 4:**

But we went back to it in 2001. We looked at FM 3-0. It's very similar.

**Dr. Swain:**

And I was here when all those guys were doing that, and that was a deliberate—but it doesn't change what I just said. Nobody rejected the '68 manual, nobody knew it was there.

**Dr. Carafano:**

So I would agree with you in a sense that—and that was my argument, is the sense that what you had was a military that was capable of being "mo' better," right? In a narrow range, right. Now, I think there was a couple of reasons why things like Grenada and Panama and stuff didn't resonate. One was, even with the rebuilding and the money that we threw into the Army in the 1980s, there wasn't really, because you have to remember, Russia was still there, right? So that was still job one, right? And there was not the capacity, even with all the money that went in there, because you're coming from so far behind, to be able to look at those things. If you remember back, the light divisions are justified not because they're going to do stuff like Somalia and Grenada. They only got funded because they came up with a mission that worked in NATO. Now, it was bogus, and stupid, right? But that was the only way it got them funded. So, and as a matter of fact, if you looked at the total Army, and we talked about the total Army, but other than the roundout brigades, the total Army in the 1980s was still pretty not well funded and trained. Just because the money wasn't there for that. And that was a big part of that. And that's why if we're going, you know, the rocks and the shoals and everything are there. If we go into a period of downsizing here, the decision that the senior Army leaders make, and these are the kind of decisions that nobody's going to prevent them from making. Nobody's going to tell the Army how to spend its 12 bucks that it has left, right? They're going to make one of three decisions. They're going to say, OK, we're going to be a full-spectrum force, and if you try to be a full-spectrum force with no budget, you're going to be nothing. You can be all of one thing, and you may wind up fighting something else, or you can try, I mean, you know, so the strategy that the Army picks is going to be really, really critical.

**Audience Member 4:**

I agree with that totally. But, why do we deny the intellectual vision of saying, OK, we don't have the resources right now to engage in, quote, "full spectrum operations," especially conventional warfare. But why do we take it out of FM 3-0?

**Dr. Carafano:**

I completely agree with you. And that was, I think, again, was the strength of the Army and the Navy of the '20s, and '30s, and '40s, where they were conceptualizing and fighting forces that didn't exist. Except on paper. Because they thought, you know, someday we might have to do this. Which is—you know, in one sense, intellectual capital is expensive, but you know, it's a lot cheaper than buying a stealth fighter, right? So if you can keep people who can conceptualize how to fight a kind of warfare. You can't. You can build a plane, well, I don't know if we can build planes anymore. I mean, you can contract for lots of things, but you can't contract for this. And to me is giving up your intellectual capital, that's the last, I mean, that's the thing that should be behind the back door at the Alamo. And this is what's always been frustrating me about the way the Army is treated in military history. I mean, to me, this is the secret sauce. This is an intellectual weapon of incredible importance that can teach these tremendously critical skills, and at the end of the day, if you can't afford anything else, at least you could have smart people. And yet, that's one of the first things we throw under the bus.

**MAJ(P) Mountcastle:**

All right, we're going to have to wrap it up there for this panel. That was a great setup for the next following panel here. Take us into 2001 and beyond. I want to thank again our presenters here today, Dr. Swain and Dr. Carafano.

# Day 2, Panel 6: Educating Leaders for a New Era, 2002 to Present

## Mission Command: An Old Idea for the 21st Century by COL (R) Gregory Fontenot

(Submitted Paper)

My purpose in this paper is raise two questions with respect to mission command. Is this central idea of the operating concept new and second are the conditions such that the Army can assure that mission command can become a key artifact of Army Culture. My view or bias is that the Army is correct in its conviction that mission command is essential to the way the Army intends to operate, but that the idea should nonetheless be examined critically in order to understand how to implement mission command as a key operational characteristic of the force. Moreover I will argue that the conditions that obtain today and the culture of the Army today will make realizing Mission Command as a means of operation difficult.

General Martin E. Dempsey, Commanding General US Army Training and Doctrine Command, established his vision clearly for how the Army should organize and operate in his recent Kermit Roosevelt Lecture at the Royal United Services Institute (RUSI). In a pithy presentation Dempsey argued convincingly that, in the 1990s the Army, and for that matter the Defense Department became mistakenly infatuated with the potential of technology to confer a long term advantage to US forces. Fundamentally, the judgment reached about the efficacy in the so called revolution in military affairs proved mistaken. According to Dempsey, the reaction of our opponents coupled with the continued ambiguity associated with combat operations led him to draw conclusions that he articulated at RUSI as six lessons.[1]

The need for exercising mission command which he characterized as "implying decentralization of capability and authority" is one of these six vital lessons that will drive how the Army should organize and operate. Further mission command, according to Dempsey, "implies that collaboration and trust are as important as command and control. It is about understanding the context of operations, and it recognizes that what comes from the lowest tactical echelon is as important as what comes from the highest strategic echelon. Today leaders at every echelon are co-creators of this context."[2] But, Dempsey goes further much further when he defines mission command as including "sharing and mitigating risk." Dempsey is absolutely right for Mission Command to become a fact of life in the Army trust and collaboration is required. Together these hallmarks of mission command demand sharing the risks of the decision that any leader takes at any echelon.[3]

The Army Capstone Concept and the Army Operating Concept go further still. Operational Adaptability is central to the Army Capstone Concept. Within the capstone concept mission command is a Core Operational Action. The Army Operating Concept is the primary document for implementing the essence of the Army Capstone Concept. Here too mission command is central to enabling what the Army now describes as full spectrum operations. In this document, mission command is defined as:

Mission command is the exercise of authority and direction by the commander and the commander's staff to integrate the warfighting functions using the operations process and mission orders to accomplish successful full-spectrum operations. Mission command enables agile and adaptive leaders and organizations to execute disciplined initiative within commander's intent as part of unified action in a complex and ambiguous environment. Mission command is critical to Army forces' ability to develop the situation through action and seize, retain, and exploit the initiative.[4]

Both the capstone concept and the operating concept are certain in the conviction that OIF/OEF, the Second Lebanon War and generally things that have happened since 2003 are as the capstone manual asserts "Harbingers of Future Conflict."[5] The concept, asserts, breathlessly that OIF demonstrates that the US Army must face "a broad range of enemy organizations that possess a wide array of capabilities (emphasis in the original)." Yet nothing in the capstone concepts examples are new. The Germans faced both conventional and unconventional forces in Russia just as the Israelis did in the second Lebanon War. Hamas conducted what could be described as web or archipelago defense which arguably the Germans invented as an asymmetric response to overwhelming Russian superiority in numbers. In my view, the Army Capstone Concept suffers from a metaphorical short term memory problem. The "harbingers" the authors chose suggest no deep reading of our history or even of reports of experiments that the Army itself conducted.

Whether the concept's authors are right in identifying the "harbingers" of future war in the period 2016-2028 or not is central to evaluating whether Mission Command can be implemented. An examination of how the Army has thought about command is a useful place from which to determine whether Mission Command is a new idea or an old idea dusted off for reuse is pertinent. From this we may conclude something about the efficacy of the idea as perceived in the past and the conditions in which the Army imagined decentralized operations and unit command initiative as most useful. For this purpose a cursory review of the Army's conceptual thinking about the nature of warfare as represented in the fundamental document of Army operations—Field Manual 100-5 Operations, later 3-0. We could start with Von Steuben but instead will only go back as far as FM 100-5 Field Service Regulations: Operations published on May 22, 1941. That document is far more prescriptive than descriptive given the development of a mass Army ultimately placing 12 million men in the field operating in multiple theaters simultaneously. Despite the "recent" discovery of complexity in the new Army operating concept World War II could be said to have been both grand in scale and complex as it involved everything from amphibious assault to military government in active combat theaters.

The Army asserted on page 18 of the 1941 manual that soldiers should be trained in such a way as to "integrate individuals in a group…without destroying the initiative of the individual."[6] Commanders, this same manual asserted, must communicate their decisions to subordinates, "by clear and concise orders, which gives them freedom of action appropriate to their professional knowledge, to the situation, to their dependability and to the teamplay (sic) desired.[7] This very directive manual further "directs" for the provision of initiative especially in operations where the commander cannot directly influence the action because of separation of units or because the commander has chosen to weight the main effort, in part, by his presence.⁸ This sounds, without resorting to anachronism, more than a little like mission command on occasion when decentralized operations are imperative or just the best course of action. Fundamentally, the 1941 manual assumed that there would be times when decentralized operations would be demanded by the either the conditions in the field or because of difficulty in communication. So in 1941 the Army believed that Mission Command or something like it might be required because of physical separation or tactical conditions. World War II soldiers were expected to act on their initiative when required.

What about that most Cold War of Cold War manuals—FM 100-5 Operations published in 1 July 1976. Even this very narrow manual, roundly criticized at the time and since, accounts for a full spectrum of operations noting that "The US Army may find itself at war in any of a variety of places and situations, fighting opponents which could vary from the highly mechanized forces of the Warsaw Pact to light, irregular units in a remote part of the less developed world."⁹ In the next paragraph the manual admits that the Army and thus 100-5 is structured and oriented on the Warsaw Pact as the "most demanding mission the US Army could be assigned."¹⁰ This manual is absolutely focused on the Fulda Gap but lists among the How to Fight manuals doctrine on everything from desert warfare to counter guerilla warfare. The Active Defense as this doctrinal statement was called absolutely required and depended on commander's initiative stipulating the need to assume risks and asserting that Colonels maneuvered while Captains fought battles because the Army in Europe had to fight outnumbered and win.¹¹ Mission command then had a place here as well.

While the Active Defense focused fundamentally on the tactical level the next two manuals articulated an operational focus. Ultimately, the concepts found in the 82 and 86 editions built from common framework the euphemism for which is AirLand Battle. The 1986 manual began with articulating a spectrum of warfare ranging from nuclear warfare to "terrorist activities (that) resist conventional military solutions. Between these extremes lies a wide range of possible conflicts which may escalate toward nuclear warfare and which will almost always involve counterterrorist activities."¹² The 1986 manual was bereft of "mission command" as a term but described command and control in terms easily understood as "mission command." The AirLand Battle required flexibility and/or variation introduced by subordinates. The manual waxed eloquently on how to create the conditions in units to facilitate exercising, leadership from any critical point on the battlefield. The section on command and control defined it as a system that would produce plans or orders that left, "the greatest possible freedom to subordinate leaders."¹³ Thus even during the Cold War the idea of decentralization of decisions and even operations were not an anathema to the Army.

US Army Training and Doctrine Command (TRADOC) published the last "legacy" manual and in fact the last FM 100-5 in 1993. This edition of the manual attempted to restore balance in Army thinking about the conflict articulating a "range of military operations," operations other than war, conflict in which hostilities might occur and war, "the use of force in combat operations against an armed enemy."¹⁴ Although there were other important ideas introduced in this manual it reflects a frustration with the Army's growing reliance on technology that General Fred Franks, commanding general of

TRADOC, resolved to down play command and control as a system which by then had so much else hung on it that what had been C2 was by 1993 C4ISR.[15] Franks reacted to what later became known as information based warfare with the same skepticism that Dempsey has about the Revolution in Military Affairs some 18 years later. In short he would have no C to the nth power acronyms so he invented the term Battle Command. Franks considered leaving control out of the manual altogether. In the end, he defined Battle Command so that it could not be conflated as even first among equals in a command and control system. Chief among those things he believed pertained to commanders were the need to think and act as "simultaneous activities" along with visualizing the battlefield and providing clear direction in battle.[16] Flexibility and operating within a superior's intent were central to Franks' ideas on Battle Command as he articulated them in the 93 manual. Although decentralized operations or command never appears in the manual it was a matter of intense discussion because Franks thought he saw signs of requirements for very small formations to operate remotely and without direct supervision—specifically company and perhaps even smaller units.[17]

So what does all of this mean? First mission command is clearly not a new idea nor is the idea that Army units should be adaptable or able to conduct decentralized operations. So what? The so what is that the Army needs to confront some basic facts about the nature of the control function of command and the way in which technology has fundamentally altered the way the Army operates both in terms of the degree of centralization and specificity and level of supervision that ensued from these changes. As late as the invasion of Iraq officers routinely followed their own judgment generally assuming if things turned out well they would be supported.

George Armstrong Custer perhaps epitomized the Civil War Army's near shibboleth of personal initiative required by poor communications but also encouraged as a matter of culture. One of the officers present at General Terry's final council of war during the Campaign of the summer of 1876 that led to Custer's defeat described the session in the following way, "It is understood that if Custer arrives first he is at liberty to attack at once if he deems prudent."[18] But the culture of initiative did not stop at regimental level. Lieutenants routinely exercised their initiative often in operations they led across enormous distances out of touch with their commanders for weeks on an end. Both the culture of command and the facts of the control system in the 19th century Army required "mission command" and decentralization. For the most part it worked, at the Little Big Horn it did not. Decentralization and mission command were practically the only way the late 19th century US Army could operate.

But what of the so called legacy Army whose last hurrah was the invasion of Iraq? The control system, by then euphemistically called network centric warfare, included Future Battle Command Brigade and Below, FBCB2, which enabled someone with access to a monitor watch the events of that war as they unfolded from a seat on the third floor of the Combined Arms Research Library. Despite this transparency, on 7 April 2003 Colonel David Perkins, commanding 2nd Brigade 3rd Infantry Division, exceeded his orders and instead of conducting a limited objective "Thunder Run" turned right instead of left and seized much of downtown Baghdad. When asked when he knew that Perkins and 3rd ID had committed to this effort, Lieutenant General William S. Wallace, commanding V Corps, responded that, "I first knew they were going all the way was when I watched the blue icons turn and head downtown."[19]

These two examples, while anecdotal, suggest how both culture and the tools of control can interact. In 1876 Terry had neither the means nor the intent to control Custer. Both he and Custer understood that Custer-when given his head-would do what he liked. Moreover Terry only knew where he expected Custer and not necessarily where the 7th Cavalry actually was during most of the campaign. For these and other reasons the Battle of the Little Big Horn has remained a matter of debate to this very day. Alternatively vilified or praised each of the major protagonists roles have continued to proved grist for discussion. Should Terry have give Custer specific orders, should Reno and Benteen, once joined have marched north to Custer's aid and would it have made a difference if they had? In 2003, Wallace enjoyed a tremendous advantage over Terry. He knew exactly where Perkins was and had the means to intervene. Wallace chose not to do so which implies a level of trust and confidence he did not glean from the control mechanisms that he had.

What Wallace might have done had Perkins lost a great many soldiers or had been defeated is a matter for speculation but it is hard to believe that he would not have been criticized for not intervening. In short, Wallace, by actively deciding not to intervene, chose to share or at least underwrite the risks that Perkins took. That is an act of courage increasingly difficult to take in this age of instant communication that makes it possible for tactical unit actions to be litigated in the media practically from the moment medical evacuation helicopters lift off with wounded.

The means to affect positive control as a consequence of instantaneous communication will act as a powerful drag on initiative when coupled with the nearly simultaneous capacity to criticize decisions without understanding context. Swearing by decentralized operations and mission command will be far easier to execute in power point briefings than in the field.

At the outset the Army needs to accept the risk that enabling initiative entails along with the benefit. In 1962, General Lyman L. Lemnitzer offered the following assessment which applies still;

Initiative is the agent which translates imagination into action. It must be used intelligently lest it becomes irresponsibility or even insubordination, but it must be used courageously when the situation warrants. Military history provides innumerable examples of commanders, who, confronted with unforeseen circumstances, have adhered slavishly to instructions and, at best, have lost an opportunity; at worst they have brought on defeat.[20]

Lemnitzer did not confront the difficulty of operating with a dramatically improved control system.

The capacity to do as Wallace did in 2003 could become more not less difficult. There is no reason to believe that our capacity to see blue, at least and to improve communications coupled with the tendency to investigate everything will decline in the future. If these conditions persist how will officers generate the capacity either to afford subordinates the opportunity to exercise mission command or to return to my thesis the time and space to

PANEL 6

reflect on their operational experience. Learning organizations, as the Army aspires to be, are able learn during execution. Bu learning lessons may take second place to responding to a cacophony of requests for information from higher headquarters, the media, families and who knows who else.

Engendering the philosophy of Mission Command within the Army will require the Army to educate not only soldiers but policy makers on the idea. Transparency afforded by mass communications and digital recorders in the hands of soldiers and journalist will assure that we litigate every tactical decision for which there is a bill to pay. The appearance of precision in control as exemplified by things like Command Post of the Future and the means to know where units are coupled with both sides developing audio and visual records of the fighting will make platoon leaders decisions grist for the 24 hours news cycle. The United States Army lost a great many soldiers killed during a rehearsal for the Normandy Invasion but that disaster did not become widely known in the public until after the war. We remain embroiled now in several controversies involving small unit engagements such as Wanat. To what extent these kinds of disputes will effect decision makers is not yet understood, but it hardly supports the concept of driving decisions down to the lowest level.

Managing the expectations of policy makers will not be as hard as managing the expectations of the American public. How do we account for tactical misjudgment in an era where family members are convinced incompetence or even criminal negligence is the only reasonable explanation for a child's "unnecessary" death in combat? This is an Army problem if the Army really means to share the risks of decisions and yet enable lowest unit possible to make tactical decisions. There will be and there as has been enormous pressure to mitigate risk. A sure fire way to do that is through centralized decision making—but that system will limit initiative and render decentralized operations very difficult.

Dempsey has rightly identified the central difficulty in making mission command a fact rather than aspiration in the Army—sharing risk. Dempsey will need to lead the campaign to consider the implications of what he proposed the Army needs to do versus what may be required of it. We who serve the Army should wonder aloud whether we really mean to embrace mission command or whether the risks will exceed our capacity. Mission command requires time for commanders/leaders to estimate their situation, understand what has transpired and be afforded the cover of their superiors in order to do either or both of these things. This old idea continues to have value perhaps even more now than previously but it is a difficult one to indulge in the conditions that obtain now. We will know what the Army means to do by watching what our senior leaders do and juxtapose against what they say.

## Notes

1. General Martin E. Dempsey, Kermit Roosevelt Lecture as printed in Royal United Service Institute, "Journal" June-July 2010, Vol. 155, No. 3, 6-9.
2. General Martin E. Dempsey. 8-9.
3. General Martin E. Dempsey. 9.
4. TRADOC Pam 525-3-1, The United States Army Operating Concept: 2016-2018, 19 August 2010, p12. See also TRADOC Pam 525-3-0, The Army's Future Force Capstone Concept (Executive Version) Operational Adaptability: Operating under Conditions of Uncertainty and Complexity in an Era of Persistent Conflict, 2016-2028, 7 December 2009.
5. Capstone Concept section 2-3 p13.
6. War Department, FM 100-5 Operations, May 22, 1941, 18.
7. War Department, 29.
8. War Department, 112
9. Department of the Army, FM 100-5 Operations, 29 April 1977 p.1-2.
10. Department of the Army.
11. Department of the Army, see especially chapters 3, 5 and 12.
12. Department of the Army FM 100-5 Operations, May 1986, 1.
13. Department of the Armys, 21.
14. Department of the Army, FM 100-5 Operations, 14 June 1993, 2-1.
15. C4ISR is command, control, communications, intelligence, surveillance and reconnaissance.
16. Department of the Army, FM 100-5, Operations, 14 June, 1993. P. 2-27. Personal knowledge as General Franks. Chief of the Training and Doctrine Command, Command Planning Group.
17. Personal conversations with General Franks.
18. Nathan Philbrick, *The Last Stand; Custer, Sitting Bull and the Battle of the Little Bighorn*, New York: Viking, 2010, 99
19. Gregory Fontenot, E. J. Degen and David Tohn, *On Point the United States Army in Operation Iraqi Freedom*, Leavenworth, Kansas: Combat Studies Institute, 2004, 349.
20. Printed on the 1962 CGSC graduation program.

# Day 2, Panel 6: Educating Leaders for a New Era, 2002 to Present

## A New "Melody Report" Educating Officers for the 21st Century by Kevin Benson, Ph.D.

(Transcript of Presentation)

**Dr. Benson:**

I found out about doing this, working on something with Don Wright, and at the end of the little talk, Don said, "Oh, Kevin, thanks so much for stepping up to give a presentation at the CSI symposium." And I said, "What CSI symposium?" I'm here because Greg's wingman dropped out, and I'm proud to be here. And I'm also proud to, number one, follow Greg, and number two, be the only guy standing in between you and a cold drink, because I'm the last speaker, so let me get at it.

I assert that it is time to reflect on the focus of our education, and what full spectrum operations means for our general staff officers. Last week, I had the privilege of spending time with the first core staff leading a symposium, where they very proudly told me that they were going to be the first major operational headquarters to refocus on full spectrum operations. And when I suggested that, you know, I think our doctrine kind of declines full spectrum operations as inclusive of that which you are not going to focus on anymore, COIN and stability operations, everyone kind of looked at me like, what are you talking about? And I left convinced that at first core, full spectrum operations, at least there as a euphemism for the high intensity clash of titans. I'm also happy to be here, as Pete knows, this gives me a chance to polish one of my pet rocks. And these are my major points. I discovered the Malloy Report when I was doing my dissertation research. In 1933, Col. George Marshall writes about (inaudible) into the college, all the way to, I think it's time for a new report, and I'll show you why. This is what Marshall wrote, in essence. I found this in our wonderful Combined Arms Research Library. Does this sound familiar? Does it look familiar? Here are his criticisms.

There are three charts. I would point out that number one really looks like my campaign. Sandstorms, traffic at (inaudible), units getting lost, a core forward (inaudible), and oddly enough, all of us in that little plans group of mine knew things like this were going to happen, but we were so clouded by the uncertainties (inaudible). Second set here, in *The Logic of Failure*, Dietrich Dorner wrote that the best managers in these experiments were the ones who asked the most questions. So, how do we square this with mission orders and mission command? Where is the balance between enough questions for situational awareness, and micromanagement? How do we tell the difference? You know as Greg suggested, litigation begins with the arrival of dust off, how does this affect operating within the commander's intent, and mission command? How do we rate orders that encouraged risk taking, and linking tactical success to attaining operational and strategic objectives. You know, there was that anti-Powerpoint rant by the US Army Reserve colonel. He went out right about it. The confusion between the battle update brief, the commander's update brief, as we called it, the Third Army daily battlefield update assessment. And yet, none of us really knew how to do assessments, believe me, I watched those. How many of our officers leave staff college understanding how to do that? But the most important one, and this is huge, was that number 13. And keep that in mind when you get to the—when I show you the Malloy Report. When I went to staff college, every unit in our garrison was at 100%, with a 100% OR rate. Yet historically, we know that's not accurate. My godson got back a month ago from being a platoon leader in a rifle platoon in Afghanistan. Uncle Kevin, you know, on paper, I have 35 soldiers. From day one until day last, he never had 35 ever, but we were game at 100%, with a 100% OR rate. Probably shouldn't do that. You know, for my own personal satisfaction, during the opening stages of this campaign that's now over, kind of sort of, I did a little back of the envelope calculation. And personally, at least to myself, to my satisfaction proved the efficacy of the 0.01% disease nonbattle injury rate. It actually proved out, based on casualty reports that we had. And I venture to say, it is still true. So again, what does that do for our war game? How do we teach war gaming here now? We don't know the answer to that.

And [Meyer] to Malloy now. This is what I found very interesting, almost 50 years later, General Meyer (inaudible) my research, I did not find out who brought this to Meyer's attention. Yet, I've seen all of the papers, he did direct General Malloy, Assistant (inaudible) of the Army at the time, to come out here, use Marshall's critiques as his basis for assessing what the college was doing. And you can see what he reported. So this also came in handy to General Sorley, then colonel, as he was writing his report to establish the School of Enhanced Military Studies, because he cited Malloy's report as support for the need for second year of study, given the complexity, there's that complexity word, that was growing. Here's one of his findings. The college could also do, I would offer, with some (inaudible) from folks not here on the statement of their mission, and the scope, and its purpose. What constitutes full spectrum operations in the 21st century? We can devise that mission statement here, but it really does need to be validated somewhere else. What courage and DA level is required to ensure our best tacticians and logisticians come to the staff college to teach those tactics? Tactics, we all know this, includes core operations. (inaudible) But how many of our students here understand that tactics goes beyond battalion, especially, and you'll see this later, when it appears that everybody campaigns? You know, while we are no longer, you can see up here, this is one of my favorite ones. (inaudible) You know, while we're no longer in the business of learning how to kill Russians, we are certainly still in the business of learning how to kill the enemy for the republic. And given that need, how does our curriculum address the hunting and skills to balance offense, defense, stability operations, or civil support operations in the continental United States? And of course, with this last one, like Jim pointed out, we also have to ask so what? This is just a major griping in the (inaudible) to fill out a form, but there's something to that. Because in addition to all of this, how do we establish conditions for honest feedback, and a mechanism to act upon it? So, (inaudible). [laughter] No, that's all right.

In 2009, I worked for Greg [Fontenot], by the way, I had the privilege of going to lead another seminar at the 3d Infantry Division, preparing for yet another deployment in Iraq. In 2009, I asked the question that is just an open question, what constitutes the center of gravity in Iraq right now? And without hesitation, the major popped up and said,

"Sir, it's the people!" And I said, "Well, we've had a successful reinforcement." All of the developments, don't you think it's time to reassess the center of gravity? I mean, this is going to help you develop your major operations plan for the division. "Sir, it's the people." Well, why? "Well sir, that's what Infantry 24 says." OK. Thank you very much, and we sort of moved on because I was running into a brick wall. But as some of us in this room know, read anything, do brigades campaign? Not according to our doctrine, but I guarantee you there are officers who will assert that oh yeah, I wrote my brigade campaign plan. Really? Who guarantees that that campaign plan is (inaudible). There's that 20th century term (inaudible) something else. How do we educate people to understand it?

Which is why I return to, I think it's time for another Malloy Report. Why is that? These are our conditions. We know that these things are happening, I'll pick up on some of the things that have been said here. We are going to enter another recentering again. This week, for those of you who live around here, the *Kansas City Star* headlined the story about the increasing levels of indiscipline in the United States Army. I read that, I read the story, I couldn't find the report, but it sounded like, and I could've closed my eyes and substituted some words, and that was when I was a lieutenant. So how are we going to, you know, how are we going to address this? Recentering is going to require, among other things, I offer, a rigorous reassessment of the education that prepares our officers to be general staff officers, because we must link tactical success. My Lieutenant Godson told me, hey, we never lost a firefight, never. Which reminded me of the little story that Harry Summers included in the top part of his book, the North Vietnamese colonel and him, and you know what that was. We defeated you all the time in battle. Yes, that's true, and it's also irrelevant. Our general staff officers have to take this wonderful range of tactical experience, I would offer, small unit tactical experience, and based on their education and experience, be able to step back from one company to 100. From one battalion to up to four. If, in fact, this is....

Note: this transcript was produced from a poor quality recording and corrupted file. Unfortunately due to technical difficulties, the final eight minutes of Dr. Benson's presentation were lost.

## Day 2, Panel 6: Educating Leaders for a New Era, 2002 to the Present

### Questions and Answers
(Transcript of Presentation)

### COL (R) Greg Fontenot
### Kevin Benson, Ph.D.

### Moderator: Mr. John McGrath

Note: unfortunately due to technical difficulties, the entire question and answer session was lost.

## Day 3, Panel 7: Sister Services Perspectives

## Historical and Cultural Foundations of Navy Officer Development by Gene R. Andersen, Ph.D.

(Submitted Paper)

I must begin by thanking Ken Gott and CSI for inviting me to participate in this conference. It is an honor to share this stage with such an eminent lineup of experts. This is my first visit to Fort Leavenworth, and I am grateful to have had this brief window into the perspective of the Army. I must emphasize that my opinions are my own, and not necessarily those of the Naval War College or the Navy. Lastly, I am not a historian, except in the most amateur sense. My field is leadership and leader development, and my responsibilities at the Naval War College include the electives program in leadership and ethics, as well as a student research project in leadership at the operational level of war.

Yesterday, General (Retired) Gordon Sullivan, former Chief of Staff of the Army, powerfully evoked some key touchstones of the Army's institutional culture and ethos, and he pointed to the Army's history as a key source of those touchstones. Edgar Schein, in his book Organizational Culture and Leadership (3d edition, 2004), calls these touchstones artifacts of an institution's culture. Schein argues that these identifiable structures, stories and rituals are the most obvious indicators of an organization's culture, while its espoused beliefs and values form a deeper stratum of the culture and both of those levels point to the underlying assumptions that are the true foundations of the organization's sense of itself and view of its environment.[1]

This perspective has been my approach to understanding why the four Department of Defense services have such fundamentally different officer development processes and methodologies, and why none of the services could successfully adopt one of the other services' system. The Navy in many ways has the most unusual of these systems, since the Navy has no leadership doctrine or leader development doctrine, has no single officer short of the CNO who is in charge of officer development and has no officer development requirements that cannot be waived. I think the answers to why this is so are embedded in the Navy's institutional culture, which is largely the product of the Navy's history. Navy Officer Leader Development is a product of the Navy's history and culture, and driven by the Navy's underlying assumptions about what the Navy is and the world the Navy inhabits.

### The Army, Air Force and Marine Corps

As context, consider the following thumbnail sketches of the Army, Air Force and Marine Corps approaches to leader development as seen in this light. These are necessarily brief and built upon generalizations about very large, diverse and complex organizations, but I think they may be helpful in understanding why each service develops officers the way it does.

The Army's underlying assumption is that it is a very large organization comprised of a multitude of small units that need to work effectively together in predictable ways as a combined arms team despite routinely being geographically dispersed. Some values that go with this are professionalism, consistency and organizational alignment. The artifacts that observers see are doctrine which is generally prescriptive (with FM 6-22 as the core for leader development), detailed organizational structure (TRADOC, Army Leader Development Office), a credentials-based view of education, and required classroom courses at nearly every paygrade (demonstrating a high commit to career-long formal leader development).

The Air Force views itself as a highly technological organization that is deeply dependent on individual thinking (hardly surprising for an organization whose key image is the fighter pilot). A key value is therefore individual effectiveness, and the artifacts we see are a leader development process driven by behavioral scientists (leadership is taught at the Air Force Academy by psychologists, not line officers) and based on enduring competencies (the Air Force has the most complex and detailed set of leader competencies), concept-driven professional military education (aerospace power), and a deep commitment to ongoing education (Air University).

The Marine Corps views itself as a low-resource organization that needs to push decisions to the lowest possible level ("The Strategic Corporal"), with junior personnel taking unsupervised action. This requires a deep inculcation in Marine values and a Marine mindset ("Every Marine a rifleman"), which is largely achieved by an immersion in Marine Corps heritage (most Marines know such stories as Presley O'Bannon and the march to Derna, John Basilone at Guadalcanal, Chesty Puller at the Chosin reservoir, and John Ripley at the Dong Ha bridge). The artifacts we therefore see are a development process driven by storytelling in the field (which more than 20% of the curriculum at The Basic School), doctrine that is generally descriptive rather than prescriptive (and driven more by philosophy than process), historically-themed professional military education, and crucible experiences.

Hopefully this brief look at the other services will help you to better see why I have chosen to focus where I have in looking at the Navy's officer development process in light of its culture and history.

**Command at Sea**

The Navy's perspective on officer development is founded in its focus on command at sea. In his Guidance for 2009, CNO Admiral Gary Roughead referred to the Navy's "culture of command that has been the foundation of our Navy's successes for more than two centuries" as a key to executing the sea services' Cooperative Strategy for 21st Century Seapower (2007).[2] Navy Regulations says "The commanding officer and his or her subordinates shall exercise leadership through personal example, moral responsibility and judicious attention to the welfare of persons under their control or supervision. Such leadership shall be exercised in order to achieve a positive, dominant influence on the performance of persons in the Department of the Navy."[3] I quote that because, in the 153 pages of the Navy Regulations, that is the only real discussion of leadership in the Navy. The Navy does not have an official definition of leadership, a top level instruction on leadership or leader development, any written doctrine on leadership, an officer charged with all officer development, a truly integrated system of professional schools, or much regard for its own heritage and history. To understand why the Navy has succeeded despite all this, let's take a quick look back to the beginnings of the Navy.

The roots of the US Navy are deeply embedded in the operation of frigates. Prior to the Civil War the Navy built few ships of the line, and none of those ever saw combat. Instead, from the earliest days of the American Revolution, the Navy built and operated frigates, most famously the "six frigates" of Ian Toll's history of the early 19th century Navy.[4] These ships, including the 44-gun Constitution, United States and President and the 36-gun Constellation, Chesapeake and Congress, were designed for independent operations at sea.[5] Intended to be fast enough to outrun any ship of superior force and both stout enough and heavily armed enough to defeat any ship that could sail with them, these ships engaged in individual missions from Nova Scotia to the Caribbean and from the US coast to the English Channel and into the Mediterranean. This created a leadership culture where captains received individual orders, sailed over the horizon in pursuit of those objectives, and returned when they believed they were finished. Squadrons were seldom assembled, and when they were, they were marked by continual infighting among the ship captains over strategy, tactics and seniority.[6]

The Navy's culture of command is therefore based on independence of action, command by negation, forehandedness and initiative.[7] Navy captains maintained immense authority over their crews and their operations, and were expected to respond effectively to changing circumstances without any guidance from senior officers.[8] This culture permeates every watchstanding function of the Navy as well, requiring junior officers standing deck watches, operating aircraft or operating small boats to act in the same spirit.[9]

Command is therefore the ultimate career objective in the Navy, and it is always viewed as the ultimate test of an officer's worth and potential. Navy line officers who are not selected for command have little chance of selection to flag rank and are typically assigned to less significant jobs. As a result, command has also become the ultimate filter in an officer's career. Success in command will usually carry an officer to the next grade; failure in command nearly always is career-ending. This is why the Navy fires so many commanding officers, by the way. Any failure of character, tactical competence, technical skill or leadership while in command is disqualifying for the next job and will usually lead to a relief for cause. Navy Times reported on Monday on the Navy's 15th relief for cause of 2010;[10] a 2009 Navy Times investigation documented an average of more than one relief for cause a month going back to 1999.[11] Though press coverage of firings often implies that the Navy's officer development system is somehow broken, the fact is that such reliefs for cause are part of the system, not a breakdown of the system.[12]

**Technical Competence**

In contrast to the armies of the eighteenth century, the navies of the eighteenth century were highly technological organizations with extensive developmental requirements for both officers and enlisted Sailors. The three-masted square-rigged sailing ship was the greatest technological achievement of the era prior to the steam engine, and it required a large, well-trained and highly specialized crew to operate it. Officers were expected to master all the tasks of basic seamanship (which included mastery of the entire system of spars, lines and sails that provided propulsion and maneuverability), naval gunnery (which required mastery of the ballistic trajectory of cannon balls launched from a platform moving in three dimensions), open water navigation (which required mastery of astronomy, the use of the sextant and spherical trigonometry) and more minor tasks like the operation of small boats, the use of the system of signal flags and shipboard damage repair. By World War I, this list included steam engineering, and shortly thereafter the operation of shipboard aircraft. By the Cold War, nuclear propulsion had joined the list, along with complex combat systems and air, surface and subsurface sensor systems.

This resulted in an officer development process that focused on technical and tactical competence, and in an enlisted force that became progressively more specialized. It also resulted in an officer development process that has always been largely conducted at sea (though this is much less the case in naval aviation). This system was largely dependent on passing expertise from more senior officers to more junior officers via a rigorous system of on-the-job training.

It is perhaps noteworthy that the Army had a drill manual from Baron von Steuben onward, and that text was updated by a series of luminaries in Army history across the nineteenth century.[13] A comparative Navy publication would perhaps be a manual on seamanship; the Navy had none until Stephen Luce wrote one in 1862 (more than 80 years after von Steuben), and his text remained the standard with only minor updates through the end of the nineteenth century. Luce also was a leading force in the establishment of the US Naval Institute in 1873, created the Navy's first shore training establishment for enlisted personnel (the forerunner of today's Navy Boot Camp) in 1882—a century after the Navy's founding—and founded the Naval War College in 1884.[14]

The Navy did not possess any ashore training location for officers until the establishment of the Naval Academy in 1845, more than four decades after the establishment of the Military Academy at West Point. Senior Navy leaders opposed the establishment of the Naval Academy, the Naval War College and the Naval Postgraduate School. The cultural result of all this is a Navy leader development process that is founded in the belief that going to sea is always the best and most effective way to develop as an officer as a professional and as a leader.

**Doctrine and the Lack Thereof**

The cultural belief that leaders are made at sea and commanding officers are best qualified to determine what development individual officers require and how that should be accomplished is key to answering the question of why the Navy has no doctrine for leadership or leader development, or even a service-wide definition of leadership. This perspective carries ashore in the Navy operation of its principal schoolhouses, most of which receive little guidance from higher authority on what they should teach or how they should teach it. The Navy has no parallel organization to the Army's Training and Doctrine Command (TRADOC).[15] Instead, school commanding officers in the Navy have wide latitude to adjust curriculum and standards based on their own professional experience. Navy doctrine is therefore largely limited to operating manuals for systems and platforms. The Navy published a series of capstone doctrine publications in 1994; they are brief, have never been substantively updated and are widely ignored (even in the Naval War College's curriculum).[16]

As a more specific example, consider the Army's publication on command philosophies, which is more than 100 pages long.[17] The Navy has no parallel instruction, nor does it perceive that it is in any way lacking because it does not. Students in the Prospective Commanding Officer course at the Navy's Command Leadership School (CLS) are required to write a command philosophy. Students are provided with several command philosophy documents that the CLS staff considers to be good, but they are not given any specific guidance for creating a command philosophy, nor is their final product inspected against any standard other than the judgment of the instructors that it is a credible document.

**Conclusion**

The Navy views itself as a highly technological organization that depends on leaders to make decisions, solve problems and take action. This requires maximizing the operational experience of leaders through sea assignments and on-the-job training, and the enforcement of cultural norms derived from command at sea, including forehandedness, initiative, adaptability and focus on mission accomplishment. All of this results in a focus on service at sea, a general conviction that education should be technical and a personnel system that rewards sustained superior performance rather than specific credentials.[18] It is perhaps worth noting that the current Chief of Naval Operations is not a graduate of the Naval War College and does not hold a master's degree. He has, however, held six operational commands, most of them at sea.[19] There are two current Navy four-stars (ADM James Stavridis, EUCOM, and ADM Patrick Walsh, COMPACFLT) with earned Ph.D.'s, but both achieved that despite the Navy's officer development system, not because of it, and both made their careers at sea.[20] This is because the Navy views time in the classroom as time away from the fundamental requirement to go to sea and learn by firsthand experience. As a result, the Navy still tends to think of education as a cost, rather than as an investment in the future of the officer and the service.

The Navy views its people as a highly flexible resource, and assumes that Sailors can master most any job. The Navy's N1 used a PowerPoint slide in recent years that summarized the training and development issues associated with sending Sailors to Provincial Reconstruction Teams with a bullet point that said we have good Sailors and they will figure it out.[21] And they have, though perhaps at some significant cost to the mission.

Today's Navy officer development system provides career-long development opportunities both in and out of the classroom, but its emphasis is on experience tours (preferably at sea or in the Pentagon), informal mentorship and self-development. Classroom training is available at key career steps (Division Officer, Department Head, Executive Officer, Commanding Officer, Major Command), but only the command courses are not easily waiverable. Education opportunities are tied to specific milestones (JPME I, JPME II, Master's degree) but officers are strongly encouraged to attain such credentials by distance learning wherever possible.[22], Primary PME is available only online via the Navy's web portal; completion is required for entry into the Naval War College.[23] Individual officer development is broadly overseen by community managers at the Navy Personnel Command, but is specifically the responsibility of each individual officer. Course directors have broad authority over curricular changes and Instructors have significant freedom in executing the curricula. This system maximizes flexibility, limits classroom time, and places a premium on individual initiative.

The Navy's principal challenge in this area today is the breakdown of the environment that made this system such a success during the Cold War. The war on terror has taken Navy people out of their community career paths and sent them to unusual jobs, reducing the consistency of the experience base in the Navy's officer corps. Budget limitations have reduced steaming days and flight hours, limiting the exposure of junior officers to key evolutions and challenges. And the skyrocketing costs of shipbuilding and aircraft production have seriously reduced the size of the operating force. The future will require the Navy to replace some time on the bridge and in the cockpit with time in the classroom, just as happened in the 1930's. It remains to be seen how we will accomplish that.

# Notes

1. "Organizational Culture and Leadership, 3rd ed." Edgar Schein, 2004.
2. NO Guidance for 2009, November 2008, page 1.
3. Navy Regulations, 1990, Chapter 8, article 0802.
4. "Six Frigates: The Epic History of the Founding of the US Navy" Ian W. Toll, W.W. Norton & Company, 2008.
5. Authorized in 1794, the six ships were built in six shipyards in six states under the oversight of famed naval architect Joshua Humphreys.
6. See, for example, "Captains Contentious: The Dysfunctional Sons of the Brine" Louis Arthur Norton, University of South Carolina Press, 2009.
7. As opposed to command by direction. Command by negation implies broad delegation of tactical choices to subordinate commanders based on a clear statement of the commander's intentions and objectives. The commander then acts as necessary to negate or disapprove actions with which he/she does not concur.
8. Including very broad non-judicial punishment authority when at sea.
9. Hence Navy pilots sign for their aircraft and approve their own flight plans from their initial qualification.
10. "Navy Sacks Three Leaders in One Day" William McMichael and Gidget Fuentes, Navy Times, 19 September 2010.
11. "Why So Many Skippers Get Fired" Andrew Tilghman, Navy Times, 14 September 2009.
12. "CO Firings Have Roots in Flawed Screening Process" Navy Times, 14 September 2009.
13. The instructions of von Steuben were originally written in 1778-79.
14. "Sailors and Scholars: The Centennial History of the US Naval War College" John Hattendorf, Mitchell Simpson and John Wadleigh, Naval War College Press, 1984, pages 5-21.
15. The Naval Education and Training Command (NETC) in Pensacola, Florida, has no role in creating doctrine, no policy role beyond administration of its subordinate schools, and little authority over the Naval Academy, Naval War College and Naval Postgraduate School (which are all considered to be Echelon II commands responsible directly to the OPNAV staff).
16. Navy Doctrine Publications 1-6.
17. AR 600-20 of 18 April 2008 is 138 pages long.
18. The Naval Academy has enforced a minimum percentage of each class choosing engineering, science and math majors formost graduating classes since the adoption of the majors program there in 1973.
19. Official biography, ADM Gary Roughead, Chief of Naval Operations.
20. "Another Crossroads? Professional Military Education Two Decades After the Goldwater-Nichols Act and the Skelton Panel" House Armed Services Subcommittee on Oversight & Investigations, April 2010.
21. The Navy's N1 is responsible for manpower, personnel, training and education of the total force.
22. The Navy does not consider Intermediate Level Education or Senior Service College to be career milestones or development requirements.
23. The Navy Primary Professional Military Education course consists of approximately 75 hours of online content in over 100 course modules available on the Navy Knowledge Online (NKO) portal. It has been available since May 2006.

## Day 3, Panel 7: Sister Services Perspectives

## "It was More Than Just Doctrine!" Reflections on the Preparation of the US Marine Corps and Its Officers for World War II by Donald F. Bittner, Ph.D.

(Submitted Paper).

*But in 1921, [future General Jerry] Thomas faced important decisions that would shape the rest of his career. Once a part of the Marine that had been – the Marine Corps of World War I and the Caribbean interventions – Thomas was now an officer in the Marine Corps that was, not the Marine Corps envisioned in War Plan ORANGE.[1]*

*Alan R. Millett*

### Prologue: Now or Then?

Concerns about war, budget issues, the nation's role in the world, a service's place in the defense establishment, changing technology, uncertainty about the future, a complex and challenging international situation, service force structure, and institutional survival. Is this the post Vietnam War era and the role of the Marine Corps in the late 20th century?[2] The early years of the second decade of the 21st century and a post Iraqi-Afghanistan world?[3] Or, does this also describe the Interwar years of the 1930s and the challenges associated with that era? In the years between World Wars I and II, wherefore the Corps and its evolution?

### The Corps and Preparing for War—Pre-1941-I

In the immediate post World War I years, none of what occurred during World War II with respect to the Marine Corps and its amphibious warfare capability—and how this would evolve—was evident. In fact, a career officer of the Corps in the early 1930's contemplating the future of his service could have postulated three options: A traditional role associated with ships detachments and barracks duty ashore, a colonial constabulary mission linked to the "Small Wars," and, for the few visionaries, a projected mission of amphibious assault.

Of these, for a Corps with an average strength of 16,093 for the fiscal year of 1932, only the first two of these stated roles were addressed in the annual report of the Major General Commandant of the Marine Corps.[4] In his 1932 report to the Secretary of the Navy, Major General Ben H. Fuller noted that Marine detachments were on 36 vessels of the Navy (including the frigate *USS Constitution*, but excluding the aviation units on the carriers *Lexington* and *Saratoga*), and in barracks at various naval stations and bases in the United States. Marine units were also serving ashore in both barracks duty and "Small Wars" roles in China (Peking and Shanghai); Haiti; Nicaragua; Guantanamo, Cuba; the Canal Zone; Guam; Hawaii; and The Philippines. The closest to landing operations was a comment that a provisional battalion of Marines with supporting artillery had embarked on the battleships *Arkansas* and *Wyoming* for "intensive training aboard those vessels in the Atlantic, Caribbean, and Pacific waters." Fuller also reported that a regimental headquarters, a battalion, and battery of artillery had participated in "joint Army-Navy exercises in Hawaiian waters"—with the goal of training "the services involved in the coordination and cooperation necessary in joint maneuvers."[5]

Since 1945, the answer to the then issue of the immediate future of the Marine Corps is clear. So much so that in 2009 and 2010, senior Marine officers still speak of the development of amphibious warfare [assault] doctrine at the Marine Corps Schools at the Marine Barracks, Quantico, Virginia, during the Interwar years—as if that was all to the issue of developing that capability that emerged before and during World War II. Indeed, during the 1933-34 Academic Year, the Marine Corps Schools suspended classes under the orders of the Assistant Commandant of the Marine Corps and devoted their attention to developing a draft landing operations doctrine. This built on the additional duty committee endeavors led by Major Charles Barrett which had commenced in 1931.[6] From this came the "Tentative Manual for Landing Operations," which through refinement via further work resulted in U.S. Navy official doctrine *Landing Operations Doctrine, United States Navy, Fleet Training Publication 167* in 1938.[7] However, there was indeed more to it than doctrine.

Missions and roles had to be established, and this gradually occurred.[8] In 1900, the General Board of the Navy assigned an advanced base mission to the U.S. Marine Corps; in 1922, the Major General Commandant of the Marine Corps, John A. Lejeune, then defined the functions of the Marine Corps to include ships detachments, guards at naval bases, garrisons in foreign areas, expeditionary operations, and forces for the fleet for shore operations in support of the fleet; and, in 1927, the Joint Board of the Army and Navy assigned to the Marine Corps the role of maintaining forces in support of the fleet for the seizure of advanced bases and limited supporting land operations as essential for a naval campaign. Amidst this, in 1921 Lieutenant Colonel Pete Ellis drafted *Advanced Base Operations in Micronesia, 1921*—a projected plan for the Marine Corps role in the U. S. Navy's War Plan Orange.[9]

This, however, did not make a capability. Force structure was needed to conduct such operations, and this gradually evolved. In 1900 the Advanced Base Force was formed, which by 1913 had become the Base Defense Force. In 1923, the Marine Corps Expeditionary Force was established (one each, based respectively at Quantico on the east coast and San Diego on the west coast). However, in 1933 a further significant changed occurred: The formal creation of the Fleet Marine Force, under the operational command of the Commander-in-Chief, U.S. Fleet, for planning and operational purposes.[10] From this would evolve the Marine Corps amphibious warfare operational capability of World War II embodied in an eventual two amphibious corps with associated troops, six divisions, five aircraft wings, and 20 defense battalions—but all of that was in the distant future.

Linked to these events would, of course, be training. Due to various commitments, e.g. World War I and after that conflict the "small wars", work in landing operations before the mid-1930s was very intermediate. Still, the Corps did what it could. Hence, limited exercises were conducted before the First World War and others in the 1920s. From the mid-1930s, more extensive and focused fleet exercises were held. Overall, regardless of where they were held in the western Pacific, Hawaii, and the Caribbean, plus some training at Quantico; these drills revealed deficiencies in Tactics, Techniques, and Procedures which were associated with the evolving landing operations capability—as well as the collaboration of the U.S. Navy and U.S. Marine Corps team.[11] Future General H. M. Smith, who participated in the Hawaii exercises, developed candid conclusions about the then capability of the Corps to conduct such an operation. As his biographer wrote, "Under the conditions then obtaining, he thought the amphibious assault impossible. The Marines would have been wiped out. Vast improvements were necessary."[12] This would occur, and as part of this process a significant shift in concept ensued: From seizing a temporary naval base in a benign environment and then defending it, to landing from the sea against a defended area where a needed base, naval or air, was needed.

A need for specialized equipment as well as training for the evolving mission also became very apparent. This involved more than small units weapons and communications equipment; that would come over time, as would developing aspects of Tactics, Techniques, and Procedures associated with control of naval gun fire, close air support, planning the loading of vessels, embarkations and debarkation from shipping, and communications for command and control. Other aspects were more fundamental. If the amphibious assault is viewed as a maritime version of World War I trench warfare, challenges indeed loomed. The defender would be operating from prepared positions awaiting the landing force. For the latter, it would be "going over the top" from a maritime "trench"—and the basic challenge of surviving the "no man's land", i.e., the ship-to-shore movement, between its maritime trench line and landing on a defended beach, i.e., a break-in via penetrating the surf zone, crossing the beach, and then penetrating inland.

How was this to be done? Certainly not by the age of sail and small wars type of shipping and landing craft previously available, as shown at Gallipoli—at least not against an enemy as capable and prepared as the Japanese (and later Germans) would be. Gradually, the answers evolved: Attack amphibious transports and cargo ships to carry the landing force into the objective area.[13] How, then, to move it from the ships (i.e., the maritime trench line) to the shore, i.e., beach? From civilian industry, eventually, came the answer: The eventual classic Landing Craft Vehicle/Personnel developed by Andrew Jackson Higgins in New Orleans, and the Tracked Landing Vehicle, from Donald Roebling in Florida.[14]

**The Corps and Preparing for War—Pre-1941—II**

Roles and mission, doctrine, structure, training, and equipment were all important, but who would lead a changed organization? This entailed the right men in the right place, and officers who were prepared to command such operations. This meant men of capability who could be identified, educated, properly assigned, and selected for promotion. Beyond initial recruitment, this meant a needed promotion reform in the United State Marine Corps—and this did not occur until 1934 under a new commandant, Major General John Henry Russell.[15]

Prior to his assuming office, promotion in the Corps was based on vacancy and seniority. When vacancies occurred, the officer at the top of the seniority list received promotion to the new vacancy. With Russell, he pushed for reform, a system based on merit by board selection.[16]

Panel 7

In advocating this change, Russell had to educate both houses of Congress on the why and implications of such a change. He stressed that the officer Corps situation was the "most serious problem confronting the Marine Corps since I joined in 1894." He informed appropriate committees of each chamber that he had overage colonels (52 to 62 of age) and Lieutenant Colonels (49 to 57), while 70% of his captains were over 40 and 37% of his First Lieutenants were over 35. Hence, the Corps could not go to war with such a situation.[17]

In addition to his staff providing more specifics, the *New York Times* supported such reform by reporting that if the situation would not change, an officer would service 140 years before being eligible for Brigadier General, and a Captain would serve 55 years in that grade.[18] Amongst young officers, the Naval Academy jib of the early 1930s seemed to be true when Midshipmen opting for the Navy joked with their soon to be Marine officer brethren, "I'll see you in 20 years when we're both Captains."[19] The issue was both physical and professional fitness. Once reform of the promotion system had been implemented, the Commandant succinctly compared and contrasted the old and new systems. In his final report to the Secretary of the Navy, General Russell in 1936 wrote, "Another serious defect of the seniority system was that an able, zealous, active and efficient officer could not be promoted over the head of another who lacked such qualifications. Mediocre officers were promoted as rapidly as the most efficient and there was not incentive to excel."[20] Serving officers of the time, especially capable and ambitious ones, certainly were aware of and talked about the situation—but stayed in because they were young, enjoyed what they were doing, and found duty in the Corps rewarding.[21]

Of course, statistics could be misleading—but officers remained in grades under the old system for long periods of time. Robert Devereux, the Marine commander at Wake Island, served five and a half years as a 2$^{nd}$ Lieutenant, and ten and a half as a 1$^{st}$ Lieutenant. Future General Jerry Thomas served 15 years as a 2$^{nd}$ and 1$^{st}$ Lieutenant. World War I hero and Marine Corps novelist (and artist) John Thomason served 14 years as a Captain, and General Oliver P. Smith, the eventual commander of the 1$^{st}$ Marine Division at the Chosin Reservoir, 17 years as a Captain. For field grade officers, a similar situation existed: Future General H. M. Smith was a Major for 13 years, and General Roy Geiger, an amphibious Corps commander in World War II and short time commander of 10$^{th}$ Army at Okinawa, 13 and a half years.[22]

Russell succeeded where his predecessors, including John A. Lejeune, had failed. Congress passed the reform and it was signed into law. Immediately, promotion boards were formed and selection based on merit was implemented. Selected officers advanced years before they would have under the old system—and their names are those of senior commanders of World War II. For example, H. M. Smith, 13 years a Major, was promoted to Colonel after only three years in grade as a Lieutenant Colonel. Smith was only one such officer so promoted because of ability and potential for future service. Besides H. M. Smith, the colonel's board in 1934 selected future generals Clayton Vogel and Charles F. Price, while that for Lieutenant Colonel advanced Julian C. Smith, Joseph Fegan, A. A. Vandergrift, Roy Geiger, Charles Barrett, Harry Schmidt, William Rupertus, and Pedro del Valle. This process continued in 1935, as Fegan, Vandergrift, Geiger, and Barrett were selected for Colonel, and a second board selected Julian C. Smith and John Marston.

Meanwhile, in 1935, Majors Clifton B. Cates, Lemuel Shepherd, Graves B. Erskine, Maurine Holmes, and Leo Hermle were selected for Lieutenant Colonel.[23]

The results of the company officers' boards were equally dramatic. In 1934, only 92 of 259 Captains were selected for Major, and only 89 of 198 1st Lieutenants were picked for captain.[24] The effect on the officers corps of the Marine Corps can easily imagined, in both its positive and negative consequences and reaction.[25]

As O. P. Smith tactfully commented, "Well, yes, it was in 1934 that the selection board process was on, and that really cleaned things out, boy! It was terrific." Marine Colonel and historian Robert Heinl tactfully stated that proficient officers "found themselves promoted with bewildering speed after years of stagnation."[26]

Other officers of the time were more candid and scathing of the former system and those who had benefited from it: As Brigadier General John Letcher penned in his memoirs, the selection boards effected the "incompetent officers of the Marine corps like scythes cutting through ripe grain…there was wailing and gnashing of teeth and bitter words especially from the wives of offices who were not selected." General Merrill Twining was even more blunt, reflectively writing that the 1934 initial boards "rid us of a heavy concentration of alcoholics, functional illiterates, and incompetent slobs. It was ruthless and intended to be."[27]

Linked to this was professional military education for its officer corps. Before 1891, America's "Soldiers of the Sea" had no formal education system for its leaders. In 1891, what eventually became known as The Basic School was founded for newly commissioned 2nd Lieutenants. Not until 1920 did the Corps establish its own professional educational system for its career officers.[28] That year, a three tiered system, originally known as the Marine Corps Schools, was established at the Marine Barracks, Quantico: The Basic School (later moved to the Marine Barracks, Philadelphia, and after World War II returned to Quantico) for 2nd Lieutenants, and one year courses respectively for captains and field grade officers.[29]

Initially patterned after and using course materials from the U.S. Army system, in the 1930s the PME curriculum changed to that of a maritime service orientation. [30]

The action officer for this was Colonel Ellis B. Miller, Chief of Staff of the schools.[31] Miller had written in August 1932, "The prolonged use of this Army material, now taken from all of the Army schools, has so saturated the entire Marine Corps Schools system that its foundation is still resting on Army principles, Army organization, and Army thought." Change had to come, for as Miller emphasized, the curricula of the schools "must involve Marine organizations, Marine equipment, Marine problems, Marine operations, with a Naval, not Army, background." As he succinctly noted, "The Marine Corps is not the Army; the Army is not the Marine Corps."[32] In 1933, Ellis articulated the key points:

> The Navy is a war machine already constructed and capable of immediate action. The Marine Corps is part of that machine, must produce, on call, a well-trained force, familiar with naval methods, and organized and equipped for conducting shore operations essential to the success of the naval mission.

PANEL 7

The implications were clear: In a future war, the fleet needed bases from which to operate and their defense and/or seizure existed via the U.S. Marine Corps: "The solution of this problem was accompanied by including as a part of the fleet, a force sufficiently strong and possessed of the necessary material to seize, establish, develop, maintain, and defend a temporary base from which the fleet might operate against the enemy...."[33]

Change indeed ensued. For example, in the curriculum for the 42 week field officers course (then named Senior Course) for the 1939-40 Academic Year, course work focused on subjects related to the Marine Corps or aspects of offensive and defensive landing operations, from military history, legal principles, logistics, military intelligence, aviation, chemical warfare, engineering, infantry weapons, communications, tactics and training, to overseas operations, map problems, and map maneuvers (all but one involving landing operations or ground operations ashore).[34]

Of interest, in the 42 week course, only one problem of 57 hours was devoted to Small Wars (near the end of the academic year)—with more hours were devoted to equitation (17) than given to basic instruction in Small Wars (16, three of which were on "Pack and Other Animal Transportation in Small Wars" with two of those a "Demonstration of Pack Saddles and Pack Loads").[35]

Included in the curriculum were the Advanced Base Problems sent from the Naval War College to the Marine Corps Schools from 1931 to 1941. A "school solution" was developed by the students and faculty, and then presented at the Naval War College at Newport, the Department of the Navy in Washington, and at the Marine Barracks, Quantico. All but two of these involved locations associated with War Plan Orange (i.e., Saipan, Guam, Tinian, Truk, and the Philippines, and from the mid-1930s to 1941 involved an amphibious assault and not simply defense of an advanced naval base seized in a benign environment and then awaiting the enemy's reaction.[36] However, the effect of this professional education should not be overly emphasized nor debunked. Between 1920 and 1941, for example, in the course for field grade officers, only 330 officers graduated from it and, of these, only 186 remained on active duty during the Second World War—but they formed the nucleus of the amphibious corps, divisions, aircraft wings, defense battalions, and corps troops of World War II.[37] During the war, 11 generals commanded Marine Corps divisions, and nine graduated from its Interwar staff college; of the 14 assistant division commanders, 11 graduated from it. Thus, 20 of 25 generals who commanded divisions or were assistant division commanders graduated from the Corps' senior professional military education institution; of the other five, three served at the Marine Corps Schools as instructors on the staff. At the amphibious corps level, the Marine Corps formed two Marine Amphibious Corps, III MAC (with the former I MAC becoming III MAC) and V MAC. Six Marine generals commanded these, and four graduated from the Quantico field officers course, and the other two served on the faculty of the Marine Corps Schools.

At the regimental level, the figures are similar.[38] During World War II, the Corps raised 33 regiments (20 infantry, six artillery, four engineer, two raider, and one parachute).[39] For these, 117 regular officers commanded regiments and would have been of the grade to have attended one or more of the Corps' and/or sister service professional military education schools before the United States entry into World War II.[40] Of these, in addition to The Basic School, 70 were graduates of one or more of the Corps' professional military education schools, 14 of a Corps PME school and a U. S. Army company grade and/or field grade officers' school, 18 of schooling only in the U.S. Army system, and three of a combination Marine Corps/U.S. Army and French War College PME courses. Only 11 did not attend a Marine Corps or sister service PME course after The Basic School and two, the aforementioned mustang and another officer, had no TBS designation after their names in the official registers.[41]

**That Was Then—But What about Now?**

The international environment, society, and services are not frozen in time. Change occurs. Conditions are very different today than in the Interwar year, but several issues connect then and now. The first is identification of officers of ability and merit for advancement and positions of increased and greater responsibilities. Despite whatever faults it may have, the system of board selection, i.e., superior professional peer review, continues to function and is indeed preferred to one based only on seniority and vacancy! A human element there may be, but is there a better method of selecting future leaders?

The other linkage is professional military education (PME). The U. S. Marine Corps has indeed institutionalized this aspect of the development of its officer corps. This includes a clearly stated and understood professional training and professional military education for Captains via its career level school, the Expeditionary Warfare School, and for all Majors at its intermediate level school, the Command and Staff College. Both of these courses are offered through a Non-Resident Distant Education programs offered by the Marine Corps' Training and Education Command's College of Distant Education and Training. Eligible officers are encouraged to enroll and become professional military education complete for their appropriate rank. A fortunate few are also board selected to attend the one year resident courses of the Expeditionary Warfare School or Command and Staff College (or sister service or foreign equivalents), whether or not they have graduated from the non-resident courses.[42]

In addition, the Corps has institutionalized a professional reading program, and emphasized cross-cultural communication programs and foreign language skills.[43] A similar PME program is now extending to its enlisted ranks, with required education and training for all the Noncommissioned Officer and Staff Noncommissioned ranks.[44] Stated simply, in professional military education a shift has occurred from a selective program for a fortunate few to one of "no Marine left behind." This is further recognition of the complexity of modern warfare emphasized by former Commandant Charles Krulak's articulated concept of the "strategic corporal" —a concept known to all contemporary Marines.[45]

The second decade of the 21st century is not the Interwar years of the 20th. Thus, in June 2010 an official U. S. Marine Corps publications stressed the following point: "Often thought of exclusively as an amphibious *assault* force, the period 1942-1945 was the only time in our history that the Marine Corps was organized, trained, and equipped for that one mission and did only one mission: Amphibious *assault*."[46] Despite this, for many Marines in the immediate decades after the Second World War, the assault was what the Corps was organized and trained for (with the sustained commitment ashore in Vietnam an

PANEL 7

exception). But what of its previous history of "small wars?" This was taught to recruits and officer candidates entering the Corps as a means of emphasizing initiative, courage, and leadership—but related to the past. In the 21st century, such is not now the case—as the two traditions of the U. S, Marine Corps of "small wars" and amphibious warfare have blended into one entity doctrinally called Expeditionary Operations.[47] This means that for contemporary Marines, more is demanded of them in the profession of arms and along the spectrum of conflict—and only the best can be selected as leaders of increased responsibility and for these only the most professional and educated can succeed in such a complex reality, be they in ranks from Corporal to Sergeant Major, or 2nd Lieutenant through General.

In 1920, as the Corps was establishing its professional education system, the words of the 13th Commandant of the Marine Corps, Major General John A. Lejeune, are still relevant:

It is our aim for all of our officers to have as good opportunities to obtain a military education as the officers of the Navy and the Army. Education is absolutely essential: An educated officer makes for educated men and an ignorant officer makes for ignorant men.

Today, Lejeune's articulated concept is even more applicable to all Marines—and soldiers, sailors, and airmen. This is a point Lejeune would have recognized, for as he later continued with this theme when speaking to the Committee on Naval Affairs of the House of Representatives: "You know there used to be an old theory that the soldier ought to be ignorant and illiterate and like dumb, driven cattle. I think our experience in this war [i.e., The Great War] shows the more intelligence, the more education, and the more initiative a man has the better soldier he is."[48]

## Notes

1. Allan R. Millett, *In Many Strife: General Gerald C. Thomas and the U.S. Marine Corps, 1917-1956* (Annapolis, MD: Naval Institute Press, 1993), 87.

2. A sensation within the Corps in the mid-1970s was the Brookings study: Martin Binkin and Jeffrey Record, *Where Does the Marine Corps Go from Here?* (Washington, DC: Brookings Institution, 1976). This is still discussed by officers of that era, e.g., Dr. J, William Gordon, Colonel, USMCR (Ret.) and Dr. Donald F. Bittner, LtColonel, USMCR (Ret.), professional exchange at the Marine Corps Command and Staff College, Quantico, Virginia, 14 September 2010.

3. Even as the Corps is still committed to operations in Afghanistan (but now out of Iraq), the service is turning its attention to post-Afghanistan issues, to include mission, role, force structure, and end strength. A study group will do so at the Marine Corps Combat Development Command, Quantico Virginia, during the autumn 2010: Commandant of the Marine Corps to Executive Steering Group for Force Structure Review Group, 1520 C 06 dated 16 August 2010, Subj: "USMC Force Structure Review Group (FSRG) 2010 Charter"; the enclosure addresses roles, missions, and Corps competencies, including those mandated by law (Title 10 § 5063). For initial discussions of this, see Gina Cavallaro, "Corps at a Crossroad: Force Structure Group Tasked with Plotting the Way Forward," *The Marine Corps Times,* 30 August 2010, 16; Bob Lamonthe, "Keep the Capabilities, Trim the Excess: CMC Defines Force Review Guidelines," *The Marine Corps Times,* 6 September 2010, 16; and appropriate material pertaining to the Corps, Walter Pincus, "Eyeing the Pentagon: Gates Considers Three Changes," *The Washington Post,* 17 August 2010, A13. For a contemporary discussion of the Corps and its amphibious mission, definition of a Marine, and concern about a second land army, see Dakota L. Wood, "Caught on a Lee Shore, The American Interest – Online – September 2010, at http://www.the-american-interest.com/index.cfm. See also, Gidget Fuentes, "Relevance of MEUs Debated after Years of Fighting on Land," *Marine Corps Times,* 4 October 2010, 34. Comments by Secretary of Defense Robert Gates on the role of the Marine Corps, especially its amphibious one, made at the Command and General Staff College, Fort Leavenworth, Kansas, on 7 May 2010, and at the Marine Corps Memorial, San Francisco, California, on 12 August 2010, have especially stimulated concern, responses, and national attention. Transcripts of these remarks are available at http://www.defense.gov/Transcripts/Transcript.aspx?TranscriptID=4623, and http://www.defense.gov/speeches/speech.aspx?speechid=1498, respectively.

4. The authorized strength of the Corps in 1932: 1,030 officers, 154 warrant officers, and 17,500 enlisted.

5. *Annual Report of the Major General Commandant of the United States Marine Corps* (Washington, DC: Government Printing Office, 1932). Several years later in assessing the capability of an assembled landing force similar to that on the aforementioned battleships, the then Major Pedro del Valle wrote that "the sad condition of our landing force was made shockingly obvious." He later concluded that "thank God we never had to make this crazy landing." Lieutenant General Pedro del Valle, USMC, *Semper Fidelis: An Autobiography* (Hawthorne, CA: Christian Book Club of America), 67 and 71.

6. In addition to Major Barrett, the committee consisted of Marine officers Major Pedro del Valle and Major Lyle Miller, and Navy Lieutenant Walter Ansel.

7. *Landing Operations Doctrine, United States Navy, Feet Training Publication 167* (Washington, DC, 1938). Copies of the evolving doctrinal publication, with various committee proceedings, are in the Archives Branch of the Gray Research Center. Appropriate changes

were issued in 1941, 1942, and 1943. Significantly, the cover letter of change 1 dated 2 May 1941 included the following verbiage: "FTP-167 is intended as a guide for forces of the Navy and Marine Corps conducting a landing against opposition. It considers, primarily, the tactics and technique of the landing operation and the necessary supporting measures therefore. Purely naval or military operations are dealt with only to the extent to which these operations are influenced by the special nature of amphibious warfare." The U.S. Army adopted the doctrine as FM 31-4, *Landing Operations on Hostile Shores*, in 1942.

8. Late 19th century issues and endeavors are studied in Jack Shulimson, *The Marine Corps' Search for a Mission, 1880-1898* (Lawrence, KS: University Press of Kansas, 1993).

9. Ellis' plan has been published. See U.S. Marine Corps, FMFRP 12-46, *U. S. Marine Corps, 712H Operations Plan, Advanced Base Operations in Micronesia, 1921 (*Washington, DC, 1992). Ellis envisioned not just defense of advanced naval bases, but also their seizure; the subject of advanced bases had been studied from the first decade of the 20th century by Marine Officers at the Naval War College, to include John Henry Russell, Robert Dunlap, Dion Williams, and Ellis himself; such materials are retained in the archives of the library of the Naval War College. For a biography of Ellis, commentary on the plan, and his demise while on a not well concealed intelligence mission in the Pacific, see Dirk A. Ballendorf and Merrill L. Bartlett, *Pete Ellis: An Amphibious Warfare Prophet, 1880-1923* (Annapolis, MD: Naval Institute Press, 1997.)

10. Department of the Navy, General Order No. 241, 7 December 1941. For the complete text, see Marine Corps Historical Division, http://www.tecom.usmc mil/HD/Docs_Speeches/Thefleetmarineforce.htm.

11. These are summarized in Allan R. Millett, *Semper Fidelis: A History of the Marine Corps* (New York: Macmillan, 1980; 2nd ed., 1991), Chapters 10 and 12.

12. Norman Cooper, *A Fighting General: The Biography of General Holland M. 'Howlin' Mad' Smith* (Quantico, VA: Marine Corps Association, 1987), 51.

13. By 1944, the Haskell class Amphibious Attack Transports (APAs) and Amphibious Attack Cargo ships (AKAs), plus Amphibious Command Ships (AGCs) configured on the same hulls, had evolved - plus other amphibious craft such as the LST (Landing Ship Tanks) and Landing Ship Docks (LSDs). Many of these vessels remained in service into the Vietnam war era. Such ships carried the landing force to the theatre and then within it, i.e., movement and maneuver. APAs and AKAs could carry approximately 20 or more landing craft. For the basic characteristics of these types ships, see *Jane's Fighting Ships, 1946-47* (New York, NY: The Macmillan Company, 1947), 388-392.

14. Landing Craft Vehicle Personnels were used both in the European and Pacific theatre of operations. The classic photo: that of U.S. troops approached Omaha Beach at Normandy. The "D-Day Museum," or more accurately National World War II Museum, is located on the site of Higgins boat manufacturing company. For characteristics of these small craft, see Commander Amphibious Training Command, U.S. Pacific Fleet, *Landing Craft and Their Employment* (1965). For a detail history of this landing craft, see Jerry E. Strahan, *Andrew Jackson Higgins and the Boats That Won World War II* (Baton Rouge, LA: Louisiana State University Press, 1994).

The descendants of the LVTs (Tracked Landing Vehicle) have been called the AMTRACs (Amphibian Tractors), AAVs (Assault Amphibian Vehicles), and EFV (Expeditionary Fighting Vehicles); the last named remain in controversial development entering the second decade of the 21st century. For details on the basic procurement of the LVT and other landing craft, see Colonel Kenneth J. Clifford, USMCR, *Progress and Purpose: A Developmental History of the U. S. Marine Corps, 1900-1970* (Washington, DC: Marine Corps History and Museums Division, 1973), 48-60.

15. In addition to the law, the Interwar problem was compounded by the Russell and Neville Boards after World War I which determined who would be retained in the post-war officer corps, their rank, and their lineal list number. i.e., seniority. For a succinct discussion of this, see Millett, *In Many a Strife,* 74, 75, and 83.

16. This meant selection for promotion predicated on potential for future service based on past performance, as opposed to a reward for past service.

17. For a succinct discussion of this, see Donald F. Bittner, "John Henry Russell," *Commandants of the Marine Corps,* Allan R. Millet and Jack Shulimson, eds. (Annapolis, MD: Naval Institute Press, 2004), 245-248. For Russell's testimony, see United States Senate, "Selection, Promotion, and Retirement of Commissioned Officers of the Marine Corps. Hearing before a Subcommittee of the Committee on Naval Affairs. S. 3058, 20 April 1934."

18. "General's Rank in Marines Requires 140 Years' Duty," *New York Times,* 15 January 1934.

19. Colonel Robert D. Heinl, USMC, *Soldiers of the Sea: The United States Marine Corps, 1775-1962* (Annapolis, MD: Naval Institute Press, 1962), 316. A variation of this quotation is in Norman Cooper's biography of H. M. Smith, *A Fighting General,* 50. At that time, almost all Marine officers entered the service via the U. S. Naval Academy.

20. Major General Commandant of the Marine Corps to the Secretary of the Navy Final Report, 2 September 1936 (Typed copy). Copies of the annual reports of the Commandants of the Marine Corps are in the Archives Branch, Gray Research Center, Marine Corps University, Quantico, Virginia.

21. Memoirs and individual oral histories candidly addressed the situation. See the critical commentary in Brigadier General John Letcher, USMC, *One Marine's Story* (Verona, VA: McClure Press, 1970), 57, 104-108, and 113-114. Letcher eventually commanded 1st Field Artillery Group (V Marine Amphibious Corps) on Iwo Jima.

22. Roger Willock, *Lone Star Marine: A Biography of the Late John W. Thomason, Jr., USMC* (Princeton, NJ: Privately Published, 1961), 3 and 15; Brigadier General Robert Devereux interview with author, 17 November 1982; General Jerry Thomas letter to author, 23 December 1982; Roger Willock, *Unaccustomed to Fear: A Biography of General Roy S. Geiger, USMC* (Princeton, NJ: Haskins Press, 1968), 168; Norman Cooper, "The Military Career of General Holland M. Smith, USMC" (Ph.D. Dissertation, University of Alabama, 1974), 101 and 104; and General O. P Smith, "Oral History" (Washington: Historical Division, 1973), 12-13. General O. P. Smith also recalled future Marine Corps Generals Jerry Thomas and Mervin Silverthorne served many years in the grade 1st Lieutenant, i.e., nearly 13.

23. Reports of Proceedings of Senior Selection Boards to the Secretary of the Navy, 25 June 1934, and 7 January and 2 December 1935. U. S. National Archives, RG 127, Box 133, File 1965-75-35-10. These reports simply list the names of the officers selected. The results were also published in the *Marine Corps Gazette.*

24. Reports of Proceedings of Junior Selection Boards to the Secretary of the Navy, 25 June 1934. U. S. National Archives, RG 127, Box 133, File 1965-75-35-10. As with the senior officer boards, the results appeared in the *Marine Corps Gazette.*

25. The opponents to the reform sought their revenge in 1936 in opposing Russell's permanent promotion to Major General. This emotional, negative, and highly personal opposition received considerable publicity at the time, e.g., see appropriate coverage in the *New York Times,* proceedings in the Senate in the *Congressional Record,* and in a memoir by

Panel 7

Russell's daughter: Brooke Astor, *Footprints: An Autobiography* (New York, NY: Doubleday & Company, Inc., 1980), 85-89, and 187-193.

26. Smith, "Oral History," 13; and Heinl, *Soldiers of the Sea,* 298.

27. Letcher, *One Marine's Story,* p. 108; General Merrill Twining letter to Author, 28 December 1982.

28. For a succinct overview of the system, see Donald F. Bittner, "Marine Corps Professional Military Education" and "Quantico, Virginia," William E. Simons, ed., *Professional Military Education in the United States: A Historical Dictionary* (Westport, CT: Greenwood Press, 2000), 190-192 and 257-259, respectively. In that volume, see also "The Basic School" (76-78), "L'Ecole Superieure de Guerre" (134-135), "Amphibious Warfare School" (42-45), and "Marine Corps Command and Staff College," (186-189).

29. Announced unofficially to the Corps via "The Quantico Schools," *The Marine Corps Gazette,* Vol. V, No. 3, September 1920, 316-317. Of interest, officers were informed that "Unless under very exceptional circumstances, student officers will not be detached until they have completed their courses. The old curse of 'This is in additional to your other duties,' will not be applied to the students, for they will be assigned no duty but their school work." (317) For an over history of the Command and Staff College, see Donald F. Bittner, *Curriculum Evolution. Marine Corps Command and Staff College, 1920-1988* (Washingtn, DC: Marine Corps History and Museums Division, 1988).

30. For commentary on this by O. P. Smith, a former faculty member at the Schools, see Clifton La Bree, *The Gentle Warrior: General Olive P. Smith, USMC* (Kent, OH: Kent State Press, 2001), 6.

31. An officer now generally unknown in the Corps of the 21$^{st}$ century, insight into this dynamic and hard driving officer can be found in Lieutenant General Victor Krulak, USMC, *First to Fight: An Inside View of the U. S. Marine Corps* (Annapolis, MD: Naval Institute Press, 1984), 81.

32. Colonel Ellis Miller letter to Brigadier General J. C. Breckinridge, 15 August 1932. HAF 274. Archives Branch, Gray Research Center, Marine Corps University, Quantico, Virginia. Miller also listed 14 specific tasks which needed to be done, the foremost resting on development of a "Marine Corps doctrine."

33. Colonel Ellis B. Miller, USMC, *The Marine Corps in Support of the Fleet* (Quantico, VA: Marine Corps Schools, 1933), 12-13. The bibliography lists 77 references, including military and naval memoirs of World War I, official and unofficial histories of Gallipoli and German Baltic operations, theorists such as Mahan and Corbett, Marine Corps officers' publications, and lectures on and after operations reports from exercises in Panama (1923), Culebra (1924), and Hawaii (1925).

34. These included Gallipoli, Zeebrugge, Baltic Islands, Alhucemas, and early American landings, plus the Civil War battles of Bull Run and Chancellorsville.

35. Master Schedule, Senior Course, Marine Corps Schools, Marine Barracks, Quantico, 1939-1940." This includes a day by day, hour by hour, week by week listing of each class and subject thereof. Summary "Recapitulation" of the courses are on pages 21 to 35. This was the last complete course before World War II, as the 1940-41 Academic Year was suspended in April 1941.

36. For a summary and analysis of the Advanced Base Problems, see Donald F. Bittner, "Taking the Right Fork in the Road: The Transition of the U. S. Marine Corps from an 'Expeditionary' to an Amphibious Corps," *Battles Near and Far: A Century of Overseas Deployment,* Peter Dennis and Jeffrey Grey, eds. (Canberra, Australia: Army History Unit, 2004), 128.

37. Figures compiled from the Marine Corps monthly muster rolls, 1920 to 1941, for the Marine Barracks, Quantico, Virginia; within that command, officers were listed under Marine Corps Schools. The original muster rolls are in the National Archives, Washington D.C., with microfilm copies in the Gray Research Center, Marine Corps University, Quantico, Virginia. The Corps also sent a limited number of officers to U.S. Army PME schools, and to one foreign institution: L'Ecole Superieure de Guerre, in Paris, France. Of the latter, 11 completed the two-year course and one finished its first year. Donald F. Bittner, "Foreign Military Officer Training in Reverse: U.S. Marine Corps Officers in the French Professional Military Education System in the Interwar Years", *The Journal of Military History*, Vol. 57, No. 3, July 1993, 481-510.

Compiled from the *Register of Commissioned and Warrant Officers of the United States Navy and Marine Corps, July 1, 1941* (Washington, DC: U.S. Government Printing Office, 1941). Educational qualifications of officers of the Marine Corps on active duty were listed in it.

38. Only regimental commanders are assessed; a similar one could be made of the defense battalions, 20 of which were raised and whose commanding officers were usually of the grade of colonel or lieutenant colonel—some of whom also commanded regiments; the list of defense battalion commanding officers is in Charles L. Updegraph, Jr., *Special Marine Corps Units of World War II* (Washington, DC: Historical Division, U.S. Marine Corps, 1972), 88-92. A similar analysis could also be made of Marine Aircraft Wing and Marine Air Group Commanders.

39. Marine Corps regiments in the war: 1st to 9th: Infantry; 10th to 15th: Artillery; 16th to 19th: Engineer; and 21st to 29th: Infantry.

40. Professional schooling beyond the entry level The Basic School for 2nd Lieutenants; included the field grade officer one-year Marine Corps and one or two year Fort Leavenworth courses, and the Corps' company grade one year course and the U.S. Army career and branch schools of the infantry, cavalry, field artillery, and coast defense artillery. Due to the recent development of a Marine Corps professional education program, that service did not then have a war college; however, 15 regimental commanders were U. S. Army or U. S. Navy war college graduates, while six had completed signal and five motor transport courses at U.S. Army schools, two had engineer courses, and three courses in law. Also, one was a naval aviator and another a certified translator in Spanish.

41. All figures compiled from the names of corps, division, assistant division, and regimental commanders listed in regimental histories (1st, 2d, 3d, 4th, 5th, 6th, 7th, 8th, 9th, 10th, 11th, 12th, 14th and 25th Marines), *Special Marine Corps Units of World War II*, and the official *History of U.S. Marine Corps Operations in World War II*, vols. I to V, 1958, 1963, 1966, 1971, and 1968 respectively, all published by Historical Branch, G-3 Division, Headquarters, U.S. Marine Corps; Gordon L. Rottman, *U.S. Marine Corps World War II Order of Battle* (Westport, CT.: Greenwood Press, 2002); and the six World War II division histories published after that conflict, and then cross correlated with names and educational qualifications noted in the *Register of Commissioned and Warrant Officers of the United States Navy and Marine Corps* for the war years, primarily that for 1941. Age became a factor as the Corps expanded – and younger officers commanded regiments as the conflict progressed, hence before the war commenced most of these did not have the opportunity to attend the Corps' senior professional military education school (or a sister service equivalent).

42. The Corps' officer development program is outlined in Commanding General, Education Command, *Marine Corps Officers Professional Military Education Continuum, March 2010*. The Commanding General, Education Command, is also the President, Marine Corps University, Quantico, Virginia. www.mcu.usmc.mil

43. In many ways, this is a return to skills many Marine officers possessed in the Interwar era. Exemplifying this was Brigadier General Samuel B. Griffith, a regimental commander in

World War II, who was fluent in Chinese and after his retirement from the Corps received his D.Phil. from Oxford University – and translated Sun Tzu into English and this work is still in print. Samuel B. Griffith, USMC, *Sun Tzu: The Art of War* (New York, NY: Oxford University Press, 1963). However, for a balanced perspective on both the positives and negatives associated with such real and superficial capabilities in the pre-World War II era, see Richard L. Millett, "Conclusions: Lessons Lost and Lessons Forgotten," *Searching for Stability: The U.S. Development of Constabulary Forces in Latin American and the Philippines.* Occasional Paper 30 (Fort Leavenworth, KS: Combat Studies Institute Press, 2010), 123-131.

44. For the specifics of the Marine Corps professional military education program, see Marine Corps Order 1553.4B, MCCDC C 40 OP dated 25 January 2008, "Subj: Professional Military Education (PME)." For a further discussion of these programs, see Colonel Terence K. Kerrigan, USMC (Ret.), "College of Distance Education," and Lieutenant Colonel Dennis Haskin, USAF (Ret.), and Major Sean Griffin, USMC (Ret.), "Distance Education and Blended Learning Seminars," *Marine Corps Gazette,* Vol. 91, No. 10, October 2010, 36-35 and 46-53, respectively.

45. General Krulak repeatedly addressed the concept of the "strategic corporal" between 1995 and 1999 while Commandant of the Marine Corps. For example, General Charles C. Krulak, "The Strategic Corporal: Leadership in the Three Block War," *Marines: Official Magazine of the Marine Corps,* Vol. 28, No. 1, January 1999, 26-32.

46. Deputy Commandant for Combat Development and Integration, *Marine Corps Operating Concepts: Assuring Littoral Access...Proven Crisis Response,* 3rd ed., June 2010, p. 2. Whether conceptually or actually true or not, the key in this statement is the institutional self-identification of its role and mission during and since World War II.

47. Marine Corps Doctrinal Publication 3, *MCDP 3, Expeditionary Operations* (Washington, DC, 1998), 32. The linkage of expeditionary operations to their naval character, especially amphibious, is on pages 45-46.

48. Major General John A. Lejeune, USMC, Testimony, 26 February 1920, *Hearings before the Committee on Naval Affairs of the House of Representatives on Estimates Submitted by the Secretary of the Navy, 1920, Vol. II* (Washington, DC: Government Printing Office, 1920), 1828 and 1830. For contemporary recommendations reference the importance of education and changes pertaining to it, see Stephen J. Hadley and William J. Perry, Co-Chairmen, *The QDR in Perspective: Meeting America's National Security Needs in the 21st Century: The Final Report of the Quadrennial Defense Review Independent Panel,* Final Corrected Advance Copy (2010), xv to xvii. www.usip.org.

# Day 2, Panel 3: Changing Leadership for a Changing World Role, 1906-1939

## Questions and Answers
(Transcript of Presentation)

### Dr. Gene Andersen, Ph.D.
### Dr. Donald Bittner, Ph.D.

## Moderated by Mr. Kelvin Crow

**Mr. Crow:**

Thank you, Dr. Bittner. I'd like to exercise the moderator's prerogative by asking the first question. We have a few moments for questions and I'd like to address that to Professor Anderson. Forgive me. I had a brother who was a Naval Officer, but can you expand a little bit on command by negation? I just didn't get a good grip on that.

**Dr. Andersen:**

Command by negation is the concept in the Navy that I've given you direction. Go forth and do your job. I will tell you if something you are choosing to do is not what you should do. I mean, that's what it boils down to. It's a little bit more complicated than that but it's essentially the idea that I've given you broad instructions and if I observe that you're doing something that I don't want you to do, I will tell you not to do it, but otherwise, go do your job. That's once again simplistic like everything else I've said, but trying to take the big ideas and boil them down, that's basically how that works out.

**Mr. Crow:**

So I'm going to let you run until you screw up and then I'll talk to you.

**Dr. Andersen:**

Then I'll tell you don't do that and if you keep doing it then I'll get somebody else. Then I'll fire you. Questions gentlemen? General Brown?

**BG Brown:**

I was one of those army officers you spoke of that had the culture shock of going to the Naval War College as a relatively senior Colonel and I was struck while there, not only by the difference between my background as an Army officer and what I felt I was encountering with the naval officers, but also the rather dramatic differences between the Navy and the Marines which in my mind were even greater than the difference between the Navy and the Army. And within the Navy the rather dramatic difference between, in my view, submariners, aviation-oriented folks, and the ones who were frigates and destroyers and surface warriors. I'm wondering if the both of you could kind of comment on the extent to which those separate cultures affect the paradigm you've described, and in the case of the Marines, the extent to which the recent 50 year run of not doing any amphibious landings may or may not have watered down the effort to distinguish the Marines from the Army that you described as being so potent in this interwar period. You know, hanging onto the amphibious warfare as being the thing that made the Marines unique. It's kind of a two-part question but hopefully related.

**Dr. Andersen:**

To lead off with the culture piece, I've sort of misguided you in the sense that I talked about a Navy culture. And there's an argument to me made—and in my longer version of this talk, I make it, that the Navy doesn't really have a culture, per se. That the Navy is a collection of communities and each of those communities has a culture, and so the culture that I spoke of is really the Navy's surface culture: the culture of the frigate destroyer, cruiser world of the Navy's surface operations. And it is not really the culture so much necessarily of the aviation community, of the submarine community, or the rest of the Navy. The Navy is, to a much greater degree than any of the other services, a collection of subordinate communities. Just as an example, career management in the Navy. The community managers that own career management for each community, own officers all the way up until the point that they're selected for Admiral. So Navy captains are detailed by people who are community managers for the benefit of the community. All the way up to the captain level, their development is driven by, "What does the community perceive is good for the community?" Not for the Navy at large. There's no central management of the Navy, of Post-Command Commanders, of Captains, of any officers short of an admiral. So the Navy is really very deeply stove piped into sub-communities. And even in aviation, I'm a helicopter guy, I was a helicopter pilot, I was very different, viewed myself as being very different from tactical air guys who flew off the carrier or the maritime patrol guys who went home every day. Two very different cultures, very different communities, and we perceived ourselves to be very different, so just within the Navy there is some incredible differences.

**Audience Member 1:**

As an outsider who served with the Navy as well as the Marine Corps, I agree with what you say. I've been at the college for 36 years now and I've had offers from all these various communities and we kind of joke about the guys in the blue suits with the gold rings but I have an engineer, I've had a chaplain, I've got a submariner, I've got a helicopter pilot in the last two years, and you talk with them about surface line issues, they're not familiar with that at all. You talk to them about going to our second year course, they talk about different areas for a promotion, career development, things of this nature. As I said, how the Navy functions like this, in many ways, is a mystery. And I've been associated with the naval service since 1962. This issue of the Marine Corps not being a second land Army, it surfaced again, if you recall, during Vietnam when one of the commandants changed the designation from a MEU, MEB, and MEF. Marine Expeditionary Unit, Marine Expeditionary Brigade, Marine Expeditionary Force, to MAU, MAB, MAF with "Amphibious" replacing the "Expeditionary." There's always that concern about are we going to evolve into a second land Army, and as Colonel Miller said in the '30s and basically as General Connelly has been saying during his "commandantcy," we can't survive and we shouldn't be a second land Army. So, what you see, and especially on his concern about the Marine Corps and getting from the Navy, amphibs and getting the expeditionary fighting vehicle online as well as the Osprey to maintain that expeditionary, I'm calling it expeditionary now, amphibious is a subset of expeditionary capability. Otherwise we're very vulnerable because Congress, the public, the Secretary of Defense is going to say we can't afford two land Armies. So that's why General Connelly keeps coming back to that. We've done some analysis of our students and right now we figure one or two years from now. I'm quoting our Dean of Academics now because I had gone in a couple days ago. We were talking in seminar and my navy officer had not seen and did not even know of the Humphrey Bogart film, *The Caine Mutiny*. So it was one of these generational discussions that spun off and our dean said in a couple years all of our Marines, their total professional experiences is going to be COIN operations, sure, insurgency, functioning as a second land Army. And then I said, well, you know, remember, about five years ago we were worried how we were going to blend our officers who had been to Afghanistan and Iraq with those who had not been. Well, that was not a problem, but it's something we see being worked out, and so for those of us who've been around, we saw the same thing after Vietnam in the Brookings study, *Where Does the Marine Corps Go From Here?* And they recommended that we assume the mission of the 18th Airborne Corps Strategic Reserve. What it ended up being was a Norway commitment. I guess we still have equipment stored up there. But that's a big concern within the Marine Corps.

**Dr. Andersen:**

Just a point about history. The Navy doesn't tend to view its history as all that significant. I walked down to the bookstore here yesterday and you've got James Hornfischer's *Last Stand of the Tin Can Sailors* for sale down there, which is a great book about sort of the Navy's equivalent to the story of Joshua Lawrence Chamberlain at Little Round Top. Ernest Evans at Johnston at Leyte Gulf is a parallel story but it has very little resonance in the Navy and very few naval officers have read the book.

**Audience Member 2:**

If I can make a comment—

**Mr. Crow:**

Gentlemen, I'm sorry, it's a fascinating discussion. I know we have other folks who'd like to ask questions but I'm afraid we've run out of time for this panel. I'd like to ask you to join me in giving a warm round of applause of thanks to our panelists.

# Day 3: Featured Speaker

## US Army Leader Development: Past, Present, and Future by Brigadire General Sean B. MacFarland

(Transcript of Presentation)

## Moderated by Kendall D. Gott

**Mr. Gott:**

Welcome to the final section of the 8th annual Military History Symposium, sponsored by the Combat Studies Institute. While I have the opportunity, I want to thank you all for coming. And I'd like to thank the staff that has supported this event in its entirety. Kurt King is up there somewhere with the audio/visual crew. We have Elizabeth Brown and Jodi Becker, who have been out at the registration booth and Kevin Reed, who has been doing a lion's share of manhandling of the books and other heavy toting and lifting, and all the staff members of Combat Studies Institute served as moderators.

One of the regrets I have during these events is I do not get enough time to say hello and to chat with each and every one of you. And I regret that. But I'd just like to say how much it means to all of us that you've traveled from afar, whether it be from the CAC headquarters or all the way from the East or West Coasts and beyond. And it was really nice to have sister services here this year, as well as our friends and allies from foreign nations.

OK, again, our final panel is our own Brigadier General Sean MacFarland, who currently serves as the deputy commandant of the Command and General Staff College here at Fort Leavenworth. Sir?

**BG MacFarland:**

Thanks. Good job. I'll try to keep my remarks as brief as my bio. First of all, I'd just like to echo thanks to everybody for attending this conference. And I hope that you've found it to be worthwhile.

I feel a little under-qualified to be standing in front of you today. I'm not an historian of any note. I'm an engineering major. But I'll do what I can to talk about how history has influenced leader development. And leader development is, as you heard, my portfolio, my brief. So I'll talk a little bit about that.

First of all, I think it's important to at least acknowledge that this entire discussion is not moot, that leaders are made and not born. If leaders were only born, then this would just be a topic of eugenics and nothing more. So I happen to believe that, as the US Army believes, that we can make leaders.

Having said that, the Army's approach to leader development through the years has had its ups and downs, with a record of mixed success. And my job is, of course, to improve on that track record. And although leadership has always helped to provide the margin between battlefield success and failure, those margins are growing slimmer all the time, thanks to technology proliferation. It's leveling the battlefield between ourselves and our potential adversaries. And that makes it all the more important to ensure that we have leadership that is superior to that of our enemies.

General Winfield Scott, who led American troops in the War of 1812 and then in the Mexican-American War actually, some 35 years later, he declared it as his fixed opinion that West Point-trained officers had transformed the Army and provided the principle difference between victory and defeat in that conflict. Now that fixed opinion was shared by enough of our leadership that West Point remained the primary source of professional education within our Army for over a hundred years thereafter. Unfortunately, despite its many and necessary contributions to America's defense, the military academy by itself was far from sufficient to meet the needs of our growing nation.

hter of hundreds of thousands of American soldiers, both Union and Confederate, under the command of West Pointers on both sides of the Civil War made it clear that something was missing in our leader development model. Indeed, our professional soldiers demonstrated little or no more skill in leading large formations than the rank amateurs. Whatever primitive talent management system that we were using back in those days, especially at the outset of the war, was severely flawed.

Furthermore, our senior commanders were largely self-taught above the tactical level in the operational art. And it was said that many carried a copy of [Antoine-Henri] Jomini's book in their saddlebags about his treatment of the Napoleonic Wars. Unfortunately, the technology of the Napoleonic Wars was in the past, and the technology of the Civil War made those tactics really inappropriate for the day. And lots of American soldiers paid a heavy price for their commanders' ignorance.

After a long series of unsuccessful commanders, the Union of course finally found, through a very costly process of trial by fire and error, their leader in Ulysses S. Grant. And to borrow from the old parable, we've made him, we took the stone that the builders rejected and made him our cornerstone. Something was upside-down in how we were picking our leaders back then.

Well, at the end of the Civil War, the Army moved back to the frontier, and began fighting a series of small campaigns against Indian tribes, just as it had before the war. And intellectualism, I think, dived to a new low within the Army during those days, along with low pay hardships and slow promotions. All these factors combined to make an Army career unattractive for the best and the brightest of that generation.

So not surprisingly, the Army turned in an embarrassing performance during the Spanish-American War. And in response, Secretary of War [Elihu] Root began to reform the Army's professional military education system. Unfortunately, the First World War interrupted those reforms shortly after they began. And their impact was minimal by the time we sent our doughboys over there. Indeed, actual combat was the main schoolhouse for our leaders during the First World War, just as it was during the Civil War.

We tacitly accepted the European view, best articulated by Field Marshal Ferdinand Foch, that it takes 15,000 casualties to train a major general. Although we were among the victors, American military innovation during the campaigns of 1918 was virtually nonexistent, and our losses were once again severe. We still had a long way to go obviously in leader development. Despite our victory, though, the experiences of the First World War in the trenches was traumatic enough that the Army, along with the other services, began to focus on education, just as Secretary Root had tried to do before the war.

And as a result, military innovation actually flourished between the world wars, despite the impact of a great depression. And it was during the inter-war period that Fort Leavenworth really came into its own as the mid-grade professional education institution that we like to call the intellectual center of the Army.

I'll defer to Pete Schifferle on the history of the Command General Staff College during the inter-war years and during those wars. Suffice it to say, the investment we made during America's lean years paid great dividends in the forms of the brilliant campaigns that our Leavenworth graduates waged during the Second World War, in both the European and Pacific theaters.

However, as we saw with the Civil War victory, can be a double-edged sword. And complacency set in after the Second World War. And we narrowly escaped disaster in Korea. Fortunately, the Korean War was similar enough to the recently concluded Second World War, and we had enough residual talent and experience still in our ranks that we were able to avoid catastrophe.

Unfortunately, that was not the case in Vietnam, where sadly our inability to adapt quickly enough to the circumstances of that conflict exhausted the Americans' national will before we were able to defeat the enemy. And ultimately, that led to the defeat of our South Vietnamese allies.

Perhaps like no other conflict though, Vietnam spurred the American Army to take a hard look at itself and change. Like the inter-war period 50 years earlier, these were lean years for the military. Nevertheless, that era was marked by numerous doctrinal and technical innovations. And General Sullivan touched on that during his talk on the first day.

But among them was our recognition of the importance of the operational art. To develop successful campaigns, the Army opened the school here at Fort Leavenworth, SAMS, School of Advanced Military Studies. And in short order, its graduates were called upon to write plans for operations in Panama and Iraq, which led to our overwhelming victories in both operations, Just Cause and Desert Storm. And some of those planners' names would be familiar to you guys, like Huntoon and Rodriguez. I mean, these were the bright, young iron majors out there who took the lessons they learned here and applied them in the field. To some, it seemed like the operational art was a powerful, mysterious force. And its practitioners inevitably earned the nickname "Jedi Knights".

But SAMS is just one of the many reasons that we enjoyed so much success, and in such disparate and far-flung operations. Another was the professionalism of our non-commissioned officers. After Vietnam, we addressed one of the most glaring deficiencies of that war, and that was the disintegration of our NCO corps. One of the reforms was the institution of the NCOES beginning in 1971. And we've all heard that no plan survives contact with the enemy. The reason our soldiers were able to implement our plans so well and to adapt and overcome innumerable challenges caused by fog and friction of warfare was our professional NCO corps. Not only do we fight well at the operational level, but we completely out-classed the battle-hardened Iraqi army at the tactical level as well.

As General Freddie Franks said when asked about the American Army's technological advantage over the Iraqi army, he said, "You could have put our soldiers in their tanks and our soldiers in theirs, and the outcomes would have been the same." Our well-trained and educated NCOs were the reason that he could make that boast.

After our victories in Panama, Iraq, and the end of the Cold War, we again fell victim to our own success. Despite entering the 21st century with quick initial victories over the Taliban regime in Afghanistan and Saddam Hussein's regime in Iraq, we failed to adapt to the growing insurgencies in both countries. We ignored the lessons of the Israeli defense force in southern Lebanon, did not prepare for a new type of irregular or hybrid warfare.

After almost losing the fruits of our 2003 victory over Iraq's armed forces to insurgency and civil war as it spread across Mesopotamia, we finally adjusted our tactics and forged a campaign that salvaged the military situation. But it was a near-run thing. It took far too long for us to adopt proper COIN TTPs [counterinsurgency tactics, techniques, procedures] in Iraq.

One of the reasons we were able to hold on despite a failing strategy and then turn the situation around was that our soldiers continued to be led by highly competent, professional junior officers and non-commissioned officers whom they respected. And they gave us senior officers the breathing space that we needed, but probably didn't deserve, to properly understand the fight we were in.

We hope to do the same in Afghanistan. But it's too soon to say whether we can or will succeed there. One thing we do know is that if we had had the same NCO corps that we had in Vietnam, it is likely that we would have been ejected from both Iraq and Afghanistan by now. And the Army would be at or past its breaking point, as it was in the '70s.

It used to be common to tell a unit that despite repeated ass-kickings at the hands of the OPFOR [opposing forces] at the combat training centers, that they're a learning organization. That wasn't much of a morale boost for rotation units, but it captured the intent of the Army's leader development philosophy. Failure was OK, as long as you learned from it.

Well, failure might be okay at a CTC [combat training center], but it's not okay on the battlefield. The American people expect us to do more than just learn from our nation's wars. They expect us to win them. And, by the way, they not only want us to just win, but they want us to do it fast, cheap, and clean. And their patience for our discovery learning process is very limited.

So how do we do that? Well clearly, we need to be more agile and adaptive. And we need to understand complex problems better and design our solutions accordingly. We have to understand our environment and think critically to succeed, both today and in the future. And that's the challenge for me and the team here at LD&E.

The Army leader development strategy that will take us through 2015 includes all four cohorts; officers, warrant officers, non-commissioned officers, and civilians. As the Army moves to fully implement the rotational readiness model we are trying to balance the three elements of learning; experience, training, and education, against the demands of persistent conflict. We started out with eight imperatives for the Army leader development strategy. The one on the bottom, the ninth, we just recently added. We really think it's important that as we enter our tenth year of constant conflict, with no end in sight, that we focus on the profession. Because the Army is beginning to show some of the strains of the burden that we're bearing.

As General [George] Casey said, we didn't become a hollow force immediately after Vietnam. That comment was made actually nine years after we got out of Vietnam. But after nine years of combat, we have not reached the point where we want to say that we're a hollow force. What we say is we're an army out of balance. And one area where that imbalance has been felt most is in our professional military education system. It's been a challenge just to get officers of all ranks and types into our schools, and then back out into the field where they're needed. That challenge has become even more acute when we transformed into a brigade-centric modular army, because that put an even greater demand on the Army for our mid-grade officers, especially majors.

And more than that, it's been a challenge just to ensure that our PME [professional military education] schools provide the right type of education and training to our officers and NCOs so that when they return to the fight, they have the tools that they need to succeed.

So what then must we teach our leaders? And how should we teach them to achieve maximum effect? Well, you can see some of the hows up above there. And what we'd like to say is that we don't teach people what to think, but we teach them how to think, which brings us to the subject of critical thinking.

Army leaders have to possess both intellectual courage and humility. They have to know how to apply these with a disciplined approach to both identify and solve the problems that we confront. And obviously this is hardly a new concept, but it also tends to be under-appreciated as a military virtue. Tennyson's poem about the charge of the light brigade immortalized a military mindset that I think is popular among many, which is, ours is not to question why, ours but to do and die. Too often, we remember this verse and not the lines that condemn the folly of that unquestioning obedience of the leaders of that charge.

So we're trying to each our officers to challenge assumptions, recognize biases, and to find the core questions to be answered. That's the key of critical thinking. History is replete with examples of commanders who fought their plan rather than the enemy, generally to their own detriment. We can only speculate how many opportunities were lost or risks unappreciated by American commanders because they didn't think critically. A recent example from our own history was our failure to recognize that growing insurgency in Iraq. We convinced ourselves that the enemy was defeated and we were only facing the ragtag remnants of a beaten army. And we persisted in that belief until we lost the initiative to the enemy. And then we had to fight hard to regain it four years after we first invaded Iraq.

Ours was to question why, not simply do and die. But we failed. *We* failed as leaders to do that effectively. It's not enough to tell an officer that he has to think critically or to give him some sort of framework to think by. We have to give him the opportunity to try and fail, and try again before we ask him to do this on the battlefield where the stakes are too high to accept failure. And our digital leader development center at the college develops scenarios and puts officers in critical decision making positions throughout the course. Our classroom instruction has shifted away from lectures, rote memorization, and approved solutions, the old green sheets, to a more open discussion that's really facilitated by an instructor, the format called the guide on the side, instead of the sage on the stage, also more properly known as learner-centric instruction.

One of the mental frameworks we're trying to each is that of design. This concept has generated a lot of discussion and some think it's a new idea. It's also generated a lot of resistance out there. But this is not a new idea. Design, the ability to understand a situation, frame the problem, and develop a solution is not new.

What's new about that? It's happened as long as commanders have led forces against an enemy, before Alexander the Great was even born. In the past, design occurred almost exclusively between a commander's ears. But today, he needs help. And staff officers trained in design can help him do that. Design assumes a greater importance when we're faced with complex situations.

Complexity is the dominant characteristic of 21st century warfare. And to those who would argue that we've always faced complex situations, I'd say that's true, but the degree of complexity is increasing. Throughout all of recorded history, we really only fought up until the past 150 years or so in just two demands, the land and the sea. About a hundred years ago, we added the air domain. About 50 years back, we added space. And about 15 years or so ago, we added cyberspace.

So if the British were to invade Boston today, Paul Revere would need a few more lanterns in the North Church steeple, you know, five if by cyberspace, something like that. But as an army, the domain of war that interests us the most is of course and always will be the land domain. Recently, we've drawn upon or been drawn into counterinsurgencies in alien lands, where we've come to appreciate the human terrain is at least as important as the physical terrain that we're fighting on. And our dismissal of Arab tribes in Iraq created conditions for our near defeat. And it was only our hard-won understanding of those tribes that later provided the key to our success.

Cultural and foreign language studies are assuming a greater importance in our military schools. And it's not as though the US has no experience with tribes. You have to wonder if our Indian wars would have lasted as long or ended so cruelly for Native Americans, not to mention for the 7th Cavalry, had we systematically undertaken to understand the tribes along our frontier. It's ironic that we discovered human terrain so far from home. As Dorothy of Kansas would say, it was in our backyard all along.

Wars is a contest of wills. Our leaders need to be able to impose their will on the enemy before the American people lose their will to continue the struggle. The challenge is growing ever more present and we have largely unsympathetic and ill-informed media maintaining an unblinking eye and non-stop commentary on everything that we're doing. The enemy knows this and exploits this. Imagine if, in the Second World War, the Nazis were able to beam videos directly into our living rooms of Hansel and Gretel sitting among the ruins of their home with their dead parents lying next to them. What would that have done to the strategic bombing campaign in the Second World War? How would it have affected it? Would Eisenhower have survived the criticism of the Torch landings, the fratricide, you know, during the Sicily landings to go on to command the Normandy invasion? Would he have lasted past D+1 at Normandy, given all the casualties we encountered on the beach on the sixth of June?

Media training for our leaders at Fort Leavenworth can help. But it really can only mitigate the effects of this media phenomenon. Unless our political masters are willing and able to create a national consensus and a sense of shared sacrifice in support of our conflicts, and they don't seem inclined to do that, the key will be for our military leaders to be able to achieve swift and decisive victory, or to reduce the cost of any protracted struggle while achieving measurable progress. That's our challenge and our dilemma.

And here at the Lewis & Clark Center, that's what we're trying to achieve. Only critical thinkers will be able to make those competing and often contradictory goals achievable. And I thank you for all of your contributions to that effort. And thanks for attending this particular conference.

## Day 3: Featured Speaker

## Questions & Answers
(Transcript of Presentation)

## Brigadire General Sean B. MacFarland
## Moderated by Kendall D. Gott

**Mr. Gott:**

We'll open this up for discussion at this time. If you have a question for the General, please raise your hand and activate your microphone when called upon.

**Audience Member One:**

Following up on your comments on the media, yesterday, we kicked around the battle of Wanat and the aftermath of the investigation, and concern for whether or not that would intrinsically have an impeding effect on the initiative and confidence of our junior officers, and whether or not we would end up with, on the battlefield, a kind of a zero defects mentality and a failsafe mentality as an impairment to our performance. What do you think of that risk? And what do you think we can do to mitigate it?

**BG MacFarland:**

Yes, sir. Well, that's a huge risk, first of all. That's what I think about the risk. What can we do to mitigate it? One of the things that we need to do is shift from a mindset of investigation to find fault to a study to learn lessons and improve. So the automatic 15-6 investigations that are triggered any time we had an engagement in Iraq where, you know, an escalation force occurred, for instance, against a civilian vehicle, even if nobody was killed, you had to do a 15-6 investigation. We opened fire against a civilian vehicle, 15-6 investigation.

Well, soldiers are inevitably going to conclude that we're playing gotcha. And no matter how many times you try to tell them that you're not, they're going to see right through you. If we can get away from that and just say, "Listen, we'll study interesting types of events on the battlefield and see what lessons we can glean from that, and then use that to prevent these types of things in the future without necessarily finding fault," then I think you might start to get a little less risk aversion.

Right now, the CAC blog site has a question on it that anybody can log in and answer. Do you think we're creating risk-averse leaders at the junior level where the rubber meets the road? And last time I checked it, granted at that point, it was pretty early, I think it was the first day, I think only 20 or 30 people responded, but the answer was overwhelmingly yes, we do think we're creating risk aversion.

And I will tell you that at the operational level, it was one of my greatest frustrations to have a risk-averse higher headquarters not wanting to experiment and adapt. And that's why it's so important for us also to explain the concept of design and critical thinking, that you can have a very risk-averse strategy that will take you straight down the path to defeat. And that risk is inherent in success. And through critical thinking, we can identify those opportunities to exploit.

So we're trying to combat that. But ultimately, we are where we are in terms of the media. And, you know, we can only, I think, affect that on the margins. They're always going to be hyper-critical of us from their uninformed perspective. And we just need to understand that that's the environment we're in. So we better be on top of our game.

So the Wanat study in particular I think brings us a great tool that we can bring into the schoolhouse here, because it's relatively recent. It resonates with our officers and NCOs. And there are tactical and operational questions there. There are ethical questions that we can talk about. It's not in the report itself, but the report can be a springboard for us to sit around and say, OK, you got a company commander who gets a silver star, and then a 15-6 investigation comes along and slaps a general officer letter of reprimand on him in his permanent file. Later, somebody else comes along and says, "No, we're not going to do that." All right, so risk aversion versus accountability, you know, where's the balance? Again, we don't tell them what to think. We teach them how to think. And we bring these questions up so that our officers are attuned to that. And then when they become senior officers, they at least understand there is a cause and effect relationship between accountability and risk aversion, so. Long way of not answering your question probably, sir.

**Dr. Hamilton:**

We spent the last two or so days talking about different educational experiences in the military from the institutional side to the education of practical experience as when the Navy goes to sea. And that's where you learn. You were arguably successful as a BCT, brigade combat team commander in making the shift from, say, kinetic operations, force protection and trying to shift the responsibility for protection to the Iraqis from that to the surge, which provided the conditions for the Iraqis to stand up better. What would you say in your educational experience really set you up to do that? Was it institutional? Was it practical experience? Was it both?

**BG MacFarland:**

It was really none of the above. It was more of the broadening experiences that I had the opportunity to have outside of what you would normally get in the course of a career. First of all, I'm not your average, well, I don't think there is such a thing as an average one-star. But I didn't get here the way, on the same timeline most people get here by. I'm strictly due course. Never been a below the zone guy.

I was picked up on my second look for battalion command, was not a first look battalion commander. When I got picked up for brigade command, they decided to inactivate the brigade I was going to. First, they decided, we're not going to change command in theater. And then they inactivated the brigade. So I became an "unslighted principal". "What are we going to do with MacFarland? Well, let's make him the fifth corps G3. He's got a year to kill," and even though that's supposed to be a former BCT commander job.

So I had some, you know, and I had the opportunity to be an aide de camp for some guys like General Shinseki and General Meigs. And I worked for Tommy Franks. And, you know, for better, for worse, all these different experiences all kind of helped me think it a little bit above the brigade level. I was able to see things from a corps or theater perspective, even if my bosses couldn't. I was used to thinking at that level, because I had all that extra time that the Army gave me by not promoting me early for anything.

So I'd say the broadening experiences were what helped me out a lot. The other thing is, I had no place to go but up. First of all, I had nothing to lose. I didn't really think I was in the hunt to become a general officer, because I'd been so delayed along the way and all that stuff, letters of reprimand, you know, as a young officer and all that.

But the other thing is, I had, you know, a problem set that was just so bad that I knew that continuing to do what we'd done in the past wouldn't work. That had been tried and it failed. So I had to try something. So I tried everything. I just threw anything I could up against the wall. And whatever stuck, we went with that. We reinforced success. And, you know, we stumbled upon this sheik who was kind of a minor figure, but he seemed like a guy that we could work with. And we just kind of once we got, you know, our foot in the door, we, you know, put the whole stack in there behind that, the lead guy's foot.

So that's kind of how we, you know, found our way out of that situation. I mean, I was trying everything, you know? You read about the tribal engagement thing because that worked. You don't read about some of the other harebrained schemes that I tried, because they didn't work and we abandoned them, you know? I'm not a brilliant guy, you know? I just was desperate. Okay.

Anybody else? Okay. Well, thanks for coming and I'll turn it back over to CSI. And hope you all get back to where you're from safely. Stay out of the (inaudible) at Fort Bliss. You know, people, I just came from Fort Bliss, and people always say, "Oh, I don't want to go to Fort Bliss. I've read about all the violence." And I said, "Hey look, all the violence is in Juarez." So El Paso's actually, like, the second safest city in America, with the exception of the AFEES facilities on Fort Bliss which are probably one of the most violent places in America, so. Thank you.

**Mr. Gott:**

Thank you again, sir. This concludes the formal program. I'd like to reintroduce Dr. William Glenn Robertson, director of the Combat Studies Institute for final remarks.

**Dr. Robertson:**

When we try to put together a symposium every year, we have two touchstones. The first is a top of current relevance, something that a very practical profession can find useful. The second is a topic that has historical depth, something that we can look at over time. Our first keynote speaker two days ago, Brigadier General Brown, laid out pretty much exactly what we were trying to do in this symposium. Because as you may recall, he said the issues of leadership and how to cultivate leaders have a timeless quality about them. And that was absolutely true.

He also said that over time, there are variables within that problem set that do make different periods unique. So there are timeless issues from the early national period of the American military establishment, but there are variables that make some of them less relevant to us today, almost 200 years later.

Over the course of these three days, we've explored some of those different time periods and some of those different variables. And there have been significant changes in national culture, in national capability, including the technological dimension, and in terms of the nature of the threat facing our country. So we've essentially looked at 200 years of Army history in terms of leader development at particular times and places in both peace and war.

For me, variables by their very nature change things over time. But at bottom, when you strip away all the extraneous things and the jargon, it comes down to this simple question: what it takes to motivate people successfully, in its rawest form, what it takes to get people to advance at the peril of their lives in the face of killing fire to do the business the nation has need of them to do.

Last March, I was privileged to be part of a staff ride for TRADOC senior leaders that looked at the Civil War campaign from Cold Harbor to the crossing of the James River in 1864. At one of our stands, we stood at the line of departure of a Pennsylvania regiment at Cold Harbor, looking across the field about 250 yards deep towards a line of entrenchments. And as I painted the picture for these senior leaders, it came down to this. What was the task that had been assigned the lieutenant colonel who was in command of that regiment?

There had been some planning, not nearly enough, at the highest levels, and at the intermediate levels. And that's leadership of a sort. But for this lieutenant colonel, it came down to what we have to do to move our regiment across 250 yards of open ground in the face of a determined enemy entrenched to the eyeballs. And they didn't falter. They didn't hesitate. They went forward.

Now, as you well know, they didn't succeed. But they gave it everything they had. The leadership was adequate to the task, though the result was not what the attackers would wish. That was 1864. The variables have changed. General MacFarland has just laid out where we are as we go forward into the next generation.

But I submit to you that the timeless part of leadership will carry forward into the next generation just as it has since the 19th century, and indeed before that, in the history of the US Army. We've tried to talk about a current, relevant issue and place it in historical context. We've had some really great speakers, some really great questions from the audience. We appreciate your coming. We look forward to having another symposium next year with a topic of current relevance, looking at through the historical lens.

So thank you all for coming. We look forward to seeing you next year.

## Day 3, Panel 8: Foreign Perspectives

## Making Australian Military Leaders: A Historical Reflection Based on the Changing Face of Wars and the Australians That are Selected to Fight Them
## by Lieutenant Colonel Craig Burn

(Transcript of Presentation)

**Dr. Wright:**

You can see the full biographies in the program, but in the order that they will speak: Lieutenant Colonel Craig Burn has served in the Australian Army's liaison to the Combined Arms Center since 2008. He is an Armor Officer who has taught at Fort Knox. Colonel Burn's experience in deploying includes Rwanda and East Timor. Colonel Jean-Claude Brejot was commissioned in 1986 after graduating from Saint-Cyr. Since that date, he has held multiple positions and deployed on a number of contingency operations, including those in the Balkans, and a period serving as an advisor in Tunisia. And Colonel Graham Norton, who was commissioned in 1985 and began a long careers as a signals officer. During this career, he deployed to the Balkans and to Afghanistan. I should say all of these gentleman serve as the liaisons from their countries military to the Combined Arms Center here at Fort Leasvenworth. Let's start with Colonel Craig Burns. Sir, the floor is yours.

**Lt Col Burn:**

Thank you, Don. Well, in the interest of time, we are going to try and hold ourselves pretty rigidly to our allocated window. I'm going to read largely my notes so I can get through it in time and make sure that we have the opportunity to grill the Brit at the end.

Thanks for the opportunity to speak as a member of this panel. Cultivating Army leaders from a historical perspective is no doubt a huge topic and I relish this opportunity to share but a few of my ideas. I'm not a historian, so my remarks will of course be based upon my experiences of over three decades in the Australian Army and through the reflections of what it means to lead Australian men and women. Please consider that my remarks are unable to be nested in the context of any Australian war of independence or civil war, as we have experienced neither. While I'll dig a little into the Australian experience of war, I will more importantly reflect upon military leadership through the prism of national character.

The leadership style for the Australian Army, as for any army, must be back cast against the character of a nation's people and the psyche associated with its sense of national security. In sharing my thoughts on the cultivation of leaders within the Australian Army, I'll skim only the wave tops of my ideas. Some may be controversial, and while I will naturally take a dig at my British colleague on one or two points, I'll avoid the well-beaten path of commenting on Australian operations under British command at Gallipoli. I will avoid it, but first dig.

Leadership is inherently a human activity, so if anything defines a leader it must be one sense of human nature and its associated behaviors. Leadership is a contextual phenomenon. That particular time, place, or situation that a group or leader finds itself in is a key determinant of who and how someone will lead. It's a social dynamic that builds its foundation in a mix of human emotion and through life's influence. We'll have defined each of the individuals in the group well before the precepts of an institutional army has touched them. The ability to counter an innate response or to strengthen one's resolve for many will not come from within one's self. It will emerge in the face of leadership and may well be assisted in its manifestation through some form of conditioning. I'm not talking about a mob or herd mentality, but with the words or acts of one person to spur the actions of another. Consider the nature of enterprise-based armies focused on miserable efficiency, equity, and [costed] outcomes. I would observe that they are less about cultivating leaders and more about developing followers. In the military context, that person responsible for assuming the leadership role will normally be appointed based upon their measured performance and experience, and then empowered through a commensurate rank. Herein lies the potential that the appointed authority is not necessarily the best leader. What they will be is the one held accountable. This is when the innate leadership foundation becomes essential. Can I have the next slide, please?

We've heard a lot of discussion through the symposium linked to generals who have most likely had far too many books written about them when you consider the heroics of many that have died under their command, and for who little, by way of writings, have been put together to reflect their leadership achievements, other than within the statistics to illustrate a point about their commander. Followers have and will always outnumber leaders. Far too few books have focused on the leadership talents of those followers. The counterpoint that I see is that of senior leadership or managers shaping organizational loyalty and culture, and drill dynamics of discipline and obedience, to achieve common purpose versus an ability to influence and channel those innate human dynamics to achieve the common purpose or the task need. It stands to reason that through inherent traits that enable leaders that emerge from doctrinal manuals, rather they're built through experience or reflection in the context of interacting with and learning about people. Yet modern armies based its measure of performance around institutional requirements. They shaped followers rather than cultivating the most effective leaders amongst their members. This is ingrained through annual assessment, that is such a determinant of career progression that they generate their own gravitational pull on assessment-driven behaviors. Seldom, if ever, are the leaders assessed by the led. In my observations, the most successful leaders are those that invest their efforts in developing emotional intelligence. That is, being a person enabled by self-awareness, self-regulation, self-motivation, or demonstrating empathy and an ability to nurture relationships through sincerity. This is, in my opinion, the absolute foundation of leadership. Those qualities can only be set very early in life, whether they are born out of adversity or a comprehensive and largely privileged upbringing. I acknowledge that these qualities alone will not make a leader successful in a military context, but I contend that if they are not evident in youth, they cannot be later trained by an ally or learnt by an adult. Precepts might be indoctrinated, but the foundation cannot be constructed after the individual has been assembled.

It is the human qualities that the Australian Army sets out to identify in any leadership candidate, as they form the foundation that can be built upon by the institution. But without, sure, we can still build leaders, but without the essential underpinning that warrant them being trusted with the lives of soldiers. These are the traits that distinguish the difference between leaders of people and leaders of organizations. Leaders of organizations are, by and large, managers. While being a manager does not preclude emotional intelligence, success in management pursuits can be based largely on academic intelligence, organizational savvy, and cunning. It is in this context that I will focus the remainder of my remarks on those aspects of leading Australian soldiers.

Where does the Australian Army draw its leaders from? In cultivating leaders, the Army sets its baseline differently from many other armies. Our post-World War II army is looking for that almost innate emotional intelligence in selecting young men and women to fulfill leadership roles in the Australian Army. Almost at no point in this process are we looking for tertiary qualifications or academic pursuits. From commissioning, we look for high school graduates that display the hallmarks of emotional intelligence, tamed with integrity, and where they have been exposed to values which are common with those of the Army and human ethics. Most often I have found in people who have been active in team sports and positions of responsibility, such as school prefecture and captaincy, school cadets, and there are many other extracurricular pursuits. Academic achievement plays a role as far as literacy and (inaudible), and beyond that achieves little in terms of advanced standing. As a result, the officer corps of the Australian Army are largely cut from the same mold of cloth. Candidates cannot recover from a life of misadventure by commissioning in the army, because those inherent traits that have facilitated poor choices in their youth are discriminators when sizing up the ability for an army to develop a person as opposed to reconstructing them.

But what of the folks they lead? Therein lies a much greater range of backgrounds against which those leaders can be challenged, and amongst from which junior leaders will naturally emerge. The Australian character was born out of adversity. Having been denied the use of North America as a penal colony, the British Empire, it was only a matter of time, went looking for options as to where it could place its ne'er-do-wells, and of course out of that circumstance Australia was colonized. But don't be mistaken; many others had set foot on Australian soil before James Cook staked his Union Jack into Sydney Cove and declared it British territory. His arrival had been preceded by the Spanish, the Portuguese, the Dutch, and the French. Of course, up until that point, nobody had been crazy enough to try and colonize the driest continent on the earth, containing the most poisonous, biting creatures that are known across the world. Notwithstanding, when you throw the deprived into circumstances of adversity and challenge them to build hope out of very little, you'll naturally see only the best of human spirit prevail. Can I have the next slide?

On the backdrop of splendid isolation, add a cricket ball, a rugby ball, a swimsuit, a homebrew kit, and you've got the makings of a great place to live and for a nation to emerge and prosper. Add to that the free settlers that have been prepared to endure months of hell as they sailed in rotting hulks across the equator, around the Cape of Good Hope, across the Indian Ocean, and then risked thousands of miles of coastal shoals to come ashore on the east coast of Australia, and you have a pretty tough breeding stock from which to raise a colonial army. It was their experiences that set so much of the character of today's Australian Army, and we work hard to reflect, 140 years on, that ethos. Those colonies then sent expeditionary forces back to the Sudan, to South Africa, and of course after federation in 1901, we built a national army that would forge its sense of true identity on the shores of Gallipoli.

Who were those men and what characterized how they would attribute themselves so well in the face of probable death and hopeless defeat? Well, they were certainly not your most politically-correct bunch of young men. They were born out of adversity and they were growing up as young men through a sense of deprivation, owning only what was achieved through work and effort, and placing no value on privilege. Where the value of trust embodied all that truly counted in a person's character. An environment where needs of the group were placed before the individual, and yet confident that the group would never ignore the individual. The Australian motto in World War II was "Fight, work, or perish." If I can digress just for the brief example of perhaps some of what we see in terms of the Australian character, an anecdote was written in the instructions for American servicemen stationed in Australia in 1942. That's a small, doctrinal, cultural awareness pamphlet that was produced at that time. Illustrates the flippant sense of humor that can often file Australians in the diplomatic states. It cites a situation in a Sydney bar where an American soldier turned to an Australian sitting next to him and said, "Well, Aussie, you can go home now. We've come over to save you." And of course the Aussie's response was, "Well, have you? And I thought you were just a refugee from Pearl Harbor." Of course there was no disrespect intended, but that was just how Australians flippantly throw something aside, and of course then get themselves in a world of strife. There was probably a brawl that ensued.

In any case, privilege through appointment is clearly rejected, and unless those privileges were earned. The sense of humor is irreverent. Identity comes from being a team player but certainly not an all-star. The [inaudible] syndrome, which remains central today in the Australian societal value system, was the mentality that ensured no one person got ahead of the pack without brining the team with them. Inherited traditions of officer selection, based on the rules of aristocracy and life's opportunities, would then give way to selection of officers from the ranks that were proven in terms of leadership and greater abilities.

But unlike the societal forces of today, it was never about finding the weakest link and voting them off the island. It was about reinforcing the weakest link, if and when it was revealed. The combination of hard work, commitment to the team, a self-deprecating attitude, and implicit trust was undoubtedly the foundation of mateship, a trait amosngst Australian soldiers today that define who we are and how we operate. Our values are few yet all-encompassing: courage, initiative, and team work. There's no doubt that the Australian Army struggles with all the compelling mechanisms that modern business practices bring to things like ensuring branding and reputation, and linking that to roots and successes in foregone generations. All those romantic notions. It's equally challenged by the dynamics of the modern labor market. However, the success that we have enjoyed over the past 60 years is really from our approach to officer candidate selection and enshrining the philosophy that effective leaders can be developed but cannot be trained. Selection of the seed stock is critical to success, because junior leaders without that innate foundation and emotional intelligence will be mercilessly ignored. Thank you.

## Day 3, Panel 8: Foreign Perspectives

## Finding the Balance Between Timeless Fundamentals and Temporal Adjustments
## by Colonel Jean-Claude Brejot

To answer the question, I will not develop a long description of the French Army Leadership evolution for several reasons:

> I am not a historian and I am so much respectful of your erudition (scholarship) therefore I will not make the mistake of walking into your yard. I only have 20 minutes, which is also a good excuse to avoid an incriminating situation. My accent could betray the meaning of my supposedly deep demonstration, and most importantly, it is Thursday, the last day of the seminar and before lunch.

> Second, I will not use a lot of Power Point slides, not because I want to follow this new trend which consists of condemning the over use of slides but simply because…I am not able to draw a complex slide. For all these reasons, I will simply focus on some aspects of the question in order to illustrate what I'm considering as the main concern for an officer thinking about how to educate leaders which is:

> Finding balance between timeless fundamentals and temporal adjustments. To find this balance, I need to go far back into the History of my country because the way we are educating our leaders is obviously linked to our style of Command which is itself deeply influenced by our culture .

### From the Feudal Army to the Royal Army

During the Middle Age, France had a simple political structure: the feudal system with the aristocracy which has the monopoly of legitimate violence and a king with a strong moral authority but little power. The French Army at the origin is an aristocratic Army and its values are those of the knighthood, which means honor, courage and momentum. This is the matrix of the French military culture, its style of command and then the influence on leadership.

This system worked quite well until what we named the Hundred Years War (1337-1453) when we faced another system. In England, the King is strong and the aristocracy weak. We then faced an army of conscripts with Infantry (France will not have an Infantry system before the Revolution in 1789). Our Knighthood system was broken in Crecy (1346) and Agincourt (1415) battles against the English infantry. This break would allow the King of France to take control of his own Army.

Between the end of the Hundred Years War, the end of the Italian War (Marignan 1515) and the victories against the King of England, a new French style is built with the association of the momentum of Cavalry, the strength of Artillery and the first use of Infantry. A new culture is appearing with the technical arms. The geometry spirit will soon be in competition with the momentum spirit.

PANEL 8

With Louis the XIV, the aristocracy is still in charge of the Army but under the control of the King. Geometry and mathematics are now used during sieges and Cavalry and Infantry are given to the aristocracy. This warfare is becoming complex and would need officers educated to deal with this complexity. But the Aristocracy is opposed to this education. A leader in this time is a noble no matter is his ability to fight.

**The New System**

The conjunction of a period of creative thinking (tactical thoughts by de Guibert and others about the Division as the organization we know today, the first tactical command posts, etc.), technical innovations (the Artillery with the Gribeauval system) and the French Revolution which opened the ranks of officers to every citizens is at the origin of the new system.

Napoleon will rationalize the momentum created by the Revolution (I will not develop the impulse the Emperor provided by creating a modern Army with the success we all know). I will just mention that he pushed the art of war and battle very high. Leaders at this time needed to associate the momentum of the old knighthood and the geometry by knowledge. This period will last till 1815 and the end of the French Empire.

**The Return of Rigidity**

With the Restoration, which is the coming back of monarchy and the Second Empire, officers are recruited from the Middle Class which is imitating what aristocracy did in the Army before the Revolution. Strongly separated from NCOs and soldiers, these officers are themselves constituting 2 parts: the officers with momentum in Infantry and Cavalry and the officers of geometry in Artillery and Engineers. Each category has his own academy (Saint-Cyr and Polytechnique). Because of this situation, the style of warfare and the subsequent command is swaying between the crazy bravery similar to Solférino and Magenta (1859) with the Infantry in the role of the ancient Cavalry and the unadventurous rigidity causing the defeat in 1870 against the Prussians. In 1914, the excessiveness attack doctrine will return.

This was a result of a lack of diversity in the recruitment of the military elite during this time. In 1914, there were 90 officers attending the equivalent of our CGSC, Command and General Staff School. Among them, 80 were from the Infantry. These leaders were all thinking in the same way: excessiveness attack.

Between August and September 1914, the French Army is coming through the disaster at the border to the miracle of the first battle of Marne. General Joffre will replace 40% of the generals during these months. The crisis highlighted the weakness of the system but innovations and critical thinking restarted during WWI. Sometimes crisis will reveal weaknesses. General Petain found again a good balance between our opposite traditions by combining arms in a sophisticated way.

After WWI, because of the trauma and the complexity of the combined arms created by Petain, rationality and geometry is coming back again in the Army, like in the XVIII century. In 1940, the victory of the German army is the perfect illustration of a good balance between science and audacity.

## In the Modern Era

In the crisis of 1940, a new Army is borne like during the first Empire and in 1918. Recruited from all our society and selected by merit, this new generation will fight until 1962 which is the end of the Algerian war. During WWII, Armored Division and Airborne units will cultivate the tradition of audacity.

The Cold War can be seen like the coming back to "science" with the nuclear deterrence and the sterilization of tactical innovations until, for the French army, the 80s and the operations abroad.

To conclude this visit of the French History, I would say that the French Military style is a permanent arbitration between the heart which stimulates the courageous action (assault, the Last Stand Defense, the sacrifice) and the reason which supports the logical combination of arms and effects. When both cultural roots are working together, it is the time of success. But, being able to identify unbalanced organization inside his proper organization means the need to educate and prepare leaders to exercise critical-thinking.

Having said that, taking into account seriously the impact of history and culture on leader's education, I would like to conclude by two riddles. Let's just have a look on these 2 quotes.

The basics in leader's education exist as we can see with these two examples. And it can be dangerous to forget them because of the appearance of some promising technology. "Man is the prime instrument of combat" colonel Ardant du Pick had written in his Etudes, before dying leading his regiment in 1870. But, the evolution of the world around the leader must be taken into account. We all know the influence of new technology in the conduct of war. But, war is primarily a human activity.

Traditions are fundamental in the History of an Army and feed the core values of the leaders. They are undoubtedly critical in educating leaders. But they also can be a brake to change and innovation.

Finally, I decided to gather in the same slide all these famous French leaders because they have something to share: they all are at the fringes of normal French Army society. Thanks to their character, their charisma, they were able to think out of the box and influence deeply my country. It's what is at stake in leadership development, I think. We don't want to create a "Brave New World" but leaders able to decide in the dark. So leadership is according to my modest experience a balance between timeless values and adjustments to the world in which we are leaving. And culture is the only way to understand and find this balance because as General de Gaulle said in Saint-Cyr when teaching History: "The true school of leadership is general knowledge."

## Day 3, Panel 8: Foreign Perspectives

## A British Perspective by Colonel Graham Norton
(Transcript of Presentation)

One of the great advantages of going last, of course, is that I can put up my picture of a British square at Waterloo. It has absolutely no relevance to what I want to say, but I'm going to put it up. It is, as you might consider, a very British trait. You've only witnessed the very Australian trait, which is to get their retaliation in first. And it is quite true to say that the British did look at a place to put all our ne'er-do-wells and we put them in Australia. One fundamental error, we realized, was you could get out there.

I have to say I was honored yesterday to listen to General Sullivan. Indeed one of the great things about serving here at Leavenworth is the regular chance to listen to the great and the good as they come through. I noted that General Sullivan said that he'd been thinking about what he might say yesterday for some time, and I have been doing the same. I've been contemplating what I might say here for a number of weeks. You therefore might want to consider why I was still putting these notes together at 11:30 last night. I would offer two explanations to you. The first is that it could be my intent to sort of draw on some of the thoughts from other presentations, use them to help compare and contrast, thinking in both in the past and the present, on leadership from our two nations. Thus I could only be putting it together last night. The less generous of you might wish to take the view that have been taken by a number of my writing offices in the past. It's that I get by on sort of an adroit combination of laziness, panic, and bluff and not a set of qualities that either of our armies would necessarily put in the top 10, I suggest. I hope you accept the former as an explanation rather than the latter.

That said, I'm going to take a bit of a leap here, because both of my colleagues have said they're not historians, and neither am I, but I'm going to try. I recall the history of UK observers in the United States. It's not necessarily a good one. Many of you may recognize Arthur Fremantle, who was an observer with Longstreet's corps at Gettysburg. It's perhaps, all in all, remarkable that after witnessing Pickett's Charge and everything that went on that day, he returned home to England to write a book, and his underpinning premise was the certainty of Confederate victory. So with that somewhat poor record in mind, I thought I might invite you to accept a few thoughts by way of comparison between the UK and the United States with regard to leadership. Actually, I would suggest this is something of a three-way comparison: my personal experience, the thinking in the UK today, and my observations and experience in my time here with the US Army. As such, this is about perspectives. You may well disagree with some of my comments. They may be wrong. But it is the perspective and prism through which I've been looking at things. You'll notice in some areas we're challenged in the same way. In others, we differ or have differing solutions. Next slide, please.

I'm going to use this slide as a sort of pan rail to cover some of the similarities of issues that the UK is dealing with. Therefore I offer six points for potential discussion. The first bullet on leadership doctrine, historical study. Despite its history, the UK doesn't actually have huge volumes of doctrine on leadership. Lots of books, lots of pamphlets, lots of historical memoirs, but nothing that we could necessarily equate to your field manual. I'd argue that we haven't done particularly badly without it. But in contrast in my career, we've suffered particularly in the recent past, I would suggest, through a poor attitude towards historical study. My generation in particular, based primarily, I might as well start with my career in Germany against a known, we thought, threat, have shamefully, in some cases, failed to study. We heard on Monday that Frederick the Great's recognition that energetic and stupid were particularly good qualities for an infantry officer, it doesn't mean they're compulsory. And I have to say, I have served alongside officers whose deliberate not understanding, particularly of technical information, was almost a badge of honor. As an officer in Germany, if you're found to be reading doctrine in the officer's mess, you would be leaving through a window. Now, that is not the case today. I often look with considerable admiration at our young armies and the young officers in our armies, their professional dedication. But I have to say, I would judge the US Army as probably slightly ahead of my own on this. But I also submit to you, there is a limit. You can actually overdo the doctrine, and the on-the-job training that we heard about this morning has equal value.

My next point is intuition or training, and I make this point with a degree of trepidation, particularly with this audience. I know what I'm about to describe is black and white. The answer is probably a shade of gray. But I do so to provoke debate. Bottom line, the question, can you train someone to be a good leader or does there have to be some innate, intuitive, natural ability? I ask this question in light of the fact that even today there is still no requirement to have a bachelor's degree to be an officer in the British Army. Most do, but it's not required. One could argue, I believe, that the US Army approaches that you can train somebody to be a leader as long as they have sufficient intelligence. The UK view is that although we have minimum educational standards, some leaders are born and not made. Inevitably, the answer is going to be somewhere in the middle. But I make this point only to emphasize that I have, on occasion, paused to wonder whether the US Army, particularly in its officers corps, and its focus on educational qualifications has not denied itself some very, very effective potential junior leaders.

My next point really runs on from that, and that's what I like to term leadership to, from, or in, or by, the ranks. We have, in the United Kingdom, something called the late entry officer, the LE officer. This is an officer who has served some 22 years in the ranks and risen to a Regimental Sergeant Major's appointment. And at that 22-year point, he's probably about 40 years old. We commission him. We commission him as a captain, as a major. And he is commissioned to do specific jobs. He's not going to command battalions, but he is going to sit in the staff of battalions and do specific jobs for which he has spent his entire career. I draw this example only by the fact that I have witnessed and watched young, and I'll use the example of an S4 in a battalion in a very complex environment, trying to deal with a lot of problems which his commanding officers ask him to do, and he's going to be senior lieutenant or a captain. He's going to be mid-20s, maybe 30. In my army, you're going to have a 44-year-old major who's been serving the army for 22 years doing that sort of job. The "so what?" here, of course, is exactly the same as the first one.

We have this separate route, unique but separate, to allow us to pick up that talent later in life and bring them through.

Next, three areas of current work in the UK. The first is that of values-based leadership. I was very interested the day before yesterday, when General Brown mentioned underpinning values of leadership. And a card, I think, said, well, that's mine, which I've carried around for about 20 years. Given to me, and this is given to every British soldier as he goes into his basic training. I just got a copy. However, our work at the moment is driven by the requirement. And the difficult balance we have, and I think it is something that occurs through time, through history, on a regular basis, of representing a nation but at the same time being seen as a beacon, being seen as something different. We're doing a lot of work now in our values-based leadership to attract people and what we call the gatekeepers, the parents of the young 16 and 17-year-old who might want to join the army, to show that we are retaining a traditional value, but at the same time balancing that with a modern society.

We're also still facing huge challenges on operations versus in-barracks leadership. I noted the recent report, which was the health prevention report, as it happened, and the chapter it had in it on the US Army about decline and loss and failure of in-barracks leadership. We've got a generation of young officers who have spent many, many, many hours, days, and years taking the fight to the enemy in Iraq and Afghanistan, but haven't sat and managed the day-to-day problems you get with soldiers in barracks, and we are concerned that we need to revitalize that and re-understand that as tempo draws down.

Finally, this question of the balance between learning and experience. I have to say, I've enjoyed the last few days. I haven't been here for all of it. I've been somewhat disappointed in the lack of (inaudible). Just in this last half an hour. I used Jim as an example here. And don't think me anti-educational. I think the whole thing is about getting the balance. And as ever as a Brit, I'm going to finish right now with a quote from Churchill, because it wouldn't be right if I didn't. Churchill, when talking about public speaking, he said, "Say what you have to say, and the first time you come to a sentence with a grammatical ending, sit down." So I shall sit down. Thank you.

## Panel 8: Foreign Perspectives

### Questions and Answers
(Transcript of Presentation)

## Lieutenant Colonel Craig Burn
## Colonel Jean-Claude Brejot
## Colonel Graham Norton

## Moderated by Dr. Donald Wright

**Dr. Wright:**

Well, shall we let the Yanks play in this? I'll go ahead and turn the floor over to Jim.

**Jim:**

I was particularly interested in your comment about recognizing the echelon of operations versus in-barracks leadership. A couple of years ago I was visiting the US Army NCO Academy in Europe, and one of the things, actually, they were complaining about was that soldiers were getting promoted to NCO so fast. There were combat veterans they were cutting back and they knew everything about everything except how to take care of their soldiers in a noncombat environment. Yesterday I mentioned the fact that one of the challenges is as you go from an army at war to an army not at war, people miss the adrenaline, the freedom, the independence, and they have trouble adjusting. I'm interested, from all your perspectives, how do you see your armies coping with that challenge?

**Col Norton:**

I think it's a common issue that all our armies are going to come across. We (inaudible) a particular challenge. At the same time, relatively large garrisons in Germany are drawing down very much in the UK as well. We're moving from what could be regarded as a seven-day-a-week mentality, both in Germany and operations, to what is more of a five-day-a-week when you're back in your home station. The challenge as I see it as that this is where history could help. I think there's a book called *Crisis in Command*, which is very much a commentary on the post-Vietnam problems the US Army had. People are reading that to think through, what are we going to do when the pressure is off a little bit? How do we deal? I don't come forward with any great answers, other than the fact that I think it's encouraging that both our armies are acknowledging it now. Perhaps we have a chance to deal with it when it comes to be. I remember Wednesday afternoons in every (inaudible) ever written. It was always a sports afternoon. That's what you used to do. If you worked hard, you got to go home early on a Friday. I speak to young officers and young soldiers now who have been here six or seven years and they don't recognize that. Therefore it's re-inculcating that balance and that in-barracks bit, which is not—let's be frank—it's not sexy to count up that you've still got all your kit. It's not sexy to count up you've still got all your soldiers. That's the problem. How do you deal with Corporal so-and-so comes and knocks on your door on Monday morning after beating up his wife. These are the sort of challenges I think we need to see and have to deal with. We've got to look back on how we've dealt with that in the past. The biggest way we can do it is to aim off of it in the first place and understand where it's coming from.

**Col Brejet:**

I would like to insist on the notion of time. The French Army is involved in operation, as I mentioned before, since the '80s, in several theaters of operation between Africa and Lebanon and so on. When I was commanding my regiment a few years ago, four years ago, I was fighting against time, because this repetition of operation, I mean, more than to be able to deal with leadership when in barracks or when in operation. It's really a matter of time, because, to take the example of the French Army in the '80s, we had a professional part of the army and an unlisted one. The professional part was always deployed in Africa, mainly, and was fighting with the same problem of time. Today we are running after time, after time, after time, to prepare to face multitasking and for the French Army, at least, reduction of the number of soldiers we have in the French Army. We need to be able to save time and to work with priorities, because more than to deal with specific. I think leadership is the same. When a young NCO or a young officer is welleducated, he will be able to lead soldiers in garrison or in combat, depending on the experience, the environment, and so on. We all know that. But the key point for me with this experience to command a regiment is to put priorities and to save time and not to give to these young NCOs and officers too many things to do without any priority. And dealing with soldiers in garrison, if it's decided as a priority by the commanding Colonel, General, and so on, we must save time to give them time to lead soldiers. And time is crucial, as Napoleon said before, a long time ago.

**Lt Col Burn:**

For a brief Australian opinion, we come from a slightly different place. The army has grown up not as part of an empire or part of a nation that wants to be an empire. We've not been offensive. We're about working for living, not living for working. My view is that if a leader is only any good in operations and he's not able to lead his soldiers in garrison, then he's inadequate and he should be like the Navy. Walk down the plank. If the true challenge and the difficulties leading soldiers in garrison, and you have got them spun up so much for their posture in operations and you can't wean them off that and give them motivation and aspiration and something to aim for in garrison, then find yourself someone who can. Because you don't have a balanced leader. In fact, you don't have a leader. And I think, in my experience in command, I'm an armor officer, so I've lived through the world of alpha-male community peers and I've seen the way men typically take it so badly when they get a support score on command and not an operational score on command. The bottom line is command is command. It's about people. So it's got to transcend both environments. Therein lies the challenge. Frankly, from what I've seen, it's those people that work in ego-based warrior domains who are faced with greater challenges and often as leaders can transcend a number of environments and are, in fact, as pure leaders, stronger and better.

They have weaknesses and there are jobs they can't do. But if it's leadership you need to get soldiers for garrison living, and for Australia, post-Vietnam peace broke out, we didn't do anything until Somalia. We went through that phase where the best were in the schoolhouse, teaching and training. Because no one wanted to stand around the garrison painting rocks. Therein lies the challenge. I just think it's nice to make these things a problem that they shouldn't be. In fact, bringing soldiers out of theater and dealing with discipline. I'm reading the article that was referred to in the Kansas City Star during the week. The drugs, the bizarre things that are going on in the barrack blocks. Let me tell you, we have our own scandals and atrocities in Australia. Those things generally reflect a command climate. So you've got to find the commander and find out why he doesn't change the climate and where are his leadership skills.

**Dr. Wright:**

Other questions? Ben.

**Ben:**

I was intrigued by the comment about a leader should be a leader, both in operations and in garrison. However, if you take somebody that's been leading in combat operations and then you return them without any additional training or orientation to a garrison headquarters or support headquarters where it's strictly a peacetime operation, there's a bit of a culture shock there. I'm just throwing this out. Don't you think that there should be some sort of reorientation for leaders that have been, say, in the combat zone for a year or something like that? And when they come back and you give them a new assignment, say, "Hey, we really want to orient you with the new problems that are coming up with the barracks and some of the new soldiers," rather than just throw them overboard because of this inability to adjust immediately to a different environment. Don't you think there should be some kind of transition?

**Lt Col Burn:**

I do agree. Personal experience. I flew out of Rwanda. The streets were littered with bodies. The massacre of the mid-'90s. Seven months in command in that environment. I flew direct from Africa, touched down in Townsville, with a plane ticket to my home location. Lost command of my company on the air field. I was given a taxi voucher. When I got off the plane in Melbourne I went looking for a taxi that was prepared to take me the hour and a half drive to the garrison. Couldn't find one. So I've got all my battle rattle there. And all of the sudden you're left swinging. But I'd spent 20 years preparing myself to command operations at that point. It's also, as a professional, upon my shoulders to be preparing myself for transitions. It didn't make it easy and it certainly was something that I agree with you. There was no decompression time and there was no acceptance in the new environment I then went on to serve in back in Australia of where I'd been and where I'd come from. You were expected to conform to that garrison life. Tough challenge. A lot learned out of it. I don't know. Systemically, it's a hard thing to solve. I think the mettle of the leader is about also working hard within yourself to be able to solve that problem. I think the analogies we saw this morning of naval command, whereby one minute you're a ship at war, the next minute you're running a cocktail party on the poop deck in some diplomatic activity. I mean, the transition and the contrast, and in some ways the ambiguities of what you're doing in your command job and the complex operations the guys are engaged in today in Afghanistan and have been in Iraq, still in Iraq. One minute, the three blocks. They've got to transition. Call it adaptation. It's the new buzz phrase. But that's just a transition of frame of mind, expectation, and what depths of your profession and your education and your experience you can draw upon. I don't think there's a systemic solution to any of that. I think it's very much an individual thing when you're the leader and the commander.

**Col Brejet:**

I have two comments regarding your question. First of all, I totally agree with you. The transition must be prepared precisely when the combat zone or the environment is very hard for leaders and soldiers. For instance, when our units are coming back from a garrison to France after they're (inaudible), they are spending almost 10 days in an island in the Mediterranean Sea in Cyprus, in order, precisely, to prepare the transition before going back to the garrison. But that's the first part of my question. I think the key point, we have to find it in the chain of command. When I say chain of command, in the French Army, the key part of our leadership organization is this chain of command between the Chief of Staff of the Army and all his colonels commanding regiments. Inside the regiments, the link between the colonel commanding and the captain in charge. This is the main chain of command. All around, this chain of command exists, of course, but they can't interfere in this chain of command. And why I'm mentioning that—it's because when the chain of command is strong inside a regiment, inside a company, we are ready to operate this transition better than if the chain of command is not functioning very well. The more the chain of command is deep and strong, the better the transition to a war zone to a garrison. We are coming back to leadership. To be ready to exert this command, as Craig mentioned just before, it's life work to prepare leaders as a young lieutenant or captain. For me, yes, we have to try to help this transition. But even with this organization, we never replace a good chain of command with commanding directed to our soldiers, NCOs, officers, all this chain of command which is part of the efficiency.

**Col Norton:**

I would just make the point that I think you're looking at a generation here that, broadly, operational deployments was the exception. Inbarracks was probably (inaudible). Anybody who's joined any of our armies in the last nine years, it will be the other way around. I think the important thing, as I said earlier, is a recognition that there are potential issues for people to resolve is the encouraging thing. Your army has done it, my army has done it. I tend to agree with Craig. A good leader is a good leader. It doesn't make any great deal of difference. But the important thing was that it has been recognized so that something can be done about it. But we are sometimes just going to be you've got people out there who haven't done inbarracks routine. The norm for that is not the norm for us.

**Dr. Wright:**

We have time for several more questions. Yeah, Wayne.

**Dr. Hsieh:**

There are various moments in American military history, the American military has attempted to learn from all their military. I think recently, if you look at American counterinsurgency doctrine, there's been a lot of talk about David Galula or David Kilcullen or Lawrence of Arabia. And I wanted to get your perspective of how well Americans have learned from your respective military traditions, especially because there's always a potential for misinterpretation. I'm an academic. When I was in graduate school, everyone was obsessed with Michel Foucault. This French thinker would come and would sort of laugh at the Americans and say, "Well, in France this is so passé." I'm just sort of curious what your perspective is when we as Americans try to adapt your ideas. Do we get it? Or do we sort of half get it or do we miss a lot of the context?

**Col Norton:**

I'll use a very contemporary example. This is something that my Chief of the Army has said in this building. You are very good, and have been over the last few years. Very, very good at spotting and bringing forward. Certainly on the doctrinal side. I will give you COIN as an example. The UK fell into the trap and the Americans, US, played to that. The Brits had been doing counterinsurgency for years and years and years. They know what they're doing. They did Malaya, so they know what they're doing. We got ourselves in a position where we were believing our own publicity. What you were able to do was take it and overtake it. FM 3-24 was undoubtedly ahead of what we had. In that respect, very, very good indeed, in terms of identifying and pulling the good. The difficulties, of course, is what you judged, it's all circumstance-based and it's all nationally-based. So sometimes you need a panel like this to suggest that the emperor's got no clothes in certain areas, because we all get into our own national group thinking. But I have been particularly impressed at the ability to identify and move quickly to do things. FM 3-24 is as good an example I can possibly think of, of picking up some good stuff that we had got, learning from what we did, and overtaking it.

**Col Brejet:**

I totally agree with Graham. You are much better than the French Army to learn the lessons of the past. I can tell you that without any problem. I have a great example with David Galula, for instance. Because we didn't know this author before you, it was mentioned by George Petraeus and FM 3-24 and so on. We rediscovered our own history, thanks to what you did here. I think you are very good teaching and studying history, much better than my own country is doing, to be honest. Maybe because the fame of France is sometimes to be arrogant, so maybe we don't need to study history, and it's a mistake. And to be honest, in my career I learned history by myself. We are in this generation where maybe in your country, the same, Graham, we didn't have formal or academic courses in history in my career. I did that by myself, because we are all considering without learning history, we are a bad leader. But I think you are doing very well regarding that.

**Lt Col Burn:**

Learning from history for Australia is a difficult thing. We don't have much of a history. Pretty new country. I've worked in the ABCI program now extensively for the last five years. We were constantly working on interoperability issues between five armies. The thing that fascinates me is that we all, unashamedly, within the ABCI community, plagiarize each other's doctrine. It's amazing in concepts and a whole range of other things. So on one hand you're trying to work interoperability at a procedural level. But also doctrine is just a whole bunch of jigsaw pieces and we reassemble them, depending on what the political spin is of the day. I'm often fascinated, though, when we hand things to the US, that ultimately when it's put through the US machine, there can be no attribution to any other nation other than itself. Whereas in Australia it's a badge of honor to say, "We've studied the US approach and we believe there's something in this and we will adopt this," and sometimes word-for-word, procedure-for-procedure. Other times, we clearly have to put a few more ays and mates and things in it. So I don't understand it. Plus I'll also note that, and it's occasional observation, but I think if we watch FM 3-24 going through, it's flips and throws, again. I don't understand why doctrine, which is supposed to be more of an enduring writing, needs to be held on to like a rattle shift. Whenever we want to induce a cultural change, and I'm speaking also of my own army, whenever we want to generate an immediate cultural change, somehow to get it through the government circles and the metrics that tilt politicians that generals are doing their job, that somehow we have to throw another copy of a doctrinal manual somewhere on a congressman's table in order to legitimize the fact that we're taking some action to change something. When in actual fact, that 80% solution that sits in your doctrine, and in your educational, if it's to make sure that people can contextualize that with what today's need is, is perhaps a more efficient approach. But the political nature of Western modern armies is change takes us in a different path. I'm not sure how the navy does it. I think my navy is pretty much the same. But in the army, and for the sake of two lines in one paragraph, in one chapter, and four paragraphs in another, we'll turn the pressures again and take it through a very intense staff process. In terms of how we share those ideas, I think within many of the armies, we share them more often than any of us even realize. But in terms of attribution, we'll quote a British general and then call him the Australian governor general rather than telling people he was a British general. We'll steal ideas and thoughts and then try, so we're all doing the same. But we certainly do, I think, swap ideas. Guys like Dave Kilcullen come to the top. We had a similar fellow doing similar work with the US State Department during Vietnam and in Burma before that, and through Vietnam. And those people crop up. People with great ideas that resonate in the time. It's not about sharing ideas. They are in some ways savants in their own little world and are of value to people.

**Dr. Wright:**

We have time for one more question.

**Audience Member 1:**

In a couple of our exchanges earlier, we've kind of belabored the issue of when officers should go back to school, and whether or not it was training that was sufficiently in advance of their utilization or whether it was training just in time. In our own experience, or in my experience, went to the basic course just coming in, went to the advance course just making captain, went to Leavenworth just a little bit after making major, and then the war college after making colonel. So you had this spread of schools, each of which seemed to be comfortably in advance of utilizing the skill that you had, or at least I thought it would. Within your armies, when do your guys go to school and why?

**Col Brejet:**

In the French Army, we have about the same system. Lieutenants in the academy, captains to prepare for a company command. We have just a difference. It's when we, as major or young lieutenant colonel, we are coming to the equivalent of CGSC. In France, we have a two-year education. The first year is for each army, and mainly for the army, because navy and air force aren't doing that. So we have one year CGSC just dedicated to the army for tactical and first approach of strategy. And we have a second year, which is totally joined with all of our services. So the only difference compared with the system developed in the army. And we also have an equivalent of war college, but with some few colonels attending this course. So basically except this joint college in Paris, the main difference with the army system. Why are we developing that? I think in the same way you are doing it. It's to prepare for next command time, depending on the potential of each officer to follow this course in order to command and command in command. Am I answering your question, sir?

**Audience Member 1:**

Yeah, thank you.

**Lt Col Burn:**

We, likewise, have a very refined system and a continuum of educative development. I highlighted that we select our candidates in spite of education. We look for leadership traits and we take them from their (inaudible). Some of those officer candidates, having been selected, are then immediately thrown into university study before they commission. Others are thrown into military training, commissioned, and then it's up to them, really, through their career to back cast and regain their tertiary studies if they wish. But we have two continuums. We have an allbranch, or what we call allcorps continuum, and we have a branch-specific continuum. They run in parallel as you pass through gates in time and rank, are fairly comprehensive, and continuously under review. But your touch points are basic levels of training. When we do our commissioning training, everyone graduates as an infantry platoon commander. List special weapons top qualifications, but that is the level male/female, infantry platoon commander basic. Then when you leave that commissioning school and you go off to do your branch qualification, the infantry guys just do special weapons, but there's not a great deal more for them to do. From that point forward, again there's a captain-level course which prepares you for sub-unit command or company-grade command, which for us is done as a major. So by the time you command that company, you've got a few more years of experience under your belt and you command as a major. Again, similar parallels through staff college, preparing you for unit command. War college is a final level. So very much the same. What we don't do that I think the US system does so well, is really put the badge of respect and recognition on tertiary education and facilitate people to get back in and study. We tend to throw that then back to the individual and say, "Yeah, you can do it and we'll help fund you in your own time." But there's no real opportunity to get out of your cut and thrust of "up or out" in the career-based system and take two years out to study. If you do that, you're left behind. When you come back in, your peer group is so far ahead of you in terms of the perceived experience and progression. In that aspect, we are very weak in terms of postgraduate studies.

**Col Norton:**

Our model, again, is virtually the same. Focused on the levels of command. Everything passed out of Sanders, passed out at the same standard. You do some special arms stuff. Your next major benchmark is your (inaudible) equipment. UK's ICSC corps comes here for two weeks and does a joint course with Ireland. Thereafter, it's training for unit command, and then potentially brigade command as well. I would reemphasize what Craig has said. Despite my comments earlier on about the level of education you need to get in, we don't necessarily put as much value on self-betterment and education in the civilian environment to the same extent as the United States Army does. I will point just one thing. There is an officer on the current CGSC course who's about to write a monogram on exactly this issue of comparison of junior officer to mid-officer training across the two armies, which might be of interest if and when he finishes it.

**Lt Col Burn:**

Your last part there about civilian education. When we do our staff college, if you do, like here, the extra couple of units, you can be accredited a master's-level qualification. That sits there and that's valuable to those who elect to do the extra bit of work. That was my first master's. My second I did on my own time at night school, like a lot of people do, and did my master's in international law, quite separately. The army will recognize it in terms of putting it on your dossier, but in terms of them thinking about that, in terms of your employment or how that may be an asset to them, it's completely lost on them. They couldn't care less.

**Dr. Wright:**

We are out of time. Join me in thanking our panelists for this.

# Appendix A Conference Program

| Day 1 |
|---|
| Tuesday, 21 September 2010 |

**0730-0800 Registration**

**0800-0815 Administrative and Opening Remarks**

**Keynote Address**
**0815-0945 Keynote Presentation**
    **BG(R) John S. Brown:**
        *Cultivating Army Leadership: An Historical Overview*

**0945-1000 Break**

**Panel 1**
**1000-1130 Antebellum Officer Education, 1800-1865**

    Looking Beyond West Point: Life in the Old Army as Education for War. Dr. Wayne Wei-siang Hsieh

    *The Development of Successful Non-professional Officers in the Army of the Tennessee, 1861-1863.*     Dr. Steven E. Woodworth

    Moderator: Dr. Donald P. Wright

**1130-1300 Lunch**

Appendix A

**Panel 2**
**1300-1430 Emergence of a Modern Officer Corps, 1866-1905**

*The 1891 Infantry Tactics.* Dr. Perry D. Jamieson

Dr. Todd Brereton

Moderator: Dr. Curtis King

**1430-1445 Break**

**Panel 3**
**1445-1615 Changing Leadership for a Changing World Role, 1906-1939**

*The Leavenworth Schools, Professional Military Education, and Reform in the Old Army, 1900 to 1917.*
Dr. Tim Nenninger

*So Rigorously Trained and Educated: Leader Development in the US Army, 1919 to 1939.*
Dr. Peter Schifferle

Moderator: Dr. Rick Herrera

**1615-1630 Administrative Announcements**

Conference Program

## Day 2
## Wednesday, 22 September 2010

**0730-0830 Registration**

**0830-0845 Administrative Announcements**

**0845-1000 Featured Speaker**
   GEN(R) Gordon Sullivan: *History Strengthens*

**1000-1015 Break**

### Panel 4
**1015-1145 Conventional and Unconventional Challenges of the Cold War, 1945-1975**

   *Soldiering as an Affair of the Heart.* Dr. Lewis Sorley

   *Leadership: DePuy, Slim, and You.* Dr. Henry Gole

   Moderator: Mr. Robert Ramsey

**1145-1300 Lunch**

### Panel 5
**1300-1430 Rebirth of the US Army, 1976-2001**

   *Thoughts in Spring on Professional Identity.*
   Dr. Richard Swain

   Dr. James Carafano

   Moderator: MAJ(P) Clay Mountcastle

**1430-1445 Break**

Appendix A

**Panel 6**
**1445- 1545 Educating Leaders for a New Era, 2002 to Present**

*Mission Command: An Old Idea for the 21st Century.* COL(R) Greg Fontenot

*A New "Meloy Report" Educating Officers for the 21st Century.* Dr. Kevin Benson

Moderator: Mr. John McGrath

**1545-1600 Administrative Announcements**

Conference Program

---

## Day 3
## Thursday, 23 September 2010

---

**0730-0830 Registration**

**0830-0845 Administrative Announcements**

### Panel 7
**0845-1000 Sister Services Perspectives**

    Dr. Gene Andersen

    *There Was More to It than Doctrine? Reflections on the Preparations in the 1930s of the Marine Corps for Future War.* Dr. Donald Bittner

    Moderator: Mr. Kelvin Crow

**1000-1015 Break**

### Panel 8
**1015-1130 Foreign Perspectives**

    *Making Australian Military Leaders; A Historical Reflection Based on the Changing Face of Wars and the Australians That are Selected to Fight Them.* Lt.Col Craig Burn

    *Finding the Balance Between Timeless Fundamentals and Temporal Adjustments.* Col Jean-Claude Brejot

    *A British Perspective.* Col Graham Norton

    Moderator: Dr. Donald Wright

**1130-1300 Lunch**

### Featured Speaker

**1300-1430 BG Sean B. MacFarland**: US Army Leader Development: Past, Present and Future

**1430-1500 Closing Discussion and Remarks**

## Appendix B Biographies

**Dr. Gene R. Andersen** is a retired naval aviator and a Section Head, Department of Leadership, Ethics & Law, US Naval Academy, 1997-2000 and the Primary Professional Military Education Program Project Leader, Center for Naval Leadership, 2003-2005. His publications include *Formal Mentoring in the US Military: Research Evidence, Lingering Questions and Recommendations*, Naval War College Review; *How to Make Mentoring Work*, US Naval Institute Proceedings, April 2009; *Leadership and Human Behavior*, Pearson Custom Publishing, 1999.

**Dr. Kevin Benson** served in the U.S. Army for 30 years. His final assignment in the Army was serving as the Director, School of Advanced Military Studies at Fort Leavenworth Kansas, from 2003-2007. He was the C/J 5 (Director of Plans) for Third US Army and the Combined Forces Land Component Command at the beginning of Operation Iraqi Freedom, from July 2002 to July 2003. He is now employed by McNeil Technologies and teaches at the U.S. Army University of Foreign Military and Cultural Studies at Fort Leavenworth, Kansas.

Kevin is a 1977 graduate of the United States Military Academy. His military education includes; the U.S. Army Armor Officer Basic Course, US Marine Corps Amphibious Warfare School, US Army Command and General Staff College, and the School of Advanced Military Studies. He also attended the Massachusetts Institute of Technology Security Studies Program as a War College Fellow in 2001. He earned a Ph.D. in American history from the University of Kansas.

**Dr. Donald F. Bittner** from St. Louis/Columbia, Missouri, is a Professor of Military History with the Marine Corps Command and Staff College. He has served Marine Corps University in and out of uniform since 1975 and has 20 years of Federal Service.

**Colonel Jean-Claude Brejot** Jean-Claude Bréjot was the chief of the Army Intelligence Doctrine office in the Army Doctrine Center located in Paris (CDEF) Prior his assignement to CAC. CDEF is in the French Army the equivalent of CAC for Doctrine, Lessons Learned and Simulation.

His prior deployments and assignments include command of 402nd Air Defense Artillery Regiment, Châlons en Champagne, France, chief of plans for 1st Division (Etat-major de force numéro 1), Besançon, France, chief of plans for European Union Operation Concordia, Skopje, Macedonia, Military Assistant for the Commanding General of Multinational Division South-East, Stabilization Force (SFOR) in Mostar, Bosnia, Military Advisor for the Commanding General of the Tunisian Staff College in Tunis, Tunisia, Operations Officer of 9th Marines Division (9ème Division d'Infanterie de Marine), Nantes, France, Planning Officer of Brigade Janus, Implementation Force (IFOR), Mostar, Bosnia, Military Assistant for the Commanding General of Brigade Janus, Implementation Force (IFOR), Mostar, Bosnia, deputy commander and troop commander in 58th Air Defense Artillery Regiment in Douai, France, Platoon leader in 54th Air Defense Artillery Regiment in Hyères, France.

APPENDIX B

His awards include the French Legion of Honour, the National Defense medal (Silver), the French Balkans medal, the NATO Bosnia medal, the EU Macedonia medal, the Tunisian Legion of Merit.

Colonel Jean-Claude Bréjot graduated from Saint-Cyr and was commissioned as an Artillery officer in 1986. He is also graduated from the Army Advanced Staff College and the Joint Staff College.

**Dr. Todd Brereton** received his PhD from Texas A&M University, specializing in army reform, education, and professionalization during the Gilded Age. He is presently professor of history at Iowa Wesleyan College, where he also serves as chair of his academic division. Brereton has been teaching at the college/university level since 1991, and has taught a wide variety of courses, including advanced courses in U.S. military history. He participated in USMA's military history seminar and has delivered numerous papers at academic conferences, including the Society for Military History. In addition to his work at Texas A&M, Brereton has taught at the University of Louisville, Georgetown College, and Eastern Kentucky University. He came to Iowa Wesleyan College in 2002. His present research regards the construction of nuclear weapons at the Iowa Army Ammunition Plant.

**Brigadier General (R) John S. Brown** gave more than 34 years of service to the United States Army, and now teaches as an adjunct professor and serves as a historical consultant. His most recent duty assignment (1998-2005) was as Chief of Military History for the United States Army.

Previously General Brown served as Chief of Programs and Requirements for the Supreme Headquarters Allied Powers Europe (SHAPE); Executive Officer to the Army DCSOPS; Commander of the 2d Brigade, 1st Cavalry Division in Texas and Kuwait; G3 Operations for III Corps; G3 of the 24th Infantry Division; and Commander of the 2-66 Armor Battalion in Germany, DESERT SHIELD, and DESERT STORM. General Brown has commanded armor units at every level from platoon through brigade, and has served on staffs at every level from battalion through theater.

General Brown has published, edited and lectured at home and overseas. Notable publications include *Draftee Division*, a case study of divisional mobilization during WWII, and the forthcoming *Kevlar Legions: A History of Army Transformation 1989-2005*. He authors the monthly column "Historically Speaking" in *Army* magazine, and has written numerous articles and chapters.

General Brown is physically handicapped. He has been married to the former Mary Beth Hoisington for 39 years. They have two children, a daughter who is a corporate lawyer and a son who is an army officer, and four grandchildren.

Education: B.S.-United States Military Academy, M.A.-Indiana University, M.M.A.S.-United States Army Command and General Staff College, M.A.-United States Naval War College, PhD-Indiana University

**Lieutenant Colonel Craig Burn** commenced his appointment as the Australian Army's LNO to CAC in January 2008. He is an armour officer and hales from the city of

Brisbane on Australia's east coast. He came to Fort Leavenworth from the Land Warfare Development Centre in Puckapunyal where he was the capability concept and requirements developer for two battlespace operating systems; ISR and IO. He has held an array of regimental, instructional and staff appointments and has previously served on exchange as a small group instructor at the US Armor School, Fort Knox.

LTCOL Burn is a graduate of the Australian Army Command and Staff College (Fort Queenscliff) and holds a Master of Defence Studies from the University of Canberra and a Master of Public and International Law at the Melbourne University.

His operational service include tours in the UN assistance mission in Rwanda, and in the International Force in East Timor.

**Dr. James Carafano** is one of the nation's leading experts in defense and homeland security, and directs the Heritage Foundation's Douglas and Sara Allison Center for Foreign Policy. He is an accomplished historian and teacher as well as a prolific writer and researcher on a fundamental constitutional duty of the federal government: to provide for the common defense. His research focuses on developing the national security required to secure the long-term interests of the United States - protecting the public, providing for economic growth and preserving civil liberties. Dr. Carafano's op-ed columns and commentary are published widely, including the *Baltimore Sun, Boston Globe, New York Post, Philadelphia Inquirer, USA Today* and *Washington Times* in addition to the *Washington Examiner*. He is a member of the National Academy's Board on Army Science and Technology and the Department of the Army Historical Advisory Committee. He is a senior fellow at George Washington University's Homeland Security Policy Institute.

**Colonel (R) Greg Fontenot:** Colonel Gregory Fontenot, USA Retired is the director of the University of Foreign Military and Cultural Studies at Fort Leavenworth, Ks. Colonel Fontenot was one of the authors of On Point: The US Army in Operation Iraqi Freedom. Colonel Fontenot served 28 years in the Army as an Armor officer commanding units in Europe and the United States. Colonel Fontenot led a tank task force in Desert Storm and an armor brigade in Bosnia. Other important assignments included faculty at USMA, chief of Command Planning Group TRADOC, Director of SAMS, and Commander BCTP.

frequent contributor to *Army Magazine* and *Military Review* Colonel Fontenot has delivered papers at the Marshall Awards Seminar, the American Literary Translation Association, Rand Corporation's Conference on Stability Operation, the Military Sensing Symposium, The USMA Symposium on Contemporary History and Cantigny Foundation.

**Colonel (R) Henry G. Gole (Ph.D.)** served four tours in Europe and three in Asia. He was an enlisted infantryman in the Korean War and a Special Forces officer in two combat tours in Vietnam. His doctorate is from Temple University. He has taught at several institutions of higher learning and continues to teach his elective course, Men In Battle, at the US Army War College. In addition to numerous articles and book reviews, his published work includes *General William E. DePuy, Preparing the Army for Modern War* (2008), *Soldiering: Observations from Korea, Vietnam, and Safe Places* (2005), and *The Road to Rainbow: Army Planning for Global War, 1934-1940* (2003).

Appendix B

**Dr. Wayne Wei-siang Hsieh** immigrated to the United States as an infant from Taiwan and grew up in Alhambra, CA. He received an excellent public high school education at Alhambra High School, and went on to Yale University, where he received a B.A. in History (2000). He attended the University of Virginia for his graduate work, where he received a PhD in History (2004) and worked under the direction of Gary W. Gallagher and Edward L. Ayers.

Hsieh spent the 2004/5 academic year as an Andrew W. Mellon Postdoctoral Fellow at Yale's Whitney Humanities Center, where he also taught half time in Yale's Directed Studies curriculum--a freshman Great Books program of which Hsieh is himself a proud alumnus. In August 2005 he joined the U.S. Naval Academy History Department, where he remains an assistant professor. For the 2011 calendar year, he will hold a position as a Henry Chauncey Jr. '57 Fellow in the Brady-Johnson Grand Strategy Program at the International Security Studies program of Yale University.

Between July 2008 and June 2009, Hsieh was on interagency detail with the U.S. State Department in Iraq, where he served as the Tuz Satellite Lead for the Salah ad Din Provincial Reconstruction Team. He received a Commander's Award for Civilian Service from 3 BSTB (Department of the Army), and a Meritorious Honor Award from the U.S. Department of State (Embassy Baghdad).

Hsieh has a diverse number of interests in military history, although he remains a nineteenth-century Americanist by trade and training.

**Dr. Perry D. Jamieson** received his PhD from Wayne State University and taught American military history at the University of Texas at El Paso in 1979 and 1980. Dr. Jamieson then began a long career in the United States Air Force History and Museums Program. He was serving as the Air Force's senior historian when he retired in March 2009.

Dr. Jamieson is the coauthor of *Attack and Die* (1982) and the author of *Crossing the Deadly Ground: United States Army Tactics, 1865—1899* (1994); *Death in September: The Antietam Campaign* (1995); and *Winfield Scott Hancock: Gettysburg Hero* (2003). His Air Force publications include books on the 1991 Gulf War and the 1996 Khobar Towers bombing. He is currently working on a volume on the final operations of the Civil War, which will be the last entry in the University of Nebraska Press series, "Great Campaigns of the Civil War."

Dr. Jamieson and his wife Stephanie live on the main street of Sharpsburg, Maryland and on most weekday mornings he hikes the Antietam battlefield. Every March for more than the last twenty years, he and Stephanie have spent about a week in Lakeland, Florida, the spring training home of the Detroit Tigers. Dr. Jamieson is a life-long fan of that team, the Red Wings, Pistons, and—he reluctantly admits—the Lions.

**Brigadier General Sean B. MacFarland** currently serves as the Deputy Commandant of the Command and General Staff College at Fort Leavenworth, Kansas.

He graduated from the US Military Academy at West Point in 1981 and was commissioned as an Armor officer. His command tours include service as the Commander of Joint Task Force – North; Commander of 1st Brigade Combat Team, 1st Armored Division

- the Ready First - in Tal Afar, West Ninewah province, and Ramadi, Iraq; Commander of 2nd Battalion, 63d Armor Regiment at Camp Able Sentry in Macedonia; Operations Officer and Executive Officer of the 3d Squadron, 4th Cavalry Regiment, in Schweinfurt, Germany and later Bosnia as part of the NATO Implementation Force (IFOR); and as Troop Commander in 3rd Squadron, 12th Cavalry Regiment, in Buedingen, Germany.

His other duties and assignments also include the Joint Staff; Combined/Joint Task Force 7 in Iraq, Aide de Camp, Deputy Regimental Operations Officer for the 3rd Armored Cavalry Regiment during Operation Desert Shield/Desert Storm; and Cavalry Platoon Leader and Troop Executive Officer in the 3rd Armored Cavalry Regiment at Fort Bliss, Texas.

He has served overseas in Germany, Iraq (Desert Shield/Desert

Storm and Operation Iraqi Freedom), Kuwait, and Bosnia (IFOR and SFOR). His educational degrees are a bachelor of science from the United States Military Academy, masters of science degrees from the Georgia Institute of Technology (Aerospace Engineering) and the National Defense University (National Resource Strategy), and a Master of Military Arts and Sciences degree from the US Army Command and General Staff College (Advanced Military Studies).

**Dr. Tim Nenninger:** Timothy. K. Nenninger is currently Chief of the Archives II Textual Records Reference Staff at the National Archives. He has been with the National Archives since 1970, where he has had extensive experience working with military and naval records, in professional as well as supervisory positions. From 1994 to 1997 he was an analyst on the World War II Working Group of the Joint US-Russia Commission on POWs/MIAs and was the principal author of the working group's report, "The Experience of American POWs Liberated by the Soviet Army, 1944-45." From 1997 to 2005 he was vice-president then president of the Society for Military History. During 1987-88 he was the John F. Morrison Professor of Military History at the US Army Command and General Staff College, Fort Leavenworth, Kansas. A graduate of Lake Forest College, he received his MA and PhD degrees in history from the University of Wisconsin-Madison where his specialization was the American military and has published a number of works in that field.

**Colonel Graham Norton** was educated at Leeds Grammar School and Loughbrough University before commissioning in to the Royal Corps of Signals in August 1985. With the exception of two tours at the School of Signals in Blandford as a student and an Instructor, his early regimental Service was in Germany, firstly as a troop commander in a 20th Armoured Brigade HQ and Signal Squadron and also as Adjutant with 4th Armoured Division HQ & Sig Regt.

At staff he served as an SO3 Assessments in the Yugoslav Crisis Call within the Defence Intelligence Staff, and briefly as SO2 Comms Ops at HQ LAND prior to attending the first Joint Advanced Command and Staff Course. Following Staff College he was appointed SO2 ISTAR in the operational requirements branch in MOD, before once again returning to Germany after being selected to command 4th Armoured Brigade HQ & Sig Squadron; a tour that included an operational deployment to Bosnia. Selected for promotion to Lt Col is 2001, following a 6 month detachment as SO1 Communications within HQCENTCOM's OEF headquarters, he returned once more to Germany to command 7th Signal Regiment.

Appendix B

A 14 month appointment as SO1 Policy in Personnel Services 2, responsible for the development of army discipline policy followed command. On selection for promotion to Colonel, he and his family again returned to Germany, when he was appointed ACOS G6 in the Allied Rapid Reaction Corps. This three year tour included an operational deployment to Afghanistan as the Commander of the UK's Joint Force CIS HQ.

Colonel Norton took up his current appointment in August 2009. He is married to Amanda, and they have 2 sons, both of whom attend Boarding School in England; Ben (17) and Edward (12). His interests include reading and photography, and he is a lifelong, if somewhat sad supporter of Leeds United Football Club.

**Dr. Peter Schifferle** is a graduate of the U.S. Army Armor Officer Basic and Advanced Courses, the U.S. Army Command and General Staff College and the School of Advanced Military Studies. He holds Masters Degrees from the University of North Carolina, Chapel Hill in German History, and the School of Advanced Military Studies in Theater Operations. He was awarded a Doctorate in American History from the University of Kansas in 2002. His book, *America's School for War: Fort Leavenworth, Officer Education, and Victory in World War II,* was published by the University Press of Kansas in April 2010.

Upon graduation from Reserve Officers Training Corps at Canisius College, Buffalo, New York, Peter J. Schifferle was commissioned into the Armor Branch in 1976. Dr. Schifferle served in a variety of command and staff positions in both Tank and Armored Cavalry units throughout the United States, Europe, the Middle East and the Republic of Korea, including an assignment as the 3d Armored Cavalry Regiment S4 during Operations Desert Shield and Desert Storm. Prior to his last assignment as Exercise Director, School of Advanced Military Studies, U. S. Army Command and General Staff College, he served as Chief of Plans, V Corps in Heidelberg, Federal Republic of Germany. That assignment included supervision of staff planning for Task Force Eagle as both IFOR and SFOR in Bosnia-Herzegovina in 1995 through 1997. After retirement in 2000, he was appointed the Director, Advanced Operational Art Studies Fellowship at the School of Advanced Military Studies.

Dr. Schifferle has been married for over thirty years to the former Sandra Leigh Gould. They have one daughter, Rachel, 20.

**Dr. Lewis Sorley**, a former soldier and then civilian official of the Central Intelligence Agency, is a third-generation graduate of the United States Military Academy who also holds a doctorate from the Johns Hopkins University. He has served on the faculties at West Point and the Army War College. His Army assignments also included leadership of tank and armored cavalry units in Germany, Vietnam, and the United States and staff positions in the offices of the Secretary of Defense and the Army Chief of Staff.

He is the author of a book on foreign policy entitled *Arms Transfers under Nixon* and two biographies, *Thunderbolt: General Creighton Abrams and the Army of His Times* and *Honorable Warrior: General Harold K. Johnson and the Ethics of Command.* The Johnson biography received the Army Historical Foundation's Distinguished Book Award. An excerpt of the Abrams biography won the Peterson Prize as the year's best scholarly article on military history. He has also been awarded the General Andrew Goodpaster Prize for military scholarship by the American Veterans Center.

His book *A Better War: The Unexamined Victories and Final Tragedy of America's Last Years in Vietnam* was nominated for the Pulitzer Prize. His edited work *Vietnam Chronicles: The Abrams Tapes, 1968-1972* received the Army Historical Foundation's

Trefry Prize for providing a unique perspective on the art of command. A second edited work, *The Vietnam War: An Assessment by South Vietnam's Generals*, is currently in press.

Dr. Sorley has also written *Honor Bright: History and Origins of the West Point Honor Code and System*, a book commissioned by the United States Military Academy's Simon Center for the Professional Military Ethic. At the Army's request he compiled and edited a two-volume work entitled *Press On! Selected Works of General Donn A. Starry*, published by the Combat Studies Institute Press at Fort Leavenworth.

Dr. Sorley served for a decade as Secretary of the Board of Directors of the Army Historical Foundation and is Executive Director Emeritus of the Association of Military Colleges and Schools of the United States. During the Spring 2009 semester he served as Gottwald Visiting Professor of Leadership and Ethics at Virginia Military Institute. Also in 2009 he was named a Distinguished Eagle Scout by the Boy Scouts of America.

**General (R) Gordon Sullivan** is the President and Chief Operating Officer of the Association of the United States Army, headquartered in Arlington, Virginia. Since assuming the presidency in 1998, General Sullivan has overseen the transformation of the Association into a dynamic 100,000+ individual and 500+ sustaining member organization that represents Soldiers, families, and the defense industry.

His responsibilities as President and Chief Operating Officer encompass both daily business operating and strategy planning for the largest Army-oriented non-profit association. The Association promotes and advocates programs for Soldiers and their families, creates opportunities for Army-Industry and professional dialog; advocates public awareness of Army and national security issues through its educational mission and maintains an outreach program to national leadership on critical issues pertinent to Army readiness.

Born in Boston, Massachusetts on 25 September 1937 and raised in Quincy. He was commissioned a second lieutenant of Armor and awarded a Bachelor of Arts degree in history from Norwich University in 1959. He holds a Master of Arts degree in political science from the University of New Hampshire. His professional military education includes the U.S. Army Armor School Basic and Advanced Courses, the Command and General Staff College, and the Army War College.

General Sullivan retired from the Army on 31 July 1995 after more than 36 years of active service. He culminated his service in uniform as the 32nd Chief of Staff—the senior general officer in the Army—and a member of the Joint Chiefs of Staff.

He is the co-author, with Michael V. Harper, of *Hope Is Not a Method* (Random House, 1996), which chronicles the enormous challenges encountered in transforming the post-Cold War Army through the lens of proven leadership principles and a commitment to shared values. He is the Chairman of the Board of Trustees of Norwich University and the Marshall Legacy Institute; and was formerly a director on the boards of Newell-Rubbermaid, Shell Corporation, Institute of Defense Analyses and General Dynamics.

General Sullivan is married to the former Gay Loftus of Quincy, Massachusetts; they currently reside in Alexandria, VA. He has three children and three grandchildren. He is an avid reader, amateur historian, and active sailor and sport fishing enthusiast.

APPENDIX B

**Dr. Richard Swain** is a retired officer of field artillery, a former director of the Combat Studies Institute (88-90; 92-94), a faculty member at the School of Advanced Military Studies. (94-99), and from 2002-2007 served as Professor of Officership in the William E. Simon Center for Professional Military Education at West Point. While at West Point he initiated and participated in an effort uniting faculty of the service academies to write a new edition of *The Armed Forces Officer* for instruction of cadets and midshipmen. (The book is currently in print by NDU Press/Potomac Books.) Rick is currently employed by the Leavenworth Office of Booz Allen Hamilton where he has been engaged as part of a team teaching operational design to various military clients. (Booz Allen Hamilton is in no way responsible for the paper presented here.) In 1991, Rick deployed to Saudi Arabia as the Third Army Historian. He wrote a monograph titled, *"Lucky War": Third Army in Desert Storm*. The book was published by CSI under the Leavenworth Press imprint, by the good offices of Dr. Roger Spiller. From 1999 to 2001 Rick was employed as a contract historian by General Montgomery Meigs to write an account of senior leadership in Bosnia. A version of that paper was published by SSI titled: *Neither War Nor Not War*. Rick currently resides with his wife Nancy in Lawton Oklahoma.

**Dr. Steven E. Woodworth** received his B.A. in history from Southern Illinois University in 1982 and his Ph.D. from Rice University in 1987. He is a two-time winner of the Fletcher Pratt Award of the New York Civil War Round Table for his books Jefferson Davis and His Generals (1990) and Davis and Lee at War (1995). Among his other works are Six Armies in Tennessee: The Chickamauga and Chattanooga Campaigns (1998), While God Is Marching On: The Religious World of Civil War Soldiers (2001), Nothing but Victory: The Army of the Tennessee, 1861-1865 (2006), and Manifest Destinies: Westward Expansion and the Coming of the Civil War (2010). He coauthored (with Kenneth J. Winkle) The Oxford Atlas of the Civil War (2004), which won the annual book prize of the Society for Military History. Woodworth has also received the Grady McWhiney Award of the Dallas Civil War Round Table for lifetime contribution to the study of Civil War history.

www.ingramcontent.com/pod-product-compliance
Lightning Source LLC
Chambersburg PA
CBHW080439170426
43195CB00017B/2824